Exploring the Self, Subjectivity, and Character across Japanese and Translation Texts

Studies in Pragmatics

Series Editors

Maj-Britt Mosegaard Hansen (*University of Manchester*)
Kerstin Fischer (*University of Southern Denmark*)
Anne Barron (*Leuphana University Lüneburg*)

VOLUME 20

The titles published in this series are listed at *brill.com/sip*

Exploring the Self, Subjectivity, and Character across Japanese and Translation Texts

by

Senko K. Maynard

BRILL

LEIDEN | BOSTON

The Library of Congress Cataloging-in-Publication Data is available online at https://catalog.loc.gov
LC record available at https://lccn.loc.gov/2021058048

Typeface for the Latin, Greek, and Cyrillic scripts: "Brill". See and download: brill.com/brill-typeface.

ISSN 1750-368X
ISBN 978-90-04-50585-8 (hardback)
ISBN 978-90-04-50586-5 (e-book)

Copyright 2022 by Senko K. Maynard. Published by Koninklijke Brill NV, Leiden, The Netherlands.
Koninklijke Brill NV incorporates the imprints Brill, Brill Nijhoff, Brill Hotei, Brill Schöningh, Brill Fink, Brill mentis, Vandenhoeck & Ruprecht, Böhlau Verlag and V&R Unipress.
Koninklijke Brill NV reserves the right to protect this publication against unauthorized use. Requests for re-use and/or translations must be addressed to Koninklijke Brill NV via brill.com or copyright.com.

This book is printed on acid-free paper and produced in a sustainable manner.

Contents

Preface   IX

PART 1
Introduction and Framework

1   Introduction: Exploring the Self   3
   1   Overview: Toward a Philosophical Contrastive Pragmatics   3
   2   The Self and Context in Pragmatics   6
   3   Language, Thought, and the Self   12
   4   Data   20
   5   Organization of the Book   26

2   From Traditional to Postmodern Concepts of Self in the West   29
   1   The Cartesian View and Vico's Opposition   30
   2   The Self Approached from Psychology and Philosophy   32
   3   Deconstruction of the Self   36
   4   Socially Constructed and Experienced Self   41
   5   Language and Social Identities   44

3   Framework: Subjectivity and Character   48
   1   Subjectivity   49
   2   Character   64

4   Perspectives from Translation Studies and Contrastive Pragmatics   77
   1   Discourse of Translation and Translation Studies   77
   2   Contrastive Pragmatics and Translation   90

PART 2
Background

5   Empty Self and Empty Place in Japanese Studies   101
   1   Centrality of Emptiness in Japanese Thought   102
   2   Nishida's Philosophy: Empty Self in the Place of Nothingness   106
   3   Miyazawa's Poetics: Transient Self as a Flickering Light   112

6　Concept of Self in Japanese Language and Discourse　117
　　1　Self in Traditional Language Studies　117
　　2　Watsuji's Approach: Interdependent Self in Social Space　120
　　3　The Multiplicity of Self in Japanese Discourse　125

PART 3
Analysis: Across Japanese and Translation Texts

7　Presenting Aspects of Self through Person Expressions　133
　　1　Variability in First-Person Expressions　133
　　2　Creativity in Person Expressions　145
　　3　Reflections　149

8　Perceptive and Receptive Self in Grammar　151
　　1　Unmentioned Perceptive Self　151
　　2　Receptive Emotive Self and Subjective Passives　158
　　3　Experiencing Others' Actions and Verbs of Giving　161
　　4　Reflections　165

9　Hidden but Expressive Self in the Topic-Comment Dynamism　166
　　1　Hidden Self and the Topic-Comment Dynamism　166
　　2　Hidden Self and the Staging Effect　170
　　3　Hidden Self and Nominal Predicates　174
　　4　Reflections　180

10　Transferred Self in Quotation and Inserted Speech　181
　　1　Quoting and Self　181
　　2　Transferring Self in Quotation and Inserted Speech　185
　　3　Floating Self in Internal Monologue and Conversation　189
　　4　Transferred Self and Inserted Speech　196
　　5　Reflections　200

11　Populated Self and Variation　202
　　1　Character and Character-Speak in Japanese and English　202
　　2　Populating the Self through Dialect and Effeminate *onee* Language　209
　　3　Narrating Self, Variation, and Style　214
　　4　Reflections　222

12 Empty and Populated Self in Japanese as Translation Text   223
    1   Aspects of Self and of Self's Onlooker in *The Eye*   223
    2   Expressivity in Two Translations of *Auggie Wren's Christmas Story*   230
    3   Reflections   238

PART 4
Reflections

13 Exploring the Self in Philosophical Pragmatics   241
    1   Empty and Populated Self: Summary   241
    2   Translation and Expressive Gaps   243
    3   Overcoming the Ideologies of Metalanguage   246
    4   Beyond the *Nihonjinron* Debate   248
    5   Toward an Embracing View of Self across Languages   251

Appendix: Synopses of the Works Selected for Data   255
References   261
Author Index   288
Subject Index   293

Preface

In this work, based on analyses of original and translation texts involving Japanese and English, I propose the concept of an "empty" but "populated" self. The empty and populated self is evidenced in Japanese grammar, style, and variation. Although the Japanese self is fundamentally empty, it is populated with multiple aspects such as perceptive, receptive, and hidden self. It is also populated with characters and characteristics such as the middle-aged male and the effeminate *onee* character. In the course of this book, I illustrate that this conceptualization of the Japanese self is nearly impossible to be adequately or consistently captured in English translation texts. This gives rise to an exploration of the nature and status of the speaker, the very concept of the speaking self in linguistics and pragmatics.

This work reports the usefulness of philosophical contrastive pragmatics, the framework in which original and translation texts are analyzed. This is achieved by adopting multidisciplinary methodological approaches such as discourse analysis, conversation analysis, pragmatics, sociolinguistics, translation studies, and literary studies. Hermeneutic interpretive analyses of translation texts reveal critical differences and gaps found across Japanese and English, not only in structure and use, but more fundamentally, in ontological perspectives.

Differences between the two languages were most shockingly experienced when in the mid-19th century Japan abandoned two centuries of isolationism. And it was directly experienced by a number of Japanese foreign students who faced severe linguistic and cultural differences as they traveled to the West at the end of the Edo and early Meiji periods.

Rutgers University where I have been faculty for many years was once one of the favored destinations of these Japanese students. Among those who came to the American East Coast was Taro Kusakabe, a 22-years old samurai from Echizen (Fukui), who in the fall of 1867 entered Rutgers College. Taro was an excellent student, but perhaps because of his intense program of study conducted in a foreign language as well as the difficulties of adjusting to American life, he suffered from a worsening case of tuberculosis. Taro passed away shortly before his graduation in April of 1870, but Rutgers College awarded him the degree posthumously. Ironically, the year 2020, marred by the COVID-19 world pandemic, marked the 150-year commemoration of the passing of Taro Kusakabe who is buried in Willow Grove Cemetery not far from campus.

I ponder about how he lived and reconciled the inevitable conflict between his self as a samurai and his self as an individual in a modernizing America.

He was placed at the nexus of Japanese and English languages, and was challenged into the translating process as he lived his days. As I walk through the Old Queens campus of Rutgers University where buildings Taro once studied in still stand, I think of the linguistic and cultural gaps he faced so far away from home, in the college town of New Brunswick, New Jersey.

For many years I have enjoyed teaching Japanese language and linguistics at American institutions (in chronological order, the University of Iowa, the University of Illinois at Chicago, Northwestern University, the University of Hawai'i, Connecticut College, Harvard University, Princeton University, and Rutgers University). I thank all the students and colleagues I have met at various places for their friendship, inspiration, and encouragement.

I thank Maj-Britt Mosegaard Hansen, Kerstin Fischer, and Anne Barron, editors of the *Studies in Pragmatics* series for their faith in me. I express my gratitude to Brill for having provided me the opportunity to express my academic adventures in book form. My special thanks go to Elisa Perotti at Brill for her editorial support and assistance.

I am grateful to the Turners and the people of Corning, Iowa, who, many years ago, so generously welcomed me as an American Field Service foreign exchange student. Although that one year I spent at Corning Community High School is long gone, the Midwest remains to be my American roots. I also express my heartfelt gratitude to my late parents, Tsutomu and Harue Kumiya of Yamanashi, Japan, who steadfastly supported my interest in studying abroad.

And, time and time again, thank you, Michael, for providing a warm and joyful world where I am free to pursue my academic and artistic interests.

SKM
Summer, 2021
"On the Banks of the Old Raritan"

PART 1

Introduction and Framework

CHAPTER 1

Introduction: Exploring the Self

1   Overview: Toward a Philosophical Contrastive Pragmatics

As a native speaker of Japanese, for decades, I have engaged in research in Japanese linguistics, discourse studies, and pragmatics. In the process, persistent questions on the philosophy of language have surfaced. How are we as speaking selves involved in and with language? Anyone who engages in linguistic activity, regardless of status as author, writer, narrator, speaker, or dramatic person, can be viewed as a language-involving self. How is this self realized through the use of language? In turn, this self also participates as a hearer, listener, partner, interactant, reader, or audience. Who or what is this self? Do different kinds of self emerge when different languages are employed? Do differences in meaning and expressivity across languages imply and provide evidence for contrasting ontological views?

In this work, I explore a contrastive approach to the concept of self from the perspective of philosophy and pragmatics by examining literary works selected from contemporary Japanese culture. Based on analyses of original and translated texts involving Japanese and English, I propose the concept of an empty and yet populated self. This empty and populated self is evidenced in Japanese grammar, style, and variation. Although the Japanese self is fundamentally empty, it is populated with multiple aspects such as perceptive, receptive, and hidden self. The self is also populated with characters and characteristics such as the middle-aged-male and the effeminate *onee* character. In the course of this book, I illustrate that this conceptualization of the Japanese self is nearly impossible to be adequately or consistently captured in English translation texts.

This empty self observed in Japanese discourse is located in a vacant setting, i.e., an empty place. The concept of emptiness is associated with Nishida's (1949) philosophy of "place of nothingness" as well as other related Japanese philosophical and religious views. This place of nothingness refers to a self-emerging space where the self embraces discourse interactions filled with rich expressive potential. Far from implying a negative concept, the empty place provides an opening or a clearing for the self's creative expressivity. The self, constantly responding to, interacting with, and internalizing its activated contexts, fluctuates, transforms, and emerges as it is.

Questions surrounding the self have challenged philosophers and intellectuals both in the East and the West. Curiously, each researcher who delves into this topic thinks in his or her own language. In this most basic sense, the philosophical question on the nature of the self is directly linked to language and its use. With our encounters engaging multiple languages in our world, an exploration into a philosophy of language from the perspective of Japanese grammar and discourse in a contrastive context is expected to bring some challenging insights. I trust that the pursuit of human knowledge should always return to the issue surrounding the self and language. Still, one must admit that despite its theoretical significance, in linguistics and pragmatics, the concept of self has not been fully addressed (Kecskes 2012).

In this work the intimate relationship between the self and language is explored from the perspective of philosophical pragmatics. By philosophical pragmatics I refer to the pursuit of an ontological understanding in the hermeneutic approach to language in practice. More concretely, this study takes a philosophical contrastive pragmatics approach conducting the contrastive analysis of original and translated works in literary genres. Attention is paid to how the language is formed, styled, and performed as a self-revealing phenomenon in Japanese. I focus on the Japanese features in the source text that express subjectivity as well as create characters, and how these phenomena are reflected or not in the English target text.

My analyses involve linguistic and sociolinguistic phenomena incorporating multiple frameworks, such as functional grammatical analysis, discourse analysis, conversation analysis, pragmatics, variation studies, textual analysis, and contrastive stylistics. This method is particularly valuable when translation texts are selected from different language families. The richness and weakness of each language as well as across languages are made evident, and repeatedly observed translation gaps provide sufficient grounds for exploring a philosophical interpretation of the self. A philosophical contrastive pragmatics allows the researcher to engage in philosophical inquiries on the basis of language, especially by understanding the self as a language user (or performer) placed in the context of a given situation. Adopting this framework makes an ontological inquiry as a part of pragmatics, broadening the scope of its disciplinary territory.

This approach requires culturally practiced language data for pragmatics-oriented analyses. The data selected for this study include Japanese novels written by contemporary authors such as Banana Yoshimoto, Kenzaburo Oe, Hiromi Kawakami, Miyuki Miyabe, and Keigo Higashino, along with their published English translations. In the majority of my earlier works, examples are taken from multiple genres of Japanese discourse, and I myself have provided glosses and translations. In this study, I focus on published Japanese and translated texts, minimizing the unreliability inherently associated with relying only on self-translated examples.

The data support my thesis that the Japanese language is suffused with expressions associated with subjectivity, characters, and characteristics not easily translated into English. I also examine a Japanese story with four different versions of English translation, Japanese and English translations of a Russian novel as well as two separate Japanese translations of an American short story. Critical features observed in examples taken from a total of 28 works involving bi-directional translations are offered as evidence.

Given the nature of data, some limitations of this work should be noted. First, the concept of an empty yet populated self is based on observations made in limited and specific source and target texts, thus conclusions may or may not apply elsewhere. Second, this work primarily analyzes the original Japanese text in contrast with its English translation. If the direction is reversed, the investigation through philosophical contrastive pragmatics may produce different results. Third, this work explores senses of the speaking self as evidenced in language and discourse and does not address aspects of a personhood directly involving psychological, social, and cultural phenomena. While it is hoped that this work generally adds to a fundamental understanding of the self, the linguistic self accessed through language and discourse tells only a partial story of the self and selves.

It is useful to remind ourselves that the discourse of translation entails much more than a mere transfer of corresponding words. Curiously, the absence of a corresponding translation sometimes communicates more than its presence. Consider that when translation is read as a part of the target society's literature, the missing expressivity does not evoke a sense that something is lacking. In other words, what is absent in the first place cannot be identified as being "missed." This is a part of the reality surrounding the translation itself. This awareness guides us in appreciating that language is exceedingly complex, and gaps in translation are difficult (or nearly impossible) to overcome. Differences are found in the core of messages stemming from culturally endorsed ontological views, which can be reached only through careful contrastive analyses.

We engage in language as a part of our interpersonal human experience, and this experience is often initiated as a performance in which we present our selves. At that moment, we create our selves as speakers, i.e., locutionary agents, of the language. We may intuitively experience our sense of being without using words. Yet, even in silence, we inevitably experience our selves influenced by language. That is because even our unspoken everyday experiences are fundamentally identified through the form of socially endorsed language. So is the case of our senses of self. The self emerges even when we are merely thinking or verbalizing a soliloquy, which requires a common language shared with others. We are creatures in and of language. As children of language, we cannot escape from the question surrounding the concept of self (or more accurately, multiple aspects of selves) and language. Given the recognized diversity in our global cultural environment, reaching for an understanding of the self from different perspectives should further our perception of how we as humans interact with language in diverse ways.

To explore the concept of self from the perspective of philosophical contrastive pragmatics, two related issues are discussed. First, how is the self construal related to the critical concept of context in pragmatics? Second, how is the self understood in association with the inherent relationship between language and thought? To address these questions, in what follows past studies on themes associated with the self in pragmatics, philosophy, and psychology are reviewed. These approaches provide an ontological context for the empty and populated self proposed in this work.

2   The Self and Context in Pragmatics

Context is a critical concept in the study of pragmatics. The movement in pragmatics represented by Mey (1993) defines itself as a study of language and its use in context. The approach in pragmatics places more emphasis on language usage than on its referential meaning. In Mey's view, "it is much more interesting to try and find out *why* people say something than whether *what* they say is true or false" (1993: 14, original emphasis). Emphasis on "why" directs us toward the speaker as opposed to the speech itself. This approach necessitates a critical inquiry into speaking selves, their social identities, communication purposes, and ways of meaning in interaction. Again, to quote Mey, pragmatics encompasses "the science of language seen in relation to its users" (1993: 5). For the purpose of this work, pragmatics is critical in two ways, its importance to context where linguistic activity takes place and the significance of the person who engages in language.

In this work the relationship between the language and its context is further explored so that the Japanese concept of the self is made evident in contrast with English. Instead of focusing on the meanings or functions associated with context, this work interprets meaning as ontological messages related to the speaking self. In other words, it is a philosophical approach to language from the framework of pragmatics which makes use of context as a guide for interpretation.

Context, itself, may be viewed as being external or internal (House 2006). External context involves situational and cultural factors, while internal context involves cognitive factors. Based on the external context, this work examines how the internal context operates involving cognitive, psychological, and ontological aspects. The devices providing the context reflect, activate, and project the emergent construal of the self evident in languages. Contrasting these devices brings to the fore how notions of self differ across languages guiding our task of exploring the concept of self.

2.1 Contextualization and Contextualization Cues

In pragmatics, the concept of context is more accurately understood as a phenomenon of "contextualization." Contextualization captures the dynamic relationship between context and language, and is understood to involve more than a set of pre-existing, pre-fixed discrete variables (Auer and Luzio 1992). Here, the context and language are in a mutually reflexive and interactionally influencing relationship, where language shapes context as much as context shapes language.

Contextualization is a term introduced earlier by Gumperz (1982) and it "involves the process by which we evaluate message meaning and sequencing patterns in relation to aspects of the surface structure of the message" (1982: 162). Cues signaling contextualization are characterized as:

> (...) any feature of linguistic form that contributes to the signaling of contextual presuppositions. Such cues may have a number of such linguistic realizations depending on the historically given linguistic repertoire of the participants. The code, dialect and style switching processes, (...) prosodic phenomena (...) as well as choice among lexical and syntactic options, formulaic expressions, conversational openings, closings and sequencing strategies can all have similar contextualizing functions.
> GUMPERZ 1982: 131

Studies based on contextualization cues can be traced to earlier research in intercultural communication. Gumperz and Tannen (1979) suggest the possibility of communication difficulties associated with misinterpretation of contexualization cues. They introduce the interactional effect of complementary schismogenesis, where each participant in conversation sticks to one's own contextualization cues for conventional interpretation. Under this circumstance, the participant's behavior results in interactional breakdowns. In pragmatics, contextualization and contextualization cues have also been applied for identifying differences in language performance between native and non-native speakers. These studies reveal different functions of contextualization cues, for example in French (Ducharme and Bernard 2001) and Japanese (Ishida 2006; Masuda 2016). Contextualization in a broader sense also provides a tool for investigating its relationship to social power in primary education (Dorr-Bremme 1990). In this work, focus is placed not so much on the difficulty of intercultural or cross-linguistic communication but on the concept of self supported by contextualization cues and evidenced in the discourse of literary genres.

Although studies of contextualization cues have been based on communication, especially on face-to-face conversational interaction, this work does not analyze conversational interaction per se. Its interactive nature, however, is evident in the selected data; dramatic persons interact in specific contexts in the novel, and readers interact with the producers of the original and translation texts. It is true that literary texts and translations are static in nature and they represent carefully thought-out pieces of verbal art. However, both texts require speaking selves (in terms of writer, narrator, and dramatic persons). As in intercultural face-to-face exchanges, difficulties (or gaps) in communication exist between original and translated texts. Instead of identifying these difficulties for improving intercultural understanding, for learning a second or foreign language, or for creating an appropriate translation, this work explores ontological views traceable to the features and to the contextualization cues of literary discourse.

In the contextualization research, both internal and external evidence may be sought (Gumperz 1982). Internal evidence is found in the interactional processes themselves, whereas external evidence is obtained from informants. Internal evidence is obtained by closely examining the process of exchange between participants, such as turn-taking and rhythmic coordination. In this work, only internal evidence is addressed, but evidence of a different nature. Communication in literary text does not occur in the way live conversation does, but contextualization cues in the text guide us in discovering the similarities and differences in ontological positions.

Given that context and contextualization are key to the process of translation, the concept of re-contextualization proposed by House (2006) should be mentioned. House (2006) argues that when translating, the context recognized in the source language undergoes a re-contextualization in the target language. She insists that the concept of contextualization proposed by Gumperz (1982) is not applicable to translation of written text because the interaction does not represent speech, and does not involve on-going interactions. Admittedly, literary text does not directly involve an on-going speech event. However, the translated literary text must be intimately integrated into the target language which requires another process of contextualization. The translator must create a new text that successfully balances a context across two languages. When translation involves typologically unrelated languages, as in Japanese and English, the contextualization process demands delicate adjustment and innovation. In this sense, the manipulation of context in translation embraces contextualization, re-contextualization, and new contextualization. The terminology aside, when contrasting original and translated texts in literary genres, focusing on context, contextualization cues as well as the re-contextualization process provides a useful approach in exploring how the self is projected in contrasted contexts.

2.2   Self in the Self-Contextualization Process

In my earlier studies, I have proposed a related concept of self-contextualization (Maynard 1989) along with concepts such as the speaking self and contextual transformation. This section revisits this approach in bridging the concept of self to the contextualization process.

Maynard (1989) recognizes the self situated in changing contexts of situation. Linguistic expressions are energized by its context and, in turn, the context is renewed by the very use of language. In this process we manipulate how we present our selves in a mutually complementary relationship which I call "self-contextualization." Self-contextualization asserts that a speaker self-contextualizes in verbal and nonverbal communication by perceiving, identifying, and evaluating the overall as well as immediate contexts through which the self properly locates itself. Self-contextualization involves two interacting stages, "contextual interpretation" and "contextual transformation." The first stage involves one's understanding of actual signs and other structural and interactional knowledge. The second stage requires a processing of ideas and intention to transform information in such a way as to be suitable for each exchange. Since the actual situation in communication changes from moment to moment, participants must continually self-contextualize, with each change being mutually incorporated in each other's self-contextualization (Maynard 1989).

To identify this mutually created context of interaction, one must integrate different types of information. First, linguistic knowledge such as grammatical structure, as well as the semantics of lexical units come to mind. Another type involves social and environmental information, including physical settings and sociocultural assumptions about the self and partner. Knowledge regarding discourse organization such as thematic and narrative structures must be integrated into the process of self-contextualization. In addition, self-contextualizing refers to incorporating information regarding the partner's personality and attitude as well as one's mutual feelings toward the partner

How one behaves in communication, then, is deeply influenced by the context of each situation. Although our thoughts play a role in determining our actions, those actions are always influenced by interactions with partners (or audience). And through such context-interacting behavior, we locate our own selves in multiple ways in a society. In this sense, self is always contextualized by way of language and discourse. Ultimately, the discovery of the self must be pursued from the perspective of pragmatics, foregrounding the self both as language user and context manipulator.

Language use in relation to context has become a central theme in pragmatics and discourse analysis. For example, Paltridge (2006), in his introduction to discourse analysis, develops the theme of language in social and cultural contexts including social class, gender, and ideology. Gee (2012) introduces Discourse (with a capital "D") to focus on multiple Discourses with multiple contexts in which a speaker engages in a social action. In his social linguistics, Discourses are much more than language, and they involve the speaker's participation and enactment of the right kind of person in the right kind of context. Discourses are ways of behaving, interacting, thinking, believing, and speaking, always in the process of self-contextualization.

In this work, I define the self as it emerges through language and discourse as follows. Self is a person, a locutionary agent who speaks and engages in language activity in context with the intention to communicate. In conversation, self is involved directly in the verbal act. In fictional discourse, however, the concept of self includes a variety of labels. We are aware that behind every literary work stands the writer or author. And within the narrative the author may assume the narrator's role as well as the role of any participant as a dramatic person. Another related term is the partner, who appears as a conversation participant or a reader. Our speech is always addressed to someone including even to one's self. Significantly in literary genres, partners may be not only dramatic persons but also readers outside of the novel's world.

The self is not an abstract entity. Rather, it is an actor and performer. The self is the flesh-and-blood body-engaging person who engages in language. In this regard, Merleau-Ponty (1962) offers guidance. Merleau-Ponty emphasizes that to describe the phenomenon of speech and the specific act of meaning, one must leave behind the traditional subject-object dichotomy. He laments that we have become accustomed, through the influence of the Cartesian tradition, to jettison the subject. Indeed, the reflective attitude of *cogito* has tended to purify the notions of body and mind to an extreme, and has resulted in its distinct division. A subject is merely what it thinks it is, and an object is something known to the subject. But, Merleau-Ponty reminds us that the "experience of our own body (…) reveals to us an ambiguous mode of existing" (1962: 198). In fact we have no way of knowing the self and that of the ambiguous existence, other than living it.

If language is thought to function only in terms of conveying propositional content, the thinking self is incapable of experiencing emotion, creating personally expressive forms of language, and manipulating language-involving performances. Furthermore, language conceived only as abstract thought cannot be self-manipulated as a part of performance. Merleau-Ponty emphasizes that the "word and speech must somehow cease to be a way of designating things or thoughts" and rather, they must "become the presence of that thought in the phenomenal world, and, moreover, not its clothing but its token or its body" (1962: 182).

The idea represented by Merleau-Ponty (1962) that the self is embodied has been pursued in disciplines including psychology, cognitive science, sociology, and pragmatics. These studies under the term "embodiment" take the position that the cognition depends on experiences perceived by one's body, and that the body itself is embedded in psychological and cultural context. In cognitive science it is understood "the world we construct is grounded in our experience as creatures with bodies who interact with their surroundings through physical processes involving sensory and motor activity" (Johnson 2018: 524). In investigating social interaction, Mondada (2019) emphasizes the importance of focusing not only on language but gesture, gaze, body posture, movement, and embodied manipulation of objects. This is because participants of conversation engage with their bodies for communicating and for sensing each other and the world.

Understanding the self as being embodied is essential for exploring multiple aspects of the self. We must avoid assuming that language is merely a symbolic representation of an objectively existing reality. We must reject treating language as a human faculty independent of perception, motor movement, and image formation.[1] This is because "linguistic meaning is embodied; it arises from our biological capacities and our physical and sociocultural experiences as beings functioning in our environment" (Marmaridou 2000: 4). In fact, as Burdelski (2010) reports, socializing politeness routines in the childhood education environment in Japan requires both verbal and non-verbal politeness routines as a part of embodied social action.

One may be unaware of the bodied self, but it is this self that perceives, creates, and manipulates the language in context. Our senses of self are discovered

---

[1] The concept of embodiment is applied in linguistic analysis in concrete and direct ways. For example, Zlatev and Blomberg (2016) phenomenologically investigate expressions of non-actual motion, e.g., *The road goes through the forest* on the basis of embodied subjectivity. They find that the meaning of such a sentence is intrinsically layered in human bodily experiences, emphasizing that the language is grounded in the embodied self.

in our experience made possible by the embodied self, and this self engages ideas and imagination all located in the context of communication. We become selves in context when we are engaged in communication; we become selves when we interactionally perform and are pragmatically realized. My concept of self approached from the pragmatics perspective is opposed to a concept of self that is abstract, isolated, and unchanging. I should add that my approach also embraces a self that is free and often playful, willfully deviating from established or recognized language use.

3 Language, Thought, and the Self

This section discusses the relationship between language and thought focusing on the concept of self. Initially, the controversy of linguistic relativity is reviewed and discussed, followed by an appreciation of the undeniable relationships between language and its associated ontological views. In the process, I present my position toward linguistic relativity and reflect on how it plays a role in the framework of philosophical contrastive pragmatics.

3.1 *The Linguistic Relativity Issue*

Linguistic relativity, or what Leavitt (2011) aptly refers to as linguistic relativities implying multiple versions, has a long and winding history. The linguistic relativity hypothesis has been a major topic of controversy in Western thought since the Enlightenment. It has been an enduring theme for anyone interested in linguistics, pragmatics, philosophy, anthropology, social psychology, translation studies, and cultural studies, among others.

Perhaps Whorf (1956) serves as a starting point for our discussion. Whorf presents his position in his frequently quoted excerpt as given below.

> Formulation of ideas is not an independent process, strictly rational in the old sense, but is part of a particular grammar, and differs, from slightly to greatly, between different grammars. We dissect nature along lines laid down by our native languages. The categories and types that we isolate from the world of phenomena we do not find there because they stare every observer in the face; on the contrary, the world is presented in a kaleidoscopic flux of impression which has to be organized by our minds—and this means largely by the linguistic systems in our minds.
> WHORF 1956: 212

Whorf's position stated above has, for decades, stirred positive and negative responses from scholars, and the controversy of whether people who speak different languages think differently lingers on today. Linguistic relativity assumes that languages can differ significantly in lexical meanings and syntactic constructions which can affect how its speakers perceive and conceptualize the world, and accordingly, think. An extreme case of this takes the position that language shapes thought, i.e., linguistic determinism. A moderate position understands that language can influence and affect thinking.

Different interpretations of the Whorfian hypothesis aside, Whorf's analysis has come under attack (Pullum 1991; Pinker 1994), and the cognitive approach to linguistics has fueled an anti-Whorfian movement. It is argued that we need to conceptualize a category before labeling it as such, i.e., cognition or natural human instinct precedes language. Among cognitive linguists, universals took precedence over linguistic diversity to the point where some of the facts were suppressed. In a way Whorf bashing has become a pastime for many scholars (Leavitt 2011).

On the other hand, since the days of Whorf, the notion of linguistic relativity has persisted, if only in the shadow of dominant linguistic approaches. For example, Lyons (1994) shares his thought as the following.

> I do subscribe, however, to a more moderate version of Whorfianism (...), according to which the *language* to which one is exposed—the language that is the product of the use of a particular *langue*—facilitates one way rather than another of categorizing phenomena and talking about them.
> LYONS 1994: 12–13, original emphasis

Interest in linguistic relativity has continued as evidenced by the availability of edited volumes revisiting the issue (Gumperz and Levinson 1996; Pütz and Verspoor 2000). Linguistic relativity has recently experienced a substantial resurgence in scholarly interest (Everett 2013; Lucy 2016). Empirical studies involving many different languages have uncovered subtle but convincing interactions between language and thought, leading to more nuanced versions of the hypothesis. After examining recent empirical research, Everett (2013) finds that many studies support the theme endorsed by linguistic relativity in various degrees and forms. Given the discoveries made in experimental psychology, anthropology, and ethnomethodology in recent years, linguistic relativity is now generally viewed as being undeniable. Whorf has made a comeback, indeed.

Everett (2013) distinguishes classical Whorfianism from the work of contemporary researchers (i.e., Neo-Whorfian scholars) who seek to substantiate a moderate version of the relativity hypothesis. Everett reviews research on spatial orientation, the construal of time, numerical cognition, the perception of colors, the categorization of objects among others, and concludes that they provide evidence to support different kinds of linguistic relativity, some representing a comparatively weak variety but some others having a major impact on human cognition. He takes the position that a majority of the data examined suggests that systematic differences in linguistic practice can and do create divergent cognitive habits. Everett endorses the relativistic position but cautions by reminding us that "careful examinations of the relevant data often suggest that more nuanced approaches to the answer (rather than a vociferous 'yes' or 'no'), and to the formulation of the question itself, may be warranted" (2013: 1).

Valid or not, the linguistic relativity hypothesis remains an open question. Many languages (including Mandarin and English, two major languages) are examined, but many others are not. Empirical evidence reported so far offers undeniable support for linguistic relativity, but more studies involving unexamined languages and discourse genres are required. It is reasonable to grant that some degrees of cognitive universals exist. For it is not the case that form and use of language determine what people can possibly think or experience. Humans share some cognitive capacities regardless of languages spoken. Still, specific languages do influence what people usually and habitually think and experience; some languages require certain kinds of cognitive processes while others do not. These differences across languages lead to variabilities in certain nonlinguistic cognitive activities as well. I do not prescribe to the extreme view that language determines thought, but neither can I absolutely deny the concept of linguistic relativity.

An empirical study involving Japanese and English supports this position. Imai and Mazuka (2007) examine how the labels and the count-mass structure in Japanese and English are associated with different construals of individuation. Their conclusions on linguistic relativity are two-fold. Although the distinction concerning individuation of objects is universally shared, linguistic relativity is partially observed at different developmental stages among Japanese speakers as well as across Japanese- and English-speaking subjects. The conclusion drawn by Imai and Mazuka (2007) offers substantial support for the position that human cognition is neither entirely universal nor entirely relative. Linguistic relativity plays multiple roles in complex ways and influences the speaker's cognitive processes.

When accessing linguistic relativity, Whorf's (1956) more moderate phrase "fashions of speaking" makes sense. Whorf suggests language as a whole (not just a lexical item or a grammatical structure) encourages certain ways of viewing the world. I have examined discourse phenomena from the perspective of pragmatics across Japanese and English in many of my earlier works (Maynard 1989, 1993a, 1993b, 2000, 2002), and have identified differences as fashions of speaking. In this work, the Japanese empty and populated self is understood to represent, motivate, and reflect a fundamental element of Japanese fashions of speaking.

In addition, it is important to remind ourselves that relativistic phenomena may exist among speakers of the same language, particularly when aspects of linguistic practices significantly vary. It should also be emphasized that not all elements of human cognitive processes are singularly determined by the speaker's native language. Furthermore, people often learn multiple languages and incorporate new features into their native languages, leading to multiple language-and-thought relationships.

A critical point when questioning the scope of linguistic relativity involves the influence of language when it is not used for communication. My position is that language influences thought while not in active use, and the concept of self in Japanese is sustained as a basic ontological understanding. The effects of language are not only deeply rooted but also form long-term habits of thought; they are not temporary thought patterns that come to be only during actual interaction. On this issue Reines and Prinz (2009) as well as Wolff and Holmes (2011) offer further guidance.

Reines and Prinz (2009) focus on two theses, i.e., Habitual Whorfianism and Ontological Whorfianism. Habitual Whorfianism refers to the position in which "languages influence psychological processes because they instill habits of thought that lead us to think in certain ways by default" (2009: 1028). Ontological Whorfianism refers to the position in which "languages influence psychological processes because they lead us to organize the world into categories that differ from those we would discover without language" (2009: 1029). They argue that these two Whorfian theses offer the most promising interpretations of the evidence provided by recent empirical research. After reviewing some representative empirical results such as grammatical gender (Spanish and German), frame of reference (Tzeltal), special categories (Korean), and noun types (Yucatec Maya), they conclude that language shapes the categorical boundaries that constitute our subjective organization of the world, and it influences our ontologies. Thus, their answer to the question is positive; language influences cognition while not in use.

The process of how the self is experienced and understood can be approached in the same manner. Although the self emerges through language use, it lingers on beyond the moment of its use. The Japanese language makes it possible for its speakers to attend to features of the world that embrace the empty and populated self. These features become habitual, and reinforce a specific way of conceptualizing the self. The Japanese language imposes the types of category boundaries unavailable otherwise. In this sense, language is not merely a vehicle for expressing thoughts; it enables its speakers to habitually conceptualize their selves in their own ways.

Another study exploring the function of language in relation to linguistic relativity offers a further supportive insight. Wolff and Holmes (2011) identify the possible effects of language on thought across a wide range of domains, including motion, color, spatial relations, and number. They conclude that although the literature on linguistic relativity remains contentious, there is growing support for the view that language has a profound effect on thought. Lamenting the idea that linguistic relativity is taken as a mere weak form of linguistic determinism, they argue that the strong-weak distinction oversimplifies a more complicated picture, and it ignores what is emerging in recent research. Their survey of the field suggests that the following five versions of the Whorfian hypothesis have garnered convincing empirical support.

1. Thinking occurs before language use (thinking for speaking).
2. Linguistic and nonlinguistic codes compete against each other (language as meddler).
3. Linguistic codes extend nonlinguistic thinking (language as augmenter).
4. Thinking is directed toward properties highlighted by language (language as spotlight).
5. Language engages a schematic mode of processing (language as inducer).

The concept of the Japanese self lingers on and facilitates specific ways of thinking. Japanese words and structures may highlight specific properties, where linguistic signs may act as a spotlight, augmenting certain aspects of the self by making them more salient than others. Self-expressions in Japanese may induce a given mode of processing, which may persist even when Japanese speakers engage in other nonlinguistic tasks. The Japanese language induces a kind of self which becomes a resource for speaking, which in turn continues its process of meddling, augmenting, spotlighting, and inducing certain ways of being. In this circular manner involving the process of language and thought, the Japanese language is intimately associated with the concept of the self. The self as proposed in this work serves as a flowing cognitive undercurrent situated in a Japanese ontological understanding.

3.2 *Language and Ontological Views*

The relation between language and ontology has been approached from philosophical and psychological perspectives, some of which are presented below. Discussing language and thought in association with the self, Heidegger (1971

[1959]) offers some philosophical insight. Heidegger's hermeneutic phenomenological approach in his ontology of Being is most directly presented in his work *On the Way to Language* (1971 [1959]). Before reviewing his position on language and thought, his approach to language itself should be introduced. In essence, Heidegger thinks that one should not understand language as existing in the abstract nor as an object existing out there; instead, one should investigate language as practiced in our ordinary lives.

Referring to Humboldt's view of language not as *ergon* but as *energeia*, Heidegger (1971 [1959]) insists that language should be viewed not as a product, but as a speaking activity, and proposes that the way to understand language must be based on what he calls "Saying" or "Showing."[2] Saying and Showing foreground the person who engages in language in the actual situation of interaction through a process of what he calls "Appropriation." Appropriation "yields the opening of the clearing in which present beings can persist and from which absent beings can depart" (1971 [1959]: 127). And it is a process through which all present and absent beings are brought into where "they show themselves in what they are, and where they abide according to their kind" (1971 [1959]: 127). Heidegger finds a significant importance in language whose practice instantiates the Appropriation process itself. He concludes by proclaiming that "(L)anguage is the house of Being because language, as Saying, is the mode of Appropriation" (1971 [1959]: 135).

Understanding the relationship between language and Being in this way, Heidegger (1971 [1959]) identifies language as a source for his philosophy, and issues the following statement connecting how language is designed to reflect the fundamental nature of humanity.

> The ability to speak is what marks man as man. This mark contains the design of his being. Man would not be man if it were denied him to speak unceasingly, from everywhere and every which way, in many variations, and to speak in terms of an "it is" that most often remains unspoken. Language, in granting all this to man, is the foundation of human being. We are, then, within language and with language before all else.
> HEIDEGGER 1971 [1959]: 112

A related critical point Heidegger (1971 [1959]) makes lies in the cross-linguistic variability of the relationship between the self and language. In Heidegger's view, all human languages are true languages but this holds true only when

---

[2] Humboldt's position is explained in Mueller-Vollmer and Messling (2017).

they are used in specific societies as they adhere to their particular destinies. Accordingly, languages contain different designs or plans that guide us to different ontological views. Heidegger insists that a natural language would never occur in and of itself without a destiny, stating "(A)ll language is historical, even where man does not know history in the modern European sense" (Heidegger 1971 [1959]: 133). Approaching language as a participatory event (of Saying and Showing), Heidegger recognizes the destined variability across languages.

Another important approach toward language and the concept of self comes from a social psychological perspective, particularly Vygotsky (Lucy and Wertsch 1987). Vygotsky (1962 [1934]) addresses the relationships among language, thought, and society in the context of child development. As I have touched upon in my earlier studies (Maynard 1993a, 2002), Vygotsky (1962 [1934]) addresses the issue of semiotic mediation in the context of child development. In Vygotsky's view, the cognitive development of an individual child is accomplished through a process of internalization of language, which is first used by the child in the socialization process. Vygotsky emphasizes that the higher psychological processes an individual attains directly reflect the social processes in which that individual has participated during earlier developmental stages, especially through the use of language. When Vygotsky takes a position that "all higher mental functions are internalized social relationships" (Wertsch 1979: 164), we are reminded that human beings retain the functions of social interaction even in our innermost private spheres. Once speech is internalized, it continues interacting with human consciousness and regulating cognitive activity. If so, one's ontological view is dependent on one's language and language-engaging interactional experiences.

Although Vygotsky himself does not refer to the language in literary genres, when Vygotsky uses the term "word," he means more than the morphological unit. The term "word" used by Vygotsky "does not refer solely to morphological units; rather, phrases, sentences, and entire texts fall under this category as well" (Wertsch 1979: 158). Japanese literary works and their translation texts selected for this study are expected to provide a reasonable resource for investigating the relationship between language and its ontological view.

At this point, for further clarification of the relationship between language and ontology, perhaps a comparison between Vygotsky and Whorf is useful. Although they worked in different intellectual settings, each viewed language as a social and cultural phenomenon, and understood individual thought to be socially influenced, serving as a mediator between the self and society. Vygotsky, in his sociocultural, historical, and ontological approach to the mind, was interested in the developmental stages of the form and function of speech in a single language. In contrast, Whorf, with his view that human languages are different in important ways, was interested in documenting the diversity of language forms. Vygotsky focused on diachronic changes within a single language, and Whorf, on synchronic comparisons across languages. In Vygotsky's view, language transforms thought in the process of socialization, and this facilitates and promotes the development of human consciousness resulting in the emergence of higher conceptual forms (Lucy and Wertsch 1987). Viewing that language constrains thought, influencing it in culturally specific patterns, Whorf interprets the influence of language on thought in terms of its implications for limiting human awareness.

For the purpose of this work, Vygotsky and Whorf offer complementary interpretive resources. By combining both, it is possible to understand the language-and-thought relationship both diachronically (historically and intra-linguistically) and synchronically (comparatively and inter-linguistically). This work takes into account both the Vygotskian understanding of language's psychosocial messages, and the Whorfian theme of cross-linguistic variability.

Finally, Taylor (2016) should be mentioned for advancing an interesting approach toward language and ontology. In his earlier study, Taylor (1985) insists that the expressive dimension is fundamental to language and therefore is more important than the designative dimension. He criticizes the Cartesian view of language that focuses on the propositional meaning where the method of isolating terms and tracing correlations with objects plays a central role. Regarding the root of this mistaken position, Taylor argues that "(T)his was grounded in the view, common to Descartes and his empiricist critics, that the contents of the mind were in principle open to transparent inspection by the subject himself" (Taylor 1985: 241).

In *The Language Animal*, Taylor (2016) interprets the Whorfian hypothesis not in terms of designative dimensions (such as simplified concepts of time and color), but more in terms of expressive functions. In his view, the cultural differences observed today lie deeper than those surface lexical items, and complex differences expand to ethical, social, and political dimensions. We are language animals who use language creatively and interpersonally, far beyond the designative dimension, and in this process the language serves as a constitutive means for the self.

We are of language and are defined in terms of language more deeply than commonly understood. Along with this position, the relationship between language and ontology appears in a different light and bears a renewed philosophical significance. It implies that languages are expected to lead to different ontological views, i.e., "ontological relativity," where one can discover philosophical messages of language both on micro- and macro-levels. Given that past studies on language, thought, and self primarily focused on speech and interaction, focusing on the literary text and its translation in this work expands the scope of analysis. In the course of this volume, not just one linguistic phenomenon but a wide range of linguistic devices and discourse strategies on multiple levels are examined. Most relevantly, this work asks the ontological question incorporating Japanese intellectual traditions that have been underrepresented in the linguistic relativity debate. It is hoped that this work paves the way for moving the debate on the language-and-thought controversy away from an extreme polarization of perspectives, but rather, toward a productive discussion on the nature of languages' undeniable influence on cognition and emotion. In the process we come closer to embracing the varied manners in which humans relatively conceive, perceive, and experience their selves in multiple ways across languages and cultures.

4   Data

4.1   *Study of Literary Works*

Data for this study are selected from literary genres. This is because the literary text, such as the novel, provides relatively restriction-free space where one's inner thoughts and feelings are richly expressed. Ostensibly objective writings such as news reports or legal documents do not strongly reflect the writer's personal attitude and therefore are not suitable for an ontological pursuit.

Lukács (1971) and Bakhtin (1981) approach the novel as a resource for literary and philosophical studies. Lukács (1971), in his attempt to find the novel's social and historical significance, positions the novel as a means through which a problematic individual reveals his or her self, stating that it is the road "towards clear self-recognition" (1971: 80). Discourse of the novel is expected to provide a useful site for exploring the concept of self.

Interestingly, Lukács (1971) compares Dostoevsky's novels with traditional Romantic novels claiming that Dostoevsky's works defy genre identification. Still, it is in Dostoevsky's works that Bakhtin (1981) pursues his philosophy of language. Bakhtin views the novel as a kind of linguistic behavior, as a verbal event. To fully understand it, we must incorporate the surrounding contextual information. The novel offers an information-rich text that reflects the social context of which it is a part. For example, direct quotation appearing in the novel does not merely represent conversation performed by dramatic persons within the novelistic universe, but, significantly, it reflects and endorses the sociocultural and philosophical values of its time.

For Bakhtin (1981), discourse of the novel is uniquely rich and alive, possessing critical qualities absent in other genres. The novel is always in the process of forming, and only the novel is receptive to innovative linguistic forms and new textual interpretation. In fact Bakhtin insists that to study genres other than the novel (e.g., epic) is to study dead language, and to study the discourse of the novel is to study a language that is alive, young, and currently forming. Discourse of the novel is free, and remains receptive to social changes and adjustments people make in their lives. Novels incorporate voices of people who use varied language styles with complex and overlapping features. Bakhtin insists that novels remain semantically receptive to languages of other genres because they maintain a timely relationship with a constantly changing reality, and their expressions are an approximation of ordinary everyday language.

As summarized above, of all genres, literary genres selected for this study are suitable for philosophical contrastive pragmatics. Most fundamentally, literary text is ideal as a data source because it often allows the researcher access to inner feelings of the author, narrator, and dramatic persons, all closely associated with ontological perspectives.

I must add here that discourse of the novel constitutes an undeniable part of language culture. As I discuss in the course of this volume, novels represent mediated discourse containing stereotyped expressions such as gender- and age-associated variations, often no longer in use in ordinary language practice. One may argue that discourse of the novel, for not consisting of naturally occurring speech, fails to supply adequate data for a philosophical pragmatics approach. However, I emphasize that language in Japanese literary genres is a part of language practice forming a significant phenomenon of the Japanese language culture, thus providing a reasonable resource for this work.

I have selected literary works whose published translations are readily available. Self-produced Japanese examples with self-produced English translations are likely to ignore language phenomena beyond the researcher's immediate access. Data created by third parties provide the distance necessary for objective analyses, and this feature supports pragmatics analysis for which the manipulation of data should be minimized. Although the usefulness of translation texts is recognized, I am aware that the reliability of the translation text itself remains controversial. In this regard, Kawahara's (2011) summary on the history of equivalence offers guidance. In the past, scholars who paid attention to equivalence between two languages tended to seriously doubt the possibility of translation. A more recent approach, however, is to appreciate equivalence in terms of the translation's social function. Different types of translation texts have come to be valued for what they serve. Still, issues of accuracy, usefulness, as well as naturalness remain unresolved (Baker 1992). Obviously, translation texts are not entirely problem-free, but it is also the case that the text created by a translator can avoid the bias of researcher-centeredness. I will revisit this controversy more thoroughly in Chapter 4.

Variability presents another potential problem in using translation texts as data. Translation texts are produced by different individuals with varied backgrounds, and the same source text may produce different results. However, one can identify generalizable differences across source and target texts. For example, Osawa (2010), from the perspective of comparative literature, persuasively isolates differences between original Japanese novels and English translations. The gap he finds is caused by the following features of the English translation text; (1) use of additional explanation, (2) shorter sentences, dividing long sentences into shorter ones, (3) a changed tone of style, translation being more casual, and (4) avoidance of certain descriptions sensitive to the target audience.[3] When these tendencies are observed consistently across multiple works, despite obvious individual and situational variation, it is possible to generalize cross-linguistic differences. The translator, being proficient in two languages, possesses a certain sense of naturalness associated with each language. When contrasting original and translation texts, a number of consistent corresponding features become apparent. It is fair to conclude that translation texts provide reasonable data for philosophical contrastive pragmatics.[4]

4.2   *Selection*

Although in the past linguistic analyses of Japanese novels have been limited to a small number of classical works, I have selected literary works representing mass and popular culture as listed below. As exemplified by many of my own research designs (Maynard 2000, 2002, 2012, 2014, 2016, 2017), I have made an effort to analyze discourse that reflects today's Japanese language culture. Note that multiple translations are available for the Japanese story *Ginga Tetsudoo no Yoru* listed below; four different translations are selected for analysis. Works, totaling to 28, are listed separately according to genres, and are ordered by the original author's last name followed by the translated work.

1. contemporary novels:
   - Kawakami, Hiromi: *Sensei no Kaban*
   - Powell, Allison Markin: *The Briefcase*

---

3 These features are associated with translation universals discussed in Chapter 4.
4 I should mention here that the use of translation texts adds not only to philosophical contrastive pragmatics but to multiple disciplines. For example, translation data are analyzed to understand cross-linguistic variations in discourse (Teich 2003) and to reveal cases of language contact (Kranich 2014).

- Oe, Kenzaburo: *Torikaeko Chenjiringu*
- Boehm, Deborah Boliver: *The Changeling*
- Yoshimoto, Banana: *Kitchin*
- Backus, Megan: *Kitchen*
- Yoshimoto, Banana: *Tsugumi*
- Emmerich, Michael: *Goodbye Tsugumi*

2. light novels:[5]
   - Nomura, Mizuki: *"Bungaku Shoojo" to Shini Tagari no Dooke*
   - McGillicuddy, Karen: *Book Girl and the Suicidal Mime*
   - Nomura, Mizuki: *"Bungaku Shoojo" to Dookoku no Junreisha*
   - McGillicuddy, Karen: *Book Girl and the Wayfarer's Lamentation*
   - Tanigawa, Nagaru: *Suzumiya Haruhi no Yuuutsu*
   - Pai, Chris: *The Melancholy of Haruhi Suzumiya*

3. mystery novels:
   - Higashino, Keigo: *Manatsu no Hooteishiki*.
   - Smith, Alexander O.: *A Midsummer's Equation*
   - Miyabe, Miyuki: *R.P.G.*
   - Carpenter, Juliet Winters: *Shadow Family*

4. stories:
   - Miyazawa, Kenji: *Ginga Tetsudoo no Yoru*
   - Bester, John: *Night Train to the Stars*
   - Neville, Julianne: *Night on the Galactic Railroad & Other Stories from Ihatov*
   - Pulvers, Roger: *Eigo de Yomu Ginga Tetsudoo no Yoru*
   - Sigrist, Joseph and D.M. Stroud: *Milky Way Railroad*

It should be noted that in *Milky Way Railroad* (Sigrist and Stroud 1996), dramatic persons appear with Japanese names; Jobanni as Kenji, Kamupanerura as Minoru, and Zaneri as Akira. Also the name of Kamupanerura's pet dog is changed from Zaueru to Pooch.

---

5 Light novels, primarily popularized since the late 1990s in Japan, are entertainment novels with anime-like illustrations that mainly target junior high school and high school boys, young adult males, and popular culture consumers. In the 2010s the genre and the market of light novels have undergone changes. Some of the light novels have enjoyed the readership of both men and women in their 40s, some even in their 50s. Light novels generally include the following features (Maynard 2012); (1) works are produced in the context of game-like-realism, (2) stories rely heavily on their characters, (3) a character database is created, (4) visual information plays an important role and is integrated into the text, (5) the stories frequently appear as a series, and (6) as popular culture entertainment, they often appear on multiple media platforms.

In Chapter 12, I analyze English and Japanese translation texts of a Russian novel. Also included are two separate translations of an American short story as listed below.

5. English and Japanese translation texts of a Russian novel:
   - Nabokov, Dmitri: *The Eye*
   - Ogasawara, Toyoki: *Me*
6. American short story and Japanese translations:
   - Auster, Paul: *Auggie Wren's Christmas Story*
   - Murakami, Haruki: *Oogii Ren no Kurisumasu Sutoorii*
   - Shibata, Motoyuki: *Oogii Ren no Kurisumasu Sutoorii*

Throughout this volume, isolated examples are presented to highlight specific phenomena. However, because contextual information available in an adjacent or nearby text is significant for interpretation, when necessary, the additional information is presented. Although only limited examples are given for making specific points, the phenomena under discussion are widely observed, and are not meant by any means to be rare occurrences. To provide broader contextual information, brief synopses of the works selected for data are presented in the Appendix. I should warn the reader that some of the discussion on data in subsequent chapters and the synopses contain spoilers.

4.3 On Data Presentation

The Romanized transliteration of Japanese words is given in phonetic orthography referred to as the Hepburn style with the following alterations. In presenting double consonants, before *cha*, *chi*, *chu*, and *cho*, *t* is added, thus instead of *icchi* 'agreement', *itchi* is used. Syllabic *n* is written *n* unless immediately preceding a vowel, in which case it is written *n'*. The glottal stop, written as small *tsu* in Japanese, is spelled out as *tt*. Long vowels are transcribed with double vowels including names of dramatic persons, e.g., Goroo, although in English translation, following the translator's method, a single vowel is used, e.g., Goro. As for Japanese proper nouns, the modified Hepburn style is used as stated above, except when established usage is available, e.g., Tokyo instead of Tookyoo. Regarding personal names, I use a single vowel in place of the original long vowel, as in Kenzaburo Oe without diacritic marks. Diacritic marks used for Japanese names are reproduced only when they appear within quoted segments. In references, Japanese names are reproduced as they appear in respective publications including diacritic marks.

Within the text, the following rules apply.
1. All Japanese examples are presented in italicized Romanization with my (often literal) English translations in single quotation marks.

2. All Japanese phrases or sentences appear in italicized Romanization with English translations in single quotation marks.
3. When Japanese phrases or sentences taken from literary works are discussed in contrast with authentic English translation, Japanese sources are specified in parentheses.

In data examples, separated from the text, the following rules apply.

1. Varied methods are used as explained below. A specific method is chosen based on what I think most reasonable and useful for the analysis.
2. Romanized transliteration of the Japanese examples may be accompanied by their published English texts with their sources specified. When multiple translations are presented for a specific source text, those translations appear as (1b), (1c), and so on. In both Japanese and English examples, quoted sentences appear marked with quotation marks even when forming a part of long quotations.
3. The division of words in transliteration is only for glossing and clarification. Although some morphemes appear attached to words and some do not, those discretionary decisions are made only for convenience. Paragraph divisions in the original and translation texts do not necessarily match; paragraph indentions are reproduced as they appear in the works examined.
4. For a few sentences where morphological and grammatical information is critical, the Leipzig glossing method is followed as much as possible. Note the following grammatical labels; GEN (genitive marker), IP (interactional particle), OBJ (object marker), and TOP (topic marker).
5. When authentic translations are unavailable, my own, often literal, translations are given in square brackets.
6. Some Japanese examples are presented with my (often literal) translations in square brackets, followed by (authentic) English translations with sources specified. In English literal translation, phrases that more directly reflect the information in the source text are parenthesized. These phrases are additions and are likely to cause unnatural English text, but presented only for clarification.
7. In many cases, only English translation texts are presented as data, but key Japanese phrases attributable to specific English translated expressions are presented in parentheses at appropriate locations. When general semantic or stylistic correspondences exist between Japanese and English texts, Japanese expressions are added in parentheses at the end of the relevant translation segments.
8. When attributable Japanese expressions are absent (as in the case of the zero-form), "zero" is used to indicate the absence.

9. In data examples, phrases and segments mentioned in the main text are presented in bold letters excluding those that appear in parentheses.

5 Organization of the Book

The 13 chapters are divided into four parts. Part 1 includes introductory Chapters 1 and 2 as well as Chapters 3 and 4 which discuss the methodological framework. Part 2, consisting of Chapters 5 and 6, provides philosophical and linguistic context for the concept of self in Japanese studies. In Chapters 7 through 11 of Part 3, I concentrate on contrastive analysis of data whose process reveals those features of the Japanese language not fully reflected in English. Translation gaps provide supporting evidence for the thesis of this work, exploring the empty and populated self in Japanese in contrast with English. Chapter 12 focusing on Japanese as translation text, reveals that the observations made in Chapters 7 through 11 also occur consistently in Japanese translation. Chapter 13 in Part 4 concludes with some final thoughts.

Chapter 1, Introduction, offers general remarks. Here I introduce a philosophical contrastive pragmatics and two critical concepts, context in pragmatics and linguistic relativity. The main theme of this work is also introduced, i.e., the Japanese empty self in the empty place, and the self that is populated with multiple aspects, characters, and characteristics. This chapter also explains the rationale for choosing literary works as data.

Chapter 2 reviews the concept of self in Western thought and linguistics. After reviewing the Cartesian view, I discuss Western approaches that challenge the traditional Western understanding of the self and language. Included are modern and postmodern deconstructionist studies from multiple disciplines such as psychology, sociology, and narrative studies. These studies provide scholarly context for exploring the concept of self from Western perspectives.

Chapter 3 focuses on the key concepts, subjectivity and character, as analytical resources. Subjectivity along with intersubjectivity offer guidance for analyzing self-expressions that indexically mark multiple aspects of the self. Character plays a role in understanding how the empty self is populated with characters and characteristics through character-speak. Also relevant for establishing the framework are two areas of research, translation studies and contrastive pragmatics involving translation text. Chapter 4 reviews perspectives from these areas of study. Translation studies provide justification and warnings when using translation texts as data, and offer an opportunity to review issues involving the Japanese language and translations of Western works.

Also discussed are research in pragmatics involving translation, i.e., contrastive translation analysis approached from literary stylistics, as well as issues related to translation universals.

In Chapter 5, I review the concept of empty self in empty place in Japanese studies. First, the influence of (zen) Buddhism to the concept of emptiness is reviewed. Then Nishida's (1949) philosophy based on the "place of nothingness" is introduced. I also discuss Miyazawa's (in Otsuka 1996) poetic interpretation of the self. Continuing within the Japanese context, in Chapter 6, I discuss how Japanese language studies have dealt with the concept of self since the Edo period. Then Tokieda's (1941, 1950) position is introduced, where self is based on the situated place. In his view, language operates within a dynamic process in which the self and situation intimately and emotively interact. In addition, Watsuji's (1990a [1962], 1990b [1962]) hermeneutic approach is discussed where an interdependent self is explored, followed by discussions on the multiplicity of self in Japanese discourse. Here I review contemporary Japanese sociological and psychological approaches to the concept of self which support the position that self is not an *a priori* theoretical construct, but emerges as being empty and populated.

In analyzing Japanese and translation texts, Chapters 7 through 11 focus on the ways in which the Japanese empty self in an empty place is populated. I discuss grammatical phenomena such as first-person references, avoidance of the transitive sentence structure, the topic-comment dynamism, and varied types of quotation and monologue. Also analyzed are speech variations as character-speak including stylistic shifts, regional dialects, and borrowed fictional varieties. I analyze data primarily taking a qualitative approach through context-based interpretation, using tools developed in multiple research areas of language studies. Different approaches are highlighted and applied to specific phenomena focused in analysis chapters.

Chapter 7 examines the empty self as presented through person-referencing terms such as the zero-form, self-referencing *watashi* 'I' and *jibun* 'self' as well as different reference forms assigned to dramatic persons. Most critically, the zero-form reveals that the Japanese self is presented as being empty, but only to be populated in the on-going discursive practice. Unlike English person-related expressions, the Japanese language, foregrounding different aspects of the self, allows for choosing fluctuating forms.

Chapter 8 concentrates on Japanese grammar where the perceptive and receptive self is captured as an experiencer of situated events and states. As evidenced by the avoidance of transitive verbs that prioritize the cause-effect schema, the Japanese self materializes with perceptive and receptive aspects through the means of perception verbs, emotive passives, and verbs of giving.

One of the most fundamental information structures in Japanese is the topic-comment dynamism which the expressive self manipulates from behind the scene. Chapter 9 explores this dynamic relationship in Japanese grammar and discourse, specifically by focusing on the use and non-use of the topic marker *wa*. The topic-comment rhetoric in discourse offers a space where the hidden self controls the staging effect. This chapter also examines the *no da* nominal predicate.

The Japanese self's transient nature is realized through quotation and related phenomena. Chapter 10 discusses varied manners of inserted speech in the Japanese language, by capturing the quoting self as a voice-manipulating self. Then I illustrate how, by cross-examining among different kinds of quotations and monologues, the self is realized as being transferred between first- and third-person perspectives. This strategy of quotation reveals the extent of freedom the self enjoys in creating differentiating yet emerging aspects of the transferred self. Chapter 11 demonstrates how the character-speak realizes the populating process of self with stereotyped characters and characteristics. Analyses include middle-aged-male language, youth language, the effeminate *onee* language as well as a variety of regional and fictional dialects.

All features analyzed in Chapters 7 through 11 are not fully and consistently reflected in English translation texts. I argue that semantic and expressive gaps are rooted in varied and sometimes radically different conceptualizations of the self that lurk beneath Japanese and translation texts.

Chapter 12 offers the contrastive analysis of Japanese as the target text. Analyses reveal that the features discussed in earlier analyses chapters are repeatedly observed in translated Japanese texts. Translation texts created in an opposite direction provide further evidence that semantic and expressive linguistic practices in Japanese differ from those in English, confirming different ontological orientations and motivations.

In the final chapter, Chapter 13, I summarize this work emphasizing the significance of the contrastive approach in the study of language and thought. In exploring the self, a new understanding is needed for establishing the theoretical notion of the self in language studies. Also in this chapter, with an awareness of and concern for using Japanese as a metalanguage for theory-building, I address the potential applicability of this study to language cultures outside of Japan, especially in the context of the *Nihonjinron* debate. I conclude this volume with an optimistic call for further advancement toward a more open and embracing appreciation of the concept of self. Understanding who the self is (or who selves are) through the hybridity of Western and non-Western approaches is hoped to transcend some of the limitations in linguistics, other language-associated fields, and beyond.

CHAPTER 2

From Traditional to Postmodern Concepts of Self in the West

To explore the self from the perspective of philosophical contrastive pragmatics, it is necessary to understand its academic context. As symbolized by Heidegger's (1971 [1959]) position that language is the house of Being, language is where one discovers one's self as a language user. This chapter briefly reviews the concept of self developed in Western academia which will provide resources associated with and leading toward the Japanese empty and populated self. It should be noted that the selection of studies to follow is known to have influenced or has been influenced by Japanese scholarly traditions. Obviously, given the aim of this work, only a brief background review is possible. These studies reveal both differences and similarities in the conceptualization of the self and identity across Japan and the West.

When thinking about the self, perhaps the most familiar and taken-forgranted understanding in the West (prominently in North America) is that of a person as a self-contained individual (Sampson 1989). Such a person is construed as a firmly bounded, highly individuated person, most aptly captured by Geertz (1984) as he criticizes such an approach. In his words:

> The Western conception of the person as a bounded, unique, more or less integrated motivational and cognitive universe, a dynamic center of awareness, emotion, judgment and action, organized into a distinctive whole and set contrastively against other such wholes and against a social and natural background is, however incorrigible it may seem to us, a rather peculiar idea within the context of the world's cultures. Rather than attempting to place the experience of others within the framework of such a conception, (...) understanding them demands setting that conception aside and seeing their experiences within the framework of their own ideas of what selfhood is. And for Java, Bali, and Morocco, at least, that idea differs markedly not only from our own but no less dramatically and no less instructively, from one to the other.
>
> GEERTZ 1984: 126

Geertz approaches the concept of self from his cross-cultural investigation in which he uncovered significantly less individualistic views. Given the contrastive mission of this work, his statement above serves as the foundation of as well as motivation for the discussion to follow. I begin by reviewing the Cartesian thesis followed by anti- and post-Cartesian arguments. Incorporating the historical background, I trace the source of the Western self in Descartes, and then contrasting it with Vico's opposition to the Cartesian position only half a century later.

1   The Cartesian View and Vico's Opposition

It was the 17th century in France when René Descartes (1596–1650) presented his thesis of rational and unitary self reached by introspection. Descartes, searching for something that lies beyond all doubt, discovers that the thinking itself is impossible to doubt, and therefore, is absolutely certain. In his work, *Meditations on First Philosophy*, Descartes (2001 [1901]) states that the initial step in philosophy requires skepticism, and therefore, one must start doubting the existence of everything. Insisting that one must doubt all knowledge and common sense, Descartes writes the following in the section titled *Concerning the Nature of the Human Mind: That the Mind is More Known than the Body*.

> But I had the persuasion that there was absolutely nothing in the world, that there was no sky and no earth, neither minds nor bodies, was I not, therefore, at the same time, persuaded that I did not exist? Far from it. I assuredly existed, since I was persuaded. (...) Doubtless, then, I exist, since I am deceived; and, let him deceive me as he may, he can never bring it about that I am nothing, so long as I shall be conscious that I am something. So that it must be maintained, all things being maturely and carefully considered, that this proposition (pronunciatum) I am, I exist, is necessarily true each time it is expressed by me, or conceived in my mind.
> DESCARTES 2001 [1901]

No matter how deep one's skepticism, the fact that one is thinking cannot be denied. As long as a person engages in thinking, this thinking person must exist. The act of thinking, in the manner of rational introspection, is the only source of self, the proof of existence. God's existence is trusted, because God is in thinking, and consequently, God cannot be a deceiver.

In Cartesian thought, a human being is divided into mind and body, with prestige given to the former. The mind is capable of creating rational thought, and therefore, the ultimate authority is given to the subject of *cogito*, the initiator of human thought. Self-introspection is prized, and interaction with others becomes less important. The thesis of *cogito, ergo sum* raises the status of introspection to its highest level. Thus Cartesian thought has become the ultimate tool for understanding the world mapped by an authoritative order. Self is understood to be a rationally thinking person isolated from and independent of others, i.e., the rational and unitary self.

The type of knowledge pursued within the Cartesian framework is rationality, i.e., an ideology of *logos*. There has been a widely held belief that one's inner thinking leads to this *logos* of clear and distinct ideas. The prioritization of rational thinking has tended to push aside humanistic knowledge, the kind of knowledge I have discussed as "the knowledge of *pathos*" (Maynard 1998a, 2000, 2002). One's humanistic knowledge including memory, psychological processes, feelings, imagination, emotion, myth, and so on, has too frequently been ignored or rejected, and deemed undeserving of scientific inquiry. In the humanities, emotion is essential, but emotion-related knowledge has been deemed unreliable. Humanistic knowledge, supported by an interpersonal relationship between "I" and "you" as characterized by Buber (1970), has been considered less trustworthy. Instead, rational thinking based on the "I-it" relationship, created solely in one's mind, has been prioritized.

Obviously, there is an irony in this thesis of *cogito*. The Cartesian thought was realized through a specific language endorsed by an inherent ideology. Thus thinking is not totally free nor absolutely clear. And more significant to this work, the thinking experience is not universal. This is because thinking must be achieved through a particular language. Each real-life language exists in its own ideological and sociocultural context. Philosophical studies on language, from whomever they originate, can never be totally free of ideology. Given this, it is not overly presumptuous to assume that for centuries the English language, or more accurately, English, German, and French, have imposed certain views of the world including the concept of self.

Although historically the Cartesian view has dominated Western sciences, there has also been a view in the West that prioritizes humanistic knowledge. Giambattista Vico (1668–1744), an Italian philosopher of the early 18th century, personifies this view just when Cartesian philosophy was beginning to take root. Vico consistently criticized the Cartesian position and doubted the thesis that the essence of humanity is objectifiable and scientifically analyzable. Instead, Vico believed that for a human being to truly understand the self, one must appreciate the meaning of history, that is, one must understand the self in one's historical context.

For Vico, whose professed academic discipline was rhetoric, it is language, rather than clear and distinct ideas, that offers the deepest well of knowledge. Language is what allows us to understand the relationship between us and the world of which we are a part. More significant to the discussion of philosophical contrastive pragmatics is that Vico (1965 [1709]) approaches the relationship between linguistic form and meaning as one of interdependence. In his view, the principle of complementarity sustains, and as in the case of the interdependence between linguistic form and meaning, the relationship between language and mind is also synergistic.

Predating the Whorfian hypotheses by two centuries, Vico warned that minds are fashioned by languages just as languages are fashioned by minds, and the two are inseparable. Following this line of thinking, it is absurd to conclude, as Descartes insisted, that clear and distinct ideas are standing behind language from which a speaker strains to pull out various ideas. Rather, the meaning of language arises with the language as it is performed. Vico insists that our relationship to language in history cannot be one of simply using it, but rather, one of participating in it. Indeed, Vico was "the first linguist to point out that language is performatory in nature" (Paparella 1993: 67).

The analysis of language and philosophical contrastive pragmatics I pursue in this work are in basic agreement with Vico's view toward language and its performatory nature. When pursuing philosophical understandings in and with language, we must understand that we participate in history through language which carries in itself its culture and history. Accordingly, we must appreciate that our language constructs the very manner in which we understand our selves. Likewise, the concept of self that a researcher seeks is inherently conditioned by his or her language, or languages, as well as sociocultural background. In language studies, unless we reach for ordinary language realized through participation among people, a mere abstract thinking may only add to the Cartesian introspection-based rationality, which may or may not reflect how people use language. In this work, as I have advocated in my earlier works (Maynard 2000, 2002), I explore a humanistic and philosophical approach to linguistics and pragmatics.

2 The Self Approached from Psychology and Philosophy

To continue with the historical background of the Western self, in the rest of this chapter I trace the history from four perspectives. Initially in this section I review the self approached from psychology and philosophy focusing on Hume (1963) and James (1904, 1929, 1984 [1890]). In the second section, I discuss the postmodern deconstruction of the self attributed to Heidegger (1962) and Derrida (1978). Then in the third section, socially constructed and experienced self is discussed focusing on positions taken by Gergen (1996) as well as Holstein and Gubrium (2000). Finally, in the fourth section, I touch upon studies exploring language and identity (Bell 1999; Bucholotz 1999; Blommaert 2007; Bucholtz and Hall 2009; Zeman 2018). All of these views resonate with but differ from the Japanese empty and populated self.

2.1 Hume and Self as a Bundle of Perceptions

David Hume (1711–1776) from the 18th century England, issues the fundamental challenge of questioning the very status of the thinking person. For Hume, the self is someone who transforms through experiences and feelings as a bundle of perceptions, an idea clearly in opposition to the Cartesian position. Hume insists that truth cannot be obtained through rational thinking, but only through experience. This is because human thought is ruled not by reason, but by a perception-based emotion.

This prioritization of experience is applicable to the concept of self. Self is one who receives information experiencing the world through the body, formed as a bundle or a collection of perceptions. Hume (1963) in his work *A Treatise of Human Nature*, confesses that "I never can catch *myself* at any time without a perception, and never can observe anything but the perception" (Hume 1963: 174, original emphasis), and defines the self in terms of perception or bundle of perceptions. In his words:

> I may venture to affirm of the rest of mankind that they are nothing but a bundle or collection of different perceptions, which succeed each other with an inconceivable rapidity and are in a perpetual flux and movement. (…) The mind is a kind of theater, where several perceptions successively make their appearance, pass, re-pass, glide away, and mingle in an infinite variety of postures and situations. There is properly no *simplicity* in it at one time nor *identity* in different, whatever natural propension we may have to imagine that simplicity and identity.
>
> HUME 1963: 174, original emphasis

Hume's view of the self with rapidly changing perceptions and in a state of perpetual flux and movement challenges the Cartesian thesis. He offers a definitive statement on the self as the following.

> When I turn my reflection on *myself*, I never can perceive this *self* without some one or more perceptions, nor can I ever perceive anything but the perceptions. It is the composition of these, therefore, which forms the self.
>
> HUME 1963: 309, original emphasis

For Hume, the mind itself, far from being an independent source of authority, is simply a bundle of perceptions without any logical connection or cohesive unification. Consequently, one can conclude that human existence remains receptive and passive; the Cartesian self cannot be automatically presumed. Regarding the scientific method as well, rejecting the analytical thinking dominant in modern sciences, Hume prioritizes human experience.

Interestingly, Giles (1993) offers an insight connecting Hume to Buddhism. Giles argues that although some critics characterize Hume as a reductionist who, after all, theoretically allows for the existence of self, if one closely reads Hume's works, it is possible to interpret his position as that of a "no-self" theory, an approach practiced in Buddhism. According to Giles, Hume does not view the self reduced simply to a bundle of perceptions, rather the self exists in the form of perception. That is to say, Hume strongly supports the position wherein the entity of a self is rejected altogether, demonstrating a polar opposite to the Cartesian position. Giles continues to explain that what Hume sees in the concept of self is the constructed self-image reached by condensing multiple experiences into an image of ideas.

It is reasonable to accept the position that the self exists as one's experience-based self image, where no definable self is to be found. One's self image changes from one moment to the next in perpetual transformation. Indeed, it is difficult, if not impossible, to identify a consistent and unitary self in any such mixed bundle of experiences.

2.2   *James and the World of Pure Experience*

Another figure in opposition to the Cartesian position is Henry James (1843–1916), the 19th century American philosopher and psychologist who sought the concept of self in a world of pure experience. James (1904), based on his radical empiricism, calls his approach a "mosaic philosophy" and explains it as the following.

> In actual mosaics the pieces are held together by their bedding, for which bedding of the Substances, transcendential Egos, or Absolutes of other philosophies may be taken to stand. In radical empiricism there is no bedding; it is as if the pieces clung together by their edges, the transitions experienced between them forming their cement.
> JAMES 1904: 568

James admits this metaphor may not be entirely accurate, but he insists that "the metaphor serves to symbolize the fact that experience itself, taken at large, can grow by its edges" (1904: 568).

James, in *Psychology Brief Course* (1984 [1890]), in his chapter titled *Self*, proposes that the self is experienced in an intersubjective relation between "I" and "Me." He treats the self as known (or the Me), i.e., the empirical ego, and the self as knower (or the I), i.e., the pure ego. In other words, the I is the pure ego who experiences the Me as an object, although for James, Me and I are not separate, but simply form "discriminated" aspects of the self. In the first section titled *The Me and the I*, James states the following.

> Whatever I may be thinking of, I am always at the same time more or less aware of *myself*, of my *personal existence*. At the same time it is *I* who am aware, so that the total self of me, being as it were duplex, partly known and partly knower, partly object and partly subject, must have two aspects discriminated in it, of which for shortness we may call one, the *Me* and the other, the *I*.
> JAMES 1984 [1890]: 159, original emphasis

James approaches the concept of Me from three dimensions; (1) its constituents, (2) the feelings and emotions they arouse (self-appreciation), and (3) the acts to which they prompt (self-seeking and self-presentation). The constituents of the Me are then divided into three classes; (1) the material Me (the body and clothing), (2) social Me (the recognition received from others), and (3) the spiritual Me (the entire collection of the states of consciousness, psychic faculties, and dispositions taken concretely). A recognition of these multiple and overlapping aspects of the self in and of itself is in clear opposition to the Cartesian position.

James' view toward the self is based on his radical empiricism which prioritizes one's personal experience. Radical empiricism understands that the human experience leads to a distinction between I and Me, and not the mind that justifies *cogito*. In an article titled *A World of Pure Experience*, James (1904) presents his view of radical pragmatism against Rationalism. He criticizes Rationalism claiming that it "tends to emphasize universals and to make wholes prior to parts in the order of logic as well as in that of being" (1904: 533). Underlying his pragmatism is the thought that the self emerges only through pure experience, and accordingly, James states:

> The instant field of the present is always experienced in its 'pure' state, plain unqualified actuality, a simple *that*, as yet undifferentiated into thing and thought, and only virtually classifiable as objective fact or as some one's opinion about fact.
> JAMES 1904: 564, original emphasis

In James' view, the person who understands the concept of Me is not established; it exists only as a passing state of consciousness. Self is held within "a system of memories, purposes, strivings, fulfilments or disappointments" (James 1904: 535). The self's consciousness flows from one moment to the next as a stream, and although there is continuity, it does not exist as an object. He warns that stream of consciousness exists only in a fleeting moment by writing *"The simplest thing, therefore, if we are to assume the existence of a stream of consciousness at all, would be to suppose that things that are known together are known in single pulses of that stream"* (James 1984 [1890]: 178, original emphasis).

James (1904) further discusses life itself as being in a constant state of flux. The metaphor he introduces is a thin line of flame advancing across a dry field. We live in this line simultaneously looking backward and forward. We are of the past, as much as of the future, constantly transforming in a changing world. Again, this image of self is far from a rational, unitary, and stable self. James expresses his thought in the following words.

> Life is in the transition as much as in the terms connected; often, indeed, it seems to be there more emphatically, as if our spurts and sallies forward were the real firing-line of the battle, were like the thin line of flame advancing across the dry autumnal field which the farmer proceeds to burn. In this line we live prospectively as well as retrospectively. It is 'of' the past, inasmuch as it comes expressly as the past's continuation; it is 'of' the future in so far as the future, when it comes, will have continued it.
> JAMES 1904: 568–569, original emphasis

By casting doubt on objectivity, James challenges the Cartesian position. In his section titled *What Objective Reference Is*, James argues "the objective reference which is so flagrant a character of our experience involves a chasm and a mortal leap" (1904: 562) and calls for its rejection. James also reminds us that our "fields of experience have no more definite boundaries than have our fields of view" (1904: 562). In his thinking, the notion of knowledge is always in transition and is dependent purely on experience.

3   Deconstruction of the Self

Questioning the Cartesian self has turned into a sweeping denial of the very existence of self in certain corners of 20th century Western academia. Deconstructionism, a perspective developed within post structuralist literary criticism and language studies, challenges all notions that involve the primacy of the subject or author. This threatening perspective presents an unsettling picture of the world and brings about a sense of insecurity to a monolithic conceptualization of the self.

In reference to deconstructionism, Heidegger (1962) is introduced here for the following reasons. First, his phenomenological philosophical position serves to push forward the postmodern movement of deconstruction. Second, his view toward Being offers insight to and is agreeable with the kind of self pursued in this study. Third, Heidegger is known to have been influenced by and to have influenced Japanese philosophers of the Kyoto school (Yuasa 1987). Two affiliated philosophers, Nishida and Watsuji, are focused in Chapter 5 and Chapter 6, respectively.[1]

Heidegger (1962) contends that Western philosophy has neglected the concept of Being because it was considered too obvious to even investigate, and he argues for the destruction of traditional philosophy. Distinguishing between ontic and ontological, Heidegger insists on the significance of the ontological quest, rather than the ontic. In discussing the nature of Being, the ontic approach questions the physical and factual elements of Being. On the other hand, in following an ontological approach, the nature of as well as the meaningful structure of existence become the focus. Thus, ontology focuses on investigating the foundation of Being, or the concept of Being itself. With this ontological approach in questioning what it means for something to be, Heidegger launches his attack on Descartes.

Heidegger opposes a subject-object dichotomy, where the former is assumed on the basis of introspection. In his view, the Cartesian consciousness cannot be isolated from the consciousness of something or by someone. But, the Cartesian self is assumed to exist prior to the self's engagement in thinking or doubting. Because of this assumption, the self-introspection process itself fails to define the self; self's existence is already assumed prior to any introspection.

The same manner of thinking applies to objects other than the self. In Heidegger's view, we do not start with the recognition of objects or appreciate the use of these objects after finding their functional value. We do not start

---

[1] Among those who studied under Heidegger are Hajime Tanabe, Shuzo Kuki, and Tetsuro Watsuji, Tanabe between 1922 to 1923, Kuki 1927 to 1928, and Watsuji 1927 to 1928, while Heidegger was at Marburg and Freiburg. Given that *Being and Time* was originally published in 1928, the intellectual interaction between Heidegger and Japanese philosophers is difficult to deny (Parks 1987).

with what Heidegger refers to as "present-at-hand," move on to what Heidegger (1962) refers to as "ready-to-hand" and then add its value-predicates. Instead, we start with the ready-to-hand, moving to present-at-hand. To quote Heidegger:

> The fact that motor-cycles and wagons are what we proximally hear is the phenomenal evidence that in every case *Dasein*, as Being-in-the-world, already dwells alongside what is ready-to-hand within-the-world; it certainly does not dwell proximally *alongside* 'sensations'; nor would it first have to give shape to the swirl of sensations to provide a springboard from which the subject leaps off and finally arrives at a 'world'.
> HEIDEGGER 1962: 207, original emphasis

Now, Heidegger's answer to the concept of self or Being emphasizes his position against traditional terms such as subject, ego, consciousness, and thinking. *Dasein*, emphasizing a sense of "being there," refers to the inherently social way of being based on *a priori* structures that facilitate a particular manner of Being. Heidegger's concept of self is better understood when broken down into three terms, Being-in-the-world, Being-toward-death, and Being-with. Being-in-the-world provides openness, a pre-intentional world, which is constituted by a certain attitude. It enables an experience that projects onto the possibilities that lie ahead or are currently hidden. He uses the term dwelling to capture the distinctive manner in which *Dasein* is in the world. Dwelling assumes that one belongs there, implying involvement. Because *Dasein*, as Being-in-the-world, is open, it is possible to take up relationships within the world.

Dasein is available in terms of possibilities in the world, and therefore, the self is always in a state of possibilities until death. This awareness that one is destined to die, i.e., Being-toward-death, requires our understanding of time, particularly the limited time of human life. *Dasein* completes itself at the termination of life, at the time of death. In this way, Heidegger emphasizes the importance of time, in our being-toward-death, and our awareness of the limitation of time at the closing of our life's possibilities.

The third term, Being-with, refers to a feature that a human being is always already with others within the world. Being-with does not refer to the sense that a human being is in proximity to others; rather, in more of an ontological sense, it means that one finds an implicit reference to others within the concept of the *Dasein*. Without others of our kind we are unable to survive. Being-with offers an essential ontological basis for *Dasein*, the self and others being located together in the world. From his phenomenological perspective, on the concept of others, Heidegger offers the following statement.

By 'Others' we do not mean everyone else but me—those over against whom the 'I' stands out. They are rather those from whom, for the most part, one does not distinguish oneself—those among whom one is too. (...) By reason of this *with-like* Being-in-the-world, the world is always the one that I share with Others. The world of *Dasein* is a *with-world*. Being is *Being with* others.

HEIDEGGER 1962: 154–155, original emphasis

More concretely, Being-in-the-world is supported by the concept of care. Care is the fundamental basis of human beings in the place, and it has to do with producing something, attending to something, and looking after it. Furthermore, care has to do with making use of something as well as giving something up and letting it go. Heidegger's *Dasein*, defined by care, is engaged in this ethically concerned mode of being-in-the-world. *Dasein* clearly opposes Descartes' Rationalism which frames the self as a being with autonomous cognitive abilities.

Influenced by phenomenology, Heidegger in particular, Derrida (1974, 1978, 1981) launches an attack on traditional Western thinking by questioning all notions that involve the subject, the author, and the self. Raising serious doubts on many interpretations of the self, Derrida, standing against the traditional sense of an autonomous and stable self, invites a more fluid view.

Derrida's complex deconstructive process can be elucidated by his concept of "differance" which implies two aspects, difference and deferral.[2] Difference refers to the Saussurean notion that all language and communication exists as a system of differences. As Saussure (1966) argues, linguistic signs are arbitrary, where the distinction among signs is recognized only by their differences from other signs within a language system. The relationship between the signifier and the signified is not based on something intrinsic or essential to the sign's nature. Similar to Saussure, Derrida notes that meanings emerge in linguistic practice on the basis of differences and distinctions, not on the basis of essences or substances.

Derrida's sense of deferral points to the inherent time lag involved in meaning. It refers to a delaying mechanism, where linguistic messages "may be read

---

2 Derrida's concept, "differance" (spelled with "a") captures the deconstructive process that includes not only difference but also deferral. Differance supposes difference in the Saussurean sense as well as the sense of an inherent time lag between presence and what constitutes that presence (e.g., writing). Differance implies that whatever we take as an immediate presence of being is the outcome of a complex, never-ending process of difference supported by deferral.

only in the past" (Derrida 1978: 224). Derrida argues that in whatever we perceive to be immediate, e.g., speech, is always already past, and therefore what is present is based on what is absent. If presence always contains absence, there cannot be a neatly drawn line of opposition between what is present and what is absent. Derrida bases his challenge against the logic of identity by this mutually supporting relationship between presence and absence, i.e., his logic of supplement based on the negative dialectics. In other words, presence and absence are not opposites, but rather, presence is defined through absence, and vice versa. In terms of language, the difference between writing and speech illustrates a case in point. Writing supplements speech; it is both different from speech and yet also contains speech. Thus, writing is both speech and what speech is not. Significantly, Derrida's interest in writing over speech endorses the study of written text, in contrast to anthropological, ethnomethodological, and sociolinguistic approaches which generally and historically prioritize speech.[3] The literary text and its translation discussed in this work should not be taken only as a phenomenon of written text. Literary text echoes the spoken language in its present, future, and past.

To explore Derrida's deconstruction of the self, it is helpful to return to Geertz's (1984) description of the Western concept of personhood. The Western self is presumed to be construed as a distinctive whole, and as a bounded entity. It functions as a center of awareness and is positioned contrastively against others. Admittedly, in linguistics what is often assumed is a speaking self who engages in language and communication as a distinctive individual. Against this view, Derrida promotes a multi-dimensional subject without a center. Refusing the logic of identity, i.e., a logic of either/or, Derrida insists on the logic of the supplement of difference, i.e., a logic of both/and. In this Derridian logic, something is inhabited also by what that something is not. Thus entities are both what they are and what they are not, i.e., A is both A and not A. Under these conditions, it is difficult to maintain the concept of self as a center of awareness and as a distinctive whole contrastively positioned against others.

From the perspective of postmodernism, then, the Western self criticized by Geertz (1984) must not only be denied but deconstructed altogether. What should be understood is that the self's awareness remains decentered and open to other cultural practices and requirements. Derrida's self can never be set

---

3 In Western linguistic studies, the prioritization of speech is most prominent in conversation analysis (Schegloff 1968; Sacks, Schegloff and Jefferson 1974; Tannen 1984; Maynard 1986a, 1987a, 1989, 1990b, 1993b, 2003) and interactional linguistics (Gumperz and Tannen 1979).

apart from the multiple others who are its very essence; the self must be recognized as a mutual relationship of the other-in-self and the self-in-other. Derrida's self exists only as and in a deconstruction process where the self is and is not, in a perpetual process with no clear beginning or end. This is also the case in the Japanese sense of empty but populated self. Emptiness and populatedness are in the negative dialectics, a process of change dependent on each other's denial and affirmation in a perpetual motion. Emptiness and populatedness are not in the either-or relationship; both are embraced.

Given the crisis of the self as suggested by Derrida, the challenge for linguistics and pragmatics is to question its own theoretical assumptions and formulations. This paradigmatic renovation must begin at its very foundation, and the theoretical and analytical concepts of the self must be repeatedly questioned. In the process, the self in language and communication may emerge with new and different features, and consequently researchers may avoid automatic affirmation of the old.

I should mention here an interesting position taken from a cognitive-philosophical perspective. In a work titled *Being No-one: The Self-Model Theory of Subjectivity*, Metzinger (2003) claims that in terms of ontology "no such things as selves exist in the world," and what exists is merely "a special kind of self-models and their contents," insisting that it is this content "that makes us believe that we actually do have, or are identical to, a self" (Metzinger 2003: 626). When Metzinger denies the existence of a self, he identifies the content of his self-model as nothing but an illusionary image. Metzinger's view reminds us of Hume's view of the self which exists as one's experience-based image. If the self is an image that changes from one moment to the next as Hume suggests, Metzinger's denial of the self seems to have less of an impact. At any rate, Metzinger (2003) is clearly against the introspection-based existence of a unitary self, echoing many Western scholarly traditions that challenge the Cartesian position.

4   Socially Constructed and Experienced Self

Studies pointing to the complexity of the self and its socially and culturally motivated conceptualizations (e.g., Geertz 1984) have gained prominence over the years. Scholars following social constructionism, based on Mead (1967 [1934]) and developed further, argue that selves, persons, and psychological traits are all socially motivated. All are social and historical construals, not naturally occurring phenomena. Mead (1967 [1934]), in his theory of symbolic interactionism, understands the self as consisting of two phases, the "I" and the "me," the latter of which is in one's consciousness and evolves when one engages in an internal conversation. Here, the individual self is essentially a social construct that we perceive from others' interpretation of, and in response to, our own internal moves linked to social interactions. In concrete terms, we experience different selves when we play out our social roles such as sibling, parent, child, worker, and so on. We are different selves answering to different social constructs. According to Mead, "(w)e divide ourselves up in all sorts of different selves with reference to our acquaintances" and "(t)here are all sorts of different selves answering to all sorts of different social creations" (1967 [1934]: 142).

A study significant to our ontological theme is Gergen's (1996) social constructionist position approached from a sociological and psychological perspective. Gergen points out that society, on a global level, has been shifting from traditional psychological essentialism to what he calls the "relational sublime." Psychological essentialism is characterized by "adherence to the view that individuals possess specifically mental processes or mechanisms" (1996: 127), and this view has long served as a pivotal point in Western scholarship. Today, psychological essentialism suffers from gradual but increasingly discernible erosion. What is happening instead is a "progressive emptying of the self" (Gergen 1996: 128).

Gergen contends that technology has been the primary force in the dismantling and emptying of the self. For example, mass media endorses, in various forms, the view that relations are most important, and society at large becomes increasingly more sensitive to the process of relatedness. Gergen concludes that as we succeed in losing the self, the security of single rationalities and fixation on univocal goals are lost and the more fluid forms of relationality become evident. Our relationships become what are most important; we may indeed capture this condition as what Gergen calls "the relational sublime."

As relation is prioritized in postmodern society, the self becomes less distinct while at the same time it becomes dismantled and emptied. Still, because we feel a need to fill our empty selves, we invite others into us. This leads to what Gergen (2000 [1991]) calls the "saturated self," where the self is overwhelmed by personal relationships. A self becomes a combination of imitated others, or a pastiche of others, incorporating other's actions into one's own. Under these circumstances, the self may become a collection of others' characters. In Gergen's words:

> To put it more broadly, as the century has progressed selves have become increasingly populated with the character of others. We are not one, or a few, but like Walt Whitman, we "contain multitudes." We appear to each

other as single identities, unified, of whole cloth. However, with social saturation, each of us comes to harbor a vast population of hidden potentials (...).

GERGEN 2000 [1991]: 71

As the saturation of the self advances, one may suffer from what Gergen (2000 [1991]) refers to as "multiphrenia." Multiphrenia results from simultaneously placing importance on the multiple others within oneself, and it leads to making efforts to accommodate all those others. Ultimately, Gergen's concept of self saturated with multiple others illustrates a clear opposition to the traditional Western concept of the self.

Burke and Stets (2009) offer another example of the socially motivated self. They challenge the Cartesian tenet by insisting that the notion of a singular "identity" of self is no longer viable, and instead, multiple "identities" should be investigated. Burke and Stets explain their concept of self by describing three strands of identities, i.e., (1) person identity or one's individual self-conception, (2) role identity associated with particular roles, and (3) social identity linked to a social group. They take the position that identities coexist within a self, and that identities do not exist *a priori* in a static state or condition, rather, they materialize as appropriate in relevant contexts.

Another society-sensitive approach is taken by Holstein and Gubrium (2000) who focus on the empirical world of everyday social life. Applying narrative analysis and conversational sequencing while incorporating local cultures, they examine how selfhood and subjectivity are narratively construed in various organizational contexts. Focusing on how community members' everyday practices develop a sense of membership, they argue that the formation of identity is tied to members' storytelling which ranges from recollections of specific events to broad lifetime experiences. The self is resultant of a social construal emerging through one's narrative practice. A person's narrative is a part of stories that reflect how people in a particular community assemble and live as they respond to the varied demands of everyday social life. In their words:

> This is an eminently practical and socially variegated self, artfully and deliberately built up in various shapes and dimensions as a basis for dealing with the circumstances in which it is located. It is a self that is able to both withstand and challenge the many self-formative demands of postmodern times.
>
> HOLSTEIN and GUBRIUM 2000: 10–11

Storytelling also reflects how people engage in the everyday work of orienting to each other as selves. Holstein and Gubrium (2000) insist that we, as social actors, not only experience a sense of self, but more significantly "live by" it. By storytelling, we construct our selves while dealing with various social circumstances. Recall the traditional Cartesian self, i.e., the inferred "I" that thinks and therefore exists. Against this view, exploring the self as a social creation in the shared narrative practice portrays the socially constructed self based on everyday experience.

5   Language and Social Identities

In modern Western linguistics, recognizing the self's social identity as being central to language has not been aggressively promoted. Traditional approaches in linguistics which prioritize the propositional content have dominated the field. Nevertheless, some noteworthy predecessors have addressed the link between one's identity and one's language.

Among the predecessors, Labov (1963) and Lakoff (1973) should be mentioned. In his study of the English dialect of Martha's Vineyard, Labov (1963) finds that certain diphthongs with recognizable features would mark speakers as Vineyarders. In other words, recognizing the relationship between linguistic features and social identities, Labov notes that a phonetic choice identifies the speaker as being native to the island. Lakoff (1973) argues that linguistic features such as tag questions, hedges, intensifiers, and pause markers are linked to an inferior social role assigned to women speakers. In her view, both structure and use of language are associated with the speaker's gender identity.

In the 1970s, Social Identity Theory is developed by Tajfel (1978). Tajfel defines social identity as "that part of an individual's self-concept which derives from his knowledge of his membership in a social group (or groups) together with the value and emotional significance attached to that membership" (Tajfel 1978: 63). Social Identity Theory emphasizes that social identity pertains to the individual rather than to the social group itself, and the individual's awareness of that membership is what is essential. An individual's own knowledge of the membership as well as the particular value attached to it play critical roles in one's conceptualization of the self. Tajfel also emphasizes that the emotional involvement of belongingness is integral to the person's identity.

Emphasis on the individual within the social group in Social Identity Theory encourages interpretive examinations of what Eckert and McConnell-Ginet (1992) call "communities of practice." The concept of communities of practice is defined as "an aggregate of people who come together around mutual engagement in an endeavor" (Eckert and McConnell-Ginet 1992: 464). They point out that in the course of this endeavor, shared beliefs, norms, and ideologies emerge. This view of a social group invites investigation into its members' expressions on which to base the underlying ideologies of how an aggregate of people can form a commonality.[4]

Works from the sociolinguistic perspective also convincingly make cases where language communicates multiple identities. For example, Bell (1999) studies a Maori song performed by different subjects including a Maori opera singer with native-like pronunciation, a group in an Irish pub, an African American using recognizably AAVE (African American Vernacular English), and a young Pakeha (Anglo) male using anglicized pronunciation. Bell concludes that the performance mode chosen by the subjects is a blend of responsive and initiative styles, reflecting cultural ambivalence toward what it is to be a New Zealander. The identity of a New Zealander is a mixture of identities and of cultures between Pakeha and Maori. Styling of the other in nuanced degrees reveals ambivalent selves caught between two places, at home in neither. Bell (1999) insists that whatever style one chooses, it simultaneously reflects elements both of community and individuality, and it is in this combination of styles that certain, if not ambivalent, identities are revealed.

The ambivalent self evidenced in the phenomenon of styling the other is also observed in the language crossing phenomenon (Bucholtz 1999; Cutler 1999; Rampton 1999). For example, Bucholtz (1999) illustrates that based on a story told by a middle-class European American youth, ideologies of race and gender shape the narrative of inter-racial conflict. By including elements of AAVE as a case of language crossing, and other discursive strategies such as constructed dialogue (Tannen 1989), the boy's story positions black masculinity in contrast to white masculinity. By styling the other, the story-teller emphasizes the power of African American masculinity, while simultaneously maintaining a narrative that reveals white culture's appropriation of African American culture. Here multiple identities are experienced by a single speaker.

Zeman (2018) addresses the self concentrating on linguistic phenomena with which the self can be conceptualized (e.g. modal verbs, free indirect discourse, and the "future of fate" construction). By focusing on multiple-perspective constructions, she illustrates how the first person is split as it is viewed from external and internal perspectives. Zeman, based on analyses of literary works, concludes that the self conceptualized in language is not a sin-

---

4 Other studies in pragmatics focusing on common beliefs or ideologies linked to aggregates and groups include Verschueren (1999), Blommaert (1999), and Kroskrity (2010).

gular wholistic entity. This is because, particularly in narrative discourse, the first-person pronoun makes reference to multiple functional dimensions of the self. Although Zeman's split selves seem to oppose a wholistic identity, her notions of external and internal selves originate from (or are viewed by) the *a priori* self already assumed to exist. In this sense, her study does not in essence oppose the centrality of the self endorsed in the Cartesian tradition.

Another approach to language and identity is that of indexical order, proposed by Silverstein (2003), and further reformulated by Blommaert (2007) as "orders of indexicality." While Silverstein's analysis is focused on the use of indexical signs, Blommaert, looking specifically for the institutional context in which orders of indexicality operate, illustrates how speakers make use of the institutional context to achieve their own ends. Although different aspects associated with indexical signs are focused, Silverstein and Blommaert share the view that identities, including linguistic identities, are constructed at location where multiple related indexical signs interact. More concretely, Blommaert (2007) introduces the concept of "polycentric orientations" which provides multiple frames through which people can make sense of interactions in a socially sensitive way. People use frames to be played out while at the same time organizing relations among them. Some frames are foregrounded while others are backgrounded, and this shifting of frames characterizes the sociolinguistic process at work in a given social context. The management of the multiplicity of frames by the speaker reveals the complexity of identities associated with language.

Approaching the theme of identity from a broader perspective, Bucholtz and Hall (2009) summarize relevant approaches into five essential principles, i.e., (1) emergence, (2) positionality, (3) indexicality, (4) relationality, and (5) partialness. Identity is emergent in discourse; it does not precede it. We recognize identity as an intersubjectively achieved social and cultural phenomenon. Within identity we find broad sociological categories as well as local ethnographic and interactional positionings. The linguistic resources that indexically produce identity are broad and flexible, and because these tools are put to use in interaction, the process of identity construal essentially resides in intersubjective relations. It is particularly important to recognize the partialness principle of identity. Bucholtz and Hall (2009) argue that any construction of identity may be in part deliberate and intentional, and in part habitual and less than fully conscious. Identity may be in part an outcome of interactional negotiation and contestation, or in part an outcome of others' perceptions and representations. In addition, an identity construal may be in part an effect of larger ideological processes that influence specific interactions, implying that identity constantly shifts in the process of unfolding interactional encounters.

Five principles presented by Bucholtz and Hall (2009) make sense with respect to explaining our theme of the conceptualization of self associated with language and discourse. They comment that the age of identity is here, not only in sociolinguistics but more generally in humanities and social sciences. Scholars in pragmatics are well equipped to provide an empirically persuasive account of identity as a social, cultural, and interactional phenomenon. Note, however, that linguistic and sociolinguistic discussions of identity in the West are tied to social groups and institutions, often with political implications. In contrast, in this work, rather than investigating socially motivated identity, a philosophical exploration of ontology is the focus. The relationship between language and self is partly founded on social actions, but more deeply instilled in our metaphysical understanding of the self.

In this chapter, different, and some opposing views of the self in Western academia have been reviewed, where anti- and non-Cartesian positions abound. The concept of self has been deconstructed, and reconstructed with socially influenced variability, multiplicity, and instability. These studies illustrate that the empty yet populated self proposed in this work is no stranger to Western academia. Rather, many studies echo similar views developed in Japan reviewed in Chapters 5 and 6. Given this academic context, the time is right to critically rethink the notion of self. Thus, it is in the spirit of integration of Western and non-Western scholarly traditions that I pursue our theme of exploring the self from the perspective of philosophical contrastive pragmatics.

Given that the concept of self plays a significant role for designing an analytical framework in this work, in the next chapter, I discuss linguistic subjectivity and intersubjectivity associated with multiple aspects of the self. Also discussed is the dialogical and performing self that serves the foundation for the concept of character and characteristics.

CHAPTER 3

Framework: Subjectivity and Character

As touched upon in Chapter 1, the methodological framework selected for this work is contrastive pragmatics, particularly approached philosophically, i.e., philosophical contrastive pragmatics. Philosophical contrastive pragmatics adopts a multidisciplinary approach including pragmatics, linguistics, translation studies, and contrastive analysis among others. I also make use of methodologies applied in my earlier studies, such as conversation analysis (Maynard 1989, 1993b) and discourse analysis (Maynard 1993a, 1997a, 2004a). Regarding specific phenomena, my earlier studies on functional approaches in pragmatics and discourse analysis offer guidance. These studies include the topic-comment organization (Maynard 1980, 1981, 1982), quotation (Maynard 1991a, 1994b, 1996b, 1998c, 2005a), demonstratives (Maynard 2006), and style shifts (Maynard 1991a, 1996a, 2001a, 2004b, 2008b). The phenomenon of linguistic variation discussed as borrowed style (Maynard 2004a) and character-speak (Maynard 2012, 2016, 2017, 2019) also offers tools for analysis. As an analytical framework, the Place of Negotiation theory (Maynard 2000, 2002) provides theoretical support, and concepts of intertextuality and inter-genre expressivity (Maynard 2008a) render interpretive guidance.

The analytical approach applied in this work is interpretive and qualitative. Following the tradition of grounded theory in social sciences (Glaser and Strauss 1967), the initial inductive approach later interacts with the deductive. My past studies of Japanese discourse resulted in the discovery of multiplicity and fluidity of the self. Based on the findings of these earlier studies, I deductively hypothesized that the features of language reflecting the Japanese self are not easily translated.

This chapter presents two key concepts critical in the methodological framework of philosophical contrastive pragmatics, namely, subjectivity and character. Self-expressions in language reflect subjectivity and intersubjectivity which index multiple aspects of the self. The concept of character offers an interpretive resource for investigating how the empty self is populated with characters and characteristics by means of character-speak.

1 Subjectivity

1.1 Subjectivity in Linguistics and Related Fields

Subjectivity is a universal phenomenon in language and is central to linguistic practice. Linguistic subjectivity, subjectivity expressed through language use, communicates what kind of self emerges by way of language. Lyons (1982) characterizes subjectivity as "the way in which natural languages, in their structure and their normal manner of operation, provide for the locutionary agent's expression of himself and of his attitudes and beliefs" (1982: 102). Lyons (1994) contrasts subjecthood (the grammatical subject of the clause or sentence) with subjectivity, or more accurately, locutionary subjectivity. Locutionary subjectivity is defined as "the locutionary agent's (the speaker's, writer's, or the utterer's) expression of himself or herself in the act of utterance" (1994: 13). Self-expressions can function in many ways for the communication of personal feelings, affective states, attitudes, and perspectives. These expressions of the speaker's and writer's subjectivity are associated with linguistic phenomena such as person expressions, deictic phrases, temporal markers, modality expressions, and attitudinal adverbs.

Linguistic subjectivity offers insights to the concept of self. First, given that self-expressions differ from the propositional content of the sentence, linguistic subjectivity marks indexicality in language in that it is inherently related to the time and space where the self engages in and describes the experience. Second, as suggested by Lyons (1982), languages differ in the degree to which subjectivity is grammaticized. Languages also differ in the degree to which the marking of subjectivity is obligatory or optional. Given the theme of crosslinguistic differences in the concept of self evidenced in language, linguistic subjectivity functions as a useful interpretive tool.

As a precursor associating subjectivity and self-expression, Benveniste's (1971) work on personal pronouns merits review. Insisting that "(L)anguage is marked so deeply by the expression of subjectivity that one might ask if it could still function and be called language if it were constructed otherwise" (1971: 225), Benveniste discusses the essential difference observed between the first- and second-person on one hand and the third-person on the other. The meaning of the pronoun *I* differs depending on who speaks; the speaker could be anyone, but as soon as the person speaks, that person is designated as *I*. Likewise, the second-person partner is defined as *you* in actual interaction, and at the same time, *I* and *you* interchange constantly.

In other words, the meanings of *I* and *you* cannot be identified in the way Saussure (1966) once did, where the relationship between the signifier and the signified, although arbitrary, is established within a system and therefore identifiable in abstract terms. While the meaning of the third-person pronoun is stable and identifiable, meanings of *I* and *you* come alive only through their intersubjective relationship. Critically, "I" emerges only in the act of speaking, and only in the intersubjective relationship with "you."

Benveniste's position demonstrates a shift from a traditional cognition-based self to the pragmatics-based self. Curiously, Benveniste (1971) refers to these intersubjective expressions as being "empty." He insists that language by its nature provides empty signs such as *I* and *you* that can be realized as persons through the intersubjective relationship. We, as speakers, recognize our selves as persons only through the appropriate use of empty signs in context. Benveniste's intersubjective self is defined by language and interaction, and he makes a convincing case that linguistic expressions provide a source for our understanding of the self. His approach, however, is limited to pronouns and demonstratives. Sorely missed are other grammatical structures as well as speech styles and variations. I approach philosophical pragmatics not so much in terms of lexical items but as phenomena spanning over multiple levels including grammatical, discursive, and rhetorical practices.

Historically, linguistic subjectivity has been examined less frequently in linguistic analysis, partly because structural and formal linguistics more typically focus on propositional information. As Lyons noted, "Modern Anglo-American linguistics (...) has been dominated by the intellectualist prejudice that language is, essentially, if not solely, an instrument for the expression of propositional thought" (1982: 103). However, as Lyons (1994) recognizes, the research environment has undergone significant changes since the 1990s.

Finegan (1995) captures this development of subjectivity research by what he identifies as a humanistic linguistics approach. He cites Tannen (1988a, 1988b) and myself (Maynard 1993a) as scholars who approach subjectivity from a humanistic linguistics approach. Under this movement, language is viewed as expressions of a perceiving and feeling self and they are analyzed focusing on emotional attitudes and personal perspectives. It is this humanistic approach to subjectivity that has been and is my focus with which I continue in this work.

Since the 1990s, the fields of linguistics, sociolinguistics, and pragmatics have produced a rich body of research exploring linguistic subjectivity and the concept of self. In his work, Haiman (1998) traces Western sociological and philosophical studies where the concept of the divided self has been developed. Analysis of what Haiman calls "un-plain" speaking persuades him to introduce the phenomenon of the divided self. Un-plain speaking includes utterances such as sarcasm where the literal meaning and the intended meaning are contradictory. In sarcasm, one senses the performer's alienation from the content; the intended meaning cannot be understood if literally interpreted.

The alienation of the self and divided selves are evidenced by other linguistic expressions as well. They include (1) self-address, (2) self-reference, (3) shame, (4) stage fright, (5) other self-conscious emotions, (6) affectation and image cultivation in general, and (7) distinct representation of the self by reflexive pronouns.

In providing linguistic evidence to support his position, Haiman (1998) first discusses cases of self-expression where representation of the self either surfaces or not. For example, although (1) and (2) are both possible, (1) is a case of "nonrepresentation of the self" (Haiman 1998: 68). In (1), the speaker is not separately identified from the world he or she takes in. In contrast, (2) illustrates self-representation where the self is clearly located in an observed world.

(1) There's snow all around—.

(2) There's snow all around me.

Second, as a case of the divided self phenomenon in English, Haiman (1995, 1998) discusses reflexive pronouns, e.g., *I expect myself to win*. He takes the position that the representation of reflexivity by a separate reflexive pronoun "originally signaled the recognition of not one but two participants and thus implied some kind of detachment from the self" (Haiman 1998: 72). And he continues to argue that the use of reflexives in contemporary English is still indicative of a divided self. Haiman (1995) warns us, however, that linguistic phenomena of reflexive expressions differ across languages, and consequently, the concept of a divided self supported in many Western studies may not be universally applicable.

Broadly speaking, in approaching linguistic subjectivity, scholars have focused on concepts of perspective, affect, and modality. From cognitive linguistics, Langacker (1990) approaches the role of the structures of both grammar and semantics in terms of perspective. For example, he contrasts *The hiker ran up the hill* with *The highway runs from the valley floor to the mountain ridge* and points out that, as in this case, numerous verbs have undergone a process of subjectification. Here the movement represented by the verb *run* is the subjective path traced mentally by the person who conceptualizes the action represented by the verb *run*.

The expression "language has a heart" used by Ochs and Schieffelin (1989) represents linguistic subjectivity that focuses on affect. They point out that language users typically express affect toward their propositional content, resonating with Jakobson (1960) who distinguishes between the emotive and referential functions of language. Ochs and Schieffelin (1989) observe that

"(L)anguages are responsive to the fundamental need of speakers to convey and assess feelings, moods, dispositions and attitudes" and "(T)his need is as critical and as human as that of describing events" (1989: 9). Affect can be achieved through lexicon, grammar, and discourse as well as through gesture and other paralinguistic devices.

Now regarding modality, perhaps the most thoroughly explored aspects are modal adverbs. In the sentence *Obviously water freezes at 32 degrees Fahrenheit*, both subjective and propositional information are presented, one being that knowledge of the laws of nature are obvious to the speaker, and two, that the freezing point of water is 32 degrees. Modal adverbs such as *obviously* express the speaker's subjective judgment as to the epistemic status of the proposition, although it is not spelled out as *it is obvious to me*. Modality in a broad sense has been explored as a device to communicate intersubjective stance and positioning (White 2003). Informed by Bakhtin's (1981) and Vološinov's (1973 [1929]) notions of dialogicality and hereroglossia, Martin and White (2005) explore modality in terms of evaluation and appraisal.[1]

1.2   Intersubjectivity, Discourse, and the Self

Focus not only on subjectivity but also on intersubjectivity in discourse becomes necessary for understanding the relationship between one's language and the self. Baumgarten, House and Du Bois (2012) emphasize that subjectivity in language is supported by intersubjectivity. In their words:

> (...) subjectivity in language only exists because in an instance of discourse, speakers always posit another person external to themselves, i.e. to whom the utterance is addressed in a particular context and in relation to whom speakers position themselves through linguistic means as a person in the discourse.
>
> BAUMGARTEN, HOUSE and DU BOIS 2012: 3

Although the concept of intersubjectivity is not new, recent interest in research into actual communicational discourse of different types and languages has brought this concept into sharper focus. In a volume edited by Baumgarten, Du Bois and House (2012), researchers approach the subjectivity and intersubjectivity of self-expressions in numerous languages in different styles of spoken as well as written discourse. Baumgarten, House and Du Bois (2012) point out that subjectivity can be marked by non-linguistic devices, such as facial expres-

---

1   It is known that Bakhtin also used the name Vološinov in some of his works.

sion, gesture, and posture. However, they remind us that the most thoroughly explored individual linguistic items are modal adverbs and personal pronouns. They summarize that subjectivity expressions function as a means for communicating social relations, speaker orientation, and speaker's conceptualization of the self.[2] Regarding research designs addressing intersubjectivity, Etelämäki (2016) advocates the integration of two approaches, cognitive linguistics and interactional linguistics. As a concrete example, Herlin and Visapää (2016) trace the roots of intersubjectivity by focusing on empathy phenomenon in everyday interaction. Integrating cognitive grammar and conversation analysis, they investigate linguistic means for constructing empathy sharing in interaction.

Since the early 1990s, linguistic studies of intersubjectivity brought to the fore some fundamental ontological issues. Lyons' (1994) following remark is a case in point.

> It may also be argued, along similar lines, that in what we commonly refer to as self-expression in language there is no sharp distinction to be drawn between the self that is expressed and the expression of that self. We may go even further in our subjectivist deconstruction of the self: we can argue, as some have done, that there is no single, unitary self, which is constant across all experience and, more especially, across all encounters with others, but rather a set of selves—not one persona, but a set of personae—each of which is the product of past encounters with others, including, crucially, past dialogic, interlocutionary and collocutionary (or conversational), encounters; we can argue, in short, that locutionary subjectivity is really interlocutionary subjectivity and that, in consequence, subjectivity, in so far as it is manifest in language if not more generally, is really intersubjectivity.
>
> LYONS 1994; 14

Immediately following this statement, Lyons adds that "I am not saying that it is right to take this view, merely that it is a defensible view and that it has to be reckoned with" (1994: 14). The challenge of reckoning with the "defensible view" is part of the motivation for this work. Lyons' statement is based on stylistic differences within a single language, but the idea of intersubjectivity

---

2   I should add here that Japanese is not mentioned in this volume although subjectivity and intersubjectivity have been important topics in Japanese linguistics (e.g., Kuno 1972, 1987; Kuroda 1973; Iwasaki 1993; Maynard 1993a). Also no study is included where data consisting of literary and translation texts are examined. This work is hoped to add new perspectives to this renewed research area of subjectivity and intersubjectivity in discourse.

is critical for reckoning with cross-linguistic differences. Differences in subjectivity and intersubjectivity across languages provide evidence for appreciating different conceptualizations of the self.

When considering the interpretive process of self-expressions, we must realize that subjectivity and intersubjectivity reside in language regardless of whether they are linguistically or non-linguistically marked. An utterance is not entirely objective in the sense that it is neutral or completely free of subjectivity or intersubjectivity. Even when the content of the statement is deemed "objective," it has a subjective source in the form of the locutionary agent, i.e., the speaking self. As Baumgarten, House and Du Bois (2012) put it, the speaker's expression of objectivity "is just another type of encoding a subjective perspective in discourse" (2012: 11). All executions of language are fundamentally subjective in that they are created and performed by an embodied self who is essentially subjective as well as intersubjective. In this most fundamental sense, concepts of subjectivity and intersubjectivity provide a cautionary starting point for interpreting linguistic expressions as revelations of the self, and for our task of exploring the self.

1.3 Linguistic Subjectivity in Japanese Grammar

Historically, the Japanese language has been intimately connected with emotion with its rich capacity to communicate subjective messages. Exploration of subjectivity in Japanese, a matter of interest among traditional Japanese scholars for two centuries (Maynard 1993a), continued through the 1970s and 1980s among functional grammarians.[3] Scholars have argued that Japanese is a subjectivity-rich language (Kuno 1972, 1987; Kuroda 1973; Kuno and Kaburaki 1975); Japanese subjectivity has been explored as well in book-length studies, Iwasaki (1993) and Maynard (1993a).

Finegan (1995) quotes my work (Maynard 1993a) in which I describe the centrality of subjectivity and intersubjectivity in Japanese discourse.

> (...) when speaking Japanese, one simply cannot avoid expressing one's personal attitude toward the content of information and toward the addressee. Such a personal voice echoes so prominently in Japanese communication that often (...) rather than information-sharing, it is subtextual emotion-sharing that forms the heart of communication.
> MAYNARD 1993a: 4

---

3 Refer to Chapter 6 for related discussion on the emotivity and subjectivity in traditional Japanese language studies.

Subjectivity in the case of Japanese presents a serious contrast with the subjectivity in many other languages, including English. Partly because subjectivity is marked often in subtle ways in many languages, it has been overlooked, or deemed too complex and difficult to handle. Consequently, the theme of subjectivity has not been pursued elsewhere as vigorously as in Japanese linguistics.

In a series of works Ikegami (1993, 2004, 2006, 2011) explores Japanese linguistic subjectivity. Ikegami (2004) defines linguistic subjectivity primarily in terms of how subjectivity is realized and characterized through specific linguistic indices. He investigates how the self perceives the surrounding phenomenon and how the self constructs sentences with differing degrees of subjectivity-indexing devices. Incorporating earlier linguistic studies associated with the concept of subjectivity (Kuroda 1973; Kuno 1987), Ikegami points out that Japanese is rich with expressions that reveal subjective meanings.

Let me touch upon a few examples. First, Japanese grammar shows a subjectivity-rooted distinction in the use of adjectives. When referring to sensory experiences, one must distinguish what the self directly feels or not. Although (3) where *watashi* 'I' appears with topic marker is possible, (4) is not acceptable under ordinary circumstances. This is because someone else's feelings are not directly experienced by the self. In the Japanese language the self emerges experience-motivated and instead of (4), an expression comparable to English *He appears to be sad* must be chosen. This contrasts sharply with English where *I am sad* and *He is sad* are both acceptable.

(3) **Watashi**-wa Kanashii.
 I-TOP am sad
 'I'm sad.'

(4) *Ano otoko-wa kanashii.
 That man-TOP is sad
 'That man is sad.'

Second, because the design of language allows for it, the self does not surface in many Japanese expressions. For example (5) has no overt mention of the locutionary subject; it only indirectly reveals the speaker. The significance of the empty self, presented as the zero-form, is highly evident in this brief utterance. Based on grammatical and stylistic features, it is possible to identify the likely context of situation for (5), i.e., a female speaker addressing someone in a casual situation. The phrase *ano hito* 'that person', carries an emotive element through the use of the demonstrative *ano* 'that' (Maynard 2006). The absence of *watashi* 'I', the avoidance of the formal predicate *desu* as well as attaching the interactional particle *yo* all hint at who are involved. The self is unmentioned, but the self as a locutionary agent is indirectly but surely communicated. Ontologically speaking, the Japanese empty self, although hidden, exists behind linguistic expressions.

(5)   **Ano hito**   suki yo.
      that person like IP
      'That person (I) like.'

Many other grammatical features in the Japanese language point to the centrality of subjectivity (Maynard 1990a, 2009, 2011). For example, the Japanese passive construction, especially passives using an intransitive verb (what is usually called the passive of negative consequences), appears in the zero-form of the self, and it often conveys a negative attitudinal response to the situation. Passives conveying a positive attitude may also appear with the zero-form. Nonetheless, in these cases, the hidden and receptive self as the person who suffers or benefits from the incident is clearly implied.

    The use of verbs of giving and receiving a favor illustrates another situation of the hidden and receptive self. When the self is personally involved in the transaction, a neutral description is avoided, and instead, verbs of giving and receiving are required. Although it is acceptable in English to neutrally describe a transaction as *My friend's brother taught me English*, in Japanese the favor received by someone close to the self must be described as a favor received by the self in an expression comparable to English *I had my friend's brother teach me English*. In other words, in Japanese, the self's involvement in the situation must be communicated by using overt or covert subjectivity expressions. Regarding this phenomenon, Oe (1979) points out that the Japanese use of the zero-form for *I* indicates that the self is not objectified; rather, the self remaining subjective, experiences and observes the event on a personal basis. The self not surfacing in the language plays a major role in communication, because hidden within the self's experiences are subjective personal voices carrying relevant emotive messages.

    Anzai (1983) notes the Japanese preference toward *koto* 'matter, event' in contrast with the English preference for *mono* 'thing, object'. The Japanese language structurally centralizes the event as a whole, with the event directly and meaningfully experienced. In this type of description, the self, although not overtly mentioned, plays a comforting role by creating an ambiance where subjective interpersonal messages are shared. Japanese speakers prefer to describe the situation of the event, especially to foreground the relationships among people and things. The self, as a receptive experiencer of the event and not the centralized acting agent, richly communicates subjective messages.

Another study by Nakajima (1987) points out a similar subjectivity phenomenon in Japanese grammar. Nakajima characterizes Japanese as prioritizing situational descriptive sentences in comparison with English, which prioritizes propositional sentences. In English, as a rule, the structure is created where the agent is followed by an action, which in turn is followed by a recipient of that action. But in Japanese such a structure is often missing, where instead the situation itself attains primacy. Initially, the contextual information is given followed by a gradual circling in on other facets of the topic. Nakajima states that "Japanese avoids logical description that centralizes the agent, and rather, describes the agent-less situation first and offers a summation with the final predicate" (1987: 61, my translation). Pointing out that Japanese is "intuitive and depictive," while English is "propositional and logical" (1987: 188, my translation), Nakajima concludes that the subjectivity in linguistic interactions is foregrounded more in Japanese than in English.

Related to the subjectivity and intersubjectivity in Japanese, a few words on Japanese modality are in order. For years in traditional Japanese language studies (Yamada 1908; Tokieda 1941, 1950), the broad concept of modality has always been closely associated with linguistic subjectivity. Since the 1970's, modality has been identified as the element that constitutes a sentence along with the proposition, and the element that expresses the speaker's subjective judgments and attitudes (Nitta 1989; Masuoka 1991). Generally in Japanese language studies, modality has been understood as the subjective expression of the speaker's stance, and usually appearing as the sentence-final elements. This contrasts with the Western approach where modality is treated as a grammatical category like tense or aspect which are mainly defined through reality status (Narrog 2018). In Maynard (1993a) I take a broader approach to modality by introducing the term "Discourse Modality" defined as "the speaker's subjective, emotional, mental or psychological attitude toward the message content, the speech act itself or toward his or her interlocutor in discourse" (1993a: 38). I analyze final particles and discourse markers as the primary strategies of Discourse Modality. Narrog (2012, 2014, 2018) takes a narrower approach to modality and offers structural and functional analyses of the Japanese modality. He explores the possibility that different modal expressions operate on different layers in clause structure occupying different functional positions in the language. Horie and Narrog (2014) explore modality in Japanese from a typological perspective. Overall, scholarly interests in the concept of modality in Japanese have allowed for the concept of linguistic subjectivity to gain prominence in Japanese language studies.

Because the centrality of subjectivity in the Japanese language and discourse goes against the prominence of propositional content, and the self often remains unmentioned, the Japanese self may be considered unimportant. This, however, is far from truth; it is not that the Japanese self is actually absent. It is ironical that the Japanese language cannot avoid, although only indirectly, marking and revealing the presumably concealed subjectivity. The self may not surface in language, but it inevitably conveys the latent subjective attitude and commitment. The self here exists as a hidden embodied person who manipulates rich subjective and expressive strategies. As I have emphasized in my earlier works (Maynard 1993a, 1997a, 2000, 2002, 2004a), in Japanese, the self underlying the linguistic expression powerfully emerges in the process of the negotiation of meaning. The self undertakes this task of indirectly communicating the very self who engages in the actual communication. The Japanese self, while being heavily influenced by subjectivity and intersubjectivity, unquestionably conveys, if only indirectly, its own messages and reveals its aspects, characters, and characteristics distinct from the other.

1.4 Subjectivity, Intersubjectivity, and the Self in Japanese Discourse

In my study on Japanese discourse, I have proposed the concept of the place-sensitive self supported by linguistic subjectivity, based on the Place of Negotiation theory (Maynard 2000, 2002).[4] Because this framework is based on subjectivity and intersubjectivity, and it serves as the foundation of the rhetoric of *pathos* relevant to the Japanese self, I should start with its brief summary.

In this theoretical framework, Japanese language is interpreted in the negotiative place of communication. In the place, bounded and defined as a meaning-negotiating space, three different dimensions are projected, i.e., cognitive, emotive, and interactional. Different angles, shades, and strengths of these projections define the three spatial dimensions in different ways. The place where these projections meet and overlap is the locus of the *topica*, i.e., the negotiative place, where ultimate semantic negotiation is achieved.

Cognitive place enables participants to recognize objects and to construct propositions accordingly. In the cognitive place, how the self observes, i.e., the self's perspective, assumes significance. Primary focus is information, and in this place the self focuses on a choice of proposition and determines which

---

4 For years Japanese scholars have incorporated the concept of place (*ba*) in language studies, most notably Tokieda (1941, 1950) and Oka (2013). Additionally, the concept of place is incorporated in pragmatics-oriented studies (Fujii 2012, Saft 2014; Hanks et al. 2019), although works by Tokieda, Oka as well as my own earlier studies on the place and the negotiation of meaning (Maynard 2000, 2002) are not mentioned in these studies.

lexical items are selected. The second projection defines the emotive place, where the self's broad emotional attitudes are foregrounded. This is the space primarily concerned with psychological and emotional aspects of communication. Elements in the emotive place include emotional attitudes toward objects and persons, aroused emotional responses, a broad range of one's general feelings, as well as cultural sentiment. These attitudes and feelings are often expressed through modality-expressive vocabulary, sentence structure as well as discourse strategies (e.g., conjunctions, the topic-comment dynamic, stylistic choices, and so on).

The third projection defines the interactional place, where the partner comes into sharp focus. Within this place, a socially interactional atmosphere is created, coordinated, and managed while personal interests are being incorporated. In this interactional place, special attention is paid toward one's partners as well as toward the participants of speech. Here the main concern lies with how the self, partner, and other participants (if any) express, understand, and manage their interpersonal relations. Such relations are critical for the creation and negotiation of meanings.

The place-sensitive self in the place of communication is a person involved with each of these projections. Self not only thinks and interacts but also richly experiences emotions and feelings. It accounts for a conceptualization of the self as someone who talks, interacts, experiences, feels, and negotiates, always in relation with partners in the place of negotiation.[5] Just as language is not an abstract concept or a stable object, the self is not an abstract entity. Recognizing that language is a practice predicated upon participation, the self is understood to be performatory, interactional, and negotiative.

Based on this framework, I have proposed the rhetoric of *pathos* (Maynard 1997a, 1998a, 2000, 2002) where I focus on the hidden but expressive self in Japanese discourse. The difference between Japanese and Western discourses can be captured by the rhetoric of *pathos* in comparison with that of *logos*. In the rhetoric of *pathos*, the concept of place provides a philosophical and pragmatic foundation. In contrast, the rhetoric of *logos* situates the self relatively independent of its place. In the rhetoric of *pathos*, place is central to the foundation of self, without which the self cannot be sustained.

The rhetoric of *pathos* has been developed for the purpose of characterizing the preference of structures and strategies practiced in Japanese discourse. Discourse features I have reported in many of my studies (e.g., Maynard 1980, 1983,

---

5   As discussed in Chapter 1, I approach the self not as an identity in the abstract, but as one that is embodied. Western studies on embodiment include Merleau-Ponty (1962), Marmaridou (2000). Zlatev and Blomberg (2016), Johnson (2018), and Mondada (2019).

1989, 1991b, 1993a, 1993b, 1996a, 1997a, 1997e, 1997g, 1998b, 1999a, 1999b, 2000, 2002, 2004a, 2005a, 2012, 2013, 2014, 2016, 2017) and phenomena discussed in this work do not exist coincidentally. What unifies these features is an underlying force pulling the Japanese language toward a certain way of expressivity, the most profound of which being of an ontological nature.

In Japanese, the self frequently recedes into the background, remaining hidden. In these situations, utterances often take on the topic-comment structure. For example, the topic marker *wa* surfaces overriding case markers, and the nominalization and nominal predicate together support the topic-comment information dynamism. Other features further supporting a Japanese preference toward the rhetoric of *pathos* include fluid methods of quotation and an abundance of self-expressions communicating personal, often emotive, commentary (e.g., interactional particles and attitudinal discourse markers). In contrast, the rhetoric of *logos* prioritizes logical relations expressed in propositions where the locutionary self frequently and explicitly surfaces.[6]

That said, let me summarize for clarification purposes the characteristics of the rhetoric of *pathos* in contrast with the rhetoric of *logos*.

1. rhetoric of *pathos*:
   a. relative unimportance of language, less trust placed in language
   b. relative importance of the topic-comment relation
   c. comment-based logic/argumentation
   d. importance of context of place
   e. expressive and emotive modality effect is critical
   f. changing state conveyed in sentence construction
   g. event, often captured by nominalization and quotation, and comment toward it important
   h. relatively fluid and shifting/moving points of view
   i. conclusion presented, if at all, at the end of text
   j. essay-like progression important in text organization
   k. sharing of personal experience important
   l. aims to sympathize, co-experience, especially through shared perspectives

---

[6] Studies are available contrasting regional or national cultures and characters (Hofstede 2001; Kosulis 2002; Nisbett 2003). However, my contrast is based on language and discourse and does not address Japanese culture in general. Still, rhetorical features in Japanese can be informed by overall cultural contrasts. For example, Kosulis (2002), in comparative philosophy, makes a distinction between intimacy- and integrity-oriented cultures. The intimacy-oriented culture favors rhetoric of *pathos*, as in the case of Japan.

2. rhetoric of *logos*:
   a. relative importance of language, more trust placed in language
   b. primacy of the subject-predicate relation
   c. importance of subject-based logic/argumentation
   d. context subordinate to text
   e. informational propositional structure is critical
   f. agent's action prioritized in sentence construction
   g. agent and its action important
   h. relatively rigid and consistent points of view
   i. conclusion often presented in the beginning of text
   j. logical coherence important in text organization
   k. objective description important
   l. aims to argue, persuade

It should be noted that the rhetoric of *pathos* and the rhetoric of *logos* are not mutually exclusive and do not directly correspond to specific languages. In fact preferences and dispreferences toward either rhetoric are likely to exist within a single language. Depending on the genre, primacy may be placed on information where the rhetoric of *logos* plays a dominant role. Legal documents and procedural manuals, for example, out of necessity, prioritize information more than emotive meanings. It is also true that the relative importance placed on informational meaning, emotive meaning, and interactional meaning may shift through time, or may be expressed in different ways through history. Even when these factors are taken into consideration, I maintain that Japanese discourse shows a marked preference toward the rhetoric of *pathos*.[7]

The self endorsed through a rhetoric of *pathos* is a person who hides behind the expression and who, in addition to the propositional information, implicitly expresses a personal and emotive attitude. This self is fundamentally empty, devoid of definable *a priori* existence. The self in the rhetoric of *pathos*

---

[7] I should add that rhetorical features in the Japanese language have been investigated by scholars with some differing results. These studies include, from the perspective of discourse analysis, Hinds (1983, 1986, 1987, 1990) and from literary genres and aesthetics, Amagasaki (2002) and Sasaki (2002). Kubota (1997), criticizing Hinds' work for overgeneralization, questions the rhetorical features associated with the Japanese language and culture. Tomasi (2004) offers a historical account of how Western influences played a role in the development of Japanese rhetorical styles. My presentation of the rhetoric of *pathos* and the rhetoric of *logos* is based on limited past analyses as made clear in my previous studies, and they do not reveal stylistic contrast across all genres between Japan and the West. Depending on genres under investigation and depending on how ontological concepts are defined, different conclusions are likely to be drawn. Clearer answers may become attainable as new analyses of different genres of Japanese discourses become available.

is unspecified, hidden behind language, and yet, ultimately emerges as a richly expressive self featured with aspects, characters, and characteristics.

The self accommodating the partner uses a variety of strategies reflecting subjectivity and intersubjectivity. This accommodation, often being interpreted from historical approaches in pragmatics (Traugott 1989, 2003), suggests that the Japanese language has changed and perhaps is changing toward an even more intense intersubjectivity, i.e, intersubjectification (Onodera and Suzuki 2007). Traugott (2003) theorizes that subjectivity in language changes through history, and relevant meanings over time come to encode or externalize, more than the so-called real-world event, the speaker's perspectives and attitudes. At the same time, meanings over time come to encode the speaker's concern toward the addressee, i.e., prioritizing intersubjectification. This historical change from information-centeredness to emotion- and partner-centeredness is specifically observed in Japanese (Onodera and Suzuki 2007; Onodera 2017). Japanese grammaticalization processes have evolved toward intersubjectification, and it has taken on a form that prioritizes the self's and other's emotions, attitudes, and interactional considerations.

Although I have not conducted a historical study, I have described in Maynard (1997b), the nature of the Japanese language in the way that does not contradict either subjectification or intersubjectification processes. To quote:

> When emotionally motivated phrases are interposed at various points in talk, a very personal voice informs the communication. Sharing emotional vulnerability enhances the sense of involvement in the interaction. The significance of the propositional meaning diminishes; the personal narrative, brimming with personal and interpersonal feelings, gains ascendency over mere facts. The subjective speaking self, hiding behind a verbal veil, stands at the heart of what is actually being communicated.
> MAYNARD 1997b: 193–194

In a subjectivity- and intersubjectivity-oriented language such as Japanese, self exists in a creative flux continuously transforming in its context. Self is multiple (Maynard 2017), fluid, and mediated through linguistic and cultural factors. Most fundamentally, self must be viewed not as a theory-bound preconception, but rather, as a pragmatics-motivated performer. Following up on my earlier work on fluid orality (Maynard 2016), in Maynard (2017) I have proposed that Japanese self is multiple and complex, and that in the realization of the self, character-speak plays a major role. From the perspective of ontology, I have discussed in detail the complexities of a self that emerges in Japanese popular culture discourse. I have explored the Self-as-Multiple theory wherein multiple characters and characteristics resonate with philosophical and poetic traditions in Japan.

Expressions of subjectivity and intersubjectivity index aspects of the self. In Maynard (2002) I identify specific aspects of Japanese selves; (1) subordinate and equal selves as kinds of the socially-bound interactional self, (2) gendered selves (such as girlish, boyish, womanly, and manly selves), and (3) the playful self. Additionally in Maynard (2007), I explore selves realized by self-referencing terms. I propose that the self is divided into self-identifying objectified self and reflexively projected self and these selves are embedded within the self as a locutionary agent.

Following my earlier works including Maynard (2019), I continue to explore the concept of empty yet populated self. Initially located in an empty place, self is itself empty, but it transforms into a populated self consisting of a complex bundle of performed features. And as one of the primary resources, the moment-to-moment language practice performs a seamless populating act. The process of populating the self is evidenced in how language is designed, expressed, and managed, especially how subjective and intersubjective expressions operate. Because of this inherent association, original and translated novels can provide a metadiscourse for philosophical inquiries of the self.

This work focuses on how subjective expressions bring about varied aspects of the self across Japanese and translation texts. In this work, following philosophical and poetic perspectives, I identify transient and flickering aspects of the self. From linguistic, social, and communicational points of view, an interdependent and relational self is noted. It also recognizes a self that is performatory, interactional, and participatory in nature. Based on linguistic features, the self is also identified as being hidden, expressive, perceptive, receptive, and intersubjective. This work notes that certain linguistic phenomena also point to a floating and transferred self, one who manipulates perspectives and other rhetorical means.

The phenomenon of varied aspects of self illustrates the complexity as well as the fluidity of the Japanese self. In essence, aspects of the self offer an opportunity for making an exodus from the paradigm of the singular consistent self, allowing the self to personalize in multiple, often contradicting, ways. As explored in the next section, along with aspects of the self, the Japanese preference toward characters and characteristics is closely associated with a desire for a more fluid way of presenting one's self.

2 Character

The second key concept in philosophical contrastive pragmatics is character. In what follows, to place this concept in the Western theoretical context, I first discuss the self as being dialogical and performatory. These concepts are applicable to both Japanese and Western studies, and understanding Japanese variations in terms of these notions is expected to guide us in locating possible translation gaps. Then concepts of character, characteristic, and character-speak are discussed, followed by a brief review of studies on the character-associated features of the Japanese self.

2.1 *Background: Dialogical and Performatory Self*

Understanding the language and the self as being dialogical and performatory in nature provides a foundation to the concept of character, characteristic, and character-speak. Because data for this study are drawn from literary genres, it is helpful to draw insight on language and self from literary theories and semiotics associated with the Russian formalist movement. Particularly noteworthy is Bakhtin's work, specifically how he approaches the concept of self. Bakhtin (1981, 1986) holds the view that language is interactional and dialogic, and language simply cannot avoid reflecting multiple voices simultaneously. Multiple voices echo in one's words (including utterances of prior as well as future speakings), and these voices are supported by social heterogeneity. Voices representing various registers, classes, cultures, and sub-cultures reverberate in speech, where the voices coexist and interanimate. Bakhtin (1981), denying the world where only subjectivity and objectivity exist in a state of abstract dichotomy, conceives of the world as being dialogic where people engage in actions and activities, and where multiple kinds of consciousness interact. This is because when we experience an object, we are in a relationship with it, and as a result, "it becomes a changing moment in the ongoing event of my experiencing (thinking) it, i.e., it assumes the character of something-yet-to-be-achieved" (Bakhtin 1993: 32).

Critically, Bakhtin emphasizes the importance of linguistic activity, and proposes a model that opposes the traditional introspection-based approach. For Bakhtin, the relationship between a person and the world is the relationship of actions, not the kind supported by a dichotomy between the self and the object. The self is a person who acts toward someone, and what the person encounters is not objects out there, but the partner. After all, those objects out there must be viewed by someone, and that someone's actions and activities must not be ignored in our approach to language and literary discourse.

From this perspective, Bakhtin (1993) turns his thought to language and its evaluative and expressive meanings, and states the following.

> Similarly, the living word, the full word, does not know an object as something totally given: the mere fact that I have begun speaking about it means that I have already assumed a certain attitude toward it—not an indifferent attitude, but an interest-effective attitude. And that is why the word does not merely designate an object as a present-on-hand entity, but also expresses by its intonation my valuative attitude toward the object, toward what is desirable or undesirable in it, and, in doing so, sets it in motion toward that which is yet-to-be-determined about it, turns it into a constituent moment of the living, ongoing event.
>
> BAKHTIN 1993: 32–33

His point that beyond designation a word cannot help but express an attitude resonates with the positions I have taken over the years. Here the term "intonation" means more than a simple phonological phenomenon; it includes linguistic variations in general. Furthermore, a word is not independent of its producer or of its recipient. It is given life in an activity-filled event because it is supported by the interdependent dialogical relationship. We must not ignore that all pragmatics-motivated phenomena come alive in the place where ongoing language events occur.

This dialogical relationship Bakhtin insists on is recognized in a broad range of relationships such as self-other, signifier-signified, text-context, rhetoric-language, and speaking-writing. All these elements should be understood not as being isolated within a dualistic system, but as being based on dialogic relationships. Holquist summarizes Bakhtin's position by stating that "(W)hatever else it is, self/other is a relation of simultaneity" (2002: 19). Holquist also adds that such a relationship exists because ultimately "(S)eparateness and simultaneity are basic conditions of existence" (2002: 20). This view affords a possibility that we discover the self with multiple aspects, characters, and characteristics.

In the novel, the language used by a dramatic person is worded by the author. Thus, it is especially important to investigate the relationship between the author and dramatic persons. Bakhtin (1981) understands this critical relationship in terms of the space which the dramatic person (i.e., Bakhtin's character) occupies, that is, the character zone. The character zone offers a space where the character's voices are heard, but those voices are always negotiated (i.e., dialogized) with the author's voice.

Bakhtin's explanation of the character zone is based on his analysis of Turgenev's novels. Perhaps one example which Bakhtin cites from *Virgin Soil* will suffice. In the sentence *But Kallomyetsev deliberately struck his round eyeglass between his nose and his eyebrow, and stared at the (…) student who dared not share his apprehensions*, Bakhtin finds a typical hybrid construction (i.e., *dared not share*). This expression captures Kallomyetsev's irritation while at the same time, in the context of authorial speech, it is laced with the author's ironic tone. As a result, this expression serves two purposes, i.e., "the author's ironic transmission, and a mimicking of the irritation of the character" (1981: 318). In other words, the expression *dared not share* echoes the author's ironic voice, while simultaneously vocalizing Kallomyetsev's irritation in a space apart from the authorial territory.

As reflected in Bakhtin's following words, the importance of the character zone is undeniable.

> Character zones are a most interesting object of study for stylistic and linguistic analysis; in them one encounters constructions that cast a completely new light on problems of syntax and stylistics.
> BAKHTIN 1981: 320

To go even further, the character zone provides an analytical framework for understanding how the otherwise empty self is populated. The character zone is where voices of the self as author, narrator, and dramatic person all interact, continuously revealing aspects of the self as well as features of characters and characteristics. Accordingly, the way sociolinguistic variations and stylistic features are translated (or not) into English is critical. What transpires in the character zone in Japanese and English differs, and these differences are linked to different ideas and portrayals of the self.

The concept of dialogicality has been explored from psychology and linguistics, especially among scholars influenced by Bakhtin (1981) and Vygotsky (1962 [1934]). For example, Bertau (2014a, 2014b) reviews an implicit Cartesian view of the speaker by criticizing it as being monological. Under this traditional assumption, the speaker is the one who uses language with authority enforcing intention through coded signs. Bertau (2014a), as an editor of a special journal issue, challenges this traditional view. She reports that scholars who work within the dialogical paradigm movement take a serious look at the relationship between language and the self by acknowledging the sociality of human beings. More critically, these scholars understand that human beings are not only fundamentally social, but their sociality is the very condition of their individuality. Also emphasized in this paradigm is that the social and the individual are not in opposition to each other; rather, they are dynamically related, generating, and supporting each other. On the role of the other, Bertau argues that it is a pre-condition for the self. In her words:

> Asserting the relatedness of human beings to their consociates, to themselves, and to their specific historical and socio-cultural environment, we get a picture of humans where *otherness* plays a central role. The basic move needed in constructing an alternative to individualistic methodology is thus a shift from the self-contained I to the related self, where the other is seen as the self's pre-condition—to acquire, develop, and perform language, thinking, consciousness, as well as its self.
> BERTAU 2014a: 434, original emphasis

Understanding language from a dialogical perspective leads us to prioritize the relation itself. The relation is formed and is practiced through language which serves as the medium of human existence. We are mediated beings, experiencing the otherness that populates within us.

Two articles in this special issue on the dialogical self, Baerveldt (2014) and Shotter (2014), should be touched upon. Baerveldt (2014) emphasizes that an individual is never alone and cannot be alone. This is not because an individual is unable or unwilling to do so, but because an individual cannot be otherwise. Given this existential reality we must recognize that language sustains the very essence of our being. To quote Baerveldt:

> The self always has its accompaniment—its shadow and thus the very fact of Being is identical with Being-with-itself—thinking, reflecting, contemplating, and emoting—all of which can only be constituted in language. Therefore language cannot be a mere tool of communication or a mechanical expression of what an individual is.
> BAERVELDT 2014: 566

Similarly but more forcefully, Shotter (2014) emphasizes that human beings need to see themselves as essentially living within "back-and-forth relations with the others and otherness around" (2014: 592). Shotter (2014, 2019), emphasizing the importance of understanding the dialogical essence of human activity, proposes a methodology that accounts for behavior of human beings in what he calls "language world." He advocates a hermeneutical theorizing rather than one of traditional representation, and takes the dialogical paradigm to a meta-theoretical interpretive level.

The dialogical paradigm has been introduced in applied linguistics as well. Scholarship in second and foreign language learning has traditionally looked to linguistics and psycholinguistics for its epistemological foundations (Hall, Vitanova and Marchenkova 2005). As a result, it has followed the formalist view of language, i.e., an abstract self-contained system with a set of rules. Furthermore, the assumption has been that these systems can be extracted from their contexts of use to be studied independently. However, as Hall, Vitanova and Marchenkova (2005) report, the limitations of this model for understanding language learners' experiences have been repeatedly pointed out, and the scholars found a more convincing approach in the works of Bakhtin (1981) and Vygotsky (1962 [1934]). In contrast to an understanding of language as sets of closed systems of normative forms, Bakhtin and Vygotsky approach it as dynamic constellations of social and historical contexts. Scholars whose studies are presented in Hall, Vitanova and Marchenkova (2005) explore the dialogical paradigm in pedagogy and identify the formation of a dialogical self in multiple languages.

The concept of dialogicality discussed above offers insights to our ontological pursuit in three ways. First, we must remind ourselves that language and discourse are understood in relation to the partner, and so is the concept of the self which emerges in relation to the other. Second, the concept of heteroglossia supports the self's multiple aspects, characters, and characteristics through which multiple selves emerge with multivoicedness. Third, the dialogicality of language reminds us that the very way the empty self is populated through character-speak is motivated by multiple voices echoing across selves.

In addition to research on the dialogical self, viewing the embodied self as a performer offers support to the concepts of character, characteristic, and character-speak.[8] The field of pragmatics has always emphasized the significance of communication activity and performance in the analysis of discourse (Mey 1993; Östman and Verschueren 2010, 2011). These research traditions have insisted on the significance of language as meaningful performance, and consequently on its functions in context. In sociology, ethnography, anthropology and linguistic anthropology, the concept of performance in verbal art has consistently occupied a central stage. And the performance-centered views have been closely associated with the presentation of self, performer, and character. The source for the concept of performance is best found in Mead's (1967 [1934]) theory of symbolic interactionism mentioned in Chapter 1.

The idea that we see ourselves as performers reminds us of Goffman's (1959) idea of "theatrical performance." In fact, the notion of performance grounds Goffman's understanding of the presentation of self. When Goffman discusses one of his central concepts, impression management, he is concerned with how to manage and present the objectified self to be seen by others. Goffman (1959),

---

8 Recall that calling attention to the significance of the performatory nature of language is not new as Vico (1965 [1709]) insisted on centuries earlier.

constructing his understanding of selves in the scene of dramaturgy, introduces vocabulary normally associated with the theater such as front, backstage, setting, audience, performance, performer, and significantly to the current study, with the concept of character.

Goffman's analogy of dramaturgy is most strongly expressed when he states his thesis that life itself is a dramatically enacted thing and although all the world is not a stage, "the crucial ways in which it isn't are not easy to specify" (1959: 72). For Goffman, the essence of the self is found not within us, but in moment-to-moment performance. This means that although a self seeks to present a particular impression, the self's image ultimately depends on conformation that comes from others.

Goffman understands that life itself is enacted similarly to the dramaturgical performance, and this guides him to his understanding that the individual is a performer, and more specifically, a character in performance. Goffman summarizes his view toward the performer and character in the following way.

> In this report, the individual was divided by implication into two basic parts: he was viewed as a performer, a harried fabricator of impressions involved in the all-too-human task of staging a performance; he was viewed as a character, a figure, typically a fine one, whose spirit, strength, and other sterling qualities the performance was designed to evoke. The self, then, as a performed character, is not an organic thing that has a specific location, whose fundamental fate is to be born, to mature, and to die; it is a dramatic effect arising diffusely from a scene that is presented, and the characteristic issue, the crucial concern, is whether it will be credited or discredited.
> GOFFMAN 1959: 252–253

For Goffman, the essence of the self is discovered not in one's interior or inner self, but in one's interaction. The image of oneself is dependent on the willingness of others to go along with the particular impression that a person seeks to present. Goffman's statement that the self is a performed character and that it arises diffusely from each successive scene offers insight to the notion of the populated self. The self is a performer who is likely to take on different characters and characteristics. Just as the self in performance and the self in character are not identical to the totality of one's self, the self is multiple in its performed manifestations. It is through a person's engagement in communication as a performer that he or she emerges as a person. Concepts of dialogical and performatory self discussed in this section provide support to self's multiplicity, particularly realized as character and characteristic through character-speak.

These concepts offer interpretive resources for exploring the self, to which issue we now turn.

2.2   *Character, Characteristic, and Character-Speak*

Both Japanese and English texts feature what Ortega y Gasset (1959) calls "exuberances" and "deficiencies." When these two languages are contrasted, their respective exuberances and deficiencies are observed in sharper focus. Differences are found not only in grammatical and discourse structures but in language variation. Character-associated variations are significant because their differences offer new insight to our task of exploring the self. I have explored the concepts of character, characteristic, and character-speak in my earlier studies on the discourse of Japanese popular culture (Maynard 2016, 2017, 2019). In this work, character- and characteristic-associated phenomena are revisited in Chapter 11.

Character in essence refers to the recognized image of personhood with expected attitudinal traits, often but not exclusively developed in popular culture discourse. It includes, but is not limited to, the widely recognized types within the popular culture database and media. Traditionally, characters in popular culture include stereotypes such as the princess character, old-scientist character, diva character, youth-gang character, middle-aged-man character, housewife character, and so on.[9] The concept of characteristic captures varied features of a character. Characteristics are character-related attributes and traits stereotypically manifested in a given context. A characteristic does not singularly define the character; it is transient, surfacing to reveal a limited feature of one's character. One's character emerges as the result of repeated and consistent presentation; a characteristic, however, flashes but briefly. Character and characteristic differ in terms of focus, but the latter is a constituent of the former, and therefore, they inherently integrate and overlap. Although not mutually exclusive, character and characteristic differ sufficiently to warrant separate terms. For example, the old man characteristic is temporarily borrowed as a playful act (i.e., a case of characteristic) while in another situation it may represent a stable character-personhood, i.e., an old man character.

Characters and characteristics are created and manipulated through character-speak, consisting of multiple verbal and visual signs. Character-speak

---

9   The term "character" is used in a specific way. It is commonly used when referring to a person and a role appearing in a work of fiction. Because here the term is used in a technical sense, I avoid using "character" in the sense of a persona in fiction unless it appears in association with others' studies. In its stead, terms such as dramatic person and participant are used to refer to the primary, secondary, and other personae in literary works.

establishes, supports, changes, and transforms characters and characteristics. Devices used as character-speak are not limited to grammar, but extend to rhetorical and interactional aspects. It involves all levels of language and communication, including script, phonological structure, voice quality, lexical selection, morphology, syntax, styles, variations, rhetorical figures, discourse organization, and conversational management. In short, character-speak refers to all modes of interaction.

The concept of character-speak involves a rich creative use of fictionalized variation and rhetoric. Fictionalized variation can be associated with regional dialects, social registers, and generation-associated styles, as well as gender-evoking speech varieties. These variations are primarily chosen for expressive and playful effects to form and manipulate characters and characteristics. Rhetorical figures such as puns and irony function as character-speak as a means for establishing a creative and humor-loving character or characteristic. In addition, from a broader perspective, character-speak includes manipulation such as intertextuality and inter-genre expressivity as well as the interplay between verbal and visual signs (Maynard 2008a). All of these expressive meanings enhance the realization of characters and characteristics as they gradually take shape.

Character-speak brings to discourse different kinds of expressive meanings. For example, we find the meaning associated with socially recognized characters created by gender-evoking variation (e.g., effeminate *onee* language) and place-evoking variation (e.g. fictional regional dialects). Other variations of character-speak mark dramatic persons in literary discourse as old man character, diva character, and so on. A self may consistently use the Kansai dialect to present the Kansai character (Jinnouchi and Tomosada 2006). Or, a self in conversation who usually speaks in a youth language may occasionally and temporarily incorporate a style stereotypically associated with an old man. A young female dramatic person may use an abrupt style stereotypically linked to men's speech, or choose a style customarily identified as that of a princess. Borrowing styles from others to activate characteristics illustrates how a self uses fictional variation as an expressive strategy. It is as if other inhabitants resided within the self, if only temporarily.

Given the popularity of the character phenomenon in Japan, it is not difficult to find works surrounding this topic in Japanese language studies. Two important works should be mentioned, "role language" proposed by Kinsui (2003, 2013) and further developed by a number of linguists (Kinsui 2007, 2011), and "utterance character" discussed by Sadanobu (2011). Role language, narrower in scope, is specifically linked to a certain stereotyped character. The features I focus on include not only Kinsui's role language, but also broader discourse phenomena and features. My focus also includes phenomena where dramatic persons or narrators temporarily take on characteristics.

Sadanobu (2011) proposes a character-related approach by introducing terms such as utterance character and expression character. He discusses linguistic expressions that cover phenomena broader than Kinsui (2003). For example, the interjections *fuun* 'uh huh' and *hee* 'I see' are associated with child speech while *hoo* 'I see' and *haa* 'I get it' activate the adult utterance character. Sadanobu (2009, 2015, 2021) discusses the prosody of interjections that accompany intonation shifts and use of character particles such as *pyoon*. Although Sadanobu's broader perspective on the character phenomenon offers insight, his approach remains in basic agreement with Kinsui (2003). Sadanobu (2011) points out that the concept of "role" is purpose-driven and is unstable because it changes depending on the social context, and accordingly, he insists that it is inadequate as an analytical tool for the character phenomenon. Still, Sadanobu recognizes that Kinsui's role language in principle overlaps with his utterance character approach. As a result, again, the scope of features discussed is narrower than the phenomena discussed in my work. Differences in terms of focus between these and my approaches are discussed further in Maynard (2016, 2017).

Related to the concept of character-speak, both in recent works (Maynard 2016, 2017, 2019), and in my earlier studies (Maynard 2004a, 2005c, 2007) I have introduced the concept of borrowed styles, as a precursor to character-speak.[10] Character-speak differs from borrowed style in the following ways. Borrowed style refers to broader phenomena observed in genres of Japanese language such as magazine articles, interviews, and Internet postings. Yet studies of the borrowed style have not explored its philosophical and theoretical implications. In contrast, character-speak is a concept developed primarily by analyzing popular culture genres in association with the phenomena of characters and characteristics. Character-speak also allows for us to directly approach our theme of exploring the concept of self, guiding us to its philosophical conceptualization.

At this point I should discuss the nature of the meaning associated with character-speak and how it is interpreted. In my view, linguistic and pragmatic features of the character-speak operate as signs that involve icon, index, and

---

[10] It should be noted that both borrowed style and character-speak differ from the concept of "role language" (Kinsui 2003, 2007, 2011; Teshigawara and Kinsui 2011). For one, as explained in Maynard (2016, 2017), borrowed style and character-speak often add features to the main dramatic persons, although it is claimed that role language does not. See other reasons in Maynard (2016, 2017).

symbol. However, character-speak operates most prominently as an indexical sign. This is because the expressive meanings foregrounded by character-speak are more social, psychological, and emotional than referential. Following Peirce (1992 [1868]), an indexical sign operates as representamen associated with an object, and its meaning is mediated by way of the interpretant through multiple semiotic accumulations and repetitions. An indexical sign, bearing a contextual and mutual relationship with an object, is a sign indexed to the pragmatics of language in the Peircean sense. This contrasts with an icon that exhibits similarity to an object, and with a symbol where the sign and object connection is arbitrary and based solely on convention.

In the Peircean semiotic system, a sign (i.e., representamen) is in relation to its object on the one hand, and to an interpretant on the other. This position differs from Saussure's (1966) signifier-signified sign system, which sorely misses the third element, the interpretant. Character-speak as indexical sign is particularly sensitive to this interpretant-centered semiotic mediation. The expressive meanings the character-speak realizes are not based on stable referential information. They are transitory links to the interactional encounter, both in terms of physical and imagined space, and more concretely to place in my Place of Negotiation theory (Maynard 2000, 2002). They are especially sensitive to the recipient's recognition, acceptance, or rejection.

The relationship between linguistic means and the realization of characters and characteristics is multiple and flexible, that is, polyindexical, where the meanings appear in "indexical fields" (Eckert 2008). The expressive meanings of a character-speak gradually become foregrounded and more readily accepted, as specific character and characteristic features repeatedly function as indexical signs (Agha 2005). Character-speak features are gradually integrated and seep into the self, and the self is portrayed as a character or someone bearing a characteristic in performance. For example, in literary works regional dialects may function to realize a complex yet recognizable character- or characteristic-expressive meaning at different points in discourse.[11]

In sum, the meanings associated with character-speak are dynamic and context-mediated. Seemingly unstable interpretations of characters and characteristics are due in part to this nature of the indexical sign itself. Creators of novels take advantage of this manner of signification where readers experience creation, transformation, and manipulation of images of dramatic persons and narrators with recognizable characters and characteristics.

---

11   In addition, and more relevant to this work, expressive meanings of the character-speak are indexically associated with popular culture and concepts of character, characteristic, and character-speak are critical for analyzing its discourse (Maynard 2022a, 2022b).

2.3 Character in Japanese Society

Characters and characteristics play a significant role in Japanese culture, and this tendency is supported by psychological motivation (Maynard 2016, 2017, 2019). Characters have become critical as shown in the phenomenon of avatars inhabiting the Internet. The ubiquity of characters in Japanese society has attracted attention from psychologists, sociologists, and cultural critics. They generally raise the question of why the character phenomenon is so pervasive in Japan, and how it impacts the psychological and social makeup of the Japanese self and society. Answers to these questions simultaneously involve positive and negative attributes surrounding the character phenomenon (Maynard 2012, 2014, 2016). Regardless of the positions, undeniably the character phenomenon plays a dominant role in defining the self among the Japanese.

Saito (2011) who focuses on the character phenomenon in Japanese classroom communication, points out that character is not something one may personally control. It is a label assigned to a member of a group, referring to a behavior or role the person is expected to perform. A person tends to accept the character label willingly, because once one's own character is known, a vulnerable issue of self identity may be evaded. In this situation, a character is not something one spontaneously performs but instead, something one is forced to accept and is obliged to perform. The psychological motivation cited here partially explains why character-speak is so useful in self presentation. By accepting or performing a character label, one can possibly hide one's self and incorporate other aspects of the self (or at least one can assume so). Even when one's character is affronted or challenged, the character, being actually a mask, helps mitigate the damage. In addition, Saito (2011) notes that performances in characters prepare Japanese children to successfully engage in certain social roles in later life.

Based on a questionnaire, Aihara (2007) identifies several benefits in accepting one's role as a character. In order of preference, they include (1) comfort, (2) protection, (3) escape from real life, (4) nostalgic return to younger days, (5) confirmation of one's existence, (6) desire for passivity, strength and liveliness, as well as (7) stress relief. Aihara adds that sometimes people feel closer to characters than even to their own family members or best friend. Aihara (2007) notes that if one communicates all day long with others on social media, the "I" that sits in front of the digital device exists only as "I-performing-as-the-character." The self sitting there is soon swallowed up in the digital world by a sense of "I-equal-the-character." The I-equal-the-character encourages and is supported by an emptying of the self.

Harada (2010) offers another study advocating the benefit of performing a character. Harada contends that a new sense of a village is widespread in postmodern Japan. In what Harada calls "new village society," young people are constantly, but not necessarily deeply, connected on the Internet through mobile devices.[12] To participate in this village of websites, blogs, and Social Network Services, one must follow a set of strictly enforced rules, such as (1) promptly responding to text messages, (2) supporting others warmly, (3) going along with others, and (4) not behaving in eccentric ways. One strategy for sidestepping these expected social norms is to act out one's character. In fact, simply declaring one's character to be narcissistic excuses one for engaging in self-centered priggish behavior. In Harada's view, the concept of character serves as a liberating tool for the sometimes stifling and forced sense of participation expected in this new village.

When communicating on the Internet, one cannot help but reveal the self presented as a character or a characteristic. And such a desire to project one's character may indeed take over one's sense of self. Indeed, characters have invaded Japan and seemingly are in the process of taking over the population. It becomes more and more persuasive to view self-presentation as a process of emptying, and populating the self, a process where the self is free to play with characters and characteristics. Senuma (2007) relates to this in his discussion of how Japanese youths find a sense of self within a group. Unlike traditional ways, young people today define themselves as a character or multiple characters. Senuma explains that differentiating one's self from others in terms of characters differs from traditional methods of seeking personality or identity. Although the traditional method involves individual initiative, the character-performing self tends to be generally dependent on others, and is featured in its openness toward its multiplicity.

It should be noted that characters presented through performances in Japanese media have strongly influenced the general public's acceptance of and familiarity with the character culture. In academia as well, terms related to the concept of character have been introduced as interpretive tools for studying Japanese discourse including Japanese popular culture (Kinsui 2021, Maynard 2021, Sadanobu 2021). Frequent exposure to the entertainment world, for example, is expected to encourage a similar kind of interactional style among viewers, who tend to overlay this character-performing communication onto their everyday language practice.

---

12   Regarding the construction of identity in the digital world elsewhere of Japan, refer to Salonen (2018), Wentker (2018) as well as Kleinke and Bös (2018). These studies discuss how increased digital activities lead to a loss of traditional identity, and how new kinds of personal, group, and collective identities are negotiated online.

As reviewed above, characters have garnered sizable attention in the discussion of Japanese culture. Particularly significant to this work include the use of character for the purpose of psychological self-protection (Saito 2011), the concept of "I-equal-the-character" (Aihara 2007), and youth's self-identification as multiple characters (Senuma 2007). These studies endorse the fluidity of the Japanese self that is more of a norm than an exception, and support the idea of populating the empty self with shifting and flexible characters as well as characteristics.

In this chapter, subjectivity and character, the two key concepts useful for exploring the self are introduced. Given that these concepts have been developed in Japan and elsewhere, they provide useful interpretive resources for conducting analyses in philosophical contrastive pragmatics.

CHAPTER 4

Perspectives from Translation Studies and Contrastive Pragmatics

This chapter discusses studies and issues relevant to contrastive pragmatics analyses. Two fields of importance are reviewed, initially translation studies followed by contrastive pragmatics, especially those involving translation texts. What follows is not meant to be a full review of these fields; only issues pertinent to this work are presented.

1 Discourse of Translation and Translation Studies

1.1 Overview

With increased contacts among different languages and cultures proliferating on the Internet, translation studies have attracted researchers with varied backgrounds and interests. This trend is supported by the publication of collected studies on translation, for example, *Routledge Encyclopedia of Translation Studies* (Baker and Saldanha 2009), *Handbook of Translation Studies* (Gambier and van Doorslaer 2010), and *The Routledge Handbook of Translation and Pragmatics* (Tipton and Desilla 2019).

Translation studies have incorporated deconstruction, postcolonial as well as sociological approaches, all under the influence of the academic milieu of the 1970s and 1980s. In addition, contrastive linguistics, discourse analysis, critical discourse analysis, psycholinguistics, and cognitive linguistics have provided academic background to the field.

In the past, up until the 1970s, translation studies have concentrated on select features associated with source and target texts. Scholars were primarily interested in finding ways to resolve semantic and expressive gaps, mainly by incorporating linguistic, social, and cultural information. Although achieving an absolute equivalence of meaning across languages is difficult, or nearly impossible, the translator makes every effort to create a text in the target language as close as possible to the original. Since the 1970s approaches relevant to translation have been adopted, e.g., textlinguistics (Beaugrande and Dressler 1981), systemic functional grammar (Halliday 1985; Halliday and Hasan 1976), and pragmatics (Kranich 2016).

Within translation studies proper, approaches from functional perspectives have produced the Skopos theory (from Greek *skopós*) by Vermeer (2004

[1989]). According to the Skopos theory, appropriateness of the translation depends on how satisfactorily it serves the aim or purpose of the target language. This view that translation is controlled by varying purposes (Reiß and Vermeer 2014) has lead to the production of multiple translations. Although the prioritization of purpose in translation studies offers an interesting angle to the translation task, the Skopos theory is not directly applicable to literary texts. Three concepts associated with the Skopos theory, however, are relevant to this work, i.e., localization, domestication, and foreignization. Localization caters toward the target society and changes the original text to meet the need of the target population. One way to localize the source text is the domestication process through which readers experience a minimum of foreignness in the translation (Venuti 2008). The opposite of domestication is foreignization through which readers are overtly made aware of the source language's distinct features. Foreignization gives a positive twist in that it introduces new concepts and values absent in the target culture. These concepts are discussed when useful in the course of this volume.

The influence of postmodernism has given rise to concerns among many researchers toward the social and cultural aspects of translation. Instead of focusing on the text itself with concepts such as equivalence and shift, scholars have begun to view translation as a social action influenced by ideologies. When viewed from the perspective of cultural studies, translation is seen as another case of Western dominance over non-Western cultures. The ideology that translation is a part of cultural imperialism has initiated the theory-building in non-Western academic communities. For example, Evan-Zohar (2004 [1978, 1990]) introduces the concept of "polysystem," which under the influence of Russian formalism, considers translation in relation to the target society's overall literature and culture. Polysystem encompasses not only classical literature but a wide range of literary works such as children's stories and mass-marketed novels. Evan-Zohar insists on treating the translation texts as a part of this larger polysystem, and raises questions as to how the translated literature is treated within the target society.

Toury (2012), influenced by Evan-Zohar (2004 [1978, 1990]), proposes Descriptive Translation Studies. In this approach, translation text is interpreted within the target society under the concept of "norm," i.e., the observable regularity or patterns in translation. Descriptive Translation Studies requires researchers to find the norm by paying attention to the translated materials as a whole, rather than focusing on an individual work. Translation is understood as a part of an overall cultural system, and accordingly, reflects the norm prevalent at a given time and place. Thus, examination of multiple translated works leads to a discovery of conventionalized regularity of the translation phenomenon in the target society.

1.2   *Translation Equivalence*

When one language is replaced by a translation text, the question of equivalence becomes critical. When functional and semantic discrepancies are observed across the source and target texts, "shift" is identified. Shift occurs on as well as across lexical, grammatical, and discursive levels. Lexical meanings may be conveyed in the target language not by word but through grammatical structure.[1] Gaps observed between the original and translated texts have provoked a debate that has been continuously raised in translation studies. Source text and target text are generally understood or at least are intended to be equivalent. Obviously, translators strive to achieve equivalence to a greater or lesser extent. Although equivalence is a fundamental issue in translation studies, it continues to be controversial and unresolved.

In fact, issues related to translation equivalence have been debated for decades since the 1960s. Nida (2004 [1964]) identifies two types of equivalence, formal and dynamic. The formal equivalence focuses on linguistic forms, while the dynamic equivalence emphasizes the effects linguistic expressions bring about. Formal equivalence can be found when correspondences such as poetry to poetry, sentence to sentence, and concept to concept are observed. That is to say, "(V)iewed from the formal orientation, one is concerned that the message in the receptor language should match as closely as possible the different elements in the source language" (Nida 2004 [1964]: 156). On the other hand, in dynamic equivalence, the translator is not as concerned with matching the receptor-language message with the source-language message. The primary concern is with the dynamic relationship, and "the relationship between receptor and message should be substantially the same as that which existed between the original receptors and the message" (Nida 2004 [1964]: 156). Here, Nida shifts focus from considering purely linguistic form to taking into account the reception of the target readers.

While Nida's two types of translation equivalence are based on the interaction with target readers, House (2010) identifies two approaches to translation, i.e., overt and covert, based on the distance between source and translation text. Overt translations produce texts where the language may contain foreign elements, i.e., a case of shining through.[2] House explains in the following way.

---

1   Although the term "shift" is often used in translation studies, in this work, I avoid using it. This is because the shift in Japanese language studies has been used in association with stylistic shifts. In its stead, in reference to chasms in translation, terms such as semantic differences and expressive gaps are used.
2   The concept of shining through in translation studies refers to the hypothesis that source language influences the translation text by making it different from non-translated text. In other

> The language in overt translation may be interspersed with foreign elements from the original, which is "shining through." An overt translation is embedded in a new speech event in the target culture. It is a case of "language mention" resembling a quotation.
>
> HOUSE 2010: 245

In contrast, a covert translation consists of the text resembling the non-translated text in the target culture. "The translation is covert because it is not marked pragmatically as a translation at all" (House 2010: 245). House (2010) gives examples of covert translation such as commercial circulars, advertisements, as well as journalistic and scientific texts. In covert translation, the translator is expected to take different cultural situations into account and make an effort to reproduce the original function, what House (2010) refers to as "real" functional equivalence. Significantly, she warns that covert translations "often require subtle lingua-cultural translation problems" (2010: 245). Translation texts analyzed in this work are covert in principle. Because typologically unrelated languages are contrasted, translations are expected to be difficult, and although covert in principle, some elements may shine through as being foreign to the target text.

Equivalence plays a diminished role in translation studies as functionalist and Skopos-oriented approaches have gained prominence. Translation is deemed appropriate as long as it is satisfactory on a functional level (Reiß and Vermeer 2014). Interest in equivalence also diminished with the acceptance of Descriptive Translation Studies (Toury 2012) where emphasis was placed on the appropriateness of the translated text in the context of the target language and culture. In addition, the move away from the equivalence issue became instrumental for conducting corpus-based analyses (Baker 1993).

Although equivalence has been slighted among some scholars in translation studies, renewed interest has been observed among others. For example, Pym (2010) distinguishes between natural equivalence and directional equivalence. Natural equivalents are regarded as given, existing prior to the act of translation only to be discovered by the translator. On the other hand, with directional equivalence, equivalence is not assumed to exist prior to translation, and therefore, the translation is created only as the result of the translator's active engagement. When dealing with culturally and typologically remote languages, finding natural equivalence is expected to be more difficult than otherwise.

---

  words, the translation may be oriented more toward the source language, wherein features of the source language shine through (Teich 2003).

Pym's position adds a renewed relevance to equivalence, particularly when he insists that equivalence is a belief structure which "may be more important than any actual testing of its existence" (2010: 25). Data selected for this work require the translator's active engagement to achieve directional equivalence.

Translation equivalence is also approached from a broader pragmatics context. Koller (2011) proposes five frames of reference to define translation equivalence; (1) denotative, (2) connotative, (3) text-normative, (4) pragmatic, and (5) formal-aesthetic. She presents 14 different factors that have an impact on the notion of equivalence, among them are structural differences, different representations of reality, as well as stylistic and aesthetic norms across languages.

Particularly relevant to this work is the translation equivalence in literary text. Krein-Kühle (2014) points out that the high status of the source text as a work of art requires a rich understanding of equivalence in the translation text, and consequently, equivalence in literary genres is difficult to be fully achieved. She reveals that an even minor changes of rhythm in German translation may fail to reflect the manner of narration in the English source text. For example, due to the process of syntactic transformation and deletion of the determiner, the German translation ignores the rhythm of English phrasing and fails to create appropriate narrative scenes.

As reviewed above, approaches to translation equivalence are varied with no clear answers as to the nature of equivalence and whether or not it is achievable. Nonetheless, defining and understanding the phenomenon of translation equivalence remains a central concern. More empirical research is needed before we come to understand what is involved in translation equivalence and its possible analytical usefulness. One may also question whether equivalence should be seen as a prescriptive or descriptive concept. It is clear, however, that using it as a prescriptive tool is premature. Given that absolute equivalence is probably impossible, what is needed is a practical determination of which linguistic expressions and strategies are taken to be sufficiently comparable in their overall meaning. Obviously, word-by-word equivalence does not make sense, but when the researcher expands the unit of analysis, what Baker (1992) calls "textual equivalence" may be more reasonably pursued. Including the lexical, grammatical, as well as discourse levels and incorporating broader perspectives of pragmatics seem to be the right direction to take.

As one final thought on translation equivalence, I should point out that the relative political, economic, and cultural powers are factors. If the target language is more dominant and prestigious, the translated text tends to bear ideological and cultural values of that target society. For example, when Japanese literature is translated into English, because translators are often associated with American academia and media, their values may reflect their ideologies, and their texts may contain stereotyped images and judgmental attitudes. This imbalance of power between the source and target language influences the quality of translation, especially in terms of the achievability of equivalence itself, but more seriously, it may distort the resultant scholarship based on translation texts.

1.3 Difficulties in Translation

Not surprisingly, scholars and translators have often voiced difficulties in translation. Because my work concentrates on semantic and expressive gaps linked to translation difficulties, their positions are worthy of review. I touch upon how Jakobson, Ricoeur, and Lefevere have approached the essence of and difficulties in translation.

Jakobson (2004 [1959]) approaches translation from functional and poetic perspectives, and categorizes translation into three types, i.e., intralingual translation (rewriting), interlingual translation (translation proper), and intersemiotic translation (transmutation). He takes the position that any type of translation involves difficulties, because languages differ in what they must convey, and not necessarily in what they may convey. For example, when narrating an event, certain languages demand marking the action's completion, while others do not. Or, in some languages the narrated event is presented prior to the narrative act, but not in others. Depending on what each language requires, speakers of that language are constantly focused on these concerns. The language is coded to support such requirements and speakers process information accordingly.

Jakobson (2004 [1959]) also discusses the difficulties of translation when poetic effects are involved. He cites a well-known aphorism as he illustrates the difficulty of translating rhymes across languages.

> If we were to translate into English the traditional formula *Traduttore, traditore* as "the translator is a betrayer," we would deprive the Italian rhyming epigram of all its paronomastic value. Hence a cognitive attitude would compel us to change this aphorism into a more explicit statement and to answer the questions: translator of what messages? betrayer of what values?
>
> JAKOBSON (2004 [1959]): 143, original emphasis

Ricoeur, in his speeches given in Paris from 1997 to 1999, expresses the inherent difficulties involved in translation. As indicative of his speech titles, *Translation as Challenge and Source of Happiness*, *The Paradigm of Translation*, and *On Paradox of Translation*, Ricoeur (2006) maintains the position that translation is not something automatic or trouble-free. He insists that the translation process involves both faithfulness and betrayal, inevitably resulting in gain and loss across languages. Because no third language is available for which one can judge the accuracy or quality of translation, translation always remains a mere approximation.

However, Ricoeur also points out that this interpretation process is observed within a single language as well. Language is featured with what he calls "linguistic hospitality," the ability to explain the meaning by way of the very language. Ricouer reminds us that we utilize this reflexive capacity of language both when dealing with a single language and across languages. The difficulty in meaning exists inherently in the language itself, but when interlingual translation is in focus, as expected, semantic difficulties exponentially increase.

Our capacity in the process of linguistic hospitality offers us the means to appreciate semantic and expressive discrepancies, and invites us to make an effort to experience different viewpoints. Consequently, semantic difficulties in translation and its interpretation can lead to a new production of meaning, the process where we may appreciate the innovative wonders of language. In Ricoeur's words:

> Now, for want of a full description, we only have points of view, perspectives, partial visions of the world. That is why we have never ceased making ourselves clear, making ourselves clear with words and sentences, making ourselves clear to others who do not see things from the same angle as we do.
> RICOEUR 2006: 27

Approaching from an ideological perspective, Lefevere (1992, 2004 [1984]) characterizes translation as a kind of rewriting behavior influenced by social and political ideologies of the day. Lefevere (1992) cites Ann Frank's diary as an example. Popularized in many languages, the translated diary was not actually a translation, but was willfully rewritten according to the translator's ideology. Lefevere warns us that translation is not neutral; rather, it is a product that accommodates the translator's social and cultural values. Lefevere (1992) also reminds us that literary text is not a reproduction of reality, but is a creation of a world filled with images. The translator first understands the other in the context of the original work, and then creates the other's image in another context of the target society. Lefevere uses the term "refraction" to refer to the inevitable integration of ideologies, poetics, and cultural preferences involved in translation. Because one cannot escape from refraction in the rewriting process, we have access only to the refracted image of the other. Lefevere (2004 [1984]) insists that we must simultaneously take into consideration the system which allows for and protects translation products, and the system which opposes and inspects that very translation process. Lefevere's position has influenced critical translation studies as well as postcolonial research, for example, Venuti (1998).

Translation, in concrete terms, is influenced by economic and marketing factors, e.g., selecting specific works and seeking publishers. One must not forget that the translator makes a decision as to which parts to translate or to ignore, what words to be chosen or avoided, as well as how closely or broadly the text is translated. Although these are personal decisions, they are clearly influenced by political and social ideologies. In this sense, translation does not exist in a vacuum.

The views introduced above all share the difficulties and complexities involved in translating. The degree of difficulty is expected to be higher when translation is conducted across languages belonging to different language families. We must recognize that the translation texts selected as data for this work come with these and other difficulties. Nonetheless, semantic and expressive gaps observed across multiple translation texts provide a ground for approaching the theme of exploring the self and for drawing reasonable conclusions.

1.4 *Influence of Translation on Japanese Grammar, Style, and Genre*

Japanese rhetorical studies have traditionally been associated with poetics and Buddhist texts (Tomasi 2004). Since the beginning of the Meiji period (1868–1912) however, the works in Western languages, German, French, and English, in particular, have been extensively translated into Japanese, and they have exerted varying degrees of influence (Yagishita 2015). In the 1880s, Western influence advanced a movement called "spoken and written language unification." This movement advocated a new literary style which prioritized spoken language over traditional written style.

This new literary style developed under Western influence mobilized intellectuals to express some concern (Maruyama and Kato 1998). For example, in his writing on Western and Japanese rhetoric, Tanizaki (2010 [1934]) laments that fundamental differences between Japanese and Indo-European languages have been slighted or even outright ignored. He suggests that Japanese writers should stop incorporating Western elements, and instead, should concern themselves with resolving the grave chaos that careless and forced translations have brought to the Japanese language. Despite such warning, translation of Western scholarship into Japanese continued on well into the 1950s. Not until the 1970s did Japanese translation change in quality; translators began to prioritize Japanese over source languages, making an effort to use Japanese phrases and expressions felt to be more natural to Japanese readers (Furuno 2002).

Faced with the difficulties of translating Western languages into Japanese, scholars and translators have held opposing views. The debate between Nogami (1921) and Yanabu (2004, 2010) represents such a case. Nogami, believing that equivalence can be achieved, insists that the ideal translation is a word-to-word glossing containing about the same number of words. In fact, he states that the content of the translation must be identical, and that the quantity must be the same. This position, according to Naganuma (2013) was originally maintained by Postgate (1922), but Postgate did not have Japanese translation in mind. In reality Nogami's notion of the ideal translation is something impossible to be realized.

Yanabu (2004, 2010) opposes Nogami's view insisting that achieving equivalence is difficult, if not impossible, between Japanese and Western languages. And as an example, Yanabu (2010) introduces the case of the topic marker *wa*. Article One of the *Constitution of the Empire of Japan* appears as "The Empire of Japan shall be reigned over and governed by a line of Emperors unbroken for ages eternal" (Yanabu 2010: 23). Article One in Japanese contains a critical example of *wa* which marks the phrase *Dainippon Teikoku* 'the Empire of Japan'. The topic marker *wa* used here differs from traditional use in that it marks a piece of new information. Given that in traditional grammar, the use of *wa* is restricted to given information, attaching *wa* to *Dainippon Teikoku* 'the Empire of Japan' forces Japanese nationals to accept it as an item of given information. Yanabu notes that the constitution was based on that of the German Empire, particularly of Prussia, and the German grammatical subject was translated into Japanese with the topic marker *wa*, which has resulted in a loosening of the existing internal restriction.

As expected, the influence of translation is not limited to sentence structure. Inoue (2012) discusses the Japanese translation of Hemingway's work which has promoted a new literary style. *Buki yo Saraba*, Oda's (1930) translation of *A Farewell to Arms*, was more of a rewritten version, and not a straight translation. According to Inoue, Oda was particularly interested in Hemingway's use of the subject *he* along with a past-tense predicate; for example, *he left* was translated into *kare wa satta*, using *kare* 'he' and *satta* 'left'. The simple sentence-final verb *ta*-form corresponding to *kare wa* created a rather straightforward statement, which gave it a less sentimental and more realistic tone. Oda's translation of Hemingway has attracted some Japanese novelists and has resulted in the adaptation of this translation style in their writings, which has brought a dry and crisp effect to the Japanese writing style (Inoue 2012).

As reviewed above, the modern Japanese language has been significantly influenced by Western languages. Thus, when contrasting Japanese and English languages, it is important to remind ourselves that similarities are expected. Although contrastive studies emphasize differences, they are not polar opposites, rather, they reveal both similar and different features which themselves undergo continuing change.

Translation studies in Japan have resulted in a number of observations on the Japanese language (Kataoka 2012; Kataoka and Konosu 2014; Ogi 2017). For example, on the priority of subjectivity, Hirako (1999) comments that the Japanese language is weak in constructing objective and rational propositions. It tends to incorporate feelings and evaluation even when one should remain objective. In another study incorporating the translation phenomena, Inoue (2005) reports a number of features. For example, Japanese language uses a frequent ellipsis of the grammatical subject as well as a flexible tense system, but does not use relative pronouns. In addition, he notes that the speaker's sociolinguistic information is expressed through personal expressions and interactional particles. Incorporating these features pointed out in translation studies, this work elaborates on these and other features associated with the concept of empty but populated self as evidenced in Japanese and translation texts.

Given our theme of exploring the self, how a translation process involving the Japanese language imposes on a translator's ontology is a curious question. Sakai (1997) discusses the precarious status of the translator. A translator is internally split as he or she functions as an addressee and an addresser at the same time; the translator is an addressee of the original text and an addresser toward the reader of the translated text. This self devoid of a stable position is what Sakai (1997) calls "a subject in transit." The translator does not individually and singularly perform translation; the translation always incorporates someone else's multiple voices, and dialogically engages the assumed reader. Regarding this concept of the self, Sakai (1997) states the following.

> In a sense, this internal split within the translator is homologous to what is referred to as the fractured I, the temporarity of "I speak," which necessarily introduces an irreparable distance between the speaking I and the I that is signified between the subject of the enunciation and the subject of the enunciated.
>
> SAKAI 1997: 13

I must add here that the multiple aspects of the self recognized in a translator are not limited to those engaged in translation. The self emerges as being split, mixed, and in transit in Japanese literary genres as explored in this work.

1.5 Stereotyped Variations in Japanese Translated Texts

Another case where translation has influenced the Japanese language is in the use of stereotyped variations. In translated works, stereotyped and often exaggerated styles play significant roles in defining participants and dramatic persons. Nakamura (2013), focusing on variations such as gendered speech and dialect, points out that, unlike the everyday Japanese language, translated Japanese texts contain variations no longer in use as well as some newly created expressions. Nakamura specifically reports that certain women's language appears in translated works, although such a variety is rarely used in contemporary Japan. She finds this phenomenon in translated works spanning over 50 years, in *Gone with the Wind* published in 1957, *Harry Potter and the Sorcerer's Stone* published in 1999, and a new translation of *The Brothers Karamazov* published in 2006.

Nakamura (2013) also notes that foreigners' speech is usually translated into a stereotyped and exaggerated style. As an example, she cites an American female jazz singer's utterance translated into stereotypical women's speech featuring *kashira* 'I wonder'. *Kashira* is rarely used today by young female speakers, but it adds the stereotyped femininity the translator intends to convey. The stereotyping is not limited to women's speech as shown in (1) taken from Nakamura (2013). Although a young Japanese male is unlikely to speak in an overly casual and airheaded style, (1) is presented as such a variety used by a high school boy in Beverly Hills. In addition to the overly friendly way of introducing himself, the final particle *sa* adds almost excessive casualness to the overall tone.

(1) Nakamura (2013: 26)
Ore no namae wa Diran Makkei, koi to dansu to rokku ni muchuuna goku heikinteki na tiin eijaa sa.
[My name, Dillan McKay. An average teenager crazy about love, dance, and rock 'n' roll, (you see).]

Translators attempt to recreate the nuanced tone of the Japanese original, but in trying to match the overall atmosphere, they seem to resort to stereotyping. In turn, their exaggerated speech creates a stereotype of the translated text.[3] In this round-about way, the translation process continues to impact contemporary Japanese language culture.

---

[3] This tendency can be identified as a case of translation universal (Baker 1993) discussed later in section 2.2.

1.6   *Mistranslation and Missing Translation*

When conducting contrastive pragmatics of translation texts, one finds obvious cases of mistranslation and missing translation. These discrepancies are likely to be caused as a result of misunderstanding, carelessness, or disregard on the part of the translator, and do not necessarily reveal inherent differences across contrasted languages. One has the impression that some mistranslations and missing translations were produced on a whim. Although these cases do not represent systematic gaps, mistranslation and missing translation represent significant issues in the translation outcome. A few examples should suffice to illustrate what is at stake.

In *Ginga Tetsudoo no Yoru*, in (2a), the expression *dooka* is translated in two ways. The correct interpretation is the sense of pleading as shown by the phrase *please* in (2b) and (2c). However, in two other translations in (2d) and (2e), the translators choose expressions of conjecture. *Dooka* can be read in both ways; when *dooka* is read as *doo ka* with the question marker *ka*, it is interpreted as conjecture. However, given the context of the original work where the mother is asked if Jobanni should close the window for her, an interpretation of conjecture does not make sense. Also note that the mother adds *Moo suzushii kara ne* 'Because it's already getting cool, isn't it?' justifying her reason for asking Jobanni to close the window. *Well let me see* in (2d) and *I guess so* in (2e) must be treated as mistakes.

(2)   a. *Ginga Tetsudoo no Yoru*, 62
"Okkasan, mado o shimete okoo ka."
"Aa, **dooka. Moo suzushii kara ne.**"
[Mom, shall I close the window (for you)?]
[Yes, please. Because it's already getting cool, isn't it?]
b. *Night Train to the Stars*, 31
"Mom, shall I shut the window now?"
"Yes, **please**, it's getting quite chilly."
c. *Night on the Galactic Railroad & Other Stories from Ihatov*, 53
"Shall I close the window for you now?"
"**Please** do. It's gotten a bit chilly."
d. *Eigo de Yomu Ginga Tetsudoo no Yoru*, 39
'Should I close the window for you, Mom?'
'**Well, let me see** … it's already getting cool now, I suppose.'
e. *Milky Way Railroad*, 28
"Shall I close the window, Mom?"
"**I guess so**. It is getting cool."

Likewise, *te o ookiku futte* in (3a) is mistranslated. In this situation, where Jobanni walked out through the school gate, the action meant by *te o ookiku futte* refers to the swinging of his arms. Although one engages in the action of *te o ookiku furu* as a sign of waving good-bye, the setting of the scene created by (3a) does not support this waving interpretation. Jobanni, smarting from a sense of isolation, perhaps accompanied with mixed feelings of jealousy and hostility, shows a renewed sense of pride as he struts forward swinging his arms. This interpretation is reinforced by sentences immediately preceding (3a), which describe several boys gathering around Kamupanerura. They form a group by the cherry tree in the corner of the school playground, and are talking about going to a festival that night. Thus, the translations *gave a vigorous wave* in (3b), *gave them a wave* in (3c), and *waving his arms high in the air* in (3d) all fail to make sense. The translation *with a broad wave of his hand* in (3e) is also inadequate. Rather than *wave*, *swing* is more appropriate.

(3) a. *Ginga Tetsudoo no Yoru*, 57
Keredomo Jobanni wa **te o ookiku futte** doshi doshi gakkoo no mon o dete ikimashita.
[But Jobanni swung his arms broadly, and determinedly stomping his feet, he went away passing through the school gate.]
b. *Night Train to the Stars*, 23
Giovanni, though, **gave a vigorous wave** and marched straight on out of the gate.
c. *Night on the Galactic Railroad & Other Stories from Ihatov*, 48
Not stopping to join in, Giovanni just **gave them a wave** before rushing off into town.
d. *Eigo de Yomu Ginga Tetsudoo no Yoru*, 23
Giovanni hurried out the gate **waving his arms high in the air**.
e. *Milky Way Railroad*, 19–20
But Kenji, **with a broad wave of his hand**, hurried by and went on out the school gate.

The issue raised above is substantiated when another case of *ookiku te o futte* appears (*Ginga Tetsudoo no Yoru*, 65). The verb *swing* is selected in translations, e.g., *He strode on through town, swinging his arms* (*Milky Way Railroad*, 32).

Missing translation is often associated with information the translator perhaps finds unnecessary. Among works examined, *A Midsummer's Equation* contains a relatively high frequency of missing translation. Given that this is a mystery novel, elaborate information unrelated to the plot development may be thought unnecessary. Missing translations occur especially (1) in monologues,

(2) with idiomatic and metaphoric expressions, (3) in association with detailed information related to dramatic persons or locations, and (4) when the narrator directly addresses the reader.

For example, Kyoohei's monologue *Sasuga wa inaka da* 'After all, this place is a real countryside' (*Manatsu no Hooteishiki*, 81) is not translated at all. Also when the information given in the original text deviates from the storyline, detailed information tends to be omitted. For example, two sentences in the original (*Manatsu no Hooteishiki*, 201) that can be translated as 'Many companies handle the employee list as top secret. They claim that releasing the list would violate their privacy policy and they do not easily share that information' are completely ignored.

Cases of missing translation are observed in other works as well, although it seems to occur more frequently with mysteries. Although investigating why mistranslation and missing translation occur in certain genres or specific works is an intriguing question, it is beyond the scope of this study.

In this section, the complexity of translation has been the focus. The difficulty of selecting translation for data comes with the territory. On the other hand, the use of translation is critical for this work which aims to understand the self reflected in the gaps between source and target languages. Translation gaps, more accurately what is untranslatable, cannot be recognized prior to the translation. Translation can reveal what otherwise would remain hidden. Going beyond the limitations of monolingual analysis, translation text is required for the contrastive philosophical pragmatics.

2   Contrastive Pragmatics and Translation

This section reviews studies that incorporate pragmatics and translation texts. Initially focused are approaches from contrastive pragmatics, discourse analysis, and cross-cultural applied linguistics, followed by discourse analyses of Japanese translation. Also translation universals are introduced. Then concentrating on the methodology, corpus-based translation studies are reviewed, suggesting some difficulties of conducting contrastive analyses involving the Japanese language. Finally reviewed is a study of translation text approached from literary studies, specifically a case between an English text and its Italian translation. Reviewing these approaches and issues is useful not only for analyzing and interpreting the data selected for this work but also for understanding the translation phenomenon in a broader context.

2.1 Contrasting Translation Texts

Kranich (2016), examining popular scientific articles and business letters, approaches English and German translation discourse from the perspective of pragmatics. Following works of House (2006, 2009, 2010, 2014), especially her concepts of covert and overt translation, Kranich qualitatively and quantitatively analyzes two linguistic domains, i.e., the expression of evaluation and epistemic modality. Particularly focused on are the preferences in communication style between English and German such as directness versus indirectness, orientation toward persons versus content, implicitness versus explicitness, and verbal routines versus ad-hoc formulation. Her corpus-based analyses and interpretive considerations uncover similarities and differences in the use of evaluative adjectives and epistemic modal markers in English-German translations. Kranich emphasizes that although in the past, English-German contrasts were based on personal experience, cultural stereotypes or limited data, her results are obtained through valid qualitative and quantitative methods.

In a volume edited by Munday and Zhang (2017), textual and discourse analytic approaches in translation studies are presented. The particular approach they take is Halliday's (1985) systemic functional linguistics, and the volume covers phenomena and topics familiar in this framework such as cohesion, thematic and information structure, and modality. Data analyzed in chapters of this volume vary; some are corpus-based on large corpora while others are based on qualitative analyses conducted on retrieved examples.

Works focusing on contrastive pragmatics from the perspective of second language acquisition are available in Pütz and Aertselaer (2008). Chapters in this volume mostly fall in applied linguistics, concerning topics such as identity in the foreign language classroom, development of competence in request making, and learning cultural norms associated with discourse markers. For example, Kurteš (2008), examining morphological segments of verbal reflexivity and middleness in Serbo-Croati as discourse markers, emphasizes the importance of interpreting messages on the basis of their underlying cultural norms and values. Research in contrastive pragmatics from an applied linguistics perspective points to the significance of deep-rooted cultural differences and acquisition difficulties.

As an example of contrastive discourse analysis using Japanese and English texts, my earlier study is introduced here. In Maynard (1996a), I have analyzed Japanese nominalization (both as a nominal clause and as a nominal predicate) and English nominalization from a contrastive perspective. Data are taken from two modern novels, one Japanese and the other American, *Tanin no Kao* by Abe (1968) and *Dangling Man* by Bellow (1988). The data also include the English translation *The face of Another* by Saunders (1966) and the

Japanese translation *Chuuburarin no Otoko* by Ota (1971). For statistical purposes, the initial five hundred sentences appearing in original Japanese and English novels are examined. Expressions investigated include the nominalizers *n(o)*, *koto*, and *mono*, as well as clauses marked by *that*, *if*, *to* and the verb gerund forms.

In *Tannin no Kao*, the nominal predicate occurs in 163 of 500 sentences (32.60%), In *Face of Another*, out of 566 sentences corresponding to the original, the nominal predicate occurs only 20 times (3.53%), (χ^2=157.73, p < .01). The nominal predicate in *Dangling Man* is observed only at 13 locations out of 500 (2.60%). In *Chuuburarin no Otoko*, out of 562 corresponding sentences, the nominal predicate appears at 85 locations (15.12%), (χ^2=49.55, p < .01). Distributional preferences illustrate that the expressive effect that the Japanese nominalization brings to discourse is not fully reflected in English translation. The high frequency of nominalization in Japanese is a part of what I have termed "rhetoric of commentation" (Maynard 1996a). The observed difference attests to the diverse ways in which languages are endowed to employ different subjectivity devices that express different attitudinal messages to varying calibrations of importance and intensity. Consequently, different aspects of the narrating self are foregrounded.[4]

A few points regarding contrastive study of Japanese translation text should be noted. Translation texts used for Japanese linguistic and literary analyses in the past have routinely tended to be limited in number, and only a few paragraphs have been examined. Even in the field of translation studies, actual analysis of a wide range of translation texts has been lacking. Often the phenomena discussed fall into special cases, and do not necessarily represent frequently observed features in original nor in translation texts. Translation studies scholars analyzing Japanese (e.g., Hayakawa 2013) have recommended broad-based interpretative analysis of translation texts, the direction I am taking by examining 28 literary works and translation.

In the process of translation text analysis, one should refrain from making overgeneralizations based on too few cases. For example, in Japanese there is a recognized tendency to avoid transitive verbs with an inanimate subject

---

4   Additional contrastive discourse analyses involving the Japanese language include Maynard (1983) which discusses a grammatical feature in Japanese and English translations of Spanish and Italian literary works and Maynard (1993b) which focuses on features of Japanese and English conversation based on parallel casual conversations collected in Japan and the US. Maynard (1999a) reports analyses of Japanese original and English translation of literary genres, and Maynard (2003) offers an overview of contrastive discourse analysis. Maynard (2019) reports contrastive analysis of literary texts involving multilingual (Japanese, English, and Portuguese) and bidirectional translation texts.

where the action influences the animate object. However, exceptions do exist when one examines a broader data base. Observe (4a) where the transitive verb *hiki modoshita* 'brought back' appears with an inanimate subject, *buzaa no oto* 'the sound of a buzzer'. And this structure is precisely what English translation chooses as shown in (4b).

(4) a. *Manatsu no Hooteishiki*, 87
   (...) hikui **buzaa no oto** ga kanojo no shikoo o genjitsu ni **hiki modoshita**.
   [A low sound of a buzzer brought her thoughts back to the real world.]
   b. *A Midsummer's Equation*, 75
   The sound of a hushed buzzer brought her back to the present.

Features of the Japanese language in contrast with English explored in this work should be considered general tendencies or favored preferences. It is not necessarily the case that a wording or phrase in one language can never be expressed in another; rather, preferences exist as fashions of speaking (Whorf 1956), and those preferences reveal themselves when the language in use is carefully and extensively contrasted.

I should also offer a warning regarding one's attitude toward the translation text. A translated literary product should be viewed as a separate creative work, not as a subtext of the original. Translation requires detailed attention given to the original, and the resultant text must be treated with respect. Let me emphasize that translators face insurmountable difficulties in their tasks. It is not my intention to personally criticize the translation or the translator. Mistakes and other semantic and expressive gaps in translation that I discuss are for the purpose of exploring the concept of self across Japanese and translation texts.

2.2 *Contrastive Pragmatics and Translation Universals*

The question of whether common tendencies or universals may be observed in translations has been raised for some time. Although this work does not address the issue, it remains an intriguing question. Searching for tendencies observed in translation can be traced to Toury (1985) when he proposes the significance of general laws as a fundamental task of his proposed Descriptive Translation Studies. Then Baker (1993), finding electronic corpora to be a useful tool, proposes a series of hypotheses on universal features of translation. Included are tendencies toward simplification and presentation of explicit information as well as overrepresentation of typical features of the target language. More specifically, Mauranen and Kujamäki (2004) position the explicitation hypothesis as the process of making translations more explicit than their source texts, forcing translation texts to exhibit a higher degree of explicitness than non-translated texts.

Kranich (2016) lists the following features of translation universals.
1. Explicitation: an overall tendency to spell things out rather than leave them implicit in translation
2. Simplification: a tendency to simplify the language used in translation
3. Normalization/conservatism: a tendency to exaggerate features of the target language
4. Levelling out: a tendency of translated text to gravitate toward the center of a continuum, i.e., to avoid stylistically marked forms of expression

Concerning translation universals, Chesterman (2004) makes a distinction between s(ource)- and t(arget)-universals, the former focusing on the difference between original and translated texts, the latter focusing on differences between translation and non-translated texts. Another kind of translation universal or tendency is proposed in a study by Tirkkonen-Condit (2004) in which the comparable Corpus of Translated Finnish is used as data. Focusing on Finnish verbs and clitic pragmatic particles typical of Finnish but missing in English, she notes that these devices and meanings are underrepresented in translated Finnish. She suggests that the hypothesis of the relative underrepresentation of target language-specific features can be considered a candidate for a translation universal.[5]

Another approach to translation universals is proposed by Wierzbicka (2005, 2008). Wierzbicka (2008) criticizes the Anglocentric bias in language education, and offers an alternative to the dominant use of English, i.e., her NSM (Natural Semantic Metalanguage) model. Werzbicka (2005) insists that we run the risk of distorting universals by imposing on them the perspective embedded in that particular language. She also warns us that the same applies to our own descriptions of cultural differences. In her view, genuine universals of culture or cognition can only be formulated if we have at our disposal a universal language. In this universal language we are able to formulate generalizations while maintaining culture-independent points of view. Her NSM model is "based on the assumption that the shared core of human thought is reflected in the shared core of all languages and can be identified through empirical linguistic investigations" (2005: 259).

In a section titled *Different Cultural Models of the Person: Anglo, Korean, Japanese, Russian*, Wierzbicka discusses the Japanese word *kokoro* 'heart, mind,

---

5 Many cases of translation gaps observed in this work can be cases of underrepresentation in English translation. Underrepresentation may very well be a case of translation universal.

spirit' in contrast with *karada* 'body' and *hara* 'belly'. She points out that Japanese *kokoro* is seen as something that finds importance in "hiddenness" in the cultural model of a Japanese person. *Kokoro* is not only a part which people can't see, but also a part other people cannot know if this person doesn't want them to know. Although Wierzbicka's formula convincingly distinguishes Japanese *kokoro* from Korean *maum*, the NSM model falls short of answering the question of how other Japanese words associated with the cultural model of a person are characterized; words such as *watashi* 'I', *ore* 'I (blunt, almost always used by male speakers)', or *jibun* 'self' come to mind. How does the NSM formula distinguish among these and other numerous first-person references connected to the cultural models of the Japanese person?

The translation universals controversy persists because universals in translation are inconceivable simply because we have no way of capturing translations from all times and all languages. There is no straightforward answer to the question of whether translation universals exist or not (Mauranen and Kujamäki 2004). Identifying the totality of translation universals including the NSM model is premature and only a more tentative and open view (e.g., tendencies observed in translation) seems reasonable.

2.3 *On Corpus-Based Translation Studies*

Regarding the methodology in contrastive pragmatics involving translation, corpus-based methods are expected to make a significant contribution. The trend adopting corpus-based research in translation studies reflects the field of computer-aided corpus linguistics developed since the 1980s (Facchinetti 2007). The access to large-scale corpora has made it possible to identify not only linguistic features of one language but also phenomena across multilingual and parallel corpora where cross-linguistic contrasts can be processed.

Because the corpus-based method allows comparisons of linguistic features on a large scale, cross-linguistic analyses addressing translation universals have been conducted. In a volume edited by Hansen-Schirra, Neumann and Steiner (2012), (1) explicitation, (2) simplification, (3) normalization, (4) levelling out, (5) sanitization, and (6) shining through are examined. Also, in this edited volume specific linguistic phenomena are examined including grammatical shifts of noun phrases in English and German (Hansen and Hansen-Schirra 2012). Given that this volume's reported studies specifically focus on the language pair of English and German, both being Germanic languages, the applicability of this method to other typologically unrelated languages such as Japanese and English is uncertain. When contrasting typologically different languages, obtaining parallel and translation texts and implementing appropriate corpus designs are expected to pose more difficulties.

For example, Shimizu and Murata (2007), analyzing parallel texts of Japanese and English corpora of newspaper articles and editorials, find difficulties in obtaining conclusive results. Shimizu and Murata focus on the patterns of transitive verb followed by reflexive pronoun and by personal pronoun in English and compare these with counterparts in Japanese, e.g., the use of *jibun* 'self'. After analyzing them syntactically and semantically (mostly digitally and in part manually), they find the word-to-word correspondence is not substantiated. Phrase alignment makes more sense than word alignment, because each word is not independently selected. Instead, the choice patterns of words in a text can and often do create new and complex units in another language. Corpus-based analysis of parallel or translation texts involving Japanese is not as feasible as in the case of the German-English pair. Shimizu and Murata also report problems of compiling English-Japanese parallel corpora, including linguistic differences between the two languages, copyright issues, and quality of translation.

Although the merits of corpus-based analyses in translation studies are recognized, this work exclusively conducts qualitative analysis. In practical terms, selecting comparable linguistic units and structures for building an appropriate corpus design is difficult. This work suffers from limitations in the sense that it is not corpus-based, and it does not conduct analyses of parallel corpora. I must remind the reader that the features noted in this work of contrastive philosophical pragmatics are based only on the comparison of original and translated texts of literary genres. Consequently, those similarities and differences may not reflect general features found in other genres. Nonetheless, I must emphasize that interpretive analyses of source and target texts reveal aspects of language not easily accessed otherwise. Full integration of qualitative and quantitative contrasts in pragmatics must await future studies.

2.4   A View from Literary Stylistics

Parks (2007) takes an interesting approach to translation texts by analyzing Virgina Wolf's *Mrs. Dalloway* in contrast with *La Signora Dalloway*, the publisher Feltrinelli's Italian translation. One of the features Parks focuses on is the English past perfect tense, which appears in Mrs. Dalloway's monologue to create ambiguity. The translation, avoiding the use of the past perfect tense as well as other seemingly ambiguous expressions, tends to directly and clearly present information.[6] In other words, the translator has made a personal deci-

---

6   The tendency for presenting information clearly and directly is recognizable as a case of a translation universal of explication (Mauranen and Kujamäki 2004; Kranich 2016).

sion to eliminate ambiguity on the basis of the judgment in what, in Italian, constitutes clear, necessary, and expected information.

One example should suffice. (5) appears at the beginning of the novel, and it includes English past perfect tense, *she had burst open* and (*had*) *plunged*. These two verbs are translated into Italian past tense, i.e., *spalancava* and *tuffava*.

(5) Parks (2007: 109–110)
Mrs. Dalloway said she would buy the flowers herself.
For Lucy had her work cut out for her. The doors would be taken off their hinges; Rumpelmayer's men were coming. And then, thought Clarissa Dalloway, what a morning—fresh as if issued to children on a beach.
What a lark! What a plunge! For so it had always seemed to her when, with a little squeak of the hinges, which she could hear now, **she had burst open** the French windows and **plunged** at Bouton into the open air.

Parks (2007) provides the back-translation in (6), i.e., the English translation of the Italian translation.[7] The segment (6) reveals that the Italian translation is conducted in the past tense as in *at Bourton she threw open the shutters* and *plunged into the open air*.

(6) Parks (2007: 111)
Mrs. Dalloway said she would buy the flower herself.
As for Lucy she already had her work to do. The doors would have to be taken off their hinges; Rumpelmayer's men would arrive soon. And then, thought Clarissa Dalloway, what a morning—fresh as if it had just been created for children on a beach.
What joy! What terror! She had always had that impression, when with a light squeak of the hinges, the same that she heard right now, **at Bourton she threw open the shutters** and **plunged into the open air.**

Parks raises another relevant concern regarding exclamatory expressions in (6). The original English expressions *What a lark! What a plunge!* are translated into *Che gioia! Che terrore!*, which are then back-translated into *What joy! What terror!* Terms selected for Italian translation are descriptive expressions of emotion, thus losing the creatively indirect effect intended in the orig-

---

7 The back-translation is a useful tool for translation analysis. I have also used this analytical strategy in my earlier study (Maynard 1999a), and I use this method where appropriate in this work as well.

inal.[8] The metaphoric effect is lost, resulting in rather flat and less intriguing text.[9] Translators tend to prioritize clarity and seem to prefer straightforward expressions, a case of explicitation translation universal (Mauranen and Kujamäki 2004; Kranich 2016). This desire for clarification, however, Parks (2007) points out, destroys the original work's intended effect. Here the stylistic preference in one language must be weighed against the recognized taste in another language.

In this chapter, I have reviewed critical concepts in translation studies, such as equivalence, difficulties in translation, and missing translation. Regarding contrastive pragmatics involving translation, varied issues and approaches were discussed including translation universals, corpus-based analyses, and literary studies. Although this work does not directly address theoretical and methodological issues in translation studies, the discussion above is hoped to add to the understanding of how the translation phenomenon and contrastive pragmatics can be meaningfully synthesized.

8 Incidentally, the Japanese translation for *What a lark! What a plunge!* in *Darowei Fujin* also employs descriptive terms, i.e., *Maa yukai! Ie kara soto e tobi dashite toki no ano kimochi* 'What fun! That feeling of plunging out from the house' (Kondo 1999: 3). The translator's preference for clarity presents translation universals of explicitation and simplification (Mauranen and Kujamäki 2004; Kranich 2016).

9 This phenomenon can be interpreted as normalization and simplification translation universals (Kranich 2016).

PART 2
Background

CHAPTER 5

Empty Self and Empty Place in Japanese Studies

*The flowing river
never stops
and yet the water
never stays
the same.*

*Foam floats
upon the pools,
    scattering, re-forming,
never lingering long.*

*So it is with man
and all his dwelling places
here on earth.*
            from *Hojoki: Visions of a Torn World* (MORIGUCHI and JENKINS 1996: 31)

∴

In what follows, I review the concept of empty self and empty place in Japanese philosophy and related studies. Starting with Buddhism, I discuss its influence on Nishida's philosophy as well as Miyazawa's poetics. This chapter provides the foundation for proposing an empty self and its transition to a self populated with multiple aspects, characters, and characteristics. It also provides the theoretical background supporting those phenomena explored in Chapter 6 as well as subsequent analysis chapters. Obviously, it is impossible to fully discuss this rich history; I have chosen limited works prioritizing those studies echoing themes of Western approaches discussed especially in Chapters 1 and 2. Although the Japanese approaches are focused, their interrelations with Western scholarship are noted.

1 Centrality of Emptiness in Japanese Thought

1.1 *The Buddhist Theory of No-Self*

As touched upon in Chapter 2, Hume (1963) rejects the self defined in terms of personal identity. According to Hume, what we experience is a continuous flow of perceptions that replace one another in rapid succession. This non- and anti-Cartesian view, what may be labeled the "no-self" theory, resonates with the Buddhist tradition in India, and particularly the zen Buddhism developed in China and Japan. Mahayana Buddhism, a sect developed later in Buddhism, experienced a breakthrough in the 2nd and 3rd centuries, which eventually came to be known as zen Buddhism. Zen Buddhism emerged in China in the 5th and 6th centuries, but it was in Japan between the 11th and 13th centuries that it fully blossomed, eventually contributing to the foundation of Japanese religious and cultural traditions.

The Buddhist approach to the self is poetically expressed by Kamo no Chomei, a poet, essayist, and Buddhist monk of the Kamakura period. Kamo no Chomei begins *Hojoki*, written in 1212 A.D., with the poetic writing presented at the beginning of this chapter. His depiction of the flowing river current captures the concept of impermanence, the transitory nature of the self and of the world itself. Considered a Japanese literary classic, *Hojoki* remains a seminal part of the Japanese school curriculum, customarily recited and appreciated by the majority of Japanese people. The transitory nature of the self is integral to Japanese culture and aesthetics.

The concept of no-self appears in Buddhism texts, the Pali Canon (circa 500 B.C.) in which a distinction is made between two types of discourse, that of direct meaning and that of indirect non-denoting meaning. In the former the meaning is clear, while in the latter, the meaning requires some interpretation. For example, although we use words like *I* and *self*, because they represent indirect meanings, we should not be led into thinking that they actually refer to something; these are nothing but words. The non-denoting quality of these expressions is critical for understanding the self in Buddhism, where the self does not exist on its own.

In more concrete terms, what or who is I or self in Buddhism? Personhood in Buddhist theory comprises an aggregation of five elements, i.e., (1) physical form, (2) perceptions, (3) feelings, (4) motives, and (5) consciousness. But none of these elements considered separately or in combination can rightfully be identified with the self. In other words, a person is not a portion of his or her parts, nor is a person ultimately the total sum of his or her parts. Everything we believe exists does not actually exist, including the self. Thus, self is nothing; it is empty. The view that self is something identifiable as a uniquely definable substance is simply not evident in Buddhist thought.

Although the concept of no-self is not completely foreign to Western thought (cf. Hume 1963, Derrida 1978), it is only in the East-Asian tradition that nothingness has been extended to the conceptualization of an empty space. This emptiness, however, cannot be viewed as something missing or lacking; it is simply empty and therefore unrestricted and free. Precisely because it is not predefined or predetermined, the emptiness facilitates possibilities. Incidentally, Chinese and Japanese Kanji script for emptiness, read in Japanese as *kuu*, is identical to the symbol for sky. This suggests that the experience of emptiness is synonymous with the openness of the sky. Indeed, emptiness refers not to a void, but to an infinite source of inspiration, creation, and life. In this way, emptiness or *kuu*, based on the concept conceived in ancient Indian Buddhism, evolved into a sense of boundlessness, freedom, and ultimately a place where the self, as it is, materializes. We discover the self in its infinite possibilities.

In search of the empty self, zen Buddhism maintains that our body has to be the first as well as the final gateway. Thus, the method for understanding the no-self theory is to engage in sitting meditation. Sitting meditation is a practice that may be described as internal contemplation or inward gazing. Through this practice the internal self comes to be seen for what it is, as a mere flow of transient elements. Through contemplation in this empty space, one abandons the thought that the self exists. The self's permanence disappears. Sitting meditation serves as the ultimate vehicle for experiencing a state of no-self, reaching for enlightenment, and achieving peace of mind.

Zen does not recommend intense study of the Buddhist text. Unlike the Christian Bible or the Islamic Koran, zen has not chosen a text-centric scripture, and instead prioritizes sitting meditation. Through this technique, the self realizes there is no self to be found. Held (1997) captures this sense of emptiness in the following way.

> A space, which leaves place for everything, is empty. The happening of appearing, the laying itself open of the world, is the disclosure of that emptiness which originally yields space for everything.
>
> HELD 1997: 157

Regarding the no-self view, Held (1997) cites a well-known linguistic example. In Western languages, one expresses coldness as *It is cold*. Here only the expression with the so-called impersonal pronoun evokes the respective quality of the happening. In Japanese, the comparable expression, *samui* 'cold' is fulfilled solely by the appearance of the happening, thus resulting in no mention of *it*.[1]

---

1 The linguistic explanation given by Held here has been made in a number of Japanese

Held cites another example where a dancing event is linguistically described. In the West, it is the dancer who is the bearer of the sentence structure, but in Japanese, the fundamental element is the dancing itself. The dancer's appearance is built into the event, but the dancer is not the primary element of the perceived event.

In the context of the self's emptiness and the no-self theory in Japanese culture, one of the popular activities in Japanese religious tradition is the chanting of Heart Sutra. In this brief text, the interrelation of all things is characterized as their coloring or visibility. And the most meaningful line in the Heart Sutra explicitly identifies this coloring as being the same as emptiness or nothingness.

1.2   *Emptiness, Place, and the Dynamic Flow*

Having discussed the concept of emptiness from the Buddhist perspective, we now turn to the tradition of Japanese thought. For decades, Japanese scholars, many under the influence of the religious and cultural milieu, have commented on the Japanese sense of empty place where centralized elements are absent. Perhaps most prominent in this tradition is Nishida (1949) who is known for his concept of "place of nothingness." Nishida's work is discussed in consequent sections; here I touch upon other studies related to the Japanese view toward the empty self and the empty place.

Hiromatsu (1982) proposes that philosophy should be approached on the basis of an event-centered world view, and not the dominant philosophical approach which focuses on things and objects. Hiromatsu, insisting on relation-based ontology, reminds us that the existence of elements simply reveals the presence of their connecting points within events. In proposing his event-centered philosophy, Hiromatsu contrasts two types of philosophy, philosophy of objects versus the philosophy of nothingness, with the former associated with Western, and the latter, with Eastern approaches. He calls for acceptance of a new paradigm of philosophy similar to the Eastern philosophy of nothingness, and advocates a kind of philosophy that prioritizes intersubjective and collaborative relationships.

Machida (2003), reviewing Nishida's (1949) philosophical thought on the place of absolute nothingness, connects Western ways of thinking to monotheism, and Japanese ways of thinking to pantheism. Advocating Nishida's predicate-based self, Machida notes that the Japanese way of identifying the self

---

language studies including but not limited to Ikegami (1981), Nakajima (1987), Maynard (1990a), and Morita (1995, 1998).

allows for multiple interpretation. This open approach gives guidance and may possibly offer a solution to Western societies' social and political complications. Machida hopes for an ideal world where individuals who emerge in the place of nothingness coexist with others, while at the same time maintaining their own integrities.

Maeno (2015), claiming nothingness and emptiness characterize the core of Japanese culture, argues that Japanese people readily embrace foreign ideas making them a part of their own, i.e., Japanize them. Referring to Kawai's (1982) emptiness-at-the-center structure of Japanese culture, Maeno argues that Japanese culture is not founded on a set of principles or patterns. In addition, referring to Uchida's (2009) position that Japan tends to position itself not in the center but at the periphery, Maeno insists no grounding or prototype is evident at the center of Japanese culture. A Japanese person living in this emptiness-centered culture lacks a strong sense of self. Still, Maeno reminds us that Western analytical sciences have created more than a few problems in the world today, and that one solution may very well lie, not in an individual-centered society, but in a nothingness- or emptiness-centered society.[2]

An interesting approach from the perspective of biology is taken by Fukuoka (2009, 2011) who clearly opposes the concept of the autonomous and stable self. He asks the question "what is life?" and answers that life is a dynamic flow. In his view, a self is not a solid identifiable entity; it is a balanced state of continual change. Fukuoka applies the biochemist Rudolf Schoenheimer's theory of dynamic state to broader concepts of life and self, introducing what he calls the "dynamic equilibrium." Dynamic equilibrium refers to the idea that life is sustained in a state of flux, and does not present itself as a unified independent unit. Biologically, all components of the body are continuously degraded, synthesized, and replaced by components of nutrients we take in as food. But nutrients are not just fuel as commonly understood; they operate to replace cells to sustain life itself. This process of degradation followed by synthesis and replacement manipulates itself in a right state of equilibrium, and this balanced state is precisely what life is.

In Fukuoka's view, unlike an independent and identifiable entity, the self provides a space in constant state of renewal (Ikeda and Fukuoka 2014). Our body is regenerated from one moment to the next; today's self differs from tomorrow's self. The evidence for this position is found in Schoenheimer's scientific experiments where what a mouse intakes as food and what a mouse

---

2 Admittedly, works by Hiromatsu (1982), Machida (2003), and Maeno (2015) tend to overemphasize the differences between Japanese and Western cultures. Still, their views merit mention.

expels as waste do not match. This is because the nutrients are used for regenerating cells, organs, and the entire body. In other words, the embodied self does not exist as a solid and unchanging entity but it consists of a continual flow of eliminating and rebuilding processes. Fukuoka concludes that life is no other than a dynamic equilibrium, and consequently our self is nothing but the space that is flowingly reforming our transient states of being.

2   Nishida's Philosophy: Empty Self in the Place of Nothingness

In my exploration into the concept of the empty self in the empty place, most influential has been Nishida's philosophy as I have discussed in Maynard (2000, 2002). It is not my intention to review his extensive philosophical thought here. In what follows I discuss some of the key concepts, including pure experience, place, place of nothingness, and the logic of the absolutely contradictory self-identity. These concepts offer insight to the foundation of philosophical contrastive pragmatics and to the exploration of Japanese and translation texts in contrast.

2.1   *Pure Experience and the Place of Nothingness*

Kitaro Nishida (1870–1945) is known as one of the few scholars who founded a philosophy based on the tradition of Japanese ways of thinking. Before developing his own philosophy known as the Nishida philosophy upon which the Kyoto school of philosophy was founded, he extensively studied Western philosophies. In fact identifying Nishida's thought purely as an Eastern philosophy is misleading (Wargo 2005; Kozyra 2018). Nishida is known to have been influenced by Aristotle, Kant, and Hume, among others.

Although he was influenced by a wide range of Western philosophies, it is also true that Nishida's thought gradually turned to Japan, to Japan's religious traditions, zen Buddhism, in particular. Saeki (2014), for example, points out that the significance of Nishida's philosophy lies in his exploration of Japan-based scholarship although he was placed amidst a sea of Western intellectual influence then rampant in Japanese academia. Nishida's intention was not necessarily to oppose Western views, but he encountered in Japanese thought a way to overcome the contradictions he was forced to reckon with in Western philosophical approaches.

Nishida faces the contradiction when the objectified self of *cogito* is obtained through an abstract introspection, presumably performed by an already assumed self. This self fundamentally differs from the embodied self who experiences life, and therefore, in Nishida's view, it never exists as a person. The

Cartesian ego engages in introspection, and yet this ego is not embodied. It is unlived, and therefore cannot, in the first place, engage in self-introspection. Still, Western logic in general endorses the self as being universal, and based on this assumption it analyzes and understands life as an object in its own right. This approach does not satisfy Nishida who views the self as a part of the world, and at the same time, views the world as an internal part of the self.

In Nishida's philosophy (Nishida 1949; Dilworth 1987), the *a priori* rational and unitary self is simply not presumed. Nishida initiates his philosophical exploration by focusing on the experience of living itself, what he calls "pure experience." As Yusa (2002) notes, pure experience is an experience of the present goings-on, and it is pure in that "it has yet to split into subject and object, or into cognition, sensation, and volition" (2002: 97). This experience is the kind we undergo when we are entirely absorbed in artistic, athletic, or spiritual training. Here the self and the world are in a state of undividedness. In Nishida's view, concepts usually assumed to be distinct, such as subject and object, spirit and concrete material, or, self and natural world, are absent; these dichotomous notions are reached only after a reflective cognitive process. In pure experience, the certainty is found in the lived moment itself. Thus the priority of the self versus experience is reversed. It is not that the self exists first and experience follows; rather, pure experience exists first, and the self emerges through it. Nishida's principle denies an *a priori* self detached from experience.

What is particularly important in Nishida's thesis of pure experience is that it requires a place, a concept he focuses on in his later writings. Nishidas's concept of place was formed, in part, as an answer to the problem of knowing, and specifically as an answer to how one philosophically understands consciousness. Thus, Nishida posits the place as a field of consciousness and awareness, and declares it as the initial point of his philosophy as expressed below.[3]

> While epistemology, starting from the idea of the subject-object opposition, has previously conceived of knowing as the composition of matter by form, I would instead like to start from the idea of self-awareness wherein the self mirrors itself within.
> KRUMMEL and NAGATOMO 2012: 54

Nishida's approach to nothingness not only eliminates the presupposition of consciousness as being a substance, it also attempts to take it to another, deeper

---

[3] The quotation from Nishida (1949) is based on a translation provided by Krummel and Nagatomo (2012).

level. Since consciousness is no longer anchored to any form of subject or object, Nishida (1949) regards consciousness as an active place (*basho*) that embraces all beings, and develops his "theory of place." This locus is fundamentally the place for self-reflection, i.e., where the self is reflected in its self. Nishida explains that a philosophical inquiry should start not from the often assumed subjectivity-and-objectivity dualism. Instead, it should start from a self-awareness which can only be realized by reflecting on oneself in oneself. For self to be conscious of something is to see oneself cast upon the self's own field of consciousness. He likens this place where the self reflects on one's self to the experience of observing one's self in a mirror. In this self-reflective mirror, the self experiences a full range of knowledge, emotion, and will. But the mirror itself must be empty; it must be a total nothingness. Nishida (1949) explains:

> That which ought to be called in this sense the mirror that illuminates itself, not only serves as the *basho* of the establishment of knowledge but also establishes emotion and volition. When we speak of the content of lived experience in most cases we are already considering this in cognitive terms. This is why we think of it as alogical matter. True lived experience entails the standpoint of complete nothingness, a free standpoint separate from knowledge. Even the content of emotion-and-volition (…) would have to be mirrored in this *basho*. It is due to this that intellect, emotion, and volition are all considered to be phenomena of consciousness.
>
> KRUMMEL and NAGATOMO 2012: 53, original emphasis

Place, a field of consciousness that enables pure experience, is the precise locus of immediacy where one experiences and where one's existence comes into being. But the place itself is not restricted by anything, nor is it an existence on its own. Nishida, calling this place the "place of nothingness," identifies it as being free from restrictions, and therefore, we experience multiple aspects of the self as we transform them. This place is ground zero for the self.

As Yusa (2002) puts it, "Nishida's fundamental intuition is that things (beings) exist always in some 'place', for otherwise, the distinction between 'being' and 'nonbeing' cannot be sustained" (2002: 203). And yet, the place is not a thing. It is a "precondition for knowing and cognition" (Itabashi 2018: 104). Within the space of this place, those things occupying the space do not deny the space; they simply exist in, and are supported by the space. When we think of someone or something in action, to acknowledge the action, there must be a place where it is located. Place exists as a condition for enabling the self's existence and action.

Nishida identifies nothingness in two places, relative and absolute. The relative place of nothingness is a field of consciousness behind the existing world, and this is where one's consciousness comes into being in a self-reflecting process. The absolute place of nothingness is deeper, beyond the field of consciousness. What is found there is an absolutely free will. Nishida's concept of absolute nothingness is based on his "logic of absolutely contradictory self-identity." The logic of absolutely contradictory self-identity refers to an understanding based on the denial of each other in a relationship, i.e., of the other and of the self. Likewise, as Ikeda (2018) explains, the place of absolute nothingness is not a place of existence or a place of nothingness. Self and the other are both denied in that they are dependent on each other and yet each does not exist *a priori* in support of the other.[4] Nishida (1949) expresses this in the following way.

> But behind consciousness there must be an absolute nothing. There must be that which not only negates all being but also negates nothing.
> KRUMMEL and NAGATOMO 2012: 65

In other words, place is where its existence is totally denied, and yet at the same time its state of nothingness is also denied. Nishida views the place of nothingness not just as a place where consciousness is experienced, but where both life and death reside. The place is where the absolutely contradictory self-identity occurs, where existence and nothingness are both negated and yet embraced.

Overall, Nishida (1949) held a humanistic image of the self, as evident in his argument that one's feelings exist on a more profound level of consciousness than one's intellectual introspection. In other words, most fundamental to human consciousness are the pure feelings experienced in a concrete immediacy in a place. As Nishida theorizes, that is where one can hear voiceless voices and see formless forms. The Japanese self emerges as a feeling-experiencing person in a concrete immediacy within the place. Resonating with the teachings of zen Buddhism, the self emerges in an empty yet enabling place, as an empty yet viable existence.

---

4 Regarding Nishida's logic of absolutely contradictory self-identity, a concrete example of the rings on a tree may be useful (Ikeda 2018). Specific tree rings are formed according to the weather. The tree rings are created by nature, i.e., the tree is definable only within nature. At the same time, nature contains the tree in itself. The tree does not exist on its own without nature, and vice versa, nature does not exist on its own without the tree. This double negation is an example of the absolutely contradictory self-identity. The self is a part of nature and nature is a part of the self; likewise, the self is reflected in the place and thus a part of the place, and yet the place is a part of the self since the place exists as it is embraced by the self.

Nishida is known to have been influenced by James (1904) who introduced terms such as "pure experience" and "direct experience." However, Nishida's pure experience involves a primordial place of nothingness where subject and object are not yet in existence. One can observe methodological differences between James and Nishida as well. James' thought is based more on a psychological process, i.e., his radical empiricism. To account for the inner workings of experiences, James explores the conjunctive relations among perceived events. In contrast, Nishida's pure experience is metaphysical in that he identifies experience on the basis of the place as a philosophical notion. James was concerned about experiences more than place, while the reverse is true for Nishida.

It is not entirely out of line to speculate that James influenced Nishida regarding how religion and philosophy are intertwined. James, unlike many of the philosophers who accepted and relied on a Christian God, held a rather open mind. In fact James states that religion "shall mean for us *the feelings, acts, and experiences of individual men in their solitude, so far as they apprehend themselves to stand in relation to whatever they may consider the divine*" (James 1929: 379, original emphasis). This pantheistic approach to the divine invites non-Christian philosophers such as Nishida to integrate religiosity into philosophical thought. The relationship between the self and religious experience becomes wide open, to the extent that it does not reject atheism and pantheism where a single authoritative God is unrecognized.

Nishida's philosophy suggests a new approach to the theme of exploring the concept of self. If we simply ask who or what the self is, it is difficult to answer. But the understanding that the self emerges in the place where it undergoes experiences invites us to appreciate the significance of our verbal interaction. Linguistic subjectivity as well as language variation, especially the concept of character-speak, operate on the basis of experiential interaction defined by the place. By using various types of character-speak in the place, we emerge as selves manifesting different features, tendencies, and preferences, and consequently, realizing the self's aspects, characters, and characteristics.

2.2   The Self and the Predicating Universal

The view endorsing the centrality of place and the place-sensitive self becomes even more significant when Nishida (1949) explains the logic based on Japanese language structure. A logical calculus of "S is P" means in Japanese that S (supported by particularity) is defined by P (predicated by generally perceived features). That is, one interprets the proposition "S is P" by applying general characteristics to the particular. Nishida clarifies this by insisting that our judgment consists of subject and predicate, and the judgment is essentially based on the fact that a specific subject is enclosed and embedded in the predicating universal. Nishida's position is expressed in the following way.

> There must be a universal at the root of consciousness. When the universal serves as a *basho* wherein all that exists is implaced, it becomes consciousness. Insofar as the universal is further determined as universal, that is, insofar as it cannot become a *basho* that is truly nothing, we see substance on the outside and universal concept on the inside.
> KRUMMEL and NAGATOMO 2012: 66, original emphasis

In Nishida's view, the subject is defined by the predicating universal. The predicate, supported by generally perceived features, is rooted in the place, the field of consciousness where one can reflect on one's self. Judgment must be approached not from the subject, but from the universal, and more accurately, within the place where S and P are mutually and inclusively determining.[5]

For Nishida, the most important aspect in ontological logic is not the *a priori* awareness of the self. Instead of building a logic based on the concept of the speaking self as the center of the universe, Nishida prioritizes the predicating universal on the basis of which the self is identified.[6] In his words:

> Ordinarily we even think of the I to be a unity as a [grammatical] subject possessing various qualities like a thing. But the I is not a unity *qua* [grammatical] subject. It must instead be a predicating unity. It would have to be a circle rather than a point, a *basho* rather than a thing. The reason why the I cannot know itself is because a predicate cannot become a [grammatical] subject.
> KRUMMEL and NAGATOMO 2012: 95–96, original emphasis

The place is where things are (Nishida 1949: 227), and where their existence fundamentally is made possible. And most importantly, this place of nothingness must be supported by a transcendental predicating universal. In this manner,

---

5 Nishida's concept of self based on the predicating universal has influenced Tokieda's (1941, 1950) view toward language, especially when Tokieda introduces the concept of the situated place. The situated place has become an important concept in subsequent theories in Japanese linguistics.

6 The idea that the predicating universal is critical for understanding the meaning resonates with Fillmore's (1976) frame semantics developed in the 1970s. Although Fillmore and Nishida both argue against a truth-conditional logic, frame semantics focuses on how meaning is interpreted on the basis of required encyclopedic knowledge, while Nishida's predicating universal serves as a foundation for an ontological understanding.

Nishida makes a radical transition from Western subject-centered logic to his predicate-supported logic.

In evaluating Nishida's theory of place, Nakamura (1993, 1996) states that Nishida achieved a Copernican paradigmatic shift from a subject-centered logic to a logic supported by a transcendental predicating universal. Most importantly, Nakamura asserts that Nishida "understood the place of Nothingness, not as a place lacking in substance, but as an infinite world of possibility" (1993: 67, my translation).

Nishida's approach to philosophy has impacted the nature of Japanese scholarship in two interesting ways. First, Nishida's philosophical approach gave him the freedom to develop a kind of creative philosophy. Nishida's self-less ego is by definition free of attachment to dogmatic viewpoints (Yusa 2002). This freeing of thought has enabled Nishida to advance his philosophical vision influenced by Japanese religious and cultural traditions.

Nishida's philosophical position is significant regarding another related point. The theory of place Nishida proposes is compatible with the Japanese ways of thinking recognized in Japanese scholarship. Japanese scholarly approaches often characterized as aesthetic and literature-oriented have been criticized for lacking logical and rational thought. Given this academic context, Nishida's philosophy has been successful in that it persuasively presents Japanese philosophical thought beyond the confines of Japan. Although his manner of argument sharply contrasts with Western approaches, his logic is presented relevantly in the context of a Western philosophical framework, thus avoiding the often criticized isolationism of the Japanese scholarly tradition.

3 Miyazawa's Poetics: Transient Self as a Flickering Light

3.1 Flickering Self in Heart-Image Sketches

Kenji Miyazawa (1896–1933), poet and author of children's literature, addresses the question of self through his poetic works. His poems integrate dreams, mental images, and glimpses of reality, which Miyazawa himself calls "heart-image sketches." These images, based on direct intuitive experiences unfiltered from a cognitive process, appear and then disappear in his mind. Miyazawa's images are not ordinary, to say the least; they emerge from his unique and often sense-based intuition. Interestingly, included in his array of images is the self, for which he uses the phrase *watakushi* 'I'. For Miyazawa, the self is a flickering light, a transient phenomenon floating in nature.

Menda (2012) interprets Miyazawa's poetry in the following way. Miyazawa's sketches may be taken to be mildly scientific, yet they defy the concept of time.

His images bypass the timeline of past, present, and future, and are presented simply as they are at the moment of his inspiration. Menda concludes that "as reflected in the animism and animalism appearing in Miyazawa's poems, his images differ from ordinary images; they take the form of Miyazawa's direct experience as he simultaneously perceives the outer world and experiences the sensation as he becomes one with those external objects he perceives" (2012: 156, my translation).

Relevantly, Miyazawa's sketches resonate with the Buddhist view of the self reflecting the Buddhism he practiced.[7] Challenging the Western self, Miyazawa understands his self not as an object or a thing, but as a kind of a phenomenon. Captured in his sketches are the moment-to-moment changing states of nature, people, and events. His view of the self is given in the introduction to his collection of poetry.

> The phenomenon called "I"
> is a blue illumination
> of the hypothesized, organic alternating current lamp
> (a compound of all transparent ghosts)
> a blue illumination
> of the karmic alternating current lamp
> which flickers busily, busily
> with landscapes, with everyone
> yet remains lit with such assuredness
> (the light persists, the lamp lost)
>   SATO 2007: 63)

Here, the self is a light that incessantly flickers. Miyazawa understands the self as an image that repeatedly appears and disappears. The term *karma* used in the phrase *the karmic alternating current lamp* resonates with Buddhism. In Miyazawa's world, however, karma is something that crisscrosses, intertwines, and mingles. His self is a repetition of turning on and off the karmic lamp; his *watakushi* takes on an instantaneous image, without any physical existence. Appearing like a ghost, it is a blue light flickering on and off. Sakai (2005) writes that Miyazawa "attempts to characterize, in his heart-image, the concept of a phenomenological self constantly made anxious about external things, and

---

7   Miyazawa was born into a well-to-do family that practiced Pure Land Buddhism, but he later converted to Nichiren Buddhism, which created a rift with his family, especially with his father.

as something featured by its non-permanence, fragility, and interdependence" (2005: 161, my translation).

Miyazawa does not presuppose a unitary and stable self existing underneath the flickering self. His *watakushi* appears in his consciousness from one moment to the next, and such a changing self is appreciated as is. He does not feel his self is missing its coherence or continuity; in fact, resonating with the Japanese cultural tradition, there is no need for the self to be stable or to be attached to the place. It is true that believing in one single self forces a person to remain just that self, but, the flickering self often feels a sense of relief from constraints and restrictions. Echoing Nishida's (1949) view of self in the place of absolute nothingness, Miyazawa's transient self, allowing for its fluctuation and change, is free.

Just as Nishida was influenced by zen Buddhisim, Miyazawa was influenced by Nichiren Buddhism, and more directly by Lotus Sutra (Watanabe 2007). The religious influence is obvious in the poem cited below.

> I shall die soon
>   today or tomorrow.
> Again, anew, I contemplate: What am I?
> I am ultimately nothing other than a principle,
>   My body is bones, blood, flesh,
>   which are in the end various molecules,
>   combinations of dozens of atoms;
>   the atom is in the end a form of vacuum,
>   and so is the external world.
> The principle by which I sense my body and the external world thus and
>   by which these materials work in various ways
> is called I.
> The moment I die and return to the vacuum,
> the moment I perceive myself again,
> in both times, what is there is only a single principle.
> The name of that original law is called *The Lotus Sutra of the Wonderful Law*, they say.
>
> SATO 2007: 213

The expression *the moment I die and return to the vacuum* resonates not only with the Buddhist view but also with the Japanese aesthetics of life's transience and impermanence. Again through this poetry, we find an approach to life different from the traditional Western self, but similar to the anti-Cartesian and postmodern approaches developed in the West.

3.2   Echoes of Western Thought

Miyazawa's view of self is influenced by certain Western philosophies. It is unclear what books Miyazawa read and what Western thoughts he studied. But in his poetry, we find references to monad, a concept developed by Leibniz, and to the name James (William James). The selection of these phrases in his poetry indicates that Miyazawa's self is conceived on the basis of spiritual, phenomenological, and psychological experiences.

For example, his poem describes the self as a combined state of multiple senses, and this self emerges in an undefinable but available space he identifies as monad. Monad literally means one unit, one thing, has no division, existing as one unit as a whole. The concept of self based on this monad presupposes a coherent unitary existence uniquely distinct from others. In contrast, Miyazawa understands monad as the smallest possible unit of matter (Watanabe 2007), and identifies it with nature where he experiences a self that has no internal consistency. The phrase is used when Miyazawa senses a faint light or wind, as in his expressions, *silver monad* and *monad of the wind*.[8] Miyazawa's monad represents a space, a world filled with natural beauty, consisting of some unknown gatherings of minute particles. Miyazawa's world of monad, far from being some unitary entity, remains free, a potential space with many floating particles. It is possible to find here Miyazawa's sense of self, a self that repeatedly appears and flickers, a transient self without a coherent or stable foundation.

Miyazawa is also influenced by William James, especially by James' concept of stream of consciousness. In his poem Miyazawa uses phrases translatable as stream of consciousness along with the name James.[9] As discussed in Chapter 1, James (1984 [1890]) posits the concept of self based on changing states of consciousness. Many of Miyazawa's heart-image sketches resemble a stream of consciousness approach. Miyazawa's self is empty, not far from the phenomenon of his monad and not unlike James' stream of consciousness.

In this chapter I have reviewed the concept of the empty self in the empty place in Japanese thought. Themes covered are dynamic flow (Fukuoka 2009, 2011), the place of nothingness (Nishida 1949), and transient self as a flickering

---

8   We find the expression *gin no monado* 'silver monad' used in his poem dated May 9, 1927, and *kaze no monado* 'monad of the wind' appearing in his poem dated April 20, 1924. Japanese poetry is taken from the Aozora Bunko website, https://www.aozora.gr.jp, accessed March 1, 2019.

9   The phrase *ishiki no nagare* 'stream of consciousness' appears in his poem dated March 28, 1927, and *Jeemusu* 'James' appears in his poem dated June 22, 1924. Japanese poetry is taken from the Aozora bunko website. https://www.aozora.gr.jp, accessed March 1, 2019.

light (Miyazawa in Sato 2007). These approaches are both influenced by and influence scholarly traditions outside of Japan. While Japanese views presented above are not uniquely Japanese, philosophical and poetic particularities discussed here are foundational to the Japanese senses of self that fundamentally differ from the traditional Western self. The emptiness and unstableness provide a clearing of space allowing for transformational possibilities that afford the necessary freedom to the Japanese self.

CHAPTER 6

Concept of Self in Japanese Language and Discourse

In what follows I review traditional and contemporary studies in Japanese language and discourse that explore the Japanese concept of self. Views on self in many of the Japanese language studies differ from and yet resonate with other Western studies. In general, it is possible to position the works reviewed here in support of the empty and populated self.

1   Self in Traditional Language Studies

1.1   *Emotive Self in the Edo Period Language Studies*

It was in the Edo period (1603–1868) that serious studies on the Japanese language began. Their purpose was not to conduct grammatical analyses, but rather, to identify rhetorical and expressive strategies for creating and commenting on *waka*, a 31-syllable poem. This aesthetic approach to language has profoundly influenced the direction of subsequent Japanese language studies. Especially noteworthy is Akira Suzuki (1764–1837), who, being influenced by Fujitani (1934 [1767], 1960 [1778]), immortalized the emotive function of the Japanese language with the phrase "voices from the heart." In his *Gengyo Shishuron* 'A Theory of Four Types of Words' (1979 [1824]), Suzuki introduces the classification of four categories, i.e., nominals, adjectivals, verbals, and *te-ni-o-ha* particles which mark grammatical cases and topics. Suzuki groups the first three into one large category, i.e., referential words, and deems *te-ni-o-ha* particles to constitute an opposing category.

Referential phrases refer to objects. They are like precious beads, are like containers, and they fail to operate without *te-ni-o-ha* particles. In contrast, *te-ni-o-ha* particles have no referential function, represent voices from the heart, and are attached to referential words. They are like strings that connect precious beads, are like hands that operate the containers, and without referential words, they have nothing to be attached to. Suzuki summarizes that the voices of *te-ni-o-ha* particles distinguish and express states of one's heart, while nominals and other words are used to distinguish and describe objects.

Another interesting point found in *Gengyo Shishuron* is Suzuki's treatment of the origin of language. He explains as follows. We hear voices in the heart that express human emotions, and these voices are the origin of *te-ni-o-ha* particles. *Te-ni-o-ha* particles are the essential spirit of referential words, and by using referential words, people named things, which resulted in the creation of nouns. When nouns were connected like a strand of beads, two types of words were created, resulting in adjectives and verbs. If one traces the history of all words, one reaches two kinds of voices, that of *te-ni-o-ha* particles and that of nouns. The voice of *te-ni-o-ha* particles communicates the states of one's heart, and the voices of nouns present things and events.

Consequently, we find in Suzuki a scholar who identifies the essence of the Japanese language not in its propositional information but in its subjective modality. Self in this view of language is expressive and manages rich modal expressions originating in the emotive self. I should add here that Suzuki's voices from the heart are expressed in Japanese in other devices and strategies as well. In addition to *te-ni-o-ha* particles, the Japanese language is rich in expressions of subjectivity that echo voices from the heart, including exclamatory expressions, modal adverbs, modal auxiliary verbs, and rhetorical interrogatives (Maynard 1993a).

1.2   *Participatory Self in the Situated Place*

Another approach relevant to the Japanese self is taken by Motoki Tokieda (1900–1967) who identifies a participatory self situated in a place of communication. Tokieda (1941, 1950) develops this idea based on his theory of language, i.e, the Language-as-Process theory. In this view, language is the very process in which the self expresses ideas through verbalization. Instead of viewing language as a product (or an object) with its internal structure, Tokieda insists that language is the very psychological process that facilitates the self's expression.

Tokieda (1941, 1950) develops his theory on the basis of three elements necessary for the linguistic event to occur. They are the speaking subject, the material/object/referent, and the situated place. Language becomes personalized when someone (self) speaks to someone (situated place) about something (material/object/referent). These three elements are intimately related, and if one is lacking, the linguistic event fails to materialize. For Tokieda, the self is the person engaging in the linguistic activity in a situated place.[1] The situated place is permeated with the self's feelings and attitudes, as well as the self's perception and intention toward those objects being described.

---

1 Tokieda's self defined by the situated place is not an abstract notion but clearly refers to an embodied person. As pointed out in Chapter 1, the concept of embodiment gained theoretical and analytical significance in Western language-related sciences years later in the 1970s and on (Marmaridou 2000; Johnson 2018; Mondada 2019).

Interestingly, Tokieda (1941), following Suzuki's (1979 [1824]) work, resurrects the concept of voices from the heart by calling attention to non-referential words. In contrast to words whose primary function is referential, particles and other nonreferential words represent the personal voice, reflecting the self's thoughts, feelings, and attitudes. Tokieda insists that words do not first reproduce objects per se and convey them, rather they express the self's signification toward objects. When we communicate, we always express our personal attitude along with the emotion we are feeling in a situated place. Because of this, we must understand that the propositional meanings of words and sentences do not entirely convey their *a priori* meanings.[2] In reality we communicate meanings beyond those conventionalized words directly linked to their linguistic signs. What we communicate through language is the experience of our psychological processes. Language makes it possible for us to incorporate our subjective thoughts, while adding new meanings. Tokieda's Language-as-Process theory focuses on this self's personal involvement with linguistic expression, and as a result, the self is understood to be situation-based.

It should be emphasized here that Tokieda's situated place goes beyond our ordinary sense of place. In his view, the situated place refers not only to the physical place of social interaction but also to a rather comprehensive (almost psychological and emotional) place. As opposed to the simple notion of the place, the situated place includes the self's attitudes, feelings, and emotions directed toward these objects in the place. Also present is the partner who undeniably influences the speaking self. Within this situated place, the self understands the partner and other objects identifiable within. Tokieda insists that language is always expressed in harmony with the situated place, summarizing that "the situated place is not purely objective or purely subjective; rather, it is the world where subjectivity and objectivity fuse into one" (1941: 44, my translation).

Tokieda's inclusion of the self's attitude and emotion in the situated place resonates with Nishida's understanding of the place. Nishida's field of con-

---

2 Tokieda's (1941, 1950) Language-as-Process theory resonates with the tenet of Western linguistics developed decades later, particularly with Hopper's (1987) Emergent Grammar. Hopper argues that linguistic structure is emergent, temporal as well as deferred, and grammar and meaning only exist in the form of emerging interpretations by language users in an interaction. The similarities observed between Tokieda and Hopper can be traced to the anti-Cartesian philosophy, i.e., Nishida's (1949) concept of empty place for Tokieda, and as suggested by Weber (1997), Derrida's (1974, 1978) deconstructionism for Hopper. Tokieda's inclusion of feelings and attitude to his theory is approached in more concrete terms by interactional linguistics, e.g., Herlin and Visapää (2016) in which the relationship between empathy and language in real-life interactions are studied.

sciousness embraces not only knowledge, but also emotion and will. Additionally, we witness that Tokieda's concept of place is ontological as evidenced when he states that "the existence of the situated place is nothing more than giving testimony that we are alive" (1941: 45, my translation). This remark is reminiscent of Nishida's position regarding the concept of existence. In the first paragraph of his writing on his theory of place, Nishida states that "things that exist must exist somewhere; otherwise, it is impossible to distinguish between there is and there is not" (1949: 208, my translation).

2 Watsuji's Approach: Interdependent Self in Social Space

2.1 *Background*

Tetsuro Watsuji (1889–1960), a philosopher of ethics, presents the concept of the interdependent self, based on features of the Japanese language. As indicative of his dedication to Nishida in his work *Ningen no Gaku to Shite no Rinrigaku* 'Ethics as the Study of Human Beings' (1990a [1962]), Watsuji has followed Nishida's (1949) line of thinking in centering his philosophy on concepts such as emptiness (Nishida's nothingness), and social space (Nishida's place). Overall, Watsuji insists that human beings cannot help but find themselves in a web of interconnected action, and thus he denies the existence of a solitary independent self. As Komaki (1986) summarizes and as I explain in subsequent sections, Watsuji, in essence, proposes that self and society represent two sides of a human being in a dialectical relationship where each exists not independently but in mutual dependency. Watsuji understands that a human being requires social space which simultaneously involves a person enabled by it; neither space nor self exists without the other. Watsuji characterizes this contradictory state as emptiness, and following a hermeneutical approach in his ontological pursuit, interprets the etymological origins of Japanese self-related words.

Like Nishida, Watsuji was influenced by an array of Western scholars including classic Greek scholars, Schopenhauer, Nietzsche, and Kierkegaard, and perhaps most significantly by Heidegger. Watsuji's work is distinct from Nishida's in that he bases his ontological interpretation on certain key Japanese phrases. Watsuji takes the position that the semantic interpretation of the words we use in our human experience will lead us to an understanding of our existence.

As in the case of Nishida (1949), Watsuji's works cannot be fully evaluated without recognizing the influence of Buddhism. In his earlier career, he published works on primitive Buddhism, Japanese aesthetics, and the ancient temples of Nara. The degree of Buddhistic influence, however, remains controversial, as Dilworth (1974) notes in the following.

> Watsuji's dialectic of absolute negation ending with explicit reference to the ground of *Emptiness* (...) and what he called the "selfless emotion" of the Japanese spirit, indeed, remind us of central Buddhist idea. But at the same time it should be stressed that Watsuji's position was not essentially a Buddhistic or religious one such as worked out in the Kyoto school.
> DILWORTH 1974: 17, original emphasis

Arguing against Dilworth (1974), Lafleur (1978) insists that the Buddhist notion of emptiness is central to Watsuji's thought, and without recognition of this connection, his approach makes no sense. As shown later, Watsuji explains the meaning of human existence within the absolute negating process of emptiness in solid connection with Buddhist thought. Watsuji's concept of emptiness fluctuates (Sevilla 2016), but his most basic approach (including Buddhist concepts such as non-duality, negation, and emptiness) constitutes a critical foundation for his philosophy.

Watsuji was influenced by Heidegger particularly during his study abroad in Germany. In fact, Watsuji's earlier work, *Fuudo* 'Climate and Culture' (1935) is written in direct response to Heidegger's *Being and Time* (Carter 1996, McCarthy 2010). In Watsuji's view, Heidegger over-emphasizes temporality and slights the concept of spatiality. By focusing on the concept of social space, Watsuji suggests concentrating on the study of ethics might provide insight into positive social connections.

2.2 *Discovering Self in and with Language*

Taking the hermeneutic phenomenological approach, Watsuji finds it important to pursue his own philosophy based on the Japanese language. Watsuji (1990a [1962], 1990b [1962]) explains his ontological view in the following way. The Cartesian approach to the self lacks concreteness and reality; such self is in fact nothing but illusion. This is because if we observe real human experiences in our daily lives, we realize we are defined in relation to our partner, as shown in the case of a wife being defined in relation to her husband, and vice versa. Humans are not isolated beings, but are in relationships. People are born into place where relationships with others are enacted. Ultimately, the self is realized and enabled in its social space.[3]

---

3 Watsuji's approach resonates with sociolinguistics and pragmatics in which the situational and social contexts are deemed theoretically critical. Years after Watsuji's work, concrete

Watsuji, following Humboldt's reasoning toward society-based languages, rejects the idea of a universal language.[4] He calls for a kind of ontology that makes use of Japanese linguistic features. First, the Japanese language focuses not on objects but on relationships. In fact, he emphasizes that not only first-person references but all other person expressions in Japanese refer to the relationship itself. Second, although the lack of plural markers in language has sometimes been identified as a sign of an uncivilized language, Watsuji maintains that Japanese language's singular-plural concept simply reflects a Japanese world view. When a word *wakai shuu* 'young person, young people, a group of youth' is used, it refers to both a single youth and a group of youth. This stems from the human being's dual nature of being both individual and social, and thus the concept of youth should not be associated with a specific numerical value. Third, the lack of person-based verb conjugations in Japanese also originates in the dual nature of human action. In Japanese the action described by the verb does not specifically belong to a singular person or persons in general. Indeed, different grammatical verb conjugations across languages simply reflect varied ways of understanding human beings.

Watsuji's major work, *Ningen no Gaku to Shite no Rinrigaku* 'Ethics as the Study of Human Beings' (1990a [1962]) is in essence a critique of Western individualism. Watsuji's notion of the being as *ningen* 'human being(s)', unlike Heidegger's *Dasein*, includes both temporal and spatial aspects of the human being-in-the-world. Watsuji presents his concept of *ningen* in the framework of ethics which he approaches as a dynamic relationship of contradiction and reconciliation between the individual and society.[5] Yonetani (2000) captures Watsuji's ethics in the following way.

> A human being becomes an individual only within society, and at the same time, society exists only through actions taken among individu-

---

theoretical and methodological frameworks were developed in these fields, in interactional sociolinguistics (Gumperz and Tannen 1979; Gumperz 1982), in particular.

4 Humboldt's position is explained in Mueller-Vollmer and Messling (2017).

5 I should mention that the academic response to Watsuji's work has been mixed. The critique generally stands on the ground that his work ratifies totalitarianism and demands an individual's submission to communal or national demands, for example Sakai (1991, 1997). However, such criticism has been ignored or refuted by a number of sympathetic scholars. Zanghellini and Sato (2020), based on their close reading of the entire text of Watsuji's *Ningen no Gaku to Shite no Rinrigaku* 'Ethics as the Study of Human Beings' (1990a [1962]), conclude that Watsuji's ethics makes adequate room for individual's resistance to unjustifiable socio-ethical demands. Other sympathetic studies include Shields (2009), McCarthy (2010), and Sevilla (2016).

als. When Watsuji uses the word "ethics," he means a dynamic structure where human existence comes alive by mediating and denying the human being's both individual and social nature.
YONETANI 2000: 285, my translation

In more specific terms, approaching the matter hermeneutically, Watsuji tackles the relationship between language and philosophy in his work titled *Nihongo to Tetsugaku no Mondai* 'The Issue of the Japanese Language and Philosophy'. In this work, written in 1929 and based on his 1928 lectures, he introduces phrases such as *ningen* 'human being(s)', *seken* 'social world, public', *yo no naka* 'social world, public', *aidagara* 'betweenness', and *sonzai* 'existence, being' in his ontological exploration, which I discuss in subsequent sections.

2.3 Self as Betweenness and the Concept of Emptiness

The Japanese word *ningen* 'human being(s)' is composed of two characters, one representing person, and the other, betweenness. Taken literally, *ningen* refers to persons in betweenness. Thus, *ningen* implies the public (i.e., society), and at the same time, human being(s) inhabiting this space. What is revealed here is a dialectical unity of dual features inherent in *ningen*. On the meaning and the nature of *ningen*, Watsuji states:[6]

> The Japanese language, therefore, possesses a very significant word; namely *ningen*. On the basis of the evolved meaning of this word, we Japanese have produced a distinctive conception of human being. According to it, *ningen* is the public and, at the same time, the individual human beings living within it. Therefore, it refers not merely to an individual "human being" nor merely to "society." What is recognizable here is a dialectical unity of those double characteristics that are inherent in a human being.
> CARTER 1996: 15, original emphasis

Watsuji contends that the individual is separate from society and yet dissolves into it. Unless we recognize this dialectical nature, it is impossible to understand the essence of *ningen*. *Ningen* is an interdependent being reflecting an "embodied intersubjectivity" (Krueger 2013).

Ningen is not a metaphysical concept; it implies a kind of self involving others within a society. This relationship is further captured in the Japanese phrase

---

6 The quotation from Watsuji (1990b [1962]) is based on the translation provided by Carter (1996).

aidagara 'betweenness'. In *aidagara*, a human being cannot be regarded as an individual or a mere social entity, but rather, as a relational being connected to other human beings, nature, and society. Self cannot be assumed *a priori* as a being based on introspection; it is realized in the betweenness, in its other-dependent intersubjective relationship. The notion of *aidagara* reminds us of Nishida's pure experience. Both *aidagara* and pure experience are dialectically interpreted, both existing prior to any subject-object distinction. Nagami (1981) summarizes that for Watsuji "(*N*)*ingen* is not an individual entity but *aidagara*, a relational contact between man and nature, man and man, man and society" (1981: 280, original emphasis).

Watsuji fundamentally views *aidagara* 'betweenness' as a concept of interconnected acts of embodied selves. Referring to the Japanese phrases *aida* 'between' and *naka* 'middle, inside, between', Watsuji applies *aidagara* to the social space, and explains in the following way.

> We cannot sustain ourselves in any *aida* or *naka* without acting subjectively. At the same time, we cannot act without maintaining ourselves in some *aida* or *naka*. For this reason, *aida* or *naka* imply a living and dynamic betweenness, as a subjective interconnection of acts. A betweenness of this sort and the spatio-temporal world combine to produce the meaning conveyed by the words *se-ken* (the public) or *yo-no-naka* (the public).
> CARTER 1996: 18, original emphasis

The interrelationship of *aidagara* is also evident when we pay attention to consciousness. Watsuji explains that when we say *I become conscious of Thou*, this *I* is never determined by *I* itself. This is because "(M)y seeing Thou is already determined by your seeing me," and as a result, "my becoming conscious of Thou is inextricably interconnected with your becoming conscious of me" (Carter 1996: 33). Watsuji makes the following statement.

> This interconnection we have called *betweenness* is quite distinct from the intentionality of consciousness. Activity inherent in the consciousness of "I" is never determined by this "I" alone but is also determined by others. It is not merely a reciprocal activity in that oneway conscious activities are performed one after another but, rather, that either one of them is at once determined by both sides; that is, by itself and by the other. Hence so far as betweenness-oriented existences are concerned, each consciousness interpenetrates the other.
> CARTER 1996: 69, original emphasis

The betweenness can be understood in a broader context as well. Ultimately, Watsuji views a person as the betweenness recognized in the world we live in. For Watsuji, a person is realized through a close interaction with the climate and culture, and this understanding serves as a foundation for his ontology.

The Japanese phrase *sonzai* 'human existence' most directly refers to the concept of self-existence. Watsuji approaches this phrase hermeneutically concluding that it means the sustenance of the self in betweenness. Since betweenness presupposes actual interaction, self-existence depends on various interactions, and consequently multiple aspects of the self are interdependently nurtured. In contrast with the independent and detached self, Watsuji defines *sonzai* as the self's comprehension of being placed within human relationships. The etymology of *son* is self's sustenance, and it means maintenance of one's self against loss, while the etymology of *zai* discloses that the subject exists in some place. And based on these meanings, Watsuji defines *sonzai* as the following.

> If it is tenable to hold that *son* is the self-sustenance of the self and *zai* means to remain within human relations, then *son-zai* is precisely the self-sustenance of the self as betweenness. (...) We could also simply say that *sonzai* is "the interconnection of the acts of *ningen*."
> CARTER 1996: 21 original emphasis

Critically, Watsuji finds the concept of emptiness to be the underlying basis of human existence. At the foundation of the logical interdependence of the opposing forces of the self and society (or individual and public), lies the notion of "emptiness." As Shields (2009) puts it, "it is important to understand that *ningen sonzai* does not rely upon Being as a source of existence, but upon Nothingness or Emptiness (*kuu*)" (2009: 270, original emphasis). The significance of *kuu* 'emptiness' in Watsuji's thought cannot be underestimated; it is conceived as the Eastern counterpart to Being (Nagami 1981). Watsuji, responding to Heidegger's philosophy, returns to the concept of place that is simply empty.

3   The Multiplicity of Self in Japanese Discourse

3.1   *Deconstruction of Identity*

Scholars observing the discourse of contemporary Japan have explored the concept of self, challenging the traditional view but resonating with the postmodernism in the West. In what follows I review social, psychological, narrative, as well as literary perspectives. Ueno (2005) advocates a position that diminishes the significance of the notion of identity itself. Ueno begins her argument by citing Hall's (1996) position on the deconstruction of identity.

> It accepts that identities are never unified and, in late modern times, increasingly fragmented and fractured; never singular but multiply constructed across different, often intersecting and antagonistic, discourses, practices and positions. They are subject to a radical historicization, and are constantly in the process of change and transformation.
> HALL 1996: 4

In Ueno's view, the concept of a single identity is not required at all. Thus it should be discarded altogether, a position reminiscent of Derrida (1974, 1978). Consider that identity is a label often attached to a minority, and is conveniently manipulated by those in power. Furthermore, identity is not something stable or defined, but is in an evolving process of forming. Ueno reminds us that, in reality, people live their lives within a flux of multiple identities, and they find no urgent need for seeking a consistent single identity. In her words:

> In reality, most people lead normal social lives with no sense of deviation when they lack a consistent identity. Moreover, today as our social belongingness changes from being a member of a cohesive group to being only a segment within the group, it has become possible to live fragmented and uncoordinated identities.
> UENO 2005: 35, my translation

We need to abandon identity as an abstract metaphysical notion, and instead, we need to understand the speaker as an embodied person who, following one's free will, undergoes the process of forming multiple aspects of the self. In this manner, it is possible to take back the labeling of identity once forced upon us, for we are our own selves engaging in our own self-forming processes. And as maintained by Hall (1996), identity is an artificial condition, often used for political and self-serving purposes. Our interactions with societies change, and so do our identities; we must understand the self not in terms of a stereotyped identity but in terms of multiple, changing, and even seemingly contradictory aspects of the self.

3.2   Self in Multiple Self-Narratives

Asano's (2001) approach to narrative discourse offers insight to the concept of self. Asano argues for a close connection between the discourse of self-narratives and self-understanding.[7] We think back on our past, and arrange some incidents in chronological order in ways we can make sense of. And self-narratives are not necessarily coherently organized stories, but a collection of random episodes told in many different situations. What is happening here psychologically is the presentation of multiple selves. Self-narratives are recited in front of others, and because of this dependency on others' reactions, they tend to become less consistent. And these varied stories serve as key to understanding the self in complex ways.

Regarding the self, Asano (2001) explains that a self consists of "I" and "me," explaining in the following way.

> Self (...) refers not to a static or stable object, but to the very process where "I" and "me" are repeatedly separated and differentiated. Therefore, it is not an identity based on a simple "sameness," but is something simultaneously the self and other, something same yet different. Self must be constructed in such a paradoxically defined way.
> ASANO 2001: 248, my translation

Thus, Asano (2001) contends that the self is produced only through the process of self-narration. One's self-image is maintained through a continuous reciting of a self-narrative as a chattering in one's mind. Asano reports that his questionnaire-based research has revealed that among Japanese youth, there is less desire to maintain a coherently unified self. By asking questions regarding their behavior when they are with friends, Asano discovers that young people routinely manage different "faces" toward different friends. These faces, however, are not thought of as being fictitious; they are believed to be genuine. Results based on similar questionnaires conducted by Asano (2005) find that the tendency to believe in multiple selves has increased from 1992 to 2002. Divided and fragmented selves are not unusual among Japanese youth, and a coherent and stable self does not seem realistic in postmodern Japan. Identity has fractured into many elements, and connections among them have become increasingly flexible and varied.

---

7 It should be noted that Asano's approach is not particular to Japanese studies. As reviewed in McAdams and McLean (2013), the idea that selves are narrative constructions is not new in Western academia. Scholars have approached the narrative identity theme in different ways (McAdams 1985; Schafer 1992; Holstein and Guberium 2000), and some with criticism, e.g., Vollmer (2005). Although it is beyond the scope of this work, inquiring into the concept of self incorporating cross-linguistic narrative phenomena is expected to add new insight.

3.3 Self as Multiple "Dividuals"

A view on the self approached from the perspective of postmodern Japanese literature is noteworthy. Hirano (2012) proposes that rather than accepting the Western concept of the individual, it is possible to view the Japanese self as "dividuals." The idea was developed in his novel (Hirano 2009), in which participants in the novel live their "divs," i.e., dividuals, and not as one single consistent individual. As Hirano (2012) maintains, when the term "individual" was introduced into Japan, it was translated to mean single or sole person and with a sense of "in-dividual," one who cannot be divided further. The idea of individualism was introduced to Japan toward the end of the 19th century when Japan underwent its Westernization process; there was a strong belief that individualism would provide a necessary condition for Japan's modernization. Although the concept was then forcefully implemented, such as individualism based on Christian monotheism as well as Cartesian objectivism, it was not fully understood among Japanese intellectuals.

When the self is understood to be unitary and consistent, conflicts among different senses of self may result in psychological trauma. If one understands the self as a collection of multiple selves motivated and realized through varied communicational interactions, internal conflicts among different aspects of the self are avoided. Hirano (2012) believes that multiple dividuals exist in one's interior and are formed as a network. It is important to maintain a certain balance within one's internal psychological network, but there is no need for rigid systematization. Hirano summarizes that dividuals are what we are made of, and different dividuals become activated in specific situations. Depending on who we interact with, and depending on the physical environment which we find ourselves in, we live as different dividuals. Importantly, in Hirano's view, dividuals are just dividuals, devoid of a consistent core. Consequently, we do not necessarily exhibit our different personalities based on an identified central core.[8] Rather, we are made of a network of dividuals.

Hirano asserts that there is no single true self and that the multiple faces one wears in interaction with other people at different interpersonal situations are all true selves. Hirano describes human beings called "I" as the following.

> The person called "I" is constructed with multiple dividuals activated through interaction with others. And one's personality (i.e., individual

---

[8] Hirano's position that the self has no consistent core is in opposition to the view presented in Hasegawa and Hirose (2005). They take the position that what they call "absolute" self, which is essentially identical to the Cartesian notion of self, applies to all languages, including Japanese. Their position is revisited in Chapter 13.

feature) is based on the ratio each dividual occupies. If the ratio of different dividuals changes, naturally, so will the personality. Personality is not single or unchanging. And it does not emerge without the other.

HIRANO 2012: 8, my translation

Hirano's (2012) position of dividuals is supported by psychological and social preferences recognized among Japanese. Tsuji (1999) argues that young speakers shift and change identities quite comfortably. This phenomenon, what Tsuji calls the "flipper tendency," illustrates that Japanese speakers find comfort in selecting different identities when situated in different social groups. A speaker holding this flipper tendency possesses multiple selves, and depending on the context, readily engages in varying human relationships by switching and transforming identities. Tsuji concludes that Japanese speakers find little need to live as a single coherent self; rather, they exhibit a desire for multiplicity.

In this chapter, I have introduced self in traditional Japanese language studies, followed by Watsuji's (1990a [1962]) concept of interdependent self. Also reviewed are Ueno's (2005) deconstruction of identity and Hirano's (2012) view of self approached from literature. These views toward the self are not limited to works selected here from Japanese studies; they share similarities with Western approaches, giving the impression of mutual integration. Significantly, some of the linguistic and philosophical approaches in Japanese studies predate what later develops in Western sociolinguistics and interactional linguistics. Although Japanese scholarly work remains largely a niche interest outside Japan, recognizing differences and similarities in academia across nations, in the spirit of hybridity, is expected to add to our theme of exploring the concept of self. To appropriately answer the question of global applicability of the concepts of self reported here as well as the empty and yet populated self proposed in this work, however, must await future studies.

PART 3

Analysis: Across Japanese and Translation Texts

CHAPTER 7

Presenting Aspects of Self through Person Expressions

This chapter investigates one of the ways through which the self is linguistically presented across Japanese and English translation texts. Our ontological pursuit involves the phenomenon of linguistic subjectivity spanning lexical, grammatical, and discursive phenomena, but person expressions allow direct access to how the self is or is not portrayed across languages. Two specific phenomena are focused on, i.e., variable forms of first-person expressions and terms referring to different dramatic persons.

1 Variability in First-Person Expressions

In Japanese, a number of family terms and other self-designating nouns are used for self-reference. The use of these terms also extends to fictive circumstances, what Suzuki (1978) calls "other-oriented self designation." Although these expressions refer to the self, they are beyond our immediate concern. In this section I concentrate on limited cases of first-person referencing terms, primarily *watashi* 'I' and its non-use as the zero form, and *jibun* 'self'.

In Maynard (2007), I argue that in Japanese, a variety of first-person references project different perspectivized appearances, i.e., ways of being viewed from different perspectives, and that they linguistically realize multiple and transient selves. I also posit that different expressions reflect and reinforce multiple aspects of our selves, echoing their multivoicedness. Multiple self-appearances are presented by the zero-form, *watashi* 'I', and *jibun* 'self', and consequently different images of the self emerge. Based on the selves projected from different perspectives, the partner comes to construct specific aspects of the speaker in interaction (Maynard 2007). Linguistic forms used for self-presentation illustrate the process through which an empty self in an empty place emerges bearing its multiple aspects. The zero-form offers the clearest indication that the self is empty only to be filled with emerging aspects, while *watashi* and *jibun* mark the objectified outer self and reflexive inner self, respectively.

1.1 Background: Subjectivity in Person Expressions

Self-referencing terms in Japanese are varied, with specific forms chosen depending on how the self wants to present itself. In conversation, different forms may be chosen all within a single speaking turn, reflecting different subjectivity-supported aspects of the self, while in written discourse these forms achieve effective portrayals of the self as speaker and dramatic person. For female speakers, the usual choices are *watakushi*, *watashi*, and *atashi*; for male speakers, *watakushi*, *watashi*, *boku*, and *ore*, among others are available. Primary features associated with these self-referencing terms are *watakushi* considered to be very formal, *watashi* used in formal masculine style and formal and casual feminine style, casual *atashi* primarily used by female speakers, blunt *ore* primarily used by male speakers, and *boku* being casual, mostly used by male speakers.[1]

According to Shinmura (1998), *watashi* is both noun and pronoun. As a noun, listed meanings include (1) matters related only to oneself in the context of the general public, (2) matters that are hidden, and (3) thoughts related to one's own interest and benefit. *Watashi* is also listed as a self-referencing pronoun. It is fair to assert that, unlike the English *I*, *watashi* functions primarily as a noun, semantically implying those features listed above.

Japanese expressions of the self have been extensively studied and here I touch upon only a few works that discuss how the self selects specific forms. First-person expressions are closely related to the speaker's personal and emotional distance from the partner as well as social standing (Maynard 2007). The choice is motivated by the self's creative desire to present a specific kind of self in any given interaction. Likewise, Horii (2015) reminds us that the choice of self-expression is not automatic, sometimes posing problems for speakers. For example, a junior high school boy is ordinarily faced with a sensitive choice of *boku*, *ore*, and *jibun*. Notably, self-expressions cannot be purely objectively determined, as noted in Horii's statement below.

> The self-referencing expression is not chosen in advance on the basis of objective fact, but is decided based on each occasion. In other words, personal pronouns provide a measure for assessing the level of the subjective nature of each communication.
>
> HORII 2015: 67, my translation

---

1 The features associated with first-person pronouns given here are prescriptive in nature (Maynard 2007; Millicia 2019). Japanese pronouns are known to be used across genders, for example, *boku* by a female speaker and *atashi* by an effeminate *onee* speaker (Maynard 2007, 2016).

SturtzSreetharan (2009) examines Japanese males' uses of first- and second-person pronouns and points out that men use pronouns not so much to express masculinity but more creatively to manage and to achieve specific conversational work across various topics. Lee and Yonezawa (2008) in analyzing 12 pairs of Japanese conversation, focus on overt forms of first- and second-person expressions. They note that these expressions not only index the speaker's social relationships but also signal contrastiveness, emphasis, and level of emotional involvement. Moreover, person expressions are associated with the speaker's commitment to the utterance as observed in floor-taking strategies and the personalization of discourse topics (Lee and Yonezawa 2008).

The difficulty in translating Japanese first-person expressions has been widely noted. Translators take stylistic and interpersonal factors into account when selecting first-person equivalencies. For example, Konosu (2018) calls attention to the difficulty in choosing from multiple Japanese expressions for the English *I*, i.e., *watashi, watakushi, atai, achiki, ore, oira, oidon, washi, wate,* and *wagahai,* and states that an appropriate style is chosen depending on the specific situation created in the translation text. Likewise, Matsuoka (2016) reports that when translating the works of Shakespeare, she chooses *ore* 'I (blunt, primarily used by male speakers)' when the dramatic person refers to himself in his thoughts, *boku* 'I (primarily used by male speakers)' when conversing with his lover, and *watashi* 'I' when speaking to a superior.

Discussing the nature of indexical signs as she incorporates Japanese person-expressions in her study, Jaszczolt (2016) argues that setting up a category of indexicals in the traditional sense (Kaplan 1979) is problematic. In various natural languages it is impossible to identify a lexical element uniquely associated with a specific indexical role. Jaszczolt concludes that because indexical signs, including the pronoun *I*, lack universal support in natural languages, connecting *I* to a universal concept of the self is misguided. Christofaki (2018) analyzes first-person reference forms in Japanese, asking what "facets" of the self these forms reveal. Beyond direct referentiality, Japanese self-expressions convey conceptual and expressive meanings which communicate different facets of the self. Christofaki concludes that these facets suggest a cross-culturally comparable self, concluding that the Japanese self does not contradict a universally definable concept of the self. I question this assumption as I engage in the theme of exploring the self across Japanese and English.

From cognitive linguistics, the idea of a split self in English offers guidance to questions on the self (Lakoff 1996). Following traditional semantics, in a sentence such as *I washed myself*, *I* and *myself* are co-referential, and this is why a sentence such as **I washed me* is ungrammatical. However, as soon as we encounter sentences (1) and (2), the judgment based on co-referentiality becomes inadequate.

(1) If I were you, I'd hate me.

(2) If I were you, I'd hate myself.

Both sentences are grammatical, but semantically different. Lakoff (1996) points out that in (1), *me* refers to the objectified "me" from the point of view of "you." In (2) *myself* refers to a self that is viewed from "I" (who assumes "you"). Both *me* and *myself* are co-referential with *I*, but they are viewed differently. Here the self as evidenced in English is split into "me" and "myself."

In cognitive stylistics, Emmott (2002) takes the position that analyses of split selves in narratives require more than what cognitive linguistics offers. After reviewing developments in cognitive studies such as the container metaphor (Lakoff and Johnson, 1980), the mental space theory (Fauconnier and Sweetser 1996), and text worlds (Werth 1999), Emmott insists that a deeper understanding of the split-selves phenomenon can be reached by applying principles available in narrative theory, for example, the narrative point of view. Emmott (1997) proposes that narratives involve contextual frames, enactors as well as character constructs where enactors refer to different versions of a character in different contexts. In narrative discourse, the phenomenon of split selves is notable, especially in flashbacks (Emmott 1997) and paralysis narratives (Emmott 2002).[2]

1.2   First-Person Expressions and Aspects of the Self

Sentences (3) through (8) employ three basic forms of self-reference, the zero-form, *watashi* 'I' and *jibun* 'self'. First, in (3) and (4), the self, the locutionary person engaging in language activity, is presented in a zero-form. The self who assumes the speaker's role is hidden and only indirectly identifiable. When the speaker is objectified, *watashi* surfaces with the topic marker *wa* as in (5) and (6). *Watashi* can also appear as an object of hate as in (3), (5), and (7). In addition, the reflexive noun *jibun* may be used with the topic marker *wa* as in (7) and (8). *Jibun*, foregrounding the inner self, can also appear as an object of hate as in (6) and (8). Although (7) and (8) are less natural than others, it is not impossible to assume appropriate contexts for them.

---

[2] I should add here that, although limited, contrastive analyses of first-person pronouns across languages are available. As an example, Fløttum (2006) observes more frequent uses of first-person pronouns in Norwegian than in English academic writing, including the use of *vi* 'we' for the purpose of involving the reader as a collaborator in a joint activity.

(3) *Watashi-ga kirai da.*
    I-OBJ   hate
    '(I) hate me.'

(4) *Jibun-ga kirai da.*
    self-OBJ hate
    '(I) hate my self.'

(5) *Watashi-wa watashi-ga kirai da.*
    I-TOP   I-OBJ   hate
    'I hate me.'

(6) *Watashi-wa jibun-ga kirai da.*
    I-TOP   self-OBJ hate
    'I hate my self.'

(7) *Jibun-wa watashi-ga kirai da*
    self-TOP I-OBJ   hate
    'I myself hate me.'

(8) *Jibun-wa jibun-ga kirai da.*
    self-TOP self-OBJ hate
    'I myself hate my self.'

Semantically, it is possible to identify the objectified self associated with *watashi* and the inner self associated with *jibun* in the following sense. The inner self is viewed from the inside, has access to inner feelings, and is mostly unconcerned with others' views. On the other hand, the objectified self is viewed from the outside of the self, is used to present the self to the outside, and is concerned with how one is viewed by others. More specifically, *watashi* appears overtly when (1) the self bears the feature of the self-identifying objectified self, (2) the self is foregrounded in the context, (3) a specific mention assists discourse organization, and (4) the self's personal voice needs foregrounding. *Jibun* is used when (1) the self reflectively reaches for the inner self, (2) the inner self needs to be clearly projected (as in the case of contrast), and (3) the presentation of the reflexive inner self creates an interactionally and socially favorable effect (as in *jibun* functioning as 'I'). The zero-form appears at the zero point to present the self as a speaker, where there is no need for specific mention. At this point the self is unspecified and remains empty.

Now, regarding variability in the use of first-person expressions, I should make a few points. The same speaker may use different self-referencing terms within any given discourse. In the source text (*R.P.G.*, 115) translated as (9) and (10), Minoru, presented as *I*, answers Officer Takegami's question. In (9), Minoru refers to himself as *boku* 'I (primarily used by male speakers)' in a socially and situationally expected style. However, in (10) a different style, i.e., the blunt masculine *ore*, is used.[3] This stylistic shift is explained as *His tone had changed, and he sounded more defiant*, but the attitudinal change conveyed by first-person references in the original is not fully conveyed. Notably, the original Japanese text makes a simple descriptive statement *Boku ga ore ni kawatta* 'Boku changed to ore'. Choices of self-reference terms in the original present an ambivalent self who occasionally becomes defiant. This way of self-presentation is missing in translation, although the use of *what the hell* in (10) communicates the general effect of the blunt style.

(9) *Shadow Family*, 76
"More or less. I'm (*boku*) renting an apartment near them, or I (zero) guess they're renting it for me."

(10) *Shadow Family*, 82
"Say, Officer?"
"What?"
"This is weird. **What the hell** has my involvement got to do with anything? You have your suspect. 'Kazumi' and I (*ore*) had nothing to do with the murder." **His tone had changed, and he sounded more defiant.**

Aspects of the self presented through different self-referencing terms observed in examples (3) through (10) can be associated with different enactors referring to different versions of the dramatic person (Emmott 1997, 2002). However, while English split selves are presented from different narrative perspectives,

---

3   A phenomenon where a single male speaker shifts first-person pronouns is not unusual. For example, in a television drama, a male speaker shifts among *ore*, *boku*, and *watashi* as he awkwardly presents himself to his potential girlfriend (Maynard 2001a). In a radio program *Ijuin Hikaru to Rajio to*, broadcast on TBS, March 1, 2021, the program host, Hikaru Ijuin, mentions that he switches between *ore* and *boku*, *ore* chosen particularly when he talks about his private life. He also mixes *jibun* when he refers to his own self. The program assistant Maki Arai observes that Ijuin chooses *ore* toward a younger guest but *boku* toward an older guest. These metalinguistic comments illustrate that different aspects of the self are routinely expressed in Japanese discourse.

the kind of selves presented with Japanese subjective self-referencing pronouns more clearly convey that they are interpersonally, psychologically, and situationally engaged.

1.3 *The Zero-Form versus* watashi

In Maynard (2007), I argue that the non-use of self-referencing expressions is associated with the "zero point" of the speaker, and *watashi* and *jibun* present selves connected to that point. This self is located at ground zero and its mention is avoided. The speaker's presence is communicated through varied linguistic means, but this presence does not surface in the form of a self-referencing term. In English, the "ecological self" (Neisser 1988) is realized as the zero-form, i.e., nonrepresentation. Although other languages are expected to have strategies that similarly function, in Japanese the non-use of first-person expressions occurs with a significant frequency.

The phenomenon of the zero-form has been discussed in pragmatics and linguistics under the heading of deletion. Traditionally, deletion is explained from the perspective of information recoverability. It should be noted, however, that in Japanese, recoverability is primarily expected from one's partner, and the speaker seems to feel free to delete relevant information by assuming that the partner will satisfactorily recover it. In other words, in contrast with English which tends to place more responsibility on the speaker, a relatively weighty responsibility is demanded from the communication partner (Hinds 1987). In fact, as noted in Maynard (2000, 2002), not saying everything is sometimes considered aesthetically more pleasing in Japanese as exemplified by the rhetorical figure of *futaku*.[4]

When the referent is already established as given information, *watashi* is usually deleted (more accurately, simply unused). The process of establishing a referent in discourse is known to involve at least two stages, establishment (first-mention) and maintenance (subsequent mentions) (Hinds 1984). The use and non-use of *watashi* along with the topic marker *wa* facilitate the topic organization in discourse, and realize the staging effect (Maynard 1980, 1987b). Although *watashi* may appear in the paragraph initial position to reactivate the topic, its repeated use is often avoided.

---

4   *Futaku* 'committing, referring to' is a traditional rhetorical figure and involves a method for expressing one's feelings by borrowing from something concrete (Amagasaki 1988). In the art of Japanese *waka*, for example, one strategy is to avoid directly stating what one feels; instead, the poet may borrow something concrete taken from nature, such as cherry blossoms, the moon, or a dewdrop.

When context requires self-identification for clarification, the self-identifying objectified self surfaces as *watashi*. Contextual factors requiring self-identification are of different kinds such as narrative structure, social context where the text is produced, or the immediate context of the interaction. Under these circumstances, especially when the self is viewed from someone other than the self, or from outside, the external self becomes a part of the self's aspect. The self is separated from the zero point, generating a sense of detachment and distance. This is where *watashi*, the objectified self, emerges.

Let us contrast the use of *watashi* and the zero-form in *Kitchin*. In (11), due to English grammatical constraints, *I* is repeated nine times. This portion of the source text (*Kitchin*, 12) provides information on Yuuichi, with no mention of *watashi* or *jibun*. The frequent use of the zero-form in the original contrasts with other sections with its frequent occurences, but that contrast is unavailable in translation.

(11) *Kitchen*, 8

He was a long-limbed, young man with pretty features. I (zero) didn't know anything more about him, but I (zero) might have seen him hard at work in the flower shop. Even after I (zero) got to know him a little I (zero) still had an impression of aloofness. No matter how nice his manner and expression, he seemed like a loner. I (zero) barely knew him, really.
It was raining that hazy spring night. A gentle, warm rain enveloped the neighborhood as I (zero) walked with directions in hand.
My apartment building and the one where the Tanabes lived were separated by Chuo Park. As I (zero) crossed through, I (zero) was inundated with the green smell of the night. I (zero) walked, sloshing down the shiny wet path that glittered with the colors of the rainbow.

Regarding the use and non-use of *watashi* 'I', perhaps Nakamura's (1991) work should be mentioned here. Pointing out that contemporary writings may start with the narrator's direct discourse, non-use of *watashi* increases dramatic impact. If at the outset *watashi* is avoided, the reader is held in suspense, thus rendering the text more interesting. The more obscure the description, the more curiosity is stirred. On the other hand, continues Nakamura, when *watashi* is used at the beginning of the novel, it signals that the self is significant indicating perhaps that the self's thoughts and feelings are the focus of the novel. Thus the use and the non-use of *watashi* reveal different ways the self interacts with narrative perspectives, stirring different kinds of anticipation.

Curiously, in the original text (*Kitchin*, 6) translated as (12), *watashi* appears in the initial sentence of the novel. This usage invites the reader to speculate that the narrating self will be the central theme.

(12) *Kitchen*, 3
   The place I (*watashi*) like best in this world is the kitchen. No matter where it is, no matter what kind, if it's a kitchen, it it's a place where they make food, it's fine with me (*watashi*).

Now, in (13), translation of the source text (*Kitchin*, 16), *watashi* appears three times. Here the narrating self conscientiously reflects on the self. It is possible to avoid using *watashi*, but its use presents the objectified self in contrast with the inner self. The first *watashi* foregrounds the objectified self as experienced by the self as narrator. The second *watashi* highlights the narrative voice, and the third *watashi* is required as the object case of the verb *yonda* 'invited'. The zero-form also appears in the source text for the English translated sentence *I've been looking at*. In (13) *I* and *me* are constantly chosen, and as a result, they fail to provide varied functions that *watashi* and the zero-form bring to the source text. Consequently, gaps occur in featured aspects of the self across Japanese and English translation texts.

(13) *Kitchen*, 10
   Suddenly, to see that the world was so large, the cosmos so black. The unbounded fascination of it, the unbounded loneliness ... For the first time, these days, **I** (*watashi*) was touching it with these hands, these eyes, **I've** (zero) **been looking at** the world half-blind, **I** (*watashi*) thought. "Why did you invite **me** (*watashi*) here?"

Another motivation for using *watashi* in *Kitchin* is when the self becomes the described target. In the original text (*Kitchin*, 16), we find *watashi* functioning as a noun modified by the modification clause *nete n no ka to omotta*, i.e., *nete n no ka to ootta watashi* 'I who thought he might be asleep'. Here the self functions on two levels, as first-person narrator and as the person experiencing *omotta* 'thought'. If the subordinate clause *nete n no ka to omotte furimuku to* 'when I looked back thinking that he might be asleep' were selected, the self's portrayal approached from two perspectives would not result. This is precisely the case in the target text (14) where the subordinate clause *Wondering if he had fallen back asleep* is used, resulting in an expressive gap.

(14) *Kitchen*, 40
   There was no response whatsoever. **Wondering if he had fallen back asleep,** I (*watashi*) looked over, and there was Yuichi, gaping at me.

Watashi may also appear with the case marker *ga*. Although the English *I*, except when it is emphasized, marks given information, in Japanese, *watashi ga*, marking new information, may appear. In the original text, *watashi ga itta* 'I said' (*Kitchin*, 35) indicates surprise at one's self, where the narrating self is separated from the experiencing self. This gives the impression that the self discovers another renewed self. The English translation in (15), *I cried out joyfully*, presents *I* as given information, failing to indicate the newly discovered self communicated in the source text.

(15) *Kitchen*, 23
   "Hello? Mikage?" The sound of his voice made me want to weep with nostalgia.
   "Long time no see?" I (*watashi ga*) **cried out joyfully.**

1.4 Jibun *for the Presentation of Inner Self*

When the context is such that the speaker reflects on the self, the inner self is foregrounded. This self is viewed inwardly, and is located close to the self's interior. *Jibun* is used for conveying this perspective, presenting the reflectively projected inner self.

A few words about *jibun* are in order. *Jibun* has two primary functions, as a pronoun and as a so-called self-reflexive noun. *Jibun*, preferred among young male speakers, especially when presenting the self's own view, may appear as first-person designation in a non-reflexive context. Used frequently but not exclusively in military or athletic discourse, *jibun* communicates a sense of humbleness. *Jibun* can also be used as second-person expressions, as in *Jibun mo iki tai n daro*? 'You want to go, too, right?'. The second-person *jibun* is excluded from the current discussion.

Nagata (1999) explains differences between sentences (16) and (17) in terms of point of view; (16) is viewed from Kiyoshi's point of view, and (17), from the narrator's.

(16) *Kiyoshi-wa   jibun-no koto-ga   kininattta.*
   Kiyoshi-TOP self-GEN matters-OBJ was concerned
   'Kiyoshi was concerned (with matters) about his self.'

(17) *Kiyoshi-wa kare-no koto-ga   kininatta.*
     Kiyoshi-TOP he-GEN matters-OBJ was concerned
     'Kiyoshi was concerned (with matters) about him.'

A similar observation can be made regarding a pair of sentences using *jibun* and *watashi*. *Jibun* is chosen when the self as a narrator takes the inner and inward perspective. In (18), the self depicted by *jibun* is the reflectively approached self. On the other hand, in (19) when the self is approached from the outside and indexed as *watashi no koto* '(matters about) me', the self-identifying objectified self is foregrounded.[5]

(18) ***Watashi**-wa **jibun**-no koto-ga   kininattta.*
     I-TOP   self-GEN matters-OBJ was concerned
     'I was concerned (with matters) about my self.'

(19) ***Watashi**-wa **watashi**-no koto-ga   kininatta.*
     I-TOP   I-GEN   matters-OBJ was concerned
     'I was concerned (with matters) about me.'

Hirose (1996, 2000, 2014) discusses *jibun* and other self-referencing forms from the perspective of private and public self. The private self refers to the speaker who has no addressee in mind, while the public self is the speaker who faces an addressee or has one in mind. Hirose argues that although in English there is no expression uniquely referring to the private self, in Japanese this self is captured as *jibun*.

I should point out here that my proposal for inner and objectified outer self regarding *jibun* and *watashi* respectively is founded on the self's perspective, and is not based on whether or not the self addresses another. Consider, for example, the sentence where both *watashi* and *jibun* occur, *Watashi wa sugu ni watashi/jibun no kimochi o tsutaeta* 'I conveyed my/self's feelings right away'. Here *watashi* and *jibun* represent different kinds of self approached from different self's perspectives, both of which may be used when addressing someone. Thus, *jibun no kimochi* 'self's feelings' can be publicly announced, revealing feelings reached from the inside, personally, and reflectively. Rather

---

5 In this regard, Sano (1997) explains that when *jibun no* 'self's' is used as in *Taro wa jibun no ushiro ni hon o oita* 'Taro placed a book behind the self', the reader more intimately senses Taro's feelings than otherwise, and as a result, it expresses the self's desire for speaker-partner empathy. In contrast, when *kare no* 'his' is used as in *Taro wa kare no ushiro ni hon o oita* 'Taro placed a book behind him', such effect is absent.

than taking a dualistic approach of private and public self, which in my view does not accurately portray the nature of Japanese first-person expressions, I approach the concept of self embracing both inner and objectified selves.

It should be mentioned here that *jibun* functions differently from English reflexives. Although reflexives are used in English expressions such as *hang oneself* and *enjoy oneself*, their Japanese counterparts, *kubi o tsuru* and *tanoshimu*, do not take *jibun* or any other reflexive expression. On the other hand, a Japanese counterpart for *I like myself* can take either *watashi* (as objectified self) or *jibun* (as inner self). For example, both *watashi ga suki da* 'I like me' and *jibun ga suki da* 'I like my self' may be used, the former presenting a self-identifying objectified self, and the latter, a reflectively projected inner self. In English, this differentiation is not practiced under normal circumstances.

In (20a) we find a case where *jibun* reflectively focuses on the self's inner aspect. The expression *jibun ga jibun dearu koto* 'the fact that my self is my self' brings the inner self to the fore through a deeply introspective inner thought. The translation in (20b), *just being myself*, does not communicate this introspective tone. (20b) moderately conveys the reflexive meaning, but not quite fully; in fact its back-translation may well take instead the form *watashi ga* in *watashi ga watashi dearu koto* 'the fact that I am I'.

(20) a. *Kitchin*, 40
Jibun ga jibun dearu koto ga mono ganashiku naru no da.
[(It is that) I become sad realizing the fact that my self is my self.]
b. *Kitchen*, 26
Just being myself made me terribly sad.

(21) is the translation of Japanese text (*Kitchin*, 54–55) which mixes the zero-form, *jibun*, and *watashi*. Through these choices, the narrating self successfully introduces different aspects of the self, i.e., the hidden speaker, the reflecting inner self, and the self-identifying objectified self. In (21), *I* is repeated eight times, and the multiple aspects of the self expressed in the original work are not sufficiently presented. In the source text zero-forms are used in reference to the hidden speaker; these are associated with the verbs *kizuku* 'notice, find', *tamageta* 'was surprised', *omotta* 'thought', and *miokutta* 'watched'. *Jibun* appears twice, while *watashi* is used three times.

(21) *Kitchen*, 34–35
But then, overpowered by their enormous weight, I (zero) found that tears were pouring down my cheeks and onto my blouse.

I (zero) was surprised. Am I (*jibun*) losing my mind? I (zero) wondered. It was like being falling-down drunk: my body was independent of me. Before I (*watashi*) knew it, tears were flooding out. I (*jibun*) felt myself turning bright red with embarrassment and (*watashi*) got off the bus. I (zero) watched it drive away, and then without thinking I (*watashi*) ducked into a poorly lit alley.

As examined above, different strategies are used for the first-person reference in the Japanese text. These variable forms populate the empty self whenever appropriate. Presenting multiple aspects of the Japanese self is not evident in the target text, because the preferred form in English is the stable *I* which identifies a consistent self.

2   Creativity in Person Expressions

2.1   *Transferred Self between Perspectives*

While *Kitchin* is a first-person novel, *Torikaeko Chenjiringu* is a third-person novel, and self-referencing forms in the latter appear with curious features. In particular, the observed perspective shift is not easily translated into English, and consequent expressive gaps across Japanese and translation texts are substantial. Kogito is the main dramatic person of *Torikaeko Chenjiringu*. The story is told from the narrator's perspective but the self-referencing *jibun* also appears. In the source text (*Torikaeko Chenjiringu*, 218–219), whose English translation is given in (22), *Kogito* is used once, and *jibun* appears twice along with the zero-form. By using *jibun*, instead of third-person expressions such as *Kogito no* 'Kogito's' or *kare no* 'his', this portion is presented as Kogito's inner thoughts. At this point, the self's perspective is transferred from third-person to first-person. Empathy is encouraged as the repeated use of *jibun* invites the reader's access to the self's inner feelings.

In the target text (22), as counterparts of the original zero-form, *jibun*, and *Kogito*, *he* appears four times, and *his*, *him*, and *Kogito*, once each. Each of these expressions consistently represents a third-person point of view, and the transitory nature of the transferred self generated in the Japanese source text is absent. In the Japanese text, by using the zero-form, third-person pronouns are avoided, and as a result, the self is not foregrounded. For example, *tada jibun ni naihatsu suru mono o itsukushinde iru* 'simply finding pleasure in the things that arose in self' is translated in (22) as *concentrate on giving tender nurture to the things that arose spontaneously in him*, where the third-person point of view is maintained.

(22) *The Changeling*, 297
>Ah, that sense of distance ... **He** (zero) had a notion that while they were all still running on the same track, so to speak, the younger generation had banded together and taken the lead, and **he** (*jibun*) was lagging a full lap behind them. Thus, in order to be able to relax once again among the books to **his** (zero) longtime home in Tokyo, **he** (zero) would give up trying to catch up with the young literati who were so far ahead and would instead **concentrate on giving tender nurture to the things that arose spontaneously in him** (*jibun*). To be sure, there was a measure of sadness there, too, but it was hard to distinguish it from an agreeably cozy feeling of quiet enjoyment. **Kogito** (*Kogito*) felt as though **he** (zero) would be able to live out the days to come, alone and marooned amid the faint glimmer of twilight, as tranquilly as someone already dead.

Similar observations can be made in (23) translated from the source text (*Torikaeko Chenjiring*, 218–219). In terms of the original discourse organization, the main participant is Kogito, who is presented three times as *Kogito*. Then, when Kogito's inner thoughts are presented, *jibun* appears four times, representing the first-person inner perspective. Kogito moves between third-person and first-person points of view. In translation (23), due to the English language restrictions, the third-person perspective is consistently taken through the use of *Kogito*, *he*, *his*, *him* and *himself*. Again, lost in the target text are the fluid Japanese perspective shifts between third- and first-person. Particularly noteworthy is that in the source text, instead of Kogito, *jibun* 'self' is used. The Japanese expression *sono yoona jibun ni kore o takusoo to shite* 'he was going to pass the baton to my self who is placed in such a circumstance' is translated as *he passed the baton of his unfinished work to Kogito*. The English target text maintains the third person perspective while the Japanese text reaches Kogito's inner feelings by identifying him as self.

(23) *The Changeling*, 305–306
>**Kogito** (*Kogito*) left the huge pile of papers next to the briefcase, thinking that when Chikashi came downstairs, **his** (zero) good intentions would be immediately evident: **he** (*jibun*) had decided to answer Goro's call to action, and leaving the papers out showed, implicitly, that **he** (zero) knew what had to be done and was ready, at long last, to do it. Still, now that **he** (zero) found **himself** (zero) face-to-face with Goro's posthumous manuscript, **he** (*jibun*) felt like an inexperienced, intimidated greenhorn, and **he** (zero) had major butterflies in **his** (zero) stomach at the mere thought of how **he** (zero) was going to deal with it. As **he** (zero) so often

did these days, he (*Kogito*) felt as if he (*jibun*) were somehow suspended in limbo, and he (zero) was bedeviled by a nagging worry that (compared with the ultraworldly Goro) he (zero) hadn't yet accumulated a sufficiently rich store of life experiences to tackle this challenge. Surely that quote from Rimbaud's letter—the secret code that had struck such a resonant chord for both of them—had been written down as a warning from Goro as he passed the baton of his unfinished work to Kogito (*jibun*). Realizing Goro's intent, Kogito (*Kogito*) was seized once again by a complicated sort of stage fright, and part of him (zero) wanted very much to chicken out.

Although *Torikaeko Chenjiring* takes the third-person point of view, it is also known that the story contains personal information about its author Kenzaburo Oe. Kogito is Oe himself, and Goroo is Juzo Itami, his brother-in-law, a renowned movie director who committed suicide by leaping from a building. In the novel, some other participants can be viewed as his family members, which the novel's readers are well aware of. The novel is not considered a confessional I-novel, but it contains a substantial amount of information that can be seen as Oe's personal confession. Given this background, for the creation of the overall novel's ambience, transferring perspectives between third- and first-person becomes critical. In English translation, the novel maintains a third-person point of view throughout. Differences across Japanese and English seriously influence the novel's overall impact, and we cannot ignore these gaps in translation between the transferred self and the stable self.

2.2 *Place-Sensitive Presentation of a Dramatic Person*

Investigating how dramatic persons are presented in Japanese in contrast with English texts, I examine the case of Konoha Inoue, the first-person narrator in the *Bungaku Shoojo* series. Konoha is referred to by other dramatic persons as *Konoha-kun* (with the friendly and casual vocative *-kun*), *Inoue* (the last name), *Konoha senpai* (*senpai* here marks someone senior in the school), *Konoha* (written in the Katakana script), and an intimacy-provoking *onii-chan* 'elder brother' (with an intimate vocative *-chan*). Multiple selves presented in different forms appear in an empty place only to be populated in multiple ways, depending on others' perspectives and attitudes. Emerging aspects of the self are realized through different reference and vocative forms used by other participants under different circumstances.

In the Japanese text (*"Bungaku Shoojo" to Dookoku no Junreisha*, 13) Konoha is called *Konoha-kun* by Tooko (the main dramatic person who is one year senior to Konoha). Konoha is called *Konoha senpai* by Takeda (a first-year student and junior to Konoha) in the source text (*"Bungaku Shoojo" to Dookoku no Junreisha*, 21), *Inoue* by Kotobuki (a female classmate) in the text (*"Bungaku Shoojo" to Dookoku no Junreisha*, 42), *onii-chan* by his mother and younger sister in the text (*"Bungaku Shoojo" to Dookoku no Junreisha*, 104). In the English translation given as (24) through (28), Konoha Inoue is translated as *Konoha* and occasionally Inoue when addressed by classmates. Konoha is firmly established as a stable self located in the place, and the story develops based on this understanding.

(24) *Book Girl and the Suicidal Mime*, 10
"Take these, **Konoha** (*Konoha-kun*). This is a direct order from your president!"

(25) *Book Girl and the Suicidal Mime*, 16
"Thank you, **Konoha** (*Konoha senpai*)!"
"Sure thing. It'll be a cinch, right, **Konoha** (*Konoha-kun*)?"

(26) *Book Girl and the Suicidal Mime*, 32
"So you have to pay for her, **Inoue** (*Inoue*)."

(27) *Book Girl and the Suicidal Mime*, 75
"**Konoha** (*Onii-chan*) you have a phone call."
My mom's voice sounded from downstairs.

Furthermore, from Miu's point of view, Konoha is referred to as *Konoha* (written in Katakana). Facing the unexpected use of Katakana for Konoha written in Kanji elsewhere, the reader senses a special relationship between Konoha and Miu.[6] In the novel, when Miu recollects what happened with Konoha, and when they actually meet again in the source text (*"Bungaku Shoojo" to Dookoku no Junreisha*, 56), *Konoha* in Katakana appears. Konoha is someone Miu has always felt intimate with, and this special meaning communicated by a switch of scripts is not reflected in the English translation.

---

6 The Katakana script substituted for normally used Hiragana and Kanji signals that something is out of the ordinary. It adds effects of unexpectedness and prominence to the discourse, often suggesting that there is something potentially significant about the phrase (Yasui 2000; Ishiguro 2007; Maynard 2012). Different scripts in different fonts and sizes are used in popular culture discourse for expressive purposes (Maynard 2012; Kinsui 2021).

(28) *Book Girl and the Wayfarer's Lamentation*, 43–44
   A lovely voice like a bell made of glass called my name exactly the way she used to.
   "**Konoha** (*Konoha* in Katakana)."
   Miu looked at me joyously, her eyes sparkling.
   Her lips curved into a gentle, indulgent smile.
   "You finally came to see me, huh, **Konoha** (*Konoha* in Katakana)?"

The Japanese novel makes use of a variety of reference and vocative forms while the English version uses only *Konoha* and *Inoue*. The Japanese empty self of Konoha Inoue emerges, transforms, and shifts as it undergoes different forms. The contrastive analysis approach makes it possible for us to appreciate the different ways of self-presentation across the source and target texts.

3   Reflections

In this chapter I have focused on the presentation of the first-person self-reference and the third-person reference to the portrayals of dramatic persons. For the presentation of the first-person self, we have observed that the self is presented through the zero-form, *watashi*, and *jibun* as well as *boku* and *ore*. These varied forms make it possible to create multiple aspects in the process of populating the empty self. These observations sharply illustrate the gaps found in the English text where personal pronouns are consistently and frequently used, and consequently, a stable self is presented without the variability available in the Japanese language. The English translation *Kitchen* where *I* is traced to Japanese *watashi*, the zero-form, and *jibun* is a case in point. Recall also the case of *The Changeling* presented in (22) and (23) where the consistency of the third-person perspective is maintained. Consequently, the shift across third- and first-person perspectives in the source text is lost. I should also add that although the English phenomenon of the split self reveals the self's complexity, the use of English reflexive pronouns does not fully render the multiplicity of self's aspects realized in the Japanese text.

The presentation of dramatic persons in a novel highlights another difference across two languages. The English target text identifies participants through a repeated use of proper nouns and personal pronouns, and the place is created on the basis of these designations. Konoha in the *Bungaku Shoojo* series, however, is presented in multiple ways. In the source text, depending on who refers to Konoha, Konoha takes on different forms reflecting multiple points of view. This decision is made by the narrating self, who populates the dramatic person's empty self based on personal, contextual, and creative needs.

Self-presentation through various means in Japanese reveals how the empty self is populated in diverse ways. The place where the self emerges is not predetermined, but becomes meaningful as it is actualized through a gradually forming self; the self and the place emerge in synergistic ways. The kind of self observed in the Japanese text is far different from the self emerging in the English text, a theme I continue to explore in the subsequent chapters.

CHAPTER 8

Perceptive and Receptive Self in Grammar

This chapter examines how the Japanese self perceives, receives, and experiences within the place. Focused are expressions that imply the perceptive and receptive self, i.e., grammatical features of the passive sentence and the *-te kureru* 'someone gives to self' structure. Although the self emerges as perceptive and receptive through these expressions, English translation takes the agent-does structure where the self as the agent of action is prominently presented.

1 Unmentioned Perceptive Self

1.1 *Perceptively Experiencing the Situation*

A Japanese sentence is often structured from the perspective of the recipient of others' actions. For example, in *Ginga Tetsudoo no Yoru*, Jobanni often goes unmentioned and is only implicitly and indirectly presented as the recipient of others' actions. In contrast, in the English translation, Jobanni is often featured as the agent of action. In other words, in Japanese the perceiver's as well as the receiver's perspective is centrally focused, while in English the self as instigator is prominently identified. Of note here, as I discuss later, is that it is possible in English translation to describe or imply the self as an experiencer, and in some translations such a framework is chosen. In terms of preference, however, we find undeniable differences.

In (1a), *Zaneri ga yahari furikaette mite imashita* 'As expected, Zaneri turned around and was looking back at him, too' is a description of Zaneri's action which is observed by Jobanni. However, in translation texts (1b) through (1e), it is Jobanni's (Giovanni's) action that is centrally focused. In all translations, the transitive verb *saw* is chosen, with Jobanni being the agent of the action, as in *As he went around the corner, he looked back and saw Zanelli looking back too* in (1b). Back-translating (1b) would result in *Kare wa kado o magatta toki furikaeri, Zaneri mo furikaette mite iru no o mita* 'when he turned the corner, he looked back and saw Zaneri who turned around and was looking back at him, too,' with Jobanni as the agent of *mita* 'saw', resulting in a structure different from that of the source text.

(1) a. *Ginga Tetsudoo no Yoru*, 67
Machi kado o magaru toki, furikaette mimashitara, **Zaneri ga yahari furikaette mite imashita.**
[When he turned the corner, he looked back, and as expected, Zaneri turned around, and was looking back at him, too.]
b. *Night Train to the Stars*, 43
As he went around the corner, he looked back and saw Zanelli looking back too.
c. *Night on the Galactic Railroad & Other Stories from Ihatov*, 58
Giovanni paused to look behind him and **saw** that while Zanelli was still staring in his direction (...)
d. *Eigo de Yomu Ginga Tetsudoo no Yoru*, 55
He turned the corner, looking back at them and **saw** Zanelli looking back too.
e. *Milky Way Railroad*, 37
They all began to whistle behind his back and then, as Kenji looked behind at the next corner, he **saw** that Akira had turned around.

Let us focus on (2a) where *onaji kumi no shichi hachinin* 'seven or eight of his classmates' functions as agent of the action as well as topic. The English translation structures it so that Jobanni is the agent, except in (2d) which follows a structure similar to the Japanese text. It is not impossible in English to implicitly communicate Jobanni's perceptive experience, but the preferred translation positions Jobanni as the agent of an action as in *he found* in (2b), *he noticed* in (2c), and *Kenji found* in (2e). (2d) describes Jobanni's classmates without mentioning Jobanni as *he*, being structurally similar to the source text. Here, as in the Japanese, Jobanni is hidden but implied as a perceptively experiencing self. This structure can be considered a case of shining through (Teich 2003) in a broad sense, given that it is not a preferred structure in the target language.

(2) a. *Ginga Tetsudoo no Yoru*, 57
Jobanni ga gakkoo no mon o deru toki, **onaji kumi no shichi hachinin** wa ie e kaera zu, Kamupanerura o mannaka ni shite kootei no sumi no sakura no ki no tokoro ni atsumatte imashita.
[When Jobanni was going out of the school gate, seven or eight of his classmates, instead of going back home, gathered together with Kamupanerura being the center (of the group), near a cherry tree standing in a corner of the school ground.]

b. *Night Train to the Stars*, 23
As Giovanni was going out of the school gate **he found** that seven or eight of his classmates had not gone straight home but were gathered in a group around Campanella near an ornamental cherry tree at the edge of the school yard.

c. *Night on the Galactic Railroad & Other Stories from Ihatov*, 48
As Giovanni was passing through the school gates, **he noticed** a group of seven or eight boys standing under a cherry blossom tree in the school yard. In the center of the group was Campanella.

d. *Eigo de Yomu Ginga Tetsudoo no Yoru*, 23
As Giovanni was walking out the school gate, seven or eight children from his class were gathered in the yard, forming a circle around Campanella by the cherry blossom tree in the corner.

e. *Milky Way Railroad*, 19
As he went out the schoolhouse gate, **Kenji found** seven or eight of his classmates who, instead of going home, had gathered around Minoru by the cherry tree in the corner of the school garden.

(3a) portrays Jobanni responding to what is happening in the place. In (3b), in contrast, Jobanni's self is directly involved in the situation. In the source text, *oshigoto ga hidokatta roo* 'your work must have been hard' describes his work with no mention of Jobanni. In each English translation, however, Jobanni is addressed as *you* being the agent, e.g., *you must have worked so hard today* in (3d).

(3) a. *Ginga Tetsudoo no Yoru*, 59
"Aa, Jobanni, **oshigoto ga hidokatta roo**."
[Ah, Jobanni, your work must have been hard.]

b. *Night Train to the Stars*, 27
"Is it you, Giovanni? I'm sure **you** must be awfully tired from your work."

c. *Night on the Galactic Railroad & Other Stories from Ihatov*, 50
"Have you just returned from work? **You** must be exhausted."

d. *Eigo de Yomu Ginga Tetsudoo no Yoru*, 29
'Oh Giovanni, **you must have worked so hard today**.'

e. *Milky Way Railroad*, 24
"Ah—Kenji, **you** must have had a rough day."

The unmentioned perceptive self can also be observed in the case of existential verbs *iru* and *aru*. It is known that certain existential verbs are translated into English verbs indicating possession, as shown in (4b) through (4e), where *iru* in

(4a) is translated into *they have* and *they have got*. This phenomenon illustrates that while the Japanese self is presented as a receptive experiencer, the English self tends to be presented as the agent of action.

(4) a. *Ginga Tetsudoo no Yoru*, 61
 "Zaueru to yuu inu ga **iru** yo."
 [A dog called Zaueru, there is.]
 b. *Night Train to the Stars*, 31
 "**They've got** a dog called Sauer."
 c. *Night on the Galactic Railroad & Other Stories from Ihatov*, 53
 "**They have** a dog called Sauer (...)"
 d. *Eigo de Yomu Ginga Tetsudoo no Yoru*, 37
 '**They've got** a dog named Sauer (...)'
 e. *Milky Way Railroad*, 27
 "**They have** a dog called Pooch."

In (5a), *yasunde ita no deshita* '(it was that) she was resting' appears with the *no da* expression which adds an explanatory tone. In translation, however, *Giovanni (...) found* and *he found* are used in (5b) and (5e). In (5c), the transitive verb *to see* is chosen, again with Jobanni being the agent. In (5d), *his mother* is the grammatical subject with no mention of Jobanni, showing a structure similar to the source text. It is possible to use this structure in English, but the agent-does structure is preferred in other translations.

(5) a. *Ginga Tetsudoo no Yoru*, 59
 Jobanni wa genkan o agatte ikimasu to, Jobanni no okkasan ga sugu iriguchi no heya ni shiroi nuno o kabutte **yasunde ita no deshita.**
 [When Jobanni entered through the entranceway, (it was that) Jobanni's mother was resting with a white cloth over her in the room next to the entrance.]
 b. *Night Train to the Stars*, 27
 Giovanni stepped up indoors and found his mother in the room immediately inside, lying with a white sheet over her.
 c. *Night on the Galactic Railroad & Other Stories from Ihatov*, 50–51
 Giovanni's mother's room was the one closest to the entranceway. He went inside **to see** her resting, covered in a white sheet.
 d. *Eigo de Yomu Ginga Tetsudoo no Yoru*, 29
 Giovanni stepped up from the entryway onto the floor. **His mother** was resting in the front room with a white cloth over her face.

e. *Milky Way Railroad*, 23–24
When Kenji came in, **he found** his mother resting in the front room with a white cloth wrapped around her head.

The contrast in a preference for the self as a perceptive experiencer versus the self as an agent of action is observed in other works as well. In (6a) taken from *Manatsu no Hooteishiki*, Kyoohei's various experiences depict him as being a perceptive experiencer. Although Kyoohei's self remains unmentioned, we clearly sense his presence. *Suiheisen no ue ni wa, sofuto kuriimu no yoona kumo ga ukande iru* 'Above the horizon, a cloud resembling a soft ice cream (cone) is floating' in (6a) simply describes what comes into Kyoohei's view. The reader vicariously undergoes Kyoohei's perceptive experiences, sharing the sentiment. This situational description brings forth the *futaku* effect, as the self's personal feelings are empathetically shared with the reader.[1] English translation in (6b), *Just about the horizon he saw billowing clouds, white like ice cream*, positions Kyoohei as an overt agent.

(6) a. *Manatsu no Hooteishiki*, 413
Mado no soto o nagareru keshiki ni me o yatta. Kaimen ga hikatte ita. **Suiheisen no ue ni wa, sofuto kuriimu no yoona kumo ga ukande iru.**
[He cast his eyes on the scenery passing by outside of the window. The ocean was sparking in the sunlight. Above the horizon, a cloud resembling a soft ice cream (cone) is floating.]
b. *A Midsummer's Equation*, 358
Kyohei looked out the window and watched the scenery going by. The ocean sparkled in the sunlight. **Just about the horizon he saw billowing clouds, white like ice cream.**

The expression *soba ni hito no tatsu kehai ga shita* 'a sense of someone standing nearby was there' in the source text (7a) does not overtly mark who is experiencing this perception. Yet in the target text (7b), *Kyohei slurped at his drink, becoming aware of someone standing next to him* clearly presents Kyoohei as the agent. Here again, the unmentioned self in the original overtly appears in translation.

(7) a. *Manatsu no Hooteishiki*, 307
Juusu o nonde itara, **soba ni hito no tatsu kehai ga shita.** Kao o ageru to, Yukawa ga tatte ita.

---

1 *Futaku* 'committing, referring to' is a traditional rhetorical figure and involves a method for expressing one's feelings by borrowing from something concrete (Amagasaki 1988).

"Att, Hakase."
[While drinking juice, a sense of someone standing nearby was there. As he looked up, Yukawa was standing there.]
["Ah, Professor."]
b. *A Midsummer's Equation*, 266
Kyohei slurped at his drink, becoming aware of someone standing next to him. He looked up. "Hey, Professor!"

1.2   *Unmentioned Self and Sense-Based Expressions*

Similar to the observations above, Japanese sense-based intransitive verbs, such as *mieru* 'to be seen, something can be seen', *wakaru* 'to be understood, something can be understood', and *kikoeru* 'to be heard, something can be heard' are used without overtly mentioning the perceiving self.[2] In contrast, the English translation often prefers to foreground the experiencing person as an agent. In *Manatsu no Hooteishiki*, quite a few examples of sense-based expressions appear as Kyoohei undergoes many noteworthy experiences. The verb *mieta* 'was seen, something could be seen' in (8a) appears in the target text (8b) as a transitive verb, i.e., *he spotted*.

(8) a. *Manatsu no Hooteishiki*, 80
Nomi nagara, doo shiyoo ka to kangaete itara, Yukawa ga aruite kuru no ga **mieta**.
[While drinking, he was wondering what to do, and then Yukawa walking down the street (toward him) was seen.]
b. *A Midsummer's Equation*, 68–69
(...) considering his next move, when **he spotted** Yukawa walking down the road.

Let us contrast how two cases of the sense-based expression *wakatta* 'was understood, something could be understood' are translated. The verb *wakatta* in the source text (*Manatsu no Hooteishiki*, 412) is translated with a transitive verb as *he finally understood* in (9). In the original text, Kyoohei as the experiencing self is not mentioned, and instead, only Kyoohei's thoughts are described. Interestingly, *wakatta* in the Japanese text (*Manatsu no Hooteishiki*, 104) is not translated with Kyoohei as the subject of a transitive verb in the target text (10). The translation *The water was perfectly clear, and light from the*

---

2 For additional information on transitive and intransitive verbs, see Makino and Tsutsui (1989, 1995) and Maynard (1990a, 2009).

sun above refracted in a hundred different angles, each creating a different color is structured such that the grammatical subjects, water and light, are followed by the verb *create*. Here, as in the source text, Kyoohei is unmentioned. However, Kyoohei's implied self, clearly sensed through the use of the sense-based transitive verb *wakatta* 'was understood', is not fully reflected in the translation.

(9)   *A Midsummer's Equation*, 357
Kyohei looked up at Yukawa and took a deep breath. It felt like a little light had flickered back on in his chest. The weight he had felt pressing down on him for the last several days lifted. Now **he finally understood** (*wakatta*) why he'd needed to talk to Yukawa so much. It was because he wanted to hear this.

(10)   *A Midsummer's Equation*, 90
On his screen he could see a glimmering undersea world of reds, blues, and greens. The seafloor looked like a massive stained-glass window. **The water was perfectly clear, and light from the sun above refracted in a hundred different angles, each creating a different color** (*wakatta*).

In *Ginga Tetsudoo no Yoru*, another perception-based verb *kikoeru* 'is heard, something can be heard' illustrates a similar phenomenon. The expression *kikoete kuru no deshita* '(it was that) they (the sounds coming toward the self) were heard' in (11a) is translated as *he could faintly pick up* in (11c), *He could faintly hear* in (11d), and *very faintly he could hear* in (11e). Back-translation, e.g., *kare wa kasuka ni kiita* 'he faintly heard', results in a structure where Jobanni is the agent of the action. In the Japanese original, the unmentioned self is presented as someone who undergoes perception-based experiences. The translation *and the faint sounds of children (...) reached him* in (11b) takes a structure similar to the source text. Observing varied uses of sentence structures in translation, choices are not based only on grammatical requirements nor personal preferences. Translators seem to choose an ideal style by mixing different sentence structures and perspectives within a specific span of discourse. Nonetheless, a general preference toward perception-based experiences is recognized in the Japanese text.

(11)   a. *Ginga Tetsudoo no Yoru*, 68–69
(...) kodomora no utau koe ya kuchibue, kiregire no sakebigoe mo kasuka ni **kikoete kuru no deshita**.
[(...) (it was that) the faint sounds of children singing and whistling, and broken cries too coming toward the self were heard.]

b. *Night Train to the Stars*, 45
(...) **and the faint sounds of children singing and whistling, and broken cries, reached him** from below.

c. *Night on the Galactic Railroad & Other Stories from Ihatov*, 59
Even from way up on the hilltop, **he could faintly pick up** the sounds of children singing.

d. *Eigo de Yomu Ginga Tetsudoo no Yoru*, 61
He could faintly hear snatches of children's screams and bits of whistles and songs.

e. *Milky Way Railroad*, 40
Very faintly he could hear the whistling and singing of the children (...)

2 Receptive Emotive Self and Subjective Passives

This section focuses on subjective and emotive passives, i.e., the usage of passives where the self is emotively influenced by the result of an unavoidable action. In passive sentences, the influenced self is often unmentioned, but its emotive meanings are significant. In Japanese, both transitive and intransitive verbs are passivized to convey the self's subjective involvement. Japanese passives may sometimes be translated into English passives, but the associated emotion is only limitedly reflected in English counterparts, resulting in substantial gaps in expressive equivalence.

Onoe (1999) captures the fundamental meaning of Japanese passives as "being influenced." He explains that passives reflect a view of the self being forced into a certain position against the self's will. In a similar vein, Tsuboi (2002) states that the basic function of passives is that, by capturing the changes caused by certain action, the experiencer comments on that change. Sakahara (2003) lists the effects of passives including (1) topic shift from agent to non-agent, (2) deprioritizing the agent, and (3) a diminished sense of transitivity. In Maynard (2004a, 2005c), I have discussed rhetorical functions of passives in discourse, and listed (1) presenting a description of the resultant situation, (2) enhancing emotive expression, and (3) creating metalinguistic effects.

English passive sentences take intransitive verbs, and often describe matters with minimal emotive response. Expressions such as *Dinner is served at 7:00* and *A boy was killed in an automobile accident* indirectly present information. These passives do not foreground a sense of subjectivity where the self receptively experiences the incident. The emotive meaning of Japanese pas-

PERCEPTIVE AND RECEPTIVE SELF IN GRAMMAR 159

sives adds aspects to the otherwise empty self, populating the self with different kinds of self absent in the target text.

Let us focus on a few examples taken from *Suzumiya Haruhi no Yuuutsu*. In (12a) Kyon is the emotive self passively experiencing the consequence of Haruhi's action. The expression *Ryoote made awasareta* '(I was clasped hands) I suffered from her clasping her hands together' is translated as *She even clasped her hands together* in (12b), and *iwarete mo na* '(even though I'm told so) I suffer from her saying so' in (13a) is translated as *Easy for you to say* in (13b), where Haruhi is presented as the person doing the pleading. The verbs used in the original are *ryoote o awasu* 'to clasp hands together' and *yuu* 'to say', the former being transitive verb plus the object case and the latter, the intransitive verb. It is difficult to find corresponding passive expressions in the target text. Kyon's self emotively undergoes experiences involving Haruhi, but such portrayal is absent. Instead, English descriptions centralize Haruhi as an agent.

(12) a. *Suzumiya Haruhi no Yuuutsu*, 40
"Onegai."
Ryoote made awasareta.
["Please."]
[(I was clasped hands) I suffered from her clasping her hands together.]
b. *The Melancholy of Haruhi Suzumiya*, 25
"Pretty please?"
She even clasped her hands together.

(13) a. *Suzumiya Haruhi no Yuuutsu*, 40
Yoroshiku ne, to **iwarete mo na.**
[I'm counting on you, (even though I'm told so) I suffer from her saying so.]
b. *The Melancholy of Haruhi Suzumiya*, 25
Counting on me huh? **Easy for you to say.**

In (14a) *meireisareta ore* 'I who was ordered' is translated as *After ordering us* in (14b), wherein Haruhi is the agent. The passivity expressed in the source text is lost, and as a result, Kyon's discomfort being ordered around is not sufficiently communicated. It is possible in English to use a passive form, e.g., *After being ordered by Haruhi to follow her*, but such a passive construction is not preferred.

(14) a. *Suzumiya Haruhi no Yuuutsu*, 70
Tsuite kinasai, to **meireisareta ore** to Asahina-san o hikitsurete Haruhi ga mukatta saki wa, niken tonari no konpyuuta kenkyuubu datta.

[Taking along me and Asahina who were ordered to follow her, the place Haruhi headed was the Computer Research Society two doors down.]

b. *The Melancholy of Haruhi Suzumiya*, 45
After ordering us to follow her, Haruhi led Asahina and me to our destination, the Computer Research Society two doors down.

In *Ginga Tetsudoo on Yoru*, we find passive expressions occurring with the verb *naru* 'become'. *Naru* implies that things are destined to happen, communicating the self's passive acceptance. The combination of the passive expression and *naru* generates a receptively accepting attitude. *Itachi ni mitsukatte taberare sooni natta* 'was found by a weasel and was about to be eaten by it' in (15a) is such an example. Here the scorpion is about to suffer from the weasel's action. In its English translations two texts incorporate a passive perspective, i.e., *he found himself cornered by a weasel* in (15c) and *he was caught by a weasel and it looked like he was going to be eaten all up* in (15d). The other two texts describe the weasel as an agent of the action, i.e., *a weasel found it and was about to eat it* in (15b) and *a weasel found the scorpion and was about to eat him up* in (15e).

Likewise in another sentence in (15a), *tootoo itachi ni osaerare sooni natta* 'in the end it was about to be pinned down by a weasel' takes the combination of the passive expression and *naru*. This is translated with the weasel as an agent, i.e., *the weasel was just about to leap on it* in (15b) and *the weasel seemed to have him cornered* in (15e). In (15d), however, the scorpion is the passive recipient, i.e., *he was about to be pinned down by the weasel*. In (15c), *he ran but could not escape it* illustrates how the scorpion responds to the weasel's attack. In target texts the weasel is an agent of the action in some cases while in others the scorpion is passively influenced by the weasel.

In the source text in (15a) and elsewhere in *Ginga Tetsudoo no Yoru*, the scorpion is consistently portrayed as the receptive experiencer undergoing an unavoidable misfortune. The combination of a passive expression and *naru* emphasizes the sense of victimization, but this is not consistently portrayed in the target texts. Again, it is possible to use a passive construction in English, but it is not preferred across all texts here, and the sense of victimization is not consistently communicated.

(15) a. *Ginga Tetsudoo no Yoru*, 117
"Suruto aru hi, **itachi ni mitsukatte taberare sooni natta** n desu tte. Sasori wa isshoo kenmei nigete nigeta keredo, **tootoo itachi ni osaerare sooni natta** wa."

["Then one day, (they say that) it was found by a weasel and was about to be eaten by it. The scorpion ran and ran away, but in the end it was about to be pinned down by the weasel."]
  b. *Night Train to the Stars*, 145
  "One day **a weasel found it and was about to eat it.** So the scorpion ran and ran for all it was worth. In the end, **the weasel was just about to leap on it** (...)"
  c. *Night on the Galactic Railroad & Other Stories from Ihatov*, 101
  "Then one day **he found himself cornered by a weasel.** Fearing for his life, **he ran but could not escape it.**"
  d. *Eigo de Yomu Ginga Tetsudoo no Yoru*, 203
  'Then one day **he was caught by a weasel and it looked like he was going to be eaten all up** himself. He tried to get away with all his might and **he was about to be pinned down by the weasel** (...)'
  e. *Milky Way Railroad*, 112
  "Then one day **a weasel found the scorpion and was about to eat him up.** The scorpion ran away as fast as he could, but finally **the weasel seemed to have him cornered.**"

3 Experiencing Others' Actions and Verbs of Giving

In Japanese, the receptive self emerges when the self is personally involved in the transaction of items and services. The receptive self mostly does not surface, but plays a critical role for interpretation, because verbs of giving convey the empty self's emotive response to receptive experiences.

Now, the situation of giving an object or providing a favorable service can be described in two ways, with the verb *kureru* 'someone gives to self (or member of self's group)' and *yaru* 'self gives to someone'; this section exclusively discusses the former. *Kureru* is also used as a quasi-auxiliary form combined with a *-te* form of the verb, for example, *oshiete kureru* 'someone taught on behalf of or for the benefit of self (or member of self's group)'. When *-te kureru* is used, the consequent benefit (or occasionally harm) brought about by the action is foregrounded. Unlike a straightforward description of an event, *-te kureru* subjectively personalizes the situation, always implying something beneficial (or harmful) to the receptively experiencing self.

In *Manatsu no Hooteishiki*, Kyoohei's receptive experiencing self comes to the fore. In his monologues and internal conversations, as well as in narrative segments, his perspectives are indirectly but convincingly communicated. Although a third-person novel, its text often gives the impression of being told from Kyoohei's first-person point of view. Yet, this interpretation is not possible in English translation. In (16a), *kite kureta* with the feeling of her giving the favor of doing in *Setsuko ga sara ni kitta nashi o nosete, hakonde kite kureta* 'Setsuko brought a dish of cut pears (for the benefit of me)' describes Kyoohei's perspective of experiencing Setsuko's kind action. The English target text (16b) takes Setsuko as an agent in *Aunt Setsuko arrived with a tray of cut pears*. Although both Japanese and English sentences take Setsuko as the agent, the use of *-te kureta* adds an undeniable emotivity, i.e., Kyoohei is the recipient of his aunt's kindness.

(16) a. *Manatsu no Hooteishiki*, 157
Suruto **Setsuko ga sara ni kitta nashi o nosete, hakonde kite kureta**. Zataku no ue ni oki, hai doozo, to yuu.
[Then Setsuko brought a dish of cut pears (for the benefit of me). She places it on the low table and says, "Please have some."]
b. *A Midsummer's Equation*, 140
Aunt Setsuko arrived with a tray of cut pears, which she placed on the low table beside him, "Dig in," she said.

In (17a) we find a case where *shite kurete iru* 'he is trying to do it (for the benefit of me)' and *shite kure nai* 'he does not do it (for the benefit of me)' appear. In both cases, Yukawa, presented with the zero-form, is the agent. The significant message here is that unmentioned Kyoohei is the recipient of the action. In contrast, in (17b), *it wasn't like he'd asked anyone to go to such lengths* and *Yukawa wouldn't explain anything to him* appear where Kyoohei surfaces as *he* and *him*. What is foregrounded in the English translation is Yukawa's action that involves Kyoohei. In the original, Kyoohei's self as a receptive experiencer is indirectly but meaningfully implied. The contrast exists here between the unmentioned receptive and experiencing self versus the overtly presented self across Japanese and translation texts.

(17) a. *Manatsu no Hooteishiki*, 102
Sore na noni konna ni shinken ni, sono negai o kanae yoo to **shite kurete iru**. Sono kuse kuwashii setsumei wa **shite kure nai**.
[Despite that, he is seriously trying to make my wish come true (for the benefit of me). In spite of that, he does not give any detailed explanation (for the benefit of me).]
b. *A Midsummer's Equation*, 88–89
(...) but **it wasn't like he'd asked anyone to go to such lengths**. Lengths he didn't even understand, because **Yukawa wouldn't explain anything to him**.

Because the -te kureru expression indirectly communicates the recipient's perspective, it may reflect multiple persons' positions. (18a) taken from *R.P.G.* describes a scene where Harue is being investigated by Officer Ishizu. *Namida o yoku suitotte kureru* '(the handkerchief) sufficiently absorbs tears (for the benefit of one's self)' is translated as *It dutifully absorbed her tears* in (18b). This expression describes the incident from a third-person point of view. In the original, it is told from the first-person perspective and the empathy with the recipient of the action is prioritized. Interestingly, the first-person perspective may refer to Harue's, Ishizu's, as well as the narrator's position. That the handkerchief absorbs Harue's tears can be interpreted as beneficial to Harue, and to Ishizu who empathizes with her. The incident may also be interpreted as being beneficial to the narrator who expresses an empathetic attitude toward the incident.

(18) a. *R.P.G.*, 65
Namida o yoku suitotte kureru.
[It sufficiently absorbs tears (for the benefit of one's self),]
b. *Shadow Family*, 49
It dutifully absorbed her tears.

The verb of giving, -te *kureru*, provides an opportunity to subjectively and emotively communicate the benefit associated with others' actions. It also indirectly and implicitly communicates the relational contacts among participants, especially the nature of their interpersonal involvement. Overall, the personal relationship enacted through the act of giving populates the empty self with interpersonally-motivated emotive aspects. In this process it also contributes in adding features to the empty place as well.

As the final example of -te *kureru*, let me discuss the relationship between Konoha and Miu in *"Bungaku Shoojo" to Dookoku no Junreisha*. Examples (19a) through (22a), taken from three consecutive pages, illustrate the emotional involvement between them. Miu, the receptive experiencer of the action does not surface, and Konoha's actions are described as being beneficial to her, i.e., *kite kureta* 'kindly came (for the benefit of me)', *sasaete kureru* 'kindly support me (for the benefit of me)', *oboete ite kureta* 'kindly remembered it (for the benefit of me)', and *akete kuretara* 'if you kindly take off the lid (for the benefit of me)'. In addition, Konoha is presented as a receptive experiencing self through *yonde kureta* 'kindly read (for the benefit of me)' in (23a). In each of these Japanese sentences, -te *kureru* implies that someone does something for the benefit of one's self, without specifying the person who offers the action beneficial to one's self. In contrast, English translation texts (19b) through (23b) specifically mention *you* as the partner who functions as the agent of the action.

(19) a. *"Bungaku Shoojo" to Dookoku no Junreisha*, 79
"Konohaa ureshii, mata **kite kureta** no ne."
["Konoha, I'm so happy, you kindly came (for the benefit of me), didn't you?"]
b. *Book Girl and the Wayfarer's Lamentation*, 59
"Konoha! **You** came to see me again! Hooray!"

(20) a. *"Bungaku Shoojo" to Dookoku no Junreisha*, 80
"Daijoobu yo. Datte hora ......Konoha ga **sasaete kureru** mono."
["Everything is fine. Because, you see, Konoha, you kindly support me (for the benefit of me)."]
b. *Book Girl and the Wayfarer's Lamentation*, 59
"It's fine. See? **You'll** catch me."

(21) a. *"Bungaku Shoojo" to Dookoku no Junreisha*, 81
"Waa. Sore koocha no purin ne? Soo deshoo? Atashi no sukina omise, **oboete ite kureta** no ne."
["Wow. That's black tea pudding, isn't it? Right? You kindly remembered my favorite shop (for the benefit of me), didn't you?"]
b. *Book Girl and the Wayfarer's Lamentation*, 60
"Ohhh! That's black tea pudding! I'm right, aren't I? **You** remembered my favorite store."

(22) a. *"Bungaku Shoojo" to Dookoku no Junreisha*, 81
"(...) ......kedo, futa o **akete kuretara** ureshii na."
["(...) ......but, I'll be glad if you kindly take off the lid (for the benefit of me)."]
b. *Book Girl and the Wayfarer's Lamentation*, 60
"But I would appreciate it if **you** could take off the lid."

(23) a. *"Bungaku Shoojo" to Dookoku no Junreisha*, 84
"Sonna ni, nando mo **yonde kureta** no? Boku wa, Miu ga okotte iru ka to omotte ita."
["You read it so many times (for the benefit of me)? I thought Miu you were angry about me."]
b. *Book Girl and the Wayfarer's Lamentation*, 62
"**You** read it that many times? I thought you might be angry."

There is no English counterpart to the *-te kureru* 'someone gives to self' expression. And as a result indirectly expressing the relationship of giving and receiving the benefit is difficult; obviously repetitiously using *kindly*, *for me*, or *for the benefit of me* is awkward. Instead, the English depiction carries a more neutral tone, and consequently the self's involvement becomes less subjective.

4 Reflections

In this chapter, I have noted that the unmentioned but perceptive and receptive self across Japanese and translation texts is not fully realized. Aspects of this self are realized through the use of perception verbs, passive sentences, and receptive *-te kureru* expressions. These Japanese grammatical features can be considered a part of the linguistic subjectivity phenomenon, contributing to create subjective and intersubjective aspects of the self. It is also possible to consider those gaps recognized across Japanese and English texts as cases of translation universals. The use of fashions of speaking (Whorf 1956) in the target language leads to the explicitation and simplification of the source text. At the same time, when an unexpected sentence pattern appears, it is a case of shining through in the covert translation. With these features taken into consideration, differences in the preference toward certain expressivity are evident across Japanese and English texts. That the unmentioned Japanese self is preferably translated in English as an overt participant undeniably generates different images of the self across Japanese and English translation texts.

In Japanese the situation is described without mentioning those persons emotively involved or influenced. The Japanese self is empty and remains hidden behind the foregrounded scene. The perceptive and receptive self emerging in Japanese discourse resonates with the Western conceptualization of the perceptive and experience-based self (James 1904, 1984 [1890]; Hume 1963). The place-sensitive self in Japanese observed in this chapter is not a self actually engaging in action, rather, the self experiences what happens and is strongly and emotionally influenced by others' actions. In English translation, a preference exists where the self engages in the action and is captured within the agent-does structure. The Japanese empty self lurking behind the scene shows a sharp contrast with the overtly presented English self.

CHAPTER 9

Hidden but Expressive Self in the Topic-Comment Dynamism

1 Hidden Self and the Topic-Comment Dynamism

The topic-comment relationship is the fundamental and indispensable force in Japanese that foregrounds subjective and intersubjective features. I have repeatedly argued that the topic-comment dynamism is central to Japanese grammar and narrative discourse (1980, 1981, 1987b), in conversations (1989), and in other genres (1992a, 1997a, 1997g). The topic is marked by a number of devices such as *tte* and *mo*, but in this chapter I focus on *wa*, and introduce the "staging" effect associated with the topic-comment dynamism. In English, it is not impossible to communicate the topic-comment relationship, e.g., *This book, I really like*, or *As for this book, I really like it*. Placing a topic at the sentence-initial position with or without *as for* offers a strategy that functions similarly to some cases of the Japanese topic-comment dynamism. However, use of these English counterparts is limited, and broad-based expressive functions of the topic-comment expression cannot be easily translated.

In addition to the topic marker, this chapter discusses the phenomenon of the *no da* structure consisting of the nominalizer *no* and the commentary nominal predicate *da* (and its variants). Through these analyses I present the hidden but expressive self realized through the topic-comment dynamism which guides us to a further understanding of related aspects of the Japanese self.

1.1 *Topic-Comment Relationships in Sentence and Discourse*

I have studied the topic marker *wa* in Japanese discourse, emphasizing its functional significance (Maynard 1980, 1982, 1987b, 1990a, 1993a, 1994a, 1997a, 1997b, 1998b, 2000, 2001b, 2004a, 2009). The topic-comment dynamism provides the fundamental axis in Japanese, and its importance warrants review. In fact, few areas within the field of Japanese language studies have generated as much research and controversy as the topic-comment phenomenon, especially as it relates to the topic (or theme) marker *wa*. In traditional language studies, scholars have identified *wa* with a variety of terms, among them perhaps "relational particle" being the most widely used.

The topic marker *wa* has often been discussed in association with sentence types. Sakuma (1940) introduces a sentence type containing a proposition consisting of subject and predicate. This sentence is divided into a narrating sentence containing a verbal predicate, and a sentence structured with a nominal predicate which defines things. The nominal predicate sentence is further divided into a quality-defining sentence and a judgmental expressive sentence. Significantly, Sakuma distinguishes between a narrating sentence and a sentence that defines things by pointing out that the former takes the grammatical particle *ga*, and the latter, *wa*. His statement implies a close association between the *wa*-marked topic and the predicate type, a point I return to later. Different functions of *wa* have also been proposed in association with and in contrast with other grammatical features. For example, Mio (1948) associates *wa* with sentences bearing a theme of judgment, i.e., judgment sentence. According to Yamazaki (1965), *wa* functions in presenting and emphasizing items and ideas for discussion. Miura (1976) associates *wa* with statements bearing some universal quality.

Regarding discourse functions of *wa*, Nagano (1986) examines how the chaining of topics is distributed in discourse, while Hayashi (1992) introduces the concept of narrative stance in characterizing *wa*'s discourse functions. In addition, Hinds (1984) has analyzed the phenomenon of topic maintenance in Japanese conversation. It is through Kuno's (1972) approach to *wa* that topic marking (or thematization) has become the focus of many scholars' inquiries outside of Japan (Hinds, Iwasaki and Maynard 1987). Kuno, incorporating the Praguean concept of theme-rheme (and given-new) information, introduces functional terms associated with *wa*, e.g., anaphoric *wa*, *wa* for generic noun phrases, thematic *wa*, and contrastive *wa*.

Turning to Western scholarship, concerning the concept of theme, the best place to start is with Weil (1887 [1844]) whose work is believed to have influenced subsequent views of the Prague Linguistic Circle. Weil distinguishes two different orders that must interact as we speak, namely, the syntactic march and the march of ideas. Weil notices that "as long as thought and word followed each other closely or immediately the very instant of perception, the unity of speech would correspond exactly with the unity of thought" (1887 [1844]: 29). However, when the thought is related to the past, it is necessary in the first place for the speaker and partner to share some common knowledge. Weil concludes that in almost everything said, there is a division between "the point of departure" or "the ground upon which the two intelligences meet," and "another part of discourse which forms the statement" (1887 [1844]: 29).

Mathesius (1983 [1929]), applying Weil's terms, point of departure and statement, develops the notion of theme and rheme. According to Mathesius, theme is the part of a sentence known or at least obvious in the given situation and from which the speaker proceeds in discourse, while rheme is that part of a sentence which contains any new information to be conveyed, and which substantially enriches the knowledge of the listener or hearer. More importantly, Mathesius concurs with Weil and introduces the notion of Functional Sentence Perspective, i.e., theme and rheme under normal situations are arranged so that theme precedes rheme. Although Prague School scholars have approached the phenomenon associated with theme and rheme differently, the fundamental tenet of the thematic relation as characterized by Mathesius has largely remained intact (Firbas 1964). This sequential organization of information enables Communicative Dynamism, where theme has the lowest level of communicative force within the information structure. Both Functional Sentence Perspective and Communicative Dynamism are applicable to the level of text as well, as shown in Daneš (1974).

Now, the concept of theme is notoriously elusive and previous studies have defined it in a variety of ways. In my own work, I have used the term theme in the following sense.

> Theme is the element, in the form of a phrase or a proposition, that presents a framework to which information is linked, or to which the propositions apply, and that provides a thematic cohesion in discourse by presenting information in accordance with the information flow from known to new.
> MAYNARD 1994a: 234

In addition to theme and rheme, scholars have used topic and comment and other related terms. These include topic, or topic Chinese style (Chafe 1976), given information (Chafe 1976), topic-framework (Brown and Yule 1983), and the given-new contract (Clark and Haviland 1977). Halliday (1967) also uses the term theme as well as given information. Given this history, I have used the term topic and comment synonymously with theme and rheme, and I continue to do so in this volume.

1.2 *Subjective Expressivity in the Topic-Comment Dynamism*

Topic-comment not only arranges information flow from given to new, it also achieves a cohesion supported by a dynamism within and across sentences. Topic-comment enriches Japanese discourse with personal commentary, especially through subjective, modal, and attitudinal messages. Ultimately, the topic-comment axis, being supported by proposition-based information, functions as a means of linguistic subjectivity for expressing the self's feelings.

Significantly, the topic-comment dynamism adds features to how the self is presented. The self who instigates and controls the relationship between topic and comment is someone who extends the self into meanings that go beyond the construction of proposition. The language operates here not so much to simply present information, but to add some perspective on how the speaker relates to or feels about that information. At the same time, the self, being empty, calls attention to topic without calling attention to the self. That is, the self often remains hidden in the transaction. This process is in sharp contrast with the self who materializes in the propositional construct. In proposition-centered language, semantic interpretation is less dependent on the place, with the meaning sometimes transcending its locality. Many of the semantic and expressive gaps in translation we find in this work can be traced back to this topic-comment dynamism critically absent in English.

1.3 The Topic-Comment Structure and the Place

Example (1), English translation of the source text (*Sensei no Kaban*, 257), exemplifies a typical process of information presentation; the new information becomes given and functions as a topic. In the discourse of the novel, the topic marking often functions to set up dramatic persons. Here we observe *sensei* 'teacher' accompanied by *ga* (marking the new information) and then followed by reference forms with the topic marker *wa*, i.e., *sensei ga*, *sensei wa*, and *sensei wa*. In the English translation (1), *Sensei* leads each sentence without being marked either as given or new information, blurring the distinction made in the original Japanese text.

It should be noted that the translation text uses *Sensei* (with the capital letter regardless of its position within a sentence), and not the English translation of the word *sensei*, i.e., teacher. This decision seems to be based on the teacher being a special person. In *Sensei no Kaban*, *sensei*, instead of the expected Kanji script, is presented in Katakana. The occupation-based phrase used as a reference as well as a vocative form reinforces the impression of someone who once was a teacher.

(1) *The Briefcase*, 168
 Sensei (*sensei ga*) picked up after six rings. He picked up, but there was only silence. **Sensei** (*sensei wa*) didn't say anything for the first ten seconds or more. **Sensei** (*sensei wa*) hated mobile phones, citing the subtle lag after your voice went through as his reason.

In the source text (*Sensei no Kaban*, 113), the teacher interacts with the narrating self *watashi* 'I'. *Watashi ga kiku to* 'when I asked' indicates the subordinate nature of *watashi*, and the teacher who answers is presented as *sensei wa*. By marking the participants with *ga* and *wa*, new information (not topic) and given information (topic) are distinctively established. In English translation (2), *watashi ga* is translated as *I*, and *sensei wa*, as *Sensei*. The cases of *ga*-marked *watashi* in *watashi ga kiku to* 'as I asked' and *watashi ga tashikameru to* 'as I asked to confirm' are both translated as *I asked*, placed at the sentence-final position. Because unaccented *I* in English conveys given information, the meaning associated with *watashi ga* in the source text is not fully communicated. The back-translation of *I asked* may be either *watashi ga kiita* or *watashi wa kiita*, making no distinction between new and given information. The distinction observed in Japanese which reveals different aspects of the self does not come through in the target text. English translation may incorporate an adverb *then* at the beginning of two sentences starting with *Sensei*. This may contribute in conveying the consequent response to *I asked*. Still, the difference between the new and given information created in the source text is not fully replicated.

(2) *The Briefcase*, 72
What are you going to do with that earring? **I** (*watashi ga*) **asked**.
Sensei (*sensei wa*) thought for a moment before answering. "I think I'll keep it in my bureau. I'll take it out sometimes for amusement."
In the bureau where you keep the railway teapots? **I** (*watashi ga*) **asked**.
Sensei (*sensei wa*) nodded gravely. "That's correct. In the bureau where I keep commemorative items."

2   Hidden Self and the Staging Effect

In my earlier works (Maynard 1980, 1981, 1987b), I have studied discourse functions of *wa* in Japanese narrative discourse and have argued that *wa* functions as a "staging" device. Staging refers to a strategy through which the narrator manipulates a dramatic person's mode of appearance on the narrative stage. The staging strategy identifies which element in discourse remains on the stage. This stage which may be called the "thematic stage" is the conceptual framework within which the discourse is organized, presented, and performed. The choice of using *wa* (or *ga* or other particles instead) reflects the self's staging choice as to which elements are placed on the stage so that the discourse may evolve around them. *Wa* often marks given information, but the choice is not automatic. The given information may not appear as topic if the self chooses not to topicalize, and it may appear as a piece of new information or something to be newly focused on. In this way, the staging effect is achieved by manipulating topicalization and nontopicalization (i.e., thematization and nonthematization in my earlier works).

The discourse develops differently depending on who or what is selected as a topic at any given moment. In a novel, the topicalized participant functions as the main character positioned stage center, with the plot developing around this person. A nontopicalized person temporarily appears on the stage and provides supporting information. In terms of plot organization, the nontopicalized person often plays a minor role. Nontopicalization is achieved when topic markers are avoided, although it is possible to select them. The self who engages in this staging manipulation remains unseen, lurking behind the discourse of the novel.

This staging strategy may also be approached from the perspective of sentence types as explored by Mio (1948). Two of the sentence types related to the topic-comment relationship are sentences of immediate description and sentences of judgment. Mio (1948) characterizes these two sentence types as follows. Sentences of immediate description represent a phenomenon as it is, and the phenomenon perceived and reflected is arrived at without the process of judgment, thus no gap separates the phenomenon from its descriptive expression. Sentences of judgment are sentences expressing judgment in a proposition such as "A equals B."

Relevant to our concern here is that *ga* is typically used for sentences of immediate description when the self presents the external world as perceived, while *wa* appears in sentences of judgment when the self reports the self's judgment. In concrete terms, when a dramatic person's action is introduced with *ga*, the information is based on an immediate perception of something new (or something treated as new) deserving attention. It is vividly presented as if happening right then and there. Topicalization as well as the avoidance of topicalization realize the staging effect that enriches the narrative expressivity. This effect is critically missing in the translated English text which results in a gap of expressivity across two languages.

Let us observe (3), translation of the source text (*Tsugumi*, 156). In *Tsugumi* the main dramatic person appears with *ga* and *wa* at the position of the grammatical subject, but the selection is not strictly based on the status of given or new information. Rather, it depends on the narrating self's perspective. In the first paragraph, *Tsugumi ga* communicates a sense of surprise. In the second paragraph, *Tsugumi ga* appears within a subordinate clause, and then it is topicalized as *Tsugumi wa*. In the third paragraph, *Tsugumi ga* communicates surprise toward a new piece of information, and then it is topicalized as *Tsugumi wa*. In the target text, *she* and *Tsugumi* are used where the distinction between the given and new information does not match that of the source text. Specifically, in the English translation, *Suddenly she spoke* and *said Tsugumi* appear where the personal pronouns *she* and *Tsugumi* do not correspond to the presentation in the source text, i.e., *ga* (new information). Consequently, the topic-comment dynamism in the source text is unavailable. To place Tsugumi (the dramatic person) in a focus worthy of attention as if it were new information as in the source text, *Tsugumi suddenly spoke* and *Tsugumi said* may be used instead, although still the effect is weak.

Now, let us focus on the narrating self, *watashi* 'I' which appears with *wa* three times in the source text (*Tsugumi*, 156). These occurrences indicate that the narrating self remains throughout on stage. The novel develops from the narrating self's point of view, from which Tsugumi is intermittently introduced and marked with *ga*. As a result, Tsugumi is portrayed as someone who temporarily and suddenly appears on the stage. Yet, this observed staging effect is not rendered in English translation (3) where *I* consistently appears. Incidentally, if the narrating self changes the staging strategy and repeatedly marks *Tsugumi* with *wa*, she would remain on stage. In this circumstance we picture both the narrating self and Tsugumi being together on stage.

(3) *Goodbye Tsugumi*, 128–129

Suddenly she (*Tsugumi ga*) **spoke.** "Did that prove how strong I am, huh? Or, do you want me to do some more?" Her tone was almost entirely flat, but you could sense how much strength she was putting into her words. **I** (*watashi wa*) followed her gaze to a girl standing nearby, her face dreadfully pale. They were in the same class. She was Tsugumi's worst enemy. Turning to a girl who was standing nearby, **I** (*watashi wa*) hurriedly questioned her about what had happened. She said she wasn't quite sure but that **Tsugumi** (*Tsugumi ga*) had been chosen to represent the class in some marathon, and when she said she couldn't run, this other girl had been selected to run in her place. The other girl was really annoyed about being chosen after Tsugumi, and the rumor was that she'd asked Tsugumi to step out into the hall during recess and then made some sort of sarcastic comment. At which point, without saying a word, **Tsugumi** (*Tsugumi wa*) had picked up a nearby chair and hurled it into the glass. That was the story.

"Try repeating what you said earlier!" **said Tsugumi** (*Tsugumi ga*).

The girl couldn't reply. All around me people were holding their breath, gulping nervously. No one even went to get a teacher. **Tsugumi** (*Tsugumi wa*) seemed to have cut herself slightly when she broke the glass—there was a little blood on her ankle—but **she** (*Tsugumi wa*) didn't seem to care. She kept gazing straight at the girl. And then **I** (*watashi wa*) noticed how terrifying the look in her eyes was.

Another staging effect can be observed in (4), translation of the source text (*Sensei no Kaban*, 218). Here the reader clearly senses the narrating self consistently presented as *I*. In contrast, in the source text, the narrating self consistently appears in zero-form as a hidden self. Regarding sensei (the dramatic person) in the source text, *sensei* at the position of the grammatical subject undergoes topicalization and nontopicalization, appearing with *ga* once and with *wa* at three locations. English translations corresponding to these four sentences take on *he* and *Sensei*, but the distinction between *he* and *Sensei* fails to achieve the staging effect observed in the source text. *Sensei wa* corresponds to *he* and *Sensei*, while *sensei ga* corresponds to *Sensei*. It is possible to translate *sensei ga* as *Sensei*, and *sensei wa* as *he*, wherein the new information is translated as *Sensei*, and the given information with a personal pronoun, but such a correspondence is missing. The topic-comment dynamism associated with sensei in the source text is lost in translation. If we back-translate *Sensei* and *he* into Japanese, random usage of *ga* or *wa* is possible. Now if we change all occurrences of *sensei wa* to *sensei ga*, sensei temporarily and repeatedly appears on stage, and his action is presented as new information worthy of renewed attention. That would indeed create a different scene, reflecting a different perspective.

The lack of the staging effect through topicalization and nontopicalization in the target text results in an expressive gap. The English grammar compels the narrator to present the narrating self and participants as agents in a propositional structure where a constant and stable self is maintained. In contrast, the Japanese language allows for the self to be hidden yet expressive.

(4)   *The Briefcase*, 137
"Sensei, aren't you hot?" **I** (zero) asked, but **he** (*sensei wa*) shook his head. **I** (zero) wondered where we were. Was this a dream? **I** (zero) had been drinking with Sensei. **I** (zero) had lost count of how many empty sake bottles there had been.
"Must be littleneck clams," **Sensei** (*sensei ga*) murmured, shifting his gaze from the horizon to the tidal flat. There were lots of people gathering shellfish in the shallows.
"They're out of season, but I wonder if you can still find them around here," **Sensei** (*sensei wa*) continued.
"Sensei, where are we?" **I** (zero) asked.
"We're back again," was all **Sensei** (*sensei wa*) said in reply.

In the source text for (5), i.e., (*Sensei no Kaban*, 198), both *watashi* and *sensei* are marked with *ga*. Given that these participants have appeared many times before in the novel, they represent given information. However, here in this scene, both are consistently nontopicalized as if introduced as new information, thus creating a surprise effect. In the English translation (5), *I* and *Sensei* are consistently used as elsewhere in the target text, and thus the nontopicalization effect is lost.

(5) *The Briefcase*, 128
"It's so quiet," **I** (*watashi ga*) said, and **Sensei** (*sensei ga*) nodded.
A little while later, **Sensei** (*sensei ga*) said, "It's very quiet," and this time **I** (*watashi ga*) nodded.

It is important to note here that the staging strategy presupposes someone who is backstage pulling the strings. This someone in control is the narrating self, hidden from view yet indicating an indirect but forceful presence. In contrast, in English translation this hidden but manipulating self is not evident. It is as if texts were produced in two different dimensions, one, the source text prioritizing the empty self outside a propositional framework, and the other, the target text prioritizing the self presented as grammatical subject. The back-translation of English can produce, instead of the original *ga* sentences, *wa*-marked sentences, such as *Sensei wa itta* 'sensei said' and *watashi wa unazuita* 'I nodded'. It is difficult, if not impossible, to transfer the staging effect to the English text.

I should add that the distinction between given and new information is communicated in English through definite and indefinite articles, by choosing pronouns and proper nouns, and by placing a prominent accent on the new information. However, creating a staging effect comparable to how it means in Japanese discourse remains untenable. The gaps observed here lead to different aspects of the self across these languages. The self in Japanese remains hidden but by controlling the staging effect, it emerges in its expressivity. This contrasts with the self in English where a self as a grammatical subject as well as an agent of the action tends to consistently occupy the central stage.

3   Hidden Self and Nominal Predicates

3.1   *Expressivity of Commentary* no da *Sentences*

The nominal predicate, consisting of the nominalizer *no* and the predicate *da* (and its variations such as *desu* and *deshita*), functions in a way similar to the topic-comment dynamism. Both represent features of the rhetoric of *pathos*, which prioritizes the event captured by nominalization followed by commentary. The *no da* structure takes a clause followed by the nominalizer *no* as a topic as well as the comment provided through the commentary predicate *da*. *No da* sentences, functioning differently from sentences without, provide subjective commentary relevant to the nominalized item within discourse. As in the case of the topic-comment structure, the nominal predicate functions as a subjective expressive strategy in discourse (Maynard 2004a, 2005c).

The *no da* phenomenon has been extensively studied. For example, Kunihiro (1984), McGloin (1984), Tanomura (1990), and Noda (1997, 2012) have identified multiple functions including adding an explanatory tone, identifying the situation, marking given information, and emphasizing background information. The *no da* expression has been associated with cognitive processes of conscious judgment and mention, reflective attitude, and objectification as well as interpersonal functions such as relationship, politeness, and group authority. From the perspective of conversation analysis, Kondo (2002) points out that the *no da* expression functions less in presenting logical connectedness, and more in guiding the partner's information processing. A similar approach is taken by Nashima (2002) who insists that the pragmatic function of *no da* is not to specify the logical relation between propositions, but rather, to guide the partner in interpretation. Tsunoda (2004) points out that the *no da* effect is in the sharing of the cognitive process between self and partner. Yamaguchi (2016) mentions that the discourse function of *no da* is to specify how ultimately situations or facts should be interpreted.

I have examined *no da* nominal predicates appearing both in spoken and written discourse (Maynard 1996a, 1997a, 1997f, 1997g, 1999b). The high frequency of *no da* is observed across genres, occurring in interview discourse 25.82% (520 times of the total 2,014 sentences) and casual conversation 25.48% (317 times of 1,244) (Maynard 1992a). In expository writing, 25.97% (288 out of 1,109) end with *no da* (Maynard 1997e). The ubiquity of *no da* expressions is noteworthy, and its translation into English poses a curious question.

When using *no da*, a speaker chooses a mode of predication qualitatively different from one without. In Maynard (1992a) I argue that the sources for this difference lie in the process of (1) objectification and packaging of the event as an object through nominalization, (2) personalization of the utterance by the predicate *da*, and (3) information organization situationally and interpersonally appropriate to the topic. In concrete terms, *no da* expressions support the cohesion in discourse that connects sentences and utterances. And this connectedness is based not so much on logical reasoning, but on the self's subjective and intersubjective attitude.

In Maynard (1997e, 1997g), I analyze *no da*, focusing on the narrating self and dramatic persons. I point out that the packaging effect of the nominalizer *no* provides a sense of narrative distance as well as objectivity, and at the same time *da* conveys the self's subjective, personal, and modality-rich expressivity. When the *no da* structure is chosen, two opposing forces of distancing and personalizing are in operation. Many of the earlier studies on the *no da* expression including explanation, givenness, politeness, and emphasis can be understood as aspects related to these seemingly contradictory objectification and subjectification forces. Predicating with the nominalizer *no* is useful for expressing the self's inner thoughts and feelings. In contrast, sentences without *no da* prioritize objective and factual description. The mixture of sentence types with and without *no da* expressions characterizes the tone of the novel. The decision to choose sentence types originates in the self, and this self, although hidden, influences how the reader interprets the text.

Messages the *no da* nominal predicate conveys show strong affinity with various features of the Japanese language. For example, in Japanese communication, the self often (1) arranges information according to the given-new strategy, (2) expresses the self's opinion with personal commitment with some packaging and distancing, (3) presents one's view in a topic-comment supported manner, and (4) prioritizes subjective and intersubjective attitude in interaction. The *no da* expression fits well with these observed tendencies and preferences. The *no da* nominal predicate also makes it possible to describe what is observed not as an action but as a state of being. In this way, instead of focusing on the foregrounded self as an agent of action, the self remains behind the scenes. Given that Japanese is known to be both a topic-comment and subject-predicate prominent language (Li and Thompson 1976), the *no da* strategy is an ideal device for bridging these two distinct but synergistic ways of organizing information and revealing subjective and intersubjective attitudes.

Let us focus on some examples taken from *Ginga Tetsudoo no Yoru* and while contrasting sentences with and without *no da* in (6a), examine how they appear in English translation (6b). In the source text (6a.1), the situation surrounding Jobanni is presented, and then *no desu* 'it is that' in (6a.2) communicates additional explanatory information relevant to (6a.1). (6a.3) describes Jobanni's behavior, followed by *no deshita* 'it was that' in (6a.4) which provides the narrator's additional information. While sentences without *no da* simply make statements about what the narrating self perceives, in sentences with *no da* and *no deshita*, the narrating self offers personal commentary.

The expression *soodan rashikatta no desu* '(it is that) they seemed to be discussing' in (6a.2) is translated in (6b.2) with expressions of conjecture, *it seemed*. Similar expressions are used in other translations as well, i.e., *they seemed to be* (*Night on the Galactic Railroad & Other Stories from Ihatov*, 48), *they were no doubt* (*Eigo de Yomu Ginga Tetsudoo no Yoru*, 23), and *they seemed* (*Milky*

Way Railroad, 19). In each of these translations, the meaning of *rashikatta* 'seemed' is communicated, but the effects of *no da* are not fully captured.

Likewise, *iroiro shitaku o shite iru no deshita* '(it was that) people were making all kinds of preparations' in (6a.4) communicates the situation in which Jobanni is placed by offering additional explanatory information relevant to (6a.3). The narrating self offers commentary adding to the situational context. In contrast, in the target text (6b.4), Jobanni appears as the agent of the action as *he found*. Jobanni also appears as an agent of the action *he passed by* in the target text (*Eigo de Yomu Ginga Tetsudoo no Yoru*, 23). The situational description is given as *there, everyone was busy preparing* (*Night on the Galactic Railroad & Other Stories from Ihatov*, 49) and *had made various preparations* (*Milky Way Railroad*, 20). Again, in all these translations, the explanatory effect of *no deshita* is missing. Here we observe that the richness in meaning and expressivity of *no desu* and *no deshita* observed in the source text is lacking in translation texts.

(6) a. *Ginga Testudoo no Yoru*, 57

1. Jobanni ga gakkoo no mon o deru toki, onaji kumi no shichi hachinin wa ie e kaera zu, Kamupanerura o mannaka ni shite kootei no sumi no sakura no ki no tokoro ni atsumatte imashita. 2. Sore wa kon'ya no hoshi matsuri ni aoi akari o koshiraete, kawa e nagasu karasuuri o tori ni iku **soodan rashikatta no desu.**
3. Keredomo Jobanni wa te o ookiku futte doshi doshi gakkoo no mon o dete kimashita. 4. Suruto machi no ieie de wa kon'ya no ginga no matsuri ni, ichii no ha no tama o tsurushi tari, hinoki no eda ni akari o tsuke tari, **iroiro shitaku o shite iru no deshita.**

[1. When Jobanni was going out of the school gate, seven or eight of his classmates, instead of going back home, gathered together with Kamupanerura being the center (of the group), near a cherry tree standing in a corner of the school ground. 2. (It was that) they seemed to be discussing about an expedition to gather the gourds to be decorated with blue lights and to be released in the river for tonight's star festival.]
[3. But Jobanni swung his arms broadly, and determinedly stomping his feet, he went away passing through the school gate. 4. (It was that) then in many houses in town, people were making all kinds of preparations for tonight's Milky Way festival by hanging balls of Japanese yew needles and attaching lights on cedar branches.]

b. *Night Train to the Stars*, 23

1. As Giovanni was going out of the school gate he found that seven or eight of his classmates had not gone straight home but were gathered

in a group around Campanella near an ornamental cherry tree at the edge of the school yard. 2. **It seemed** they were discussing an expedition to gather the snake gourds that, with blue lights in them, would be set adrift on the river that night to celebrate the festival (*no desu*). 3. Giovanni, though, gave a vigorous wave and marched straight on out of the gate. 4. Outside in the street, **he found** that the houses and shops were making all kinds of preparations for their night's Milky Way Festival, decorating the whole place with balls of yew needles hung from the eaves and cedar boughs with lights attached to them (*no deshita*).

As seen above, expressive differences between sentences with and without *no da* are clear in the source text. The observed variable effects are achieved through the self's manipulation of subjectivity which implies the narrating self's presence. In contrast, in English translation, effects of *no da* sentences are absent, resulting in the text lacking in the combination of the packaged information along with its subjective personal commentary. The variability in narrative stances observed in the original are not operative in the English translation.

3.2   Use and Avoidance of no da Expressions

What is clearly observable in *Ginga Tetsudoo no Yoru* is the ubiquity of *no da* in its narrative portions. For understanding this phenomenon of *no da*, let me contrast *no da* expressions in *Ginga Tetsudoo no Yoru* with those in *Manatsu no Hooteishiki*. Both works are narrated from the third-person point of view, and both feature a boy as one of the main dramatic persons. The initial 500 sentences of both works are examined to find out whether sentences appear with or without *no da*. The frequency of *no da* expressions differ significantly. In *Ginga Tetsudoo no Yoru*, *no da* sentences occur 97 times and sentences without, 403 times, resulting in 19.4%. In *Manatsu no Hooteishiki*, the comparable figures are 16 and 484, resulting in 3.2% (χ^2 = 65.46, p < .01). *Ginga Tetsudoo no Yoru*, rich with fairy-tale like images, contains frequent *no da* expressions suitable to the story's poetic and imaginative tone. On the other hand, being a mystery novel, *Manatsu no Hooteishiki* foregrounds objective and factual information, and sentences without *no da* are preferred. The choice and mixture of sentences with or without *no da* lead to different narrative modes, presenting different kinds of the narrating self.

Next, let us contrast, in *Ginga Tetsudoo no Yoru*, the portion where the frequency of the *no da* expression substantially differs, and examine how this discrepancy is or is not reflected in the English translation. In the first paragraph of the source text (*Ginga Tetsudoo no Yoru*, 70–71) whose translation is given as (7), we find three cases of nominal predicates, *hashiri tsuzukete ita no deshita* '(it was that) the train continued to run', *suwatte ita no desu* '(it is that) he was sitting there', and *hikatte iru no deshita* '(it was that) brass buttons glittered'. These expressions are translated in *Night Train to the Stars* in (7) as *had been clattering along, Yes, he was sitting*, and *beamed*, wherein the little train, Jobanni, and brass buttons are depicted as agents of the action. The expression *Yes he was sitting* is emphatic, and this reflects a partial effect of the *no da* expression. In the third paragraph of (7) we find *It was Campanella*. This is a translation of the *no da* sentence, i.e., *Sore wa Kamupanerura datta no desu* '(It was that) it was Kamupanerura'. In English translation, the explanatory effect of the original is absent. Similar expressions are used in other translations as well: *It was Campanella! (Eigo de Yomu Ginga Tetsudoo no Yoru*, 71), and *It was Minoru! (Milky Way Railroad*, 45). Interestingly, in the target text (*Night on the Galactic Railroad & Other Stories from Ihatov*, 61) we find the italicized sentence *Why, it was none other than Campanella*, which brings about the explanatory, emotive, and emphatic effects similar to the *no da* expression.

Regarding the distribution of nominal predicates, only the first and the last paragraph contain them. In the second paragraph, information without *no da* is presented in a simple straightforward manner, while in the first and the third paragraphs with *no da*, the narrating self's subjective comments come to the fore. Although in the source text, the paragraphs with and without *no da* produce different narrative effects, these differences are not reflected in the target text.

(7) *Night Train to the Stars*, 51
When he recovered, the little train that he was riding in **had been clattering along** the tracks for some time (*no deshita*). **Yes, he was sitting** in the carriage, with its rows of small yellow lights, of a little night train, looking out of the window (*no desu*). Inside the carriage, the blue velvet-covered seats were mostly empty, and two large brass buttons **beamed** in the gray varnish of the opposite wall (*no deshita*).
In the seat directly in front of him sat a tall boy in a black, wet-looking jacket, with his head thrust out of the window watching the outside. Something about the set of the boy's shoulders was so familiar that Giovanni felt an urge to find out who it was. He was just about to stick his own head out of the window to see, when the boy drew his in and looked at Giovanni.
It was Campanella (*no desu*).

4   Reflections

This chapter has focused on two related aspects associated with the topic-comment dynamism. First, the topic-comment relationship on the level of discourse achieves the staging effect, and second, effects of *no da* nominal predicates communicate both narrative distancing and personalization. In these strategies, we sense the presence of a hidden self manipulating information through the topic-comment dynamism. In contrast, in English translation texts, the hidden self is not sensed; instead the self often appears as an agent of the action in the agent-does structure. Instead of the topic-comment dynamism, cohesion in English is primarily achieved by repeated layers of proposition-based statements. Differences we discover here are subtle, yet these differences in linguistic subjectivity are critical for how one interprets the literary text. For this reason, the translation gaps found here cannot be easily dismissed. It is true that other strategies in English may be used to fill the gap, but the effect of the topic-comment dynamism cannot be easily recreated.

Unfortunately, features directly linked to the core of the Japanese language are often ignored in English translation. They are not easily expressed in English, and even when they are, these features are not likely to be fully sensed. Consider that ironically, the missing information is not felt to be missing by English readers. What does not exist in the first place cannot be missed. Although what is missing may be the most important aspect in the source language, its absence in the target language may simply be unnoticed and left in the abyss. Buried deep at the margin of two languages is the irreconcilable difference that remains unnoticed and unappreciated. Only through a contrastive pragmatics involving translation texts, are we able to come closer to understanding some of the unappreciated gaps across Japanese and English translation texts.

In this chapter we have identified different kinds of the self across Japanese and English. In the former, the hidden but expressive self provides personal commentary. In the latter, the centralized self as agent dominates. The self realized in the topic-comment dynamism is someone who is hidden, who experiences, digests, and then conveys how the self feels. It is the kind of self who tells a story about that very self, rather than a self who organizes objectified information in the form of a proposition. It is true that narrative text, both in Japanese and English, provides a space where the self's personal and subjective voices reverberate (Bakhtin 1981). Still, those voices differ and differing aspects of the self suggest almost unbridgeable differences in the nature of language and how linguistic signs behave across Japanese and English.

CHAPTER 10

Transferred Self in Quotation and Inserted Speech

1 Quoting and Self

The act of quoting creates opportunities where different aspects of self are at play. The self that emerges during the process of quoting in Japanese reveals its multiplicity and relatively free transference across first- and third-person positions. As we continue with our theme of exploring the concept of self, examining how quotation operates across Japanese and English translation texts is expected to reveal similarities and differences that offer insight to our exploration.

1.1 *Background*

Linguistic studies on quotation have primarily been concerned with the distinction between indirect and direct speech. In pragmatics and discourse studies, much attention has been paid to communicational functions of various modes of speech associated with quotation. For example, based on his analysis of direct speech observed in southwest Scotland, Macaulay (1987) states that self-quotation is used as a kind of distancing strategy whereby the speaker presents himself or herself "as an actor in a scene" (1987: 22). Tannen (1989) argues that the overall effect of what she calls "constructed dialogue" is to create involvement. In addition, Mayes (1990) discusses discourse functions of direct quotation in English conversation listing (1) dramatization of events, (2) presentation of evidence, (3) backgrounding of unimportant information, (4) clarification, and (5) error correction.

Quotation in a broad sense is approached by Vandelanotte and Davidse (2009) in which they analyze innovative quotatives such as *be like* and *go*, and identify these as imitation clauses as opposed to traditional reporting clauses.[1] The quotation strategy in English is not limited to the traditional method, although innovative quotatives are more restricted in use. Studies on direct and indirect quotation in English also employ psychological experiments as reported in Eerland and Zwaan (2018). Given that direct speech is known to

---

1 The observation made by Vandelanotte and Davidse (2009) resonates with my research on the Japanese quotation occurring with *mitaina* '(be) like' (Maynard 2005a, 2005b). The concept of imitation is applicable to this Japanese phenomenon of the *mitaina* quotation, a strategy to integrate conversation into narrative text.

describe the situation more vividly and perceptually engaging than indirect speech, they examine effects of speech types on source memory, and conclude that although direct speech may enhance memory for how something was said, indirect speech enhances memory for who said what.[2]

Of the many studies on quotation available in the field of Japanese linguistics, perhaps Kamada (1988, 2000) and Sunakawa (1988, 1989) should be mentioned. Kamada (1988) asserts that the function of direct quotation is not merely to parrot the quotee's utterance, but rather, to offer dramatic effect by inserting one *ba* 'place or situation of talk' into another. The notion of a clash of place matrixes is further pursued in Sunakawa's work (1988, 1989). Sunakawa examines functional differences between the quotative clause *to* and the nominal clause marked by *koto* along with predicate verbs, and concludes that they differ in terms of their usage in expressing the dual places. The tradition of analyzing quotation as it relates to the situation and the place implies that quotation is a useful site for investigating the Japanese self.

Other studies include Coulmas (1986) which offers an overview of Japanese direct and indirect speech and concludes that although many sentences are structurally ambiguous, the interpretation of the clause as direct or indirect speech is usually accessible in natural discourse. Hirose (1995) distinguishes direct and indirect speech in Japanese on the basis of his concepts of public and private self, the former being a quotation of public expression, and the latter, a quotation of private expression. Further studies on Japanese quotation and the use of quotative *tte* include Hayashi (1997), Itani (1997), Suzuki (1998), Fujita (2000), and Kato (2010).

I have discussed quotation and related phenomena in a series of studies. In Maynard (1984, 1986b, 2001d), I investigate functions of quotative marker *to* and the nominalizer *koto* followed by the object marker *o*, and a combination of *to yuu koto o* in literary discourse. In these studies, I report that the quotative *to*, in comparison to other devices, provides a means for representing multiple points of view. The use of an identical particle *to* for marking both direct and indirect quotation allows for a smooth shift in perspective. Although *koto* and *to yuu koto* occur with subordinate clauses, the scope of *to* is broader, involving an entire sentence and a stretch of discourse. In Maynard (1992b, 1994b), I study the mixing of voices expressed through the combination of clause and noun connected with *to yuu* (i.e., quotative marker *to* and *yuu* 'say').

---

2 This point raised by Eerland and Zwaan (2018) is interesting cross-linguistically; Coulmas (1986) points out that a general preference for indirect reports is recognized over verbatim quotation in Japanese. More study is required, however, before discovering how Japanese perspective plays a role in enhancing different types of memory.

In Maynard (1996b) I explore the functions of self-quotation, focusing on direct-style self-quotation, direct-style self-presentation of thought as well as direct-style quotative explanation, and conclude that self-quotation allows for manipulation of multiple voices in Japanese discourse. The direct-style self-quotation, in particular, facilitates a presentation of multiple voices that transmit information on different levels. In Maynard (2005b, 2005c), I investigate conversations inserted into discourse, focusing on the expressivity of sentence-final *mitaina* '(be) like', the use of *mitaina* connected to a noun as well as *mitaina* used for structuring conversation as modifier. I point out that a conversation inserted in text, i.e., inserted speech, illustrates a merger between quotation and narration, providing a relatively flexible expressive means in Japanese.

It should be noted that the distinction between direct and indirect quotation in Japanese is less clear than in English. Direct quotation may appear without quotation marks (Maynard 1984, 1986b), or, it may be directly incorporated within a sentence (Maynard 1992b, 2005a, 2005c). I also analyze assumed quotation (Maynard 1995, 1997a, 1997h), meta-quotation (1997d), as well as monologues in Japanese girls' comics (Maynard 2016, 2017).

My studies mentioned above reveal the functions of the Japanese quotation being varied, complex, and free of certain restrictions. Quotation, allowing for rich manipulation of multivoicedness and varied manners of presentation of the self across genres, offers resources for presenting a wide range of quoting activities of the self and others. In fact, due to the relative flexibility available in Japanese quotation, its counterpart in English translation is likely to result in expressive gaps. In this chapter I contrast quoting strategies across Japanese and English translation texts, and in the process, I continue my exploration into the nature of the empty and populated self in Japanese.

1.2 *Inserted Speech in the Novel*

For understanding the quotation and the self in literary genres, works by Bakhtin (1981), Kristeva (1980), and Vološinov (1973 [1929]) offer some guidance, specifically their approach to multivoicedness and the dialogic nature of linguistic activity. When quoting, at least two voices are at play. Furthermore, each of the self's speech is filled with multiple voices, dialogized within itself as well as with others' speech. Kristeva takes the view that every text is intertextually constructed as a "mosaic of quotations," and that any text is the "absorption and transformation of another" (1980: 66). Quoting in a novel offers the phenomenon where intertextuality is overtly manipulated. What is relevant in the use of quotation is not that it simply invites another's voice, but that the speaker and the invited quotee alternate. As Unami (1991) reminds us, the person who quotes becomes a part of the quotation when, in turn, he or she is quoted by someone else. This transition by way of embedded quotations creates an intertextual effect otherwise unavailable, resulting in a multivoiced and intertextually complex discourse. Taking advantage of this expressive complexity, a speaker employs quotation and inserted speech for portraying desired aspects of the self and others.

In his discussion of direct and indirect discourse, Vološinov (1973 [1929]) states that direct discourse may appear in association with indirect discourse, as it undergoes what he calls "particularized direct discourse." The particularized direct discourse offers expressive meanings associated with the participant's portrayal of the self in the novel. Although the author manipulates direct discourse in the novel, the participant's utterances contribute to the creation of an image of the self as a character or multiple characters. In Vološinov's words:

> Another modification in the same direction may be termed *particularized direct discourse*. The authorial context here is so constructed that the traits the author used to define a character cast heavy shadows on his directly reported speech. The value judgments and attitudes in which the character's portrayal is steeped carry over into the words he utters. The referential weight of the reported utterances declines in this modification but, in exchange, their characterological significance, their picturesqueness, or their time-and-place typicality, grows more intense.
> VOLOŠINOV 1973 [1929]: 134, original emphasis

The speech with "time-and-place typicality" has a character-defining capacity, and it functions within Bakhtin's (1981) concept of character zone introduced earlier in Chapter 3. The character zone is a territory of influence, and it is most clearly defined by directly quoted speech. When dramatic persons in the novel speak in their characters enacted through character-speak, a zone is activated. Here, the self enters into a dialogic interanimation with others, and its character-associated significance grows.

Furthermore, a character zone, never completely independent or empty, is disputed and dialogically negotiated among author, narrator, and dramatic persons. In the character zone, an utterance is always oriented toward the other, and the self emerges only in the process of dialogic interanimation. The addressee may not be physically present, yet even then, words are addressed to another. Accordingly, it is worthwhile to concentrate on quotation and more broadly on inserted speech, the kind of speech through which a speaking self in the novel comes alive in relation to the partner. Studying quotation and inserted speech, because they activate the character zone where characters live, is expected to reveal different aspects of the self, characters, and characteristics emerging in the novel.

2 Transferring Self in Quotation and Inserted Speech

Quotation in original Japanese text utilizes varied means of presentation including (1) with quotation marks, (2) following a dash, (3) without any graphological marks, (4) as indirect quotation, as well as (5) a direct discourse embedded in a sentence. Self, through the use of these varied means of inserted speech, is transferred from one point of view to the next, echoing multiple quoted voices and populating its self with multiple aspects, characters, and characteristics. In English translation, devices for quotation are limited primarily to the use of quotation marks and italicization, and direct and indirect voices are most often distinctly marked. Accordingly, boundaries between the self and the other are established more clearly than in Japanese.

Of note, however, an English expression resembling that of Japanese occasionally appears. Anzai (1983) points out that representative speech in English provides similar effects, and cites the following example taken from *Yama no Oto* by Yasunari Kawabata. The sentence *Shingo wa umi no oto ka to utagatta ga yahari yama no oto datta* 'Shingo suspected that it was the sound of the sea, but it was, just as expected, the sound of the mountain' is translated by Edward Seidensticker as *Shingo wondered if he might have heard the sound of the sea. But no—it was the mountain.* Note that although the Japanese expression *yahari yama no oto datta* 'it was, just as expected, the sound of the mountain' appears as narrative discourse, it strongly communicates Shingo's direct voice. This is due to the sentential and attitudinal adverb *yahari* 'as I thought, after all, as expected' that communicates the self's subjective attitude toward the statement. Relevantly, in English translation, the expression *But no* is used to reflect Shingo's direct voice. Although the representative speech in English offers a device to move across perspectives, its use is restricted. Missing in English are the fluid merging and transferring perspectives that frequently and fluidly occur in Japanese quotation and inserted speech.

Let us start our contrast between the source and the target texts. In (1a), taken from *R.P.G.*, we find a sentence that starts with a dash, i.e., *Anta ga Kazumi kaa. Heee,* 'So you are Kazumi. I see.' This inserted speech starting with a dash indicates that it is not an ordinary quotation, but rather, a silent speech. It bears features of direct speech, marked by the particle *kaa* and an interjection *heee*, and based on contextual information, it is most reasonably interpreted as a direct quotation of an earlier utterance being presented here as a part of Kazumi's recollection. In fact, Imai, a woman who plays the role of Kazumi's mother in the made-up pseudo-family, made this comment earlier when she identified Kazumi. The gravity of this utterance, signaled through Imai's tone of voice, reverberates in the original scene, although only as a part of Kazumi's unvoiced recollection.

One method used in English translation to separate the quotation-like segment is italicization. English translation,—*So this is little Kazumi! Well, well well!* appears italicized and with a dash. However, this method fails to represent varied types of inserted speech observed in Japanese; Imai's voice as a part of Kazumi's recollection does not clearly resonate in (1b).

(1) a. *R.P.G.*, 276–277
"Imai Naoko ga?"
"Un, shashin o mita koto ga aru tte. Chichi ga miseta no yo."
—**Anta ga Kazumi kaa. Heee.**
"Waratte ta." Unadareta mama, Kazumi wa me o mihiraita. "Atashi no kao o mite, atashi o sashite, waratta."
["You mean Naoko Imai?"]
["Yeah, she's seen the photo, I was told. My father showed it to her."]
[—So you are Kazumi. I see.]
["She was laughing." With her head down, Kazumi opened her eyes wide. "She looked at my face, and pointing at me, she laughed."]

b. *Shadow Family*, 180
"She did?"
"Yeah. She said she'd seen a photo my dad showed her."
—*So this is little Kazumi! Well, well, well!*
"She laughed at me." Head lowered, Kazumi opened her eyes. "She looked at me, and pointed, and laughed."

In (2a), the father's utterance *Otoosan ga omae o mamotte yaru* 'I, your father, protect you (for the benefit of you)' is inserted without any marker. However, by lexical and stylistic choice, it is possible to identify whose direct speech it is, and this creates an atmosphere where the father utters these words right then and there in the narrative scene. The expression *mamotte yaru*, with the verb of giving, *yaru* 'self gives to someone (with the implication of offering a favor)', clearly communicates the interpersonal relationship of a daughter receiving her father's favor, which is not strongly replicated in (2b). The description, *I'll protect you. I'm your father*, simply conveys information, with little interpersonal empathy. The direct speech with the character-defining capacity is difficult to be fully translated. Here again, the translation is italicized, but Italics are used for both (1b) and (2b), although (1a) and (2a) differ in the ways the direct discourse is presented in the source text. In Japanese, partly due to linguistic and stylistic features that can convey aspects, characters, and characteristics, sentences with no overt markers may function as direct quotation, allowing for multiple voices to resonate in discourse more fluidly than in English.

Another point of interest here is the use of tense in English translation as shown in (2a) and (2b). Although the source text appears with the nonpast $(r)u$-form of the verb, i.e., *Namida ga nagareru* 'Tears flow from eyes', the English translation takes the past tense *Her tears were falling*. As shown in other examples to follow, although the tense shift between nonpast and past is observed in the source text, in the target text, the narrative past tense is generally maintained. English translation depicts the narrating self who simply reports and tells the story about past events and states.

Regarding tense in English discourse, Fludernik (2003) comments that the tense marking relates to the passing of time, sequentiality, chronology, and to expressions of subjectivity. It also offers a textual function of foregrounding and backgrounding. She notes that in certain narrative text with a sense of enhanced fictionality, the tense shifts to narrative present among different events, paragraphs, and chapters. The translation texts examined in this work tend to prefer the narrative past tense, regardless of the source text's tense. Those properties mentioned above may not be applicable to the translation text here. However, it should be noted that the function of the tense as a subjectivity strategy is available in English, if only in different ways.

(2) a. *R.P.G.*, 280
Otoosan ga omae o mamotte yaru.
"Baka mitai."
Namida ga nagareru.
[I, your father, protect you (for the benefit of you).]
["Like an idiot."]
[Tears flow from eyes.]
b. *Shadow Family*, 182
I'll protect you. I'm your father.
"What a bunch of crap."
Her tears were falling freely now.

In *Manatsu no Hooteishiki*, dramatic persons' feelings are often expressed through internal monologues as inserted speech. In (3a), *Baka ni sun na yo, to omotta* 'Don't ever take me lightly, I thought' contains direct speech with an emphatic particle *yo*, as well as a thought presentation marked with *to*. The combination of the direct voice embedded within the thought presentation is not reflected in the translation text (3b). The translation *What were you expecting?* is presented only as a silent speech that reflects Kyoohei's defiant attitude. Again, the translation is italicized, but the narrating self's intended expressivity does not clearly materialize.

(3) a. *Manatsu no Hooteishiki*, 6
"Densha no naka." Kogoe de kotaeta. Shanai de no manaa gurai wa wakatte iru.
"A, soo. Jaa, chanto noreta no ne."
"Un." **Baka ni sun na yo, to omotta.**
["On the train." I answered almost in a whisper. I know well how to behave on the train.]
["I see. So, you did get on all right, didn't you?"]
["Yeah." Don't ever take me lightly, I thought.]
b. *A Midsummer's Equation*, 4
"On the train," he said, keeping his voice down.
"Glad you got on all right."
"Yeah." ***What were you expecting?***

(4a), taken from *Tsugumi*, shows cases where direct quotations with quotation marks are embedded within a sentence. *Koko ni gohan okimasu yo!* 'I leave your lunch here' and *Tsugumi, koi no yamai na n ja nai no* 'Tsugumi, you aren't lovesick, are you?' are embedded within a sentence which provides situational descriptions. In the target text (4b), quoted segments and main clauses are divided into separate sentences, resulting in the loss of the original discourse structure. To our particular interest is that the conditional meaning associated with *to itte mitara* 'as I said so' is missing in translation. When direct speech is embedded within a descriptive statement, a juxtaposition of place occurs. The direct quotation brings the dramatic effect of immediacy while the description adds a sense of distancing. Consequently, different aspects of the self come to the fore. This seemingly contradicting effect is lost in English translation (4b) where quotation and description remain dissociated.

(4) a. *Tsugumi*, 100–101
Sonna kookei o minarete ite, natsukashii to sae omotta watashi wa oogoe de,
"Koko ni gohan okimasu yo!"
to makuramoto ni obon o oite heya o deru toki ni futo,

"Tsugumi, koi no yamai na n ja nai no."
to itte mitara kanojo wa damatta mama ude dake dashite watashi ni purasuchikku no mizusashi o nage tsuketa.
[I was used to observe such a scene, and felt even nostalgic, and in a loud voice, I said,]
["I leave your lunch here."]
[as I was leaving the room after placing the tray next to her pillow, suddenly,]
["Tsugumi, you aren't lovesick, are you?"]
[as I said so, she, without a word, extended her arm out and hurled a plastic pitcher at me.]

b. *Goodbye Tsugumi*, 82
I was so used to seeing her that way that I even started to feel a bit nostalgic.
"Hey, I'll leave your lunch here for you, okay?" I shouted, setting the tray down next to her pillow. Then suddenly, as I started out the door, I came out with this: "Hey Tsugumi, do you think maybe you're just lovesick?" Without saying a word Tsugumi whipped out her arm and hurled a nearby plastic pitcher at me.

As observed above, Japanese quoting methods in the source text are varied and flexible, while only limited methods are chosen in English translation. Different levels of the self's fluidity observed here may appear subtle, yet the unresolved gaps should not be too easily dismissed.

3   Floating Self in Internal Monologue and Conversation

Quotation may take the form of independent inserted speech representing an internal monologue as well as internal conversation. Although the internal monologue bears conversational features, it is not spoken in reality, and remains muted; it is mostly observed when the self presents its internal voice in a soliloquy. Quotation as an internal conversation occurs within a conversation, constituting a silent speaking turn. In the discourse of the novel, these appear as independent units mostly without graphological marks, not unlike narrative portions. However, they bear features of conversational interaction (e.g., speech styles and interactional particles), and are interpreted as such.

3.1 *Inserted Speech as Monologue*

In an internal monologue, the narrating self and dramatic persons engage in speech with rich linguistic and sociolinguistic variation. These monologues express what is difficult to verbalize or perhaps impossible to utter in a narrative scene. Internal monologues can be traced to the dramatic person's soliloquy performed on stage (Maeda 2004). Internal conversation rich with variation activates relevant situations, creating an atmosphere where multiple voices interanimate in the character zone (Bakhtin 1981). The conversational interaction is enacted within the narration, and the reader hears multiple voices traversing in the narrative space. It facilitates revelation of the self's characters and characteristics and realizes the transferred self between different dimensions, allowing the reader access to the self's interiority.

An internal monologue can be viewed as a mediating resource for conversation and narration, two traditionally distinct modes. The separation between narration and conversation reminds us of the differentiation Genette (1980) makes between diegesis (telling) and mimesis (showing). Diegesis is similar to telling, and mimesis, to showing, both of which are integrated into different styles of narration, poetry, and drama. The internal speech can be understood as mimesis where the self engages in a mimetic showing not only as narrator but also as dramatic person.

The tendency for novels to be mimetic may be traced to the origin of narratives. Narratives were originally performed as oral story-telling before a live audience. Even when presented in written form, the communicative goal of narration retains the sense of an oral performance. Interestingly, in Japan, it is only in modern literature that internal monologues, some appearing as internal conversation, disappeared from the text. Mitani (1996) reports, on the basis of analyzing the text of *Rashomon* by Ryunosuke Akutagawa, that the author struggled over the choice of narrative styles, specifically between modern narration and the traditional Japanese narrative method. Internal monologues appearing in *Rashomon* are produced as a result of Akutagawa's attempt to resolve this dilemma. In Mitani's words:

> Modern literature has refused to legitimatize the use of internal monologues. Without the establishment of an independent genre, the literary genre was strongly influenced by Realism and Naturalism, which maintain that the internal monologues of other people are something people could not hear. This common sense approach to life gained primacy, and the modernist approach became dominant. Consequently, in modern novels we rarely find internal text that presents one's inner thoughts. Internal monologues, if uttered in ordinary life, would be treated as an

act of an insane person, but in pre-modern classical literature, the text was divided into different narrative categories; in the notes of *The Tale of Genji*, the internal monologue was considered a legitimate technique along with the textual divisions such as text, conversation, and narration.

MITANI 1996: 223, my translation

Despite the trend of modern literature, it is also true that internal monologue has sustained throughout the history of Japanese literary genres. As I analyze in this chapter, it expresses the self's inner voice, populating the empty self with different often emotive and expressive aspects.

3.2   Across Narration and Monologue

Let us now examine cases where a distinction between narration and monologue is unclear in Japanese. (5a) can be interpreted as Chikako's monologue echoing her direct voice. In translation, however, it is presented as the content of Chikako's thoughts, as in *Chikako longed to tell the girl what it was she wanted to know*. Additionally, in the original, *Shikashi sore ni wa, hannin o mitsuke naku te wa* 'But to do that I (or we) must catch the killer' is ambiguous as to who catches the killer. It gives the impression that Chikako herself (given that she is a police officer and a member of the investigation team) is to catch the killer. In the English translation (5b), however, it is presented as *they*, from an outsider's point of view excluding Chikako.

Also noteworthy is the different tense chosen in the original and translated texts. In the source text, the nonpast $(r)u$-form is maintained, although in English the narrative past tense is chosen for the last two sentences, i.e., *Chikako longed* and *they had to catch*. As I touched upon already, the narrative tense encourages a reading that the event is reported on, and not that it is Chikako's direct voice. The perspective shift observed in the source text is not realized in the target text. The Japanese text allows for ambiguity in its perspective taking, but in English translation such an interpretation is untenable, suggesting that, in contrast with English, the Japanese self is more open to flexibility.

(5)   a. *R.P.G.*, 81

Mottomo na uttae da. Seitoona iibun da. Kazumi ga shiri tagaru koto o oshiete yari tai. **Shikashi sore ni wa, hannin o mitsuke naku te wa.**
[Totally understandable plea. A legitimate complaint. I want to tell Kazumi what she wants to know (for the benefit of her). But to do that, I (or we) must catch the killer.]

b. *Shadow Family*, 58
A thoroughly understandable plea. A legitimate complaint. **Chikako longed to tell the girl what it was she wanted to know.** But to do that, first **they had to catch** the killer.

In (6a), we find a case where perspectives are mixed and overlayed between Chikako and the narrator. Here the self is transferred in the original, but the English translation separates these voices. The expression *Harue no yuu toori da* 'It is exactly as Harue says' can be read as the direct voice of Chikako as well as the narrator's. In (6b), this sentence is translated into the third-person narrative description in past tense as *just as her mother had said*. Likewise, a perspective overlay is observed in *sono hanbun wa wakasa no sei daroo* 'half of that is perhaps due to her youth'. The speculative *daroo* here can be interpreted either as Chikako's or the narrator's voice. The English translation, *was half due to her youth*, by taking the narrative point of view, simply makes a factual statement in past tense. Here it is possible to associate the Japanese ambiguity of narrative points of view with multiple and shifting aspects of the self. In contrast, the consistent points of view supported by narrative past tense is linked to the stable self whose perspective choices come under stricter rules.

(6) a. *R.P.G.*, 83
Soo, Kazumi wa zutto okotte iru. **Harue no yuu toori da.** Jitsu wa sakki, robii de mita kanojo no kao ni, amari ni mo hakkiri to shita ikari no iro ga ukande iru koto ni, Chikako mo naishin odoroite ita. Ikari o kakuse nai, **sono hanbun wa wakasa no sei daroo.**
[Yes, Kazumi has been angry for a long time. It is exactly as Harue says. To be honest, Chikoko was surprised inside at the fact that when she saw her in the lobby, such a clear sign of anger surfaced on her face. She cannot hide her anger, half of that is perhaps due to her youth.]
b. *Shadow Family*, 59
Yes, Kazumi was in a continual state of rage, **just as her mother had said.** From the first moment she'd spotted her in the lobby earlier, deep down Chikako had been taken aback at the level of anger clearly distinguishable on the girl's face. Her unconcealed anger **was half due to her youth.**

An internal monologue in the source text is often translated into an indirect quotation and into a descriptive statement made from the third-person point of view. In (7a) taken from *"Bungaku Shoojo" to Shini Tagari no Dooke*, the internal monologue *bungeibu o tsuzukete yuku no ka naa* ...... 'Do I continue to stay with this literature club, I'm not sure, maybe I will', with the elongated interactional particle *naa*, appears as Konoha's direct speech. Its translation into indirect quotation, *I wonder if I can stay with* in (7b), does not accurately present his direct voice. The use of direct self-quotation is associated with the self's performance as an actor in the scene (Macaulay 1987), the dramatization of events (Mayes 1990) as well as revealing characters and characteristics. When direct speech is translated into an indirect quotation, these effects are weakened, and accordingly, the narrating self's degree of mimesis is diminished. Here the expressive meanings associated with direct discourse reflect multiple voices (Vološinov 1973 [1929]) and perspectives.

(7) a. *"Bungaku Shoojo" to Shini Tagari no Dooke*, 13
Kono mama kono okashina senpai to futari kiri de, **bungeibu o tsuzukete yuku no ka naa** ......
[Do I continue to stay with this literature club just two of us with this strange senior student, I am not sure, maybe I will.]
b. *Book Girl and the Suicidal Mime*, 10
I wonder if I can stay with this club if it's just me and this freakish president.

In (8a) taken from *Suzumiya Haruhi no Yuuutsu*, the direct voice in *Kokoro ga atatamaru ne* 'my heart warms up, really', with the empathy-seeking particle *ne*, is translated in (8b) into a narrative description in past tense, *It made me feel all warm and fuzzy inside*. In the original, when Kyon, as a hidden experiencer, speaks in his direct voice, a stylistic shift occurs and Kyon's friendly character comes through. In English translation, this shift is unrealized, and the third-person narration is maintained. As a result, the creative manipulation of points of view observed in the source text is ignored. Here it is possible to recognize that different kinds of character zones (Bakhtin 1981) are in operation.

(8) a. *Suzumiya Haruhi no Yuuutsu*, 155
Kondo wa kita to minami ni wakareru koto ni nari, oretachi wa minami tantoo. Sari giwa ni Asahina-san wa chiisaku te o futte kureta. **Kokoro ga atatamaru ne.**
[This time it was that we split north and south, and we are assigned to the south side. As we parted, Asahina waved her hand in small motions (for the benefit of us). My heart warms up, really.]
b. *The Melancholy of Haruhi Suzumiya*, 101
This time, we split up searching north and south. Nagato and I were responsible for the south side. Asahina waved her small hand at me before she went on her way. **It made me feel all warm and fuzzy inside.**

In (9a), *Yabai, misukasarete iru* 'Oh no, I'm seen through (she sees me through)' is an internal monologue presented as inserted speech, but its translation *This was bad—she'd seen right through me* in (9b) simply offers a situational description and explanation. The lack of internal monologue in the target text weakens its sense of involvement (Tannen 1989) clearly activated in the original. In addition, effects realized by the the nonpast (r)u-form and the passive structure are ignored in translation. The nonpast form describes the current state but English translation takes the narrative past tense, and it is integrated into the narrative-internal timeline. *Misukasarete iru* 'I am seen through (she sees me through)' is a passive of harm, but this is translated into the agent-does structure with Tooko as agent. The subjectivity echoing the direct voice in the source text is diminished due to the switch to a narrative description. Sorely missed is Konoha's direct and emotive voice echoing in his internal monologue expressed through his grammatical choice and casual speech style. Here we witness Konoha's self floating between a narrative self depicted in the first sentence and another self in the second sentence who is populated with a frank and casual youth character.

(9) a. *"Bungaku Shoojo" to Shini Tagari no Dooke*, 31
Tooko senpai ga paipu isu no ue de hiza o kakae, suzushige ni me o hosomeru no o mite, mimi ga kaa tto atsuku naru. **Yabai, misukasarete iru.**
[I see Tooko sitting on the fold-up chair hugging her knees with her eyes comfortably half-closed, my ears become burning hot with embarrassment. Oh no, I am seen through (she sees me through).]
b. *Book Girl and the Suicidal Mime*, 24
I glanced over at Tohko, who sat on the fold-up chair hugging her knees, her bright eyes crinkling, and my ears burned with embarrassment. **This was bad—she'd seen right through me.**

3.3 *Phantom Participation and Internal Conversation*

Depending on the context, internal conversations are divided into four categories. As I have discussed in Maynard (2014, 2016), these are (1) thought-presenting internal conversation, (2) adjacency-pair internal conversation, (3) solitary internal conversation, and (4) quoted-speech-responding internal conversation. Thought-presenting internal conversation is placed between direct quotations, and provides the self's inner thoughts. In adjacency-pair internal conversation, although the utterance is heard by no one, the self responds to the partner's quoted speech by taking a speaking turn. In solitary internal conversation, the self engages in a phantom speech in a silent conversation. In quoted-speech-responding internal conversation, the self speaks in a direct quotation, and is immediately followed by the self's internal speech. The reader hears internal conversations enacted in different ways as their voices interanimate in the character zone.

In Japanese, an internal speech functions as if it were part of a conversation. Let us observe two examples from *Suzumiya Haruhi no Yuuutsu*. In (10a) Kyon, the narrating self, appears as if he were participating in the conversation then and there as evidenced by Kyon's speech style *Soo kai, kimatte ru no kai. Hajimete shitta yo* 'Is that so? Obvious, is it? First time I've heard about it (you know)'. These two sentences without quotation marks are presented as a part of a thought-presenting internal conversation. Notably, in English translation in (10b), a direct quotation with quotation marks appears. An undeniable difference exists between direct quotation and internal conversation in that the former is heard but the latter is not. This distinction, however, is not replicated in translation. A gap exists in how information is given and interpersonal transactions are enacted. Consequently, in the target text we miss aspects of the self that are foregrounded in the source text.

(10) a. *Suzumiya Haruhi no Yuuutsu*, 32
"Atashi ga ki ni iru yoona kurabu ga hen, soo de nai no wa zenbu futsuu, kimatte ru desho."
Soo kai, kimatte ru no kai. Hajimete shitta yo.
["Any club I like is weird, others are all ordinary, it's obvious, isn't it?"]
[Is that so? Obvious, is it? First time I've heard about it (you know).]
b. *The Melancholy of Haruhi Suzumiya*, 20
"Any club I like is weird. Everything else is totally normal. Isn't that obvious?"
"Really? Obvious, is it? First I've heard about it."

In the source text (*Suzumiya Haruhi no Yuuutsu*, 232) whose translation appears as (11), adjacency-pair internal conversation without quotation marks is repeated four times. Their English counterparts appear in (11.2), (11.4), (11.6), and (11.8), all presented with quotation marks. In the source text, Kyon, as a narrating self, secretly participates in the conversation-in-progress. Kyon's internal conversation offers his response to Koizumi's direct quotation, and Kyon's muted utterances exist in a different dimension. In the target text, all utterances presented as direct quotations deliver Kyon's audible voice in the narrative scene. Ultimately, the intricate manipulation of voices is not accurately reflected in the target text. This is unfortunate because throughout the novel, Kyon's self continues to engage in these internal conversations. Overall, Kyon's self floats across multiple aspects including the narrating self, the self as dramatic person, and the muted self who engages in internal conversations.

(11) *The Melancholy of Haruhi Suzumiya*, 154
    1. "I brought up the anthropic principle to draw a comparison. I haven't gotten to Suzumiya yet."
    2. "So tell me already. Why do you, Nagato, and Asahina all like Haruhi so much?" (without quotation marks in the source text)
    3. "I believe her to be a charming person. But let's set that aside. Do you remember? I once said that the world may have been created by Suzumiya."
    4. "It annoys the hell out of me, but I guess I still remember." (without quotation marks in source text)
    5. "She has the ability to realize wishes."
    6. "Don't make that kind of a statement with a straight face." (without quotation marks in source text)
    7. "I have no choice but to make such a statement. The situation is changing the way Suzumiya wishes."
    8. "Like that's possible." (without quotation marks in source text)

4   Transferred Self and Inserted Speech

Torikaeko Chenjiringu contains various modes of inserted speech associated with quotation. They include (1) Goroo's voice recorded on tape, (2) Goroo's words in the drama script authored by him, (3) past conversations between Goroo and Kogito, (4) content of interviews, (5) Kogito's conversation with other participants, (6) Kogito's assumed conversation, (7) conversation among multiple dramatic persons, (8) Kogito's and other participants' internal conversation and monologue, (9) direct quotation inserted within narration, and so on. Among direct quotations we find those that occur with quotation marks, with dashes, and with no graphological marks.

    Given that varied cases of inserted speech form critical elements in the novel, gaps observed across Japanese and English translation texts are difficult to ignore. For one, internal monologues of the narrating self are often translated into third-person narrative descriptions. As a result, shifts in points of view observed within a paragraph in the source text are often ignored in the target text. For another, direct quotation, quotation without graphological marks as well as expressions bearing both direct and indirect voices in the source text are often, and seemingly randomly, translated into indirect description, direct quotations with quotation marks, or italicized sentences. Here, the intended effects in the original are diminished in their impact.

(12a.1) provides description from a third-person perspective, although (12a.2) and (12a.3) present Kogito's internal monologue from the first-person point of view. These sentences represent direct discourse accompanied with the non-past $(r)u$-form. The Japanese self is transferred from one perspective to another in the middle of the paragraph. The direct-style monologue as inserted speech in (12a.2) and (12a.3) facilitates the presentation of multiple voices and activates the dramatic effect of presenting vivid images (Maynard 1996b). At the same time, because this segment diverts from the narrative stream, it creates a sense of distance from the narrative act. The English translation consistently takes the third-person point of view, and (12a.2) is translated into the subordinate clause *He thought* in (12b.2). Sentence (12b.3), translated and placed in a new paragraph, is presented from the third-person point of view in the narrative past tense. As revealed in the consistent perspective-taking in (12b), the self portrayed in English sentences remains stable and consistent.

(12) a. *Torikaeko Chenjiringu*, 83
   1. Kogito ni wa sono Azuma Beemu fujin no yuu, Goroo no shinario ni motozuite Doitsu jin no kantoku ga toru eiga to yuu hanashi o kiita kioku wa nakatta. 2. Shikashi, ano jitsu wa ki no yowai Goroo ni, kono hito no yuuben ni sakarau kiryoku ga tsuzuita daroo ka? 3. Toku ni sono hito no musume to nanra ka no kankei ga ari, sore ga yakkaina mono to natte ite, to yuu yoona koto de areba naosara ni ......
   [1. There was no recollection on the part of Kogito that, as this Azuma Beemu women says, based on Goroo's screenplay a German director would make a film. 2. But I wonder, would Goroo who is actually weak-willed continue to have the energy to resist this woman's pushy talkativeness? 3. Especially some kind of relationship with her daughter exists and that relationship has turned problematic, and then the difficulty would even increase ......]
   b. *The Changeling*, 105
   1. Contrary to this Azuma-Bōme women's supposition, Kogito had no recollection of ever having heard anything about a plan for a German director to make a film based on one of Goro's original screenplays. 2. **He thought** it likely that Goro, who was somewhat weak-willed (or, more charitably, softhearted) and hated to say no to anyone, might simply have been unable to summon the energy to resist this woman's blandishments.

3. The likelihood increased if you considered the possibility (again, this was wild surmise) that Goro might have had some kind of involvement with the woman's daughter and that relationship had become complicated and problematic.

The segment following the dash in (13a) describes Kogito who speaks into the tape recorder as he addresses the deceased Goroo. To indicate that this is not an ordinary conversation, quotation marks are avoided. English translation (13b), however, uses quotation marks thus presenting it as ordinary direct quotation. Consequently, the expressive intent of the original is weakened. In the source text, the impression is created that Kogito is speaking to his deceased brother-in-law in a monologue, recollecting their past, perhaps with a sense of loss and regret. The English translation in direct quotation following the statement *Then he turned back to Tagame and replied in great excitement* in (13b) fails to communicate the complexity of how Kogito is feeling. The original monologue does not constitute a speaking turn; only Kogito's inner (and hidden) feelings are present. The direct quotation provided in the target text fails to capture the breadth of emotion expressed in the source text. In addition, the expression *omiyage ni moratta* 'I received as a souvenir' with the verb of receiving *morau* 'to receive' reveals an established empathy between Kogito and the professor. The translation, however, simply describes the event as *he brought back for me* with the professor as the agent of an action.[3]

(13) a. *Torikaeko Chenjiringu*, 92
Soshite tagame ni mukatte isoisoto kotaeta no da.
—Sensei no saigo no furansu taizai no toki da ne, ano toshi Pari de wa gomi shuushuunin no sutoraiki ga atta. Shigai no tokoro dokoro kara gomi o yaku kemuri ga agatte iru, Pari zenshi no miniachua no yoona e o **omiyage ni moratta**. Ima mo Seijoo no tsukue no mae ni oite aru yo.
[(It is that) then he turned back to the Tagame headset and began to willingly reply.]
[—At the time of the professor's last stay in France, you remember, that year there was a sanitation workers' strike in Paris. I received as a souvenir, a miniature painting that depicted the entire city of Paris where here and there in the streets smoke was rising from the piles of burning trash. That is still placed on the desk in front of me here in Seijoo, (you know).]

---

3 Note that (13b) contains information not directly provided in the source text, i.e., Professor Musumi. This is provided to the English reader for clarification purposes, a case of explici-

b. *The Changeling*, 115
Then he turned back to Tagame and replied in great excitement. "That must have been at the time of Professor Musumi's last stay in France! It was the year there was a trash collectors' strike in Paris. I still have a souvenir that **he brought back for me**; it's a miniature-type painting that shows the entire city of Paris, and here and there you can see smoke rising from the piles of burning trash in the streets. It's sitting on the desk in front of me, here in Seijo."

An interesting perspective shift is observed in (14a). *Kogito wa* in (14a.1) and *Kare wa* in (14a.2) present topicalized Kogito in descriptive narration, followed by (14a.3) in which the narrator offers an explanation. Then in (14a.4), the expression *ore wa*, the topicalized *ore* 'I (blunt, primarily used by male speakers)', presents Kogito's direct voice. This clear shift to an internal monologue as inserted speech is not reflected in the translation (14b.4), where the third-person perspective is continued with the expression *he was curious*.[4] In fact, the shift to the first-person is hinted earlier in (14a.2) when *jibun no* 'self's' appears. Through this expression, instead of *kare no* 'his', Kogito's privately-reached internal self emerges. In contrast, *he* is consistently used in (14b.2).

The shift from third-person to first-person observed in the source text is a case of what Watabe (2015) calls "transferred-person point of view." Watabe notes that this shift of person perspective is observed in Japanese novels starting from the 2000s. The once recognized clear separation between the narrating self and the narrated self has weakened in recent years. Watabe points out that in contemporary Japanese literature, the first-person narrative voice has taken over the traditional third-person view and this tendency is observed in Oe's recent writings. The differentiation in perspectives has diminished, and some novels have incorporated multiple-person perspectives, instead. *Torikaeko Chenjiringu* is a prime example, with the transference and merging of points of view recognized throughout the novel. This transferred self constitutes an aspect that perpetually populates the empty self, revealing its flexible nature.

---

tation translation universal (Mauranen and Kujamäki 2004; Kranich 2016). Another case of explicitation is observed in (14b) where *for agreeing to view the corpse* is added.

4 The lack of perspective shift in the English translation may be related to the explicitation, simplification, and normalization, as well as the levelling out of translation universals (Mauranen and Kujamäki 2004; Kranich 2016). Overall, maintaining the third-person perspective makes it easier for the reader to follow the narrative plot, although that may not necessarily be the only intent of the author.

(14) a. *Torikaeko Chenjiringu*, 16

    1. **Kogito wa**, Chikashi ni misukasarete iru kokoro yowasa ga ari nagara, Umeko-san ni sasowareru to isoisoto tatoo to shite ita. 2. **Kare wa**, itsumade mo seichoo shikire nu **jibun no** koto o, kakuritsu shita sabishisa de omotta no da. 3. Shikashi moo hitotsu ki ga tsuite iru koto mo atta no dearu. 4. **Ore wa**, Goroo no hoho kara mimi ni kakete tagame ni mukete hanashite ita ato ga, shoogeki ni yotte nokotte iru ka doo ka tashikame takatta no da ......

    [1. Kogito, even with awareness of his sensitive heart being looked through by Chikashi, when invited by Umeko, he was about to willingly stand up. 2. (It is that) he thought of his self with a firmly grounded feeling of loneliness as someone not being able to fully grow up. 3. But (it is that) there is one more thing he was aware of. 4. (It is that) I wanted to check whether there might be a mark stretching from his ear to his cheek caused by the shock (of hitting the ground when he committed suicide) that would indicate he had been talking into the Tagame headset.]

b. *The Changeling*, 14

    1. As Chikashi perceptively surmised, the prospect of viewing Goro's dead body filled Kogito with dread, but when Umeko voiced her request he automatically started to stand up. 2. **He** couldn't help thinking that **he** would never be mature enough to handle something like this, and **he** was engulfed by feelings of loneliness and isolation. 3. But he was conscious of another motivation for agreeing to view the corpse, as well: 4. **he was curious** whether there might be a mark stretching along Goro's cheek that would indicate he had been talking into a Tagame-type headset when he jumped.

5   Reflections

As past studies have revealed, quotation offers multiple functions in discourse. In English, self-quotation provides an opportunity to present the self as an actor in a scene (Macaulay 1987), and constructed dialogue creates involvement (Tannen 1989). English direct quotation enables the dramatization of events (Mayes 1990). English quotation functions as imitation clauses and reporting clauses (Vandelanotte and Davidse 2009) indicating innovative uses. As noted through contrastive pragmatic analyses, these functions are recognized in Japanese as well. But differences also exist. Japanese quotation crosses over perspectives and places (Kamada 1988, 2000; Sunakawa 1988, 1989), and as emphasized in this chapter, they are varied, flexible, and fluid. Form and use of inserted speech differ across Japanese and English, activating different kinds of character zones, and accordingly, recognized expressive gaps remain.

In Japanese, with internal monologue and internal conversation, the crossover between narration and quotation can be relatively easily achieved. This shifting creates a kind of discourse where the self is transferred across first- and third-person perspectives. The empty self, through different ways of telling a story, populates its self with different aspects, as it constantly transforms and moves. This floating and transferred self is difficult to materialize in English, where the distinction between first- and third-person is more strictly enforced. The stable self maintained in the English text requires divided and separate perspectives, encouraging a clearer division between the self and the other. Quotation proves to be another phenomenon that reveals different ontological foundations observed across Japanese and English translation texts.

CHAPTER 11

Populated Self and Variation

1   Character and Character-Speak in Japanese and English

Populating the empty self with aspects, characters, and characteristics is discussed earlier in Chapter 3. This chapter explores how the Japanese self is populated with characters and characteristics through character-speak in the framework of contrastive pragmatics. We focus on a number of character-associated features across Japanese and English translation texts.

1.1   Middle-Aged-Male and Old-Man Languages

Middle-aged-male language establishes a corresponding character and characteristic. In (1a) and (2a), taken from *R.P.G.*, Takegami, a middle-aged male detective interviews Kae. *Wake desu na* 'so it's that' in (1a) exhibits a typical and often stereotyped feature of middle-aged-male language, i.e., *na* or *naa* added immediately following the *desu/masu* verb ending. This speech variety is spoken when speakers reach their 40s, and more frequently in their 60s. Although only 1.3% of male speakers in their 20s use this variety, 18.4% of speakers in their 60s are known to use it (Kokuritsu Kokugo Kenkyuujo 2000). Takegami avoids this style in formal contexts, but resorts to it when he is relaxed. Middle-aged-male language foregrounds mature frankness and friendliness, and as a result of its use Takegami is identified as a man in his middle-age.

Likewise in (2a) when Takegami says *Beteran desu na* 'an old hand, then', his dialogue perfectly matches the image of such a character. He could just have easily said *Beteran desu ne*, but the choice of *na* is characteristic- and character-defining. The effect of this middle-aged-male language is unlikely to come through in translation. *So basically your work involves internal affairs* in (1b) and *That makes you an old hand, doesn't it?* in (2b) are neutral and the subtext that his speech style is undeniably associated with a middle-aged man is absent.

(1)   a. *R.P.G.*, 198
       "Ha haa. Soo suru to uchimuki no koto o shikiru **wake desu na**."
       ["I see. So it's that you handle internal affairs."]
    b. *Shadow Family*, 134
       "I see. **So basically your work involves internal affairs.**"]

(2) a. *R.P.G.*, 198–199
  "Kotoshi de juugonen desu."
  "Beteran desu na."
  ["This year makes it fifteen years."]
  ["An old hand, then."]
 b. *Shadow Family*, 134
  "This year it will be fifteen years."
  "That makes you an old hand, doesn't it?"

In (3a) taken from *Suzumya Haruhi no Yuuutsu*, an old man is introduced, and he speaks in an old-man language. Features of the old-man language include the interactional particle *noo*, and the interrogative form *ka ne*. These expressions deviate from the speech style of other dramatic persons, clearly establishing the character as that of an old man. The utterance *Ryooko-san to yuu no ka ne* 'So she's Ryooko, I see' indexes the speaker as old and male, but its English translation in (3b), *Her name's Ryoko?*, does not index age or gender. Missing in translation are a gentle demeanor along with stereotyped traditional values associated with an elderly person.

(3) a. *Suzumiya Haruhi no Yuuutsu*, 222
  "**Ryooko-san to yuu no ka ne**, ano musumesan wa. Kidate no yoi, ii ko datta **noo**."
  ["So she's Ryooko, I see, that girl. She was a good-natured, fine girl."]
 b. *The Melancholy of Haruhi Suzumiya*, 147
  "**Her name's Ryoko?** She was a good-natured, kind girl—"

1.2 Character-Speak of Special Dramatic Persons

Dramatic persons in *Ginga Tetsudoo no Yoru* come from many different backgrounds, and different speech patterns establish their characters. Let us focus on two such dramatic persons, a bird-catcher and a scholar. (4a) represents the character-speak of a bird-catcher. With the emphatic particle *ze* in *Kono kisha wa, jissai, doko made de mo iki masu ze* 'This train, you see, actually goes far, to faraway places', the bird-catcher's speech deviates from others' speech styles. In the translation, we find *you know* in (4b) and (4c), *precisely* in (4d), and *indeed* in (4e). *Ze* often marks the speaker as unsophisticated and male, but neither of these social markers comes across in translation. The use of *wasshi* 'I' also communicates a blue-collar male, but in all translations, *I'm getting off* is chosen with the neutral *I*.

(4) a. *Ginga Tetsudoo no Yoru*, 84
   "Sore wa ii ne. **Kono kisha wa, jissai, doko made de mo ikimasu ze.**" (...)
   "**Wasshi** wa sugu soko de orimasu. **Wasshi** wa, tori o tsukamaeru shoobai de ne."
   ["That's nice, isn't it? This train, you see, actually goes far, to faraway places."] (...)
   ["I'm getting off soon right over there. My business is catching birds, you see."]

   b. *Night Train to the Stars*, 79, 81
   "Now that's nice. That's just where this train is going, **you know**." (...)
   "**I'm getting off** a bit farther along the line. You see, my business is catching birds."

   c. *Night on the Galactic Railroad & Other Stories from Ihatov*, 72–73
   "Oh, that's nice. This train can really take you that far, **you know**." (...)
   "**I'm getting off** soon. I'm a bird catcher by trade, you see."

   d. *Eigo de Yomu Ginga Tetsudoo no Yoru*, 109, 111
   'That's really something. That's **precisely** where this train is going.' (...)
   '**I'm gettin' off** a bit down the track. Bird catchin's my line.'

   e. *Milky Way Railroad*, 63–64
   "That's good enough. **Indeed**, this train does go on to the end." (...)
   "**I'm getting off** just up the line here. My job is catching birds."

(5a) introduces a scholar whose character-speak includes the polite question ending with *ka ne* and the polite command form *tamae*. These expressions signal a higher status character who is mature and respected, but the English translation fails to communicate this. For example, *Hey there, stop! Don't use your pick, use a chisel instead, and carefully!* in (5c) and *Hey there! Yes, you! That's enough with the pickax! Do it gently, with a chisel!* in (5e) effectively communicate the authoritative voice. But they fail to convey the level of polite formality inherent in the source text. The back-translation is likely to take on an ordinary Japanese style, without indicating the kind of character portrayed in Japanese.

(5) a. *Ginga Tetsudoo no Yoru*, 81
   "Kono kemono **ka ne**, kore wa bosu to itte ne, oi oi, soko, tsuruhashi wa yoshi **tamae**. Teinei ni nomi o yatte kure **tamae**."
   ["This beast, you ask, this is called "bosu," you see, hey, over there, please don't use a pick, make sure to use your chisel carefully."]

b. *Night Train to the Stars*, 73
"This beast here—it's called *bos*, (hey!—stop using your pickaxes there—do it carefully, with chisels!)"
c. *Night on the Galactic Railroad & Other Stories from Ihatov*, 70
"Now, these bones you see, they're from a creature called Vos—**Hey there, stop! Don't use your pick, use a chisel instead, and carefully!**"
d. *Eigo de Yomu Ginga Tetsudoo no Yoru*, 101
"We geologists call it a "boss" ... hey, you, put down that pick! Can't you be more careful and use a chisel?"
e. *Milky Way Railroad*, 60
"This beast, now, is called a Bossy ... **Hey there! Yes, you! That's enough with the pickax! Do it gently, with a chisel!**"

1.3   *Anti-Social* yankii *Language*

Yankii language is a variety associated with a group of youth called *yankii* (Saito 2009). It takes on a blunt style (e.g., blunt negative morpheme *nee* instead of *nai*) and incorporates *yankii* slang. More broadly, *yankii* in Japanese culture refers to a group of often delinquent junior and senior high school students who can be associated with a number of anti-sociocultural values and preferences. *Yankii* members often belong to motorcycle gangs known for their outrageous and illegally modified motorcycles and automobiles. Their outfits consist of long jackets with embroidered Kanji phrases displaying their group names and mottoes. According to Nagae (2009) and Nanba (2009), a *yankii* (1) dislikes school, (2) respects the hierarchical relationship within the group, (3) resists mainstream social values, (4) tends to be politically and culturally conservative, and (5) wears altered school uniforms and other attention-catching costumes. The phrase *yankii* in a broad sense also refers to a subculture practiced by youth groups described above. *Yankii* can also refer to the said subcultural values not necessarily associated with anti-social attitudes.

Female *yankii* members incorporate blunt *yankii* language in their speech, and generally share *yankii* values. In *Tsugumi*, Tsugumi personifies the *yankii* character. She occasionally speaks in a formal style, but primarily takes on a brisque style, and her sometimes in-your-face language plays a significant role in establishing her *yankii* character. English translation (6) corresponds to the source text (*Tsugumi*, 13) which contains an example of female *yankii* speech where we find a mixture of stereotypically women's language (*atashi* 'I') and blunt style (*omaera* 'you'). The combination represents the female *yankii* style echoing both femininity and bluntness. The target text, however, does not fully incorporate these mixed attitudes. *You jerks sure are gonna feel like crap if I die tonight! Stop crying already!* in (6) exhibits the coarseness of her attitude with cursing words, but the stereotypical female *yankii* character does not fully come through.

(6) *Goodbye Tsugumi*, 6
  But even at times like that, Tsugumi sneered. "**You** (*omaera*) **jerks sure are gonna feel like crap if I** (*atashi*) **die tonight! Stop crying already!**"

Tsugumi's *yankii* language shifts to ordinary *da* style when she feels weak and vulnerable. The *da* style, not as blunt as *yankii* language, still consistently maintains her straightforward character. Occasionally, Tsugumi's speech communicates a certain kindness, however. The English translation (7) contains *Hey moron, what do you call yourself? You got some kind of name?* which shows coarseness. In the source text (*Tsugumi*, 96), the expression *Omae, nan te yuu no? Namae* 'You. What is it, your name?' contains the blunt *omae* 'you', but the use of the particle *no* adds a tinge of tenderness. English translation does not communicate Tsugumi's momentary lapse into kindness as signaled in the utterance. The same is true for *Nani? Jochuu no musuko na no? Omae* 'Is it that you're a maid's son?' in the source text which is translated as *What, is your mother a maid or something?* in (7). Tsugumi's speech in the source text contains both the particle *no* carrying a sense of tenderness and the blunt *omae* 'you', but the target text fails to catch that note of softness in Tsumugi's otherwise spunky posture.

(7) *Goodbye Tsugumi*, 79
  "Yeah, thanks, I noticed," she replied. Then she hollered into the street, "**Hey moron** (*omae*), **what do you call yourself** (*no*)? **You** (*omae*) **got some kind of name?**" (...)
  "That new hotel is gonna be my house."
  "**What, is your** (*omae*) **mother a maid or something** (*no*)?" Tsugumi chuckled.

Tsugumi's *yankii* language can be understood as gender-crossing. Regarding female speakers' coopting male speech, Chinami (2003), based on her analyses of Japanese manga discourse, understands it as a way of (1) undercutting any seriousness to the talk, (2) inviting self-disclosure, and (3) displaying raw emotion. When a female speaker adopts male speech, she is able to effectively use otherwise restricted straightforward expressions. A female's use of the blunt male style provides both camouflage and excuse for choosing non-conforming language usually unavailable otherwise. The overall effect Tsugumi's mixed styles bring to the novel does not contradict what Chinami (2003) proposes as functions of gender-crossing speech. This is not captured in the English translation.

1.4 Youth Language

Youth language is a generation-associated variety functioning as a character-speak. According to Yonekawa (2002), youth language as casual speech fosters (1) entertainment, (2) easy participation, (3) camaraderie, and (4) image-based communication. Functional features of youth language include (1) abbreviations, (2) creation of new vocabulary, (3) emphatic phrases, (4) semantic shifts, and (5) insertion of buffer zones. From a slightly different perspective, Satake (1995, 1997) explains the effect of youth language with the term "softening." He contends that young people are in general adverse to conflict. They try to avoid friction in conversation by side-stepping minor differences of opinion or misunderstanding. They adopt a softening strategy, preferring vague or indirect expressions, and thus avoid taking strong positions. The use of half-questions with rising intonation lessens the note of challenge, rendering the questioning non-confrontational. Here softening devices include *mitaina* 'seem like, (be) like' and *kekkoo* 'more or less, more than expected' as well as utterance-final speech qualification markers such as *to yuu ka*, *tte yuu ka*, and *ttsuu ka*.

Tsuji (1999), based on his questionnaire, interprets expressions such as *toka* 'or', *tte yuu ka* 'or', *tte kanji* 'feel like' and *mitaina* 'seem like, (be) like' to be linked to psychological traits found among youth. Tsuji concludes that the dichotomy animating youth language is not one of deep/shallow or strong/weak, but one of heavy or light relationships. Youth language is motivated by a psychological preference for light relationships, avoiding anything heavy, i.e., intimate or serious, and thus freeing the self from social constraints and dependencies. This youth's preference is indeed reflected in the style of light novels targeting young adult readers. Youth language found in novels populates the self with youthful characters and characteristics as illustrated in the examples to follow.

In the source text (*"Bungaku Shoojo" to Shini Tagari no Dooke*, 70) we find the use of *to yuu ka* 'or', typical of youth language. Its translation in (8), *I guess I just got a little high-strung or something*, communicates a sense of hesitation with *I guess* and *or something*. It fails, however, to communicate the presence of Japanese youth language, and fails to realize the corresponding characteristic of the self. The same point can be made regarding *tsui amaete shimatta to yuu ka* 'I was in the mood of being dependent on your good will ...' which is translated as *I guess I just got carried away with it*; it lacks the youth-associated softening effect.

(8) *Book Girl and the Suicidal Mime*, 52
"Oh, that? It wasn't anything important, really (*to yuu ka*). **I guess I just got a little high-strung or something** (*to yuuka*). I guess I was a little down because of the rain. And you looked at me so kindly ... **I guess I just got carried away with it** (*to yuu ka*). Oh geez, it's so embarrassing. Please just forget that happened."

Youth language in casual conversation in the novel adds an overall youthful characteristic and character to dramatic persons. For example, in *Suzumiya Haruhi no Yuuutsu*, Taniguchi's style creates a youth character. In the source text (*Suzumiya Haruhi no Yuuutsu*, 20), *Nanse tsura ga ii shi sa* 'More than anything, her face is pretty' and *Nna koto wakan nee shi* 'Such a thing they won't know' contain the casual and intimate style associated with young people (*tsura* instead of *kao* 'face', *nna koto* instead of *sonna koto* 'such a fact', and *wakan nee* instead of *wakara nai* 'cannot tell'). Target text (9) fails to add the character depicted through youth language.

(9) *The Melancholy of Haruhi Suzumiya*, 12
"It's because she has the looks (*Nanse tsura ga ii shi sa*). Plus she's great at sports and probably gets better grades than most. You can't tell she's a freak when she just stands there and keeps her mouth shut (*Nna koto wakan nee shi*)."

In *R.P.G.*, although Minoru chooses polite speech in the interview, he shifts to youth language in the source text (*R.P.G.*, 226). For example, the choice of *ossan*, a blunt vocative referring to a middle-aged man as well as the use of the blunt negation *ja nee no* create Minoru's character, i.e., a male teenager with attitude. Minoru's behavior of showing disrespect to the middle-aged detective is communicated in translation in the target text (10), *Come on, Officer, What are you, nuts?*, but this does not bring about a youth character. Minoru's self is portrayed differently across Japanese and English texts.

(10) *Shadow Family*, 152
"You gotta be kidding me," said Minoru. "**Come on, Officer** (*ossan*), **What are you, nuts** (*ja nee no*)?"

2   Populating the Self through Dialect and Effeminate *onee* Language

This section discusses regional dialects and the effeminate *onee* language as character-speak. A person might regularly speak in a dialect to create a local character, but the dialect is also often borrowed to add a characteristic. For example, a Tokyo native may occasionally mix in an Osaka vernacular expression, a case of "fictional dialect" where the non-native variety is borrowed to assume a character or a characteristic (Maynard 2016). The effeminate *onee* style creates a character or a temporary characteristic.

2.1   *Creating Character with Dialect*

Regional dialects in Japanese society have been considered speech styles to avoid, and people outside of Tokyo have sought to learn the so-called standard or Tokyo speech. However, this dialect-associated inferiority complex (Shibata 1958) has mostly dissipated since the 1990s. It is fair to generalize that dialects no longer convey a social stigma. Instead, dialects have become a preferred style for promoting empathy and deeper bonds among friends. Inoue, Ogino and Akizuki (2007) remark that people today choose dialects for a kind of personal joy. Indeed, it is not difficult to find regional dialects in the entertainment media, where different dialects are stereotypically associated with certain characters and characteristics. Tanaka (2011), with the term "dialect costume play," captures the expressive effects associated with dialects. Tanaka observes that speakers of the Tohoku dialect are viewed as being unsophisticated, Osaka dialect speakers as fun-loving and straightforward, and Okinawa dialect speakers as warm and tender. These stereotypes, not necessarily negative, are selected and played out to accentuate the self's characteristics under specific circumstances.

Miyake (2005) discusses cases where the Kansai dialect is used by speakers coming from elsewhere. This fictional (i.e., borrowed) Kansai dialect is frequently used by people up to their 30s, and is associated with values such as familiarity, warmth, and tenderness. Miyake, reporting that dialects are used for entertainment, relaxation, and enjoyment, identifies this phenomenon as a new strategic use. Fictional dialects create buffer zones for smoothing out potential conflicts, while keeping the conversation on friendly terms. Miyake points out that of all dialects, the Kansai dialect most strongly performs this function. Likewise, Tanaka (2011, 2014) associates borrowed dialects, i.e., what Tanaka calls "virtual" dialects, with certain recognized values. For example, we find (1) the Osaka dialect entertaining, (2) the Kyoto dialect cute and feminine, (3) Tokyo and Osaka dialects stylish, (4) the Okinawa dialect warm, (5) the Tohoku dialect down-to-earth and unpretentious, and (6) the Kyushu dialect to be somewhat macho.

Let us now examine cases where regional dialects function as a character-speak. In the source text (*Torikaeko Chenjiringu*, 34), Kogito recollects having a conversation with his mother. Although this is a third-person novel, as pointed out earlier, Oe's personal lives are interwoven in the narrative, and Kogito, as Oe himself, is presented as coming from Ehime Prefecture. The mother's speech addressing her son takes the formal *desu/masu* style with features of the Iyo dialect spoken in Ehime prefecture (i.e., the use of the progressive tense *-te oru* instead of *-te iru*, as in *-te otta*, *-te orarete*, and *-te ora zu*, and attaching an interactional particle *ya*). In the target text (11), an explanation is offered about the mother's dialect, i.e., *Kogito's mother began to speak in the local Iyo dialect, which tends to feature more exclamatory sentences than standard Japanese*. While the authenticity of this explanation is debatable, the fact that such an explanation is thought to be required can be interpreted as a case of foreignization and accomodation (Venuti 2004, 2008) as well as explicitation (Mauranen and Kujamäki 2004; Kranich 2016). The English translation of the mother's speech does not reflect its tender folksy tone, a key sentiment of the source text.

(11) *The Changeling*, 40
Later, when they were sitting across from each other at the breakfast table, **Kogito's mother began to speak in the local Iyo dialect, which tends to feature more exclamatory sentences than standard Japanese.** "I've been praying (*-te otta*) for a chance to see you since the beginning of last spring, Kogito!" she began. (It was already fall.) "And now that you're sitting (*-te orarete*) here, I still half feel as if it's my fantasy eating breakfast in front of me. It doesn't help that I can barely hear what you're saying—of course, I've gotten quite deaf; and on top of that you still don't open your mouth (*-te ora zu*) wide enough when you speak, just like when you were a child!"

The source text (*Torikaeko Chenjiringu*, 137), comparable to the translated text (12), includes direct speech from Daioo, an old gentleman who knew Kogito's father. Daioo's character-speak is explained as being *natsukashisa o mitometa koto o hitei deki nai mori no naka no akusento de* 'with the accent of people in the forest with which I could not deny feeling nostalgic'. Although Daioo's speech is translated and appropriately provides information, the direct impact of the dialect is lost. The expression *Kogito-san ga washira no koto mo, ano hi no koto mo, kesshite wasurete wa orare n no ya to anshin shimashita ga!* 'I am relieved to find out that you, Kogoto, have not forgotten about us nor about that day' includes the progressive form of *-te orare n* and the interactional particle *ya*, markers of the Iyo dialect. In the translation, *It's a great relief to me to know that you haven't forgotten about that day, or about us!*, fails to fully capture the effect of the dialect in the source text. Although Daioo's speech is identified as a dialect, his dialect-associated sentiments are not conveyed in translation. It should be noted that incorporating English regional dialects in the target text could possibly bring similar effects. However, given the specificity of the Iyo dialect, duplicating its effect would be difficult, if not impossible.

(12) *The Changeling*, 179
  Abruptly, the hitherto-silent one-armed man began to speak in a spirited, exclamatory way, with the same sweetly nostalgic deep-forest accent that Kogito would hear from the men who attacked him, twenty years later. "It's me, Daio! You know, they used to call me Gishi-Gishi! You remember (*-te orare n*), don't you, Kogito? (…) **It's a great relief to me to know that you haven't forgotten about that day, or about us (*ya*)!**"

2.2 *Effeminate* onee Language as Character-Speak

In traditional studies, men and women in Japan have been directly associated with male and female speech styles. In fact, men's and women's styles were prescribed as a part of social conventions, providing fuel to the existing gender stereotypes. Men's speech is considered to be straightforward, rational, definitive, and persistent, while women's language is associated with politeness and indirectness (Masuoka and Takubo 1992). For example, *kashira* 'I wonder', has been loosely indexed to female speakers with features such as softness and indirectness (Ide 1979). As discussed in my earlier studies (Maynard 2016, 2017, 2019), it is important to be aware that gender-associated variations are not inherently motivated by the self's biological gender (Butler 1990). Selecting certain gendered languages in Japanese involves personal, expressive, and playful factors.

As recent developments in variation studies illustrate, the relationship between linguistic forms and social meanings are considered indexical, and these relationships are fluidly multiple, and mediated by cultural and ideological factors (Eckert 2000; Okamoto and Shibamoto-Smith 2016). This notion of polyindexical is supported by "indexical fields" (Eckert 2008) where linguistic signs are not socially indexed in a fixed one-to-one relationship.

Character-speak takes advantage of the stereotyped indexical relationship through a process where repeated indexical acts conventionalize the function of a specific variation. Through what Agha (2005) refers to as "enregister," the variation comes to be associated with certain indexical values. Masculine and feminine speech styles used as character-speak fundamentally provide a creative resource, and it is through personal choice that gender-associated characters and characteristics materialize as elements of the self. Given that the data analyzed in this study are taken from literary genres, variations represent conventionalized and stereotyped use, and do not necessarily coincide with naturally-occurring usage. Nonetheless, literary works constitute a significant part of the language culture of contemporary Japan, providing a substantial resource for studying the concept of self.

Now, the effeminate *onee* style is a speech variety that crosses over traditional gender identities. Historically, the *onee* language is most directly associated with gay men and drag-queens of the early 2000s, and it narrowly refers to the particular language spoken in gay bars in Shinjuku, Tokyo where it served as a unifying force in the gay community (Maree 2013). Among these speakers, *onee* language was not seen simply as an imitation of women's language. As Maree (2008) reports, *onee* language speakers themselves acknowledge differences in their way of speaking. Two lesbians, Sayuri and Oka, report that "the major difference between the *onee* style and stereotypical women's language lies in the exaggerated intonation and extended vowels" (Maree 2008: 71). Further, Sayuri adds that the difference from stereotypical women's language is that the *onee* language consists of "overdoing by about 50 percent the way women speak" (Maree 2008: 71).

Incorporating points made regarding the *onee* language by researchers (Lunsing and Maree 2004, Maree 2003, 2013; Abe 2014; Maynard 2016, 2017), its features are summarized as listed below.

1. inflected intonation and high-pitched voice, often playful and theatrical
2. frequent use of the following features:
    a. interactional particles *yo* and *ne* immediately following nominals
    b. interactional particle *wa*, and its combination such as *wa yo* and *wa yo ne*
    c. pronouns *atashi* 'I' and *watash* 'I', and self-referencing first name
    d. expressions associated with stereotyped woman's language or feminine speech, such as an exclamatory expression *ara* 'oh', as well as *kashira* 'I wonder' added as attitudinal marker
    e. command forms such as *nasai*, and other advice-giving strategies
    f. exaggerated emotional expressions
3. choice of girlish or feminine topics or speech situations associated with traditionally female professions
4. hyper participation in conversation, often chatty
5. cynical straightforward remarks, sometimes with maliciousness expressed in opinions and comments
6. tendency to insist on one's positions and opinions

Features listed above are both strongly and moderately feminine. Strongly feminine are the high-pitched voice, the use of interactional particle *wa*, and phrases such as *atashi* 'I', *ara* 'oh, my!' and *kashira* 'I wonder'. Moderately feminine features are the interactional particle *no* (both in interrogative and non-interrogative contexts) and its combinations such as *no yo* and *no yo ne*. The interactional particle *no* is also used by male speakers, but it carries with it a sense of softness traceable to femininity. Additional features of the *onee* language used for entertainment purposes include a mixture of coarse vocabulary, blunt style that evokes masculine speech, as well as the use of self-critical and self-deprecating comments.

Incidentally, it is not impossible to employ a speech style similar to the *onee* language in English. Miyawaki (2018) gives an example *What's your name, dear?* which is translated as *Nee anta, namae wa?* with feminine features. Although feminine speech may occur in English, its use is severely restricted in comparison to the Japanese effeminate *onee* language.

In *Kitchin*, Yuuichi's mother, Eriko, who is actually his biological father, plays a critical role in the story. Eriko is presented as an *onee* character, and his *onee* language character-speak includes *atashi*, and interactional particles *no*, *wa*, and *wa ne*. In the source text (*Kitchin*, 66), we find *Atashi wa yokatta wa* 'I feel I was fortunate' with *atashi*, typically feminine first-person reference, and *wa*, typically feminine interactional particle. This is flatly translated in (13) as *I'm grateful for it*, without any indicator of femininity; Eriko's effeminate *onee* character does not materialize. Similarly, we find in the source text (*Kitchin*, 66) *Mikage no sunao na kokoro ga, totemo suki yo* with the interactional particle *yo* without the predicate *da*, which is translated in (14) as *I love your honest heart, Mikage*. The use of the verb *love* adds a touch of femininity, but the presence of an *onee* character is absent. The stereotypical effeminate expression, *Ii wa nee* in the source text (*Kitchin*, 67) appears as *You've been lucky* in (14). Again, it is difficult to sense the effeminate *onee* character here. It is not that English has no speech style similar to the Japanese *onee* language. However, hyperfeminine expressions that could imply the *onee* character are not found in the target text examined for this study, implying its stricter restrictions.

Notably, the expression *to hizu mazaa wa itta* 'his mother said' appears in the source text (*Kitchin*, 66) where indicated in parentheses in (14). This is not translated into English at all, although it reveals a curious choice of words. We find the use of English phrases *hizu* and *mazaa* presented in the Katakana script, instead of Japanese phrases such as *kare no* 'his' and *hahaoya* 'mother'. This attention-getting manipulation using English loan words communicates an unusual distancing yet attention-catching effect. This reminds the reader that Yuuichi's mother is actually his father who functions as "his mother." The fact that this sentence is missing in translation results in a gap in communication that is not insignificant.

(13) *Kitchen*, 41
"Yes. But if a person hasn't ever experienced true despair, she grows old never knowing how to evaluate where she is in life; never understanding what joy really is. **I'm grateful for it.**"

(14) *Kitchen*, 42
"I think I understand."
"**I love your honest heart, Mikage.** The grandmother who raised you must have been a wonderful person (*to hizu mazaa wa itta*)."
I smiled. "She was."
"**You've been lucky,**" said Eriko. She laughed, her back to me.

The relationship between Mikage and Eriko, Yuuichi's biological father, is developed on the basis of Eriko's cross-gendered self, and this relationship cannot be fully appreciated without the *onee* language. Due to the English translation not fully capturing how language variety operates in Japanese, the impact of the novel is attenuated.

3 Narrating Self, Variation, and Style

3.1 *Narration and Character-Speak*

This section focuses on Kyon's narration in *Suzumiya Haruhi no Yuuutsu* and discusses how the narrative style is managed in English translation. Although Kyon, a high school student, speaks in youth-oriented standard speech, he also takes on other variations. Specifically, Kyon is populated through multiple character-speak including (1) the fictional Kansai dialect, (2) old-man language, (3) blunt youth style, (4) feudal-lord style, (5) mature and respected style, and (6) casual style.

Fictional vernacular expressions *kettaina* 'strange, bizarre' in the source texts (*Suzumiya Haruhi no Yuuutsu*, 250) and *aho* 'fool' in (*Suzumiya Haruhi no Yuuutsu*, 124) are borrowed from the Kansai dialect. These phrases, standing out from the text, activate values associated with the Kansai dialect. Translation given in (15) and (16) do not reflect this, and Kyon's Kansai characteristic is not generated.

(15) *The Melancholy of Haruhi Suzumiya*, 166
Then what about me?
Why was I dragged into this bizarre (*kettaina*) mess?

(16) *The Melancholy of Haruhi Suzumiya*, 80
    Data Overmind? Humanoid interface?
    My ass (*aho*).

The expression *wai* in the source text (*Suzumiya Haruhi no Yuuutsu*, 255) is typically associated with old-man language. By borrowing *wai*, an attribute of being like a mature old man emerges as Kyon's characteristic. Also, Kyon's self is presented as someone who playfully incorporates multiple variations and styles. Its translation (17), *I'll fan myself* fails to convey this implicit and expressive message.

(17) *The Melancholy of Haruhi Suzumiya*, 169
    "Kyon, I'm hot."
    "Yeah. So am I."
    "Fan me?"
    "If I'm going to fan anyone, **I'll fan myself** (*wai*). I don't have enough energy to be wasting any on you this early in the morning."

Kyon occasionally reveals his personal feelings in a candid youth language. *Koitsu* 'this damned kid' in the source text (*Suzumiya Haruyi no Yuuutsu*, 25), *Nani ga beeru da* 'What about the veil? (What are you talking about!)' and *Ii no ka omae* 'Hey you, OK with that? (Darn it!)' in the source text (*Suzumiya Haruhi no Yuuutsu*, 108), *kono ama* 'this damned girl' and *tsumori de iyagatta* 'had the nerve to do it' in the source text (*Suzumiya Haruhi no Yuuutsu*, 136) are all blunt candid expressions. The English counterparts given in translations (18), (19) and (20) do not reflect Kyon's gruff attitude. For example, *Ii no ka omae* is translated as *Are you OK with that?* in (19). The back-translation of this English sentence can result in a variety of expressions of different politeness and formality levels. For example, *Sore de ii?* 'Is that OK?' does not communicate Kyon's attitudinal shift. A forthright speech style is not impossible in English, but Kyon's harshness is missing. In (20) although we find a cursing expression *the damn girl*, a counterpart to *tsumori de iyagatta* 'She had the nerve to go ahead with it (Darn it)!' is missing.

(18) *The Melancholy of Haruhi Suzumiya*, 15
    What exactly was she (*koitsu*) trying to accomplish?

(19) *The Melancholy of Haruhi Suzumiya*, 70
    "All right, SOS Brigade! It's finally time to unveil ourselves to the world! Everyone! Let's join together as one and give it our all!"

What do you mean by unveil (*Nani ga beeru da*)?
When I turned to look, I found that Nagato had returned to her customary position and was taking another crack at her hardcover.
You've been arbitrarily included as a member, you know. **Are you OK with that** (*Ii no ka omae*)?

(20) *The Melancholy of Haruhi Suzumiya*, 88
(…) it was revealed that **the damn girl** (*kono ama*) was going to put the pictures in that digital camera on my half-assed Web site (*tsumori de iyagatta*).

Among Kyon's character-speak in the source text (*Suzumiya Haruhi no Yuuutsu*, 253), we find the feudal-lord style *kudaranai mono dearu koto yo naa* 'it sure seems like a meaningless matter'. This style is so unusual that it catches attention. Its English translation, *it seems like such a trivial thing*, in (21), however, fails to convey this entertaining, almost comical, characteristic of Kyon's narrating self.

(21) *The Melancholy of Haruhi Suzumiya*, 168
Indeed, once the truth has been brought to light, **it seems like such a trivial thing**.

In addition, as shown below, Kyon's speech style extends to that of a mature and respected person. *Anshin shi tamae* 'Don't worry' in the source text (*Suzumiya Haruhi no Yuuutsu*, 16) as well as the use of a question marker *kai* as in *Soo kai. Kimatte ru no kai* 'Is that so? Obvious, is it?' in the source text (*Suzumiya Haruhi no Yuuutsu*, 32) clearly stand out from his other narrative segments. They add an unexpectedly mature characteristic to his narration and populate the self likewise. Again, target texts (22) and (23) fail to communicate this narrative expressivity.

(22) *The Melancholy of Haruhi Suzumiya*, 9
Rest assured (*Anshin shi tamae*), you didn't. The only thing strange here is Haruhi's mind.

(23) *The Melancholy of Haruhi Suzumiya*, 20
"Any club I like is weird. Everything else is totally normal. Isn't that obvious?"
"Really (*Soo kai*)? Obvious, is it (*Kimatte ru no kai*)? First I've heard about it."

3.2 On Style and Style Shifts

The term "style" (or speech style) in Japanese linguistics has often been used in association with verb morphology, i.e., *da* and *desu/masu* forms characterized as informal/casual/abrupt and formal/polite, respectively. In practice, style entails a complex interaction of multiple factors. For example, phonological features, vocabulary, verb morphology, sentence structure, topic selection, discourse structure, as well as regional and social dialects contribute to an overall style. The Japanese practice of shifting and mixing styles is ubiquitous, and it seems to have intensified in variety and degree in recent years. In written discourse the narrating self mixes styles across segments or even within a sentence. A dramatic person may shift styles when addressing the same partner.

The research on styles is extensive, and here I review only a limited number of studies. Perhaps I should start with Haga's (1962) work which offers a general introduction to Japanese styles. Haga, citing spoken style and written style, suggests a mixture of these styles without reason should be avoided; i.e., his "rule of consistency in sentence-final forms." Haga, however, points out several situations under which language users may purposefully mix the plain and abrupt *da* form and the formal *desu/masu* form. First, in discourse where *da* endings dominate with occurrences of sporadic *desu/masu* endings, *desu/masu* endings produce effects such as formality, humor, personal comment, and sarcasm. In a discourse segment where the *desu/masu* style dominates with sporadic *da* endings, *da* endings express interpersonal familiarity and closeness. In addition, Haga notes that sometimes the *da* and *desu/masu* mixture results from sociolinguistically uncertain circumstances, especially when the speaker fails to clearly assess the partner's relative social status.

Adding to Haga's reserch, in a series of studies I have examined styles and style shifts in Japanese discourse. In Maynard (1991a, 1991b, 1993a, 1997c, 2001a, 2001b, 2001c, 2001e), I focus on *da* and *desu/masu* verb endings, and identify their respective functions. These studies examine casual conversation as well as dialogue from fiction and literary essays in which abrupt and formal forms are mixed. I conclude that the choice of abrupt versus formal forms may be predicated upon a low versus high awareness of the partner. Low awareness situations which encourage the abrupt style occur when the self (1) is emotionally excited, (2) is involved in the event almost as if it were occurring right then and there, (3) expresses internal feelings in an almost self-addressed utterance, (4) jointly creates utterances, (5) presents the semantically subordinate information, and (6) expresses social familiarity and closeness. On the other hand, high awareness situations which promotes a formal style occur when the self expresses thoughts and presents information prioritizing social conventions and expectations.

More specifically, when *da* appears in the predominantly *desu/masu* text, the self communicates surprise, abrupt remembrance, or a sudden surge of emotion. For example, *da* is chosen in the narrative text when the self is located in the narrative scene right then and there taking a narrative-internal perspective. The choice for an abrupt style within a predominantly formal style effectuates immediacy and directness. Conversely, when *desu/masu* appears in the context of *da*, it marks a keener social awareness of convention. In a narrative text, the *desu/masu* style expresses a narrative-external voice, a voice allowing the narrating self to directly address the reader. The *desu/masu* style enhances the impression that the self, foregrounding the self's interactional attitude, is making a conscious effort to address the partner. I have also discussed, in Maynard (1997c), varieties of styles and style shifts and, avoiding the prescriptive tone associated with traditional studies, emphasize that style is chosen on the basis of social convention as well as the self's expressive desire.

I examine, in Maynard (2001b, 2001c, 2001e, 2002), a television drama series in which two people fall in love, and analyze how they shift styles depending on the degree of intimacy. I point out that the *da* style allows for direct and powerful expressions of emotion, communicating a sense of familiarity, tolerance, and indulgence. My analysis also reveals that the style shift occurs according to the chronologically documented emotional developments enacted in the drama. Also discussed are varied factors that motivate style shifts among dramatic persons. For example, when a person is vulnerable and hesitant, the speech shifts to a softer, gentler, and mostly politer style. Using the concepts of different aspects of the self (gendered, interactional, as well as girlish, boyish, womanly, manly, subordinate, and equal), I analyze fluid and shifting speech styles of dramatic persons. In Maynard (2004a, 2004b, 2005a), I examine style shifts in a variety of written discourse and propose basic styles, base-line *da*, and base-line *desu/masu*, as well as emotive *da*, and supra-polite styles.

In these studies, I interpret stylistic shifts in terms of the presentation of different selves. When interactional elements of communication are foregrounded, the self is highly aware of a socially-bound partner. When emotive features become primary, the self becomes less sensitive to social factors. When the self uses expressions aiming for a direct emotive appeal toward the intimate partner, the vulnerable and emotive self is foregrounded. Above all, in a series of studies (Maynard 1991a, 1991b, 1993a, 1997c, 1999a, 2001a, 2001b, 2002, 2004a, 2004b, 2005c), I emphasize that stylistic choices are motivated not only by social factors and constraints, but more importantly, by personal emotion and desire. In fact, stylistic choice and style mixture result from a compromise between the two opposing forces involving social norms and personal creativity. As noted by Haga (1962), and as I have explored based on a variety of genres of Japanese discourse, fluidity and variability of style are the norm, and styles, as with many other linguistic and interactional strategies, can be manipulated for a self-expression that facilitates a process of populating the empty self with different aspects, characters, and characteristics.

3.3 Narrating Self and Style Shifts

Let us now contrast styles and their shifts in the source and target texts, first by focusing on Kyon's narrative style in *Suzumiya Haruhi no Yuuutsu*. Kyon as the first-person narrator generally uses *da*, and often incorporates interactional particles which add an air of casualness, but he also shifts to *desu/masu* and blunt styles. Kyon's style shifts, however, are not generally reflected in the target text.

In source texts (*Suzumiya Haruhi no Yuuutsu*, 89) and (*Suzumiya Haruhi no Yuuutsu*, 150) we find Kyon's narrative style shifts to *desu/masu*, as in *Shoojiki tamari masen* 'Honestly, it's overwhelming' and *Ii egao desu* 'It is a nice smile'. This style diverts from an otherwise consistent *da* style. Suddenly Kyon presents his feelings with formality, as if making an announcement to the public. Readers become aware of the self who manipulates this style, although Kyon is not overtly mentioned. The corresponding English translation given in (24), *To be honest, I can't get enough of that outfit*, retains the same style as the rest of the discourse. Note also that *I* appears, indicating that Kyon functions as the agent of action, although in the original *Shoojiki tamari masen* appears with no overt use of the first-person pronoun. This contrasts with the source text where Kyon remains a receptive experiencer. Similarly, *Ii egao desu* in the source text (*Suzumiya Haruhi no Yuuutsu*, 150) conveys Kyon's attitude of formally making an announcement. This stylistic shift is not reflected in *A brilliant smile* appearing in (25).

(24) *The Melancholy of Haruhi Suzumiya*, 57
I could only stare at her in her bunny outfit.
Sorry. **To be honest, I can't get enough of that outfit** (*desu/masu* style).

(25) *The Melancholy of Haruhi Suzumiya*, 98
"Can we put this all on hold? Just set the matter of whether or not I believe you aside and put this on hold."
"OK."
Asahina smiled. **A brilliant smile** (*desu/masu* style).

Now, we turn to styles and style shifts in *Kitchin*. In the source text (*Kitchin*, 54), *munamoto ni ochite iru de wa nai desu ka* 'to my surprise, tears are pouring down on my chest' takes the *desu/masu* form. This exclamatory expression in the nonpast tense directly but formally communicates surprise. Yet, this shift is not reflected in the target text (26), i.e., *I found that tears were pouring down*, where *I* appears as an agent in a descriptive sentence in the narrative past tense.

(26) *Kitchen*, 34

But then, overpowered by their enormous weight, **I found that tears were pouring down** my cheeks and onto my blouse (*desu/masu* style).

Similarly, *ma ga sashita to yuu no deshoo* 'maybe it was that an evil took over me' in the source text (*Kitchin*, 10) is translated into a descriptive sentence, *it was like I was possessed* in (27), where the style shift is not introduced. Overall, it is difficult to translate into English the effect of stylistic choices and style shifts.

(27) *Kitchen*, 6

Bad as it sounds, **it was like I was possessed** (*desu/masu* style). His attitude was so totally "cool," though, I felt I could trust him.

Style shift becomes prominent through the use of interactional particles as well. The narrating self leaves the narrative world behind, and appears in another place where the self speaks to the reader in a conversational style. Conversational narration featured with interactional particles reveals the self's character or characteristic. For example, the use of *wa* communicates a stereotyped sense of femininity, evoking gender-associated character or characteristic. Additionally, interactional particles addressing the reader foreground the narrating self. But these nuanced shifts are integral to Japanese language and are exceedingly difficult to capture in translation.

A very casual conversational style may appear in narration, creating an overall friendly atmosphere. *Naan ni mo* 'nothing at all' with a casual tone in (28a) is such an example. Yet, its translation *I didn't think about it beyond that* in (28b) fails to create such an ambience. Back-translated, the likely expression would be something like *Sore ijoo wa kangae nakatta* 'I didn't think more about it', which does not reflect the original style. In addition, note that (28a) ends with the nominal predicate *no da*, evoking a self who manipulates the predicate.

(28) a. *Kitchin*, 13

Naan ni mo, kangaete wa i nakatta **no da**.

[(It was that) I wasn't thinking about anything at all.]

b. *Kitchen*, 8

I didn't think about it beyond that.

Use of blunt style may be metalinguistically noted, as shown in (29a). Sentences *Kookai wa saki ni tata nee n da* 'You'll regret it later for sure' and *Obaachan ni sonna kuchi o kiku na yo* 'Don't ever talk to your grandmother like that' clearly take this coarse blunt style. *Sonna kuchi o kiku na yo* 'Don't ever talk like that' is a command, but in translation in (29b), *talking to your grandfather that way* is presented as a part of the indirect statement. The part *Watashi mo mata tsukarete ita tame omowazu kitanai kotoba de omotte shimatta* 'Because I was tired, inadvertently, I thought in a filthy language' is translated in (29b) with an embedded clause within which the indirect thought is presented. The use of *I thought* in the target text reinforces a style which lacks apparent conversational features observed in the source text.

(29) a. *Kitchin*, 53
"Mada tsuka nai noo! Nemui."
Yuki-chan wa dada o kone tsuzuketa.
Gaki. **Watashi mo mata tsukarete ita tame omowazu kitanai kotoba de omotte shimatta. Kookai wa saki ni tata nee n da. Obaachan ni sonna kuchi o kiku na yo.**
["Aren't we there yet! Sleepy."]
[Yuki continued her whiny pouting.]
[Brat. Because I was tired, inadvertently, I thought in a filthy language. You'll regret it later for sure. Don't ever talk to your grandmother like that.]
b. *Kitchen*, 34
Yuki continued her whiny pouting. "Aren't we there yet? I'm sleepy."
The brat! I, too, had acted that way when I was tired. You'll regret it, **I thought, talking to your grandmother that way.**

Style shifts noted in this section express the narrating self's emotion and attitude. The subjective personal attitude exposes the interior of the hidden self, foregrounding associated aspects, characteristics, and characters. Shifting to a conversational style gives the impression that the self, as narrator, is actually engaging in a pseudo-conversation with the reader. In English, although style shifts observed in the Japanese original text are unavailable, other strategies may be chosen to communicate similar effects. For example, in (27) we find *it was like I was possessed*, which adds a conversational tone. However, incorporating varied styles is not preferred and appears only infrequently.

4 Reflections

This chapter has focused on a character-speak that populates the empty self. I have discussed the difficulty of fully translating the effect of character-speak, by illustrating examples of middle-aged-male language, old-man language, special occupation-related styles, female *yankii* language, youth language, dialects, fictional dialects, and the effeminate *onee* language.

Character-speak is used by the self not only as a dramatic person but also as a narrator. I have discussed features used for narration such as old-man language, youth blunt style, feudal-lord style, and casual speech, all of which are selected by a single narrating self. Also examined are *da* and *desu/masu* styles the narrating self uses for creating different aspects.

Differences in character-speak across the source and target texts can be understood as differences found in character zones. The Japanese character zone is broad in its capacity for active changes, while the character zone in English is apparently narrower with less possibility for the self's manipulation. By filling in the character zone with many voices of characters and characteristics, the self becomes populated. The Japanese self is enriched through linguistic features, sociolinguistic variations, styles, as well as shifts in style. The abundance and ubiquity of variation examined in this chapter illustrate the significance of this expressivity, although these features are notably absent in English translation. The fluid character zone in Japanese suggests that the Japanese self is fundamentally empty, yet is ever-changing as it is populated with varied features.

Although English translation lacks a similar character-speak, this does not mean character-speak is untenable in English. Variations are universally available across languages, but the significance they play within language, discourse, and pragmatics differs. Variations are often based on and motivated by the society in which the language is spoken, and the permissible application of variations also depends on social conventions and expectations. Given differences observed across Japanese and English texts, the gaps in translation pointed out so far are not surprising. Still, we cannot carelessly dismiss these gaps, for we must avoid distorting how the source text is intended in its fullness to mean.

CHAPTER 12

Empty and Populated Self in Japanese as Translation Text

Up to this point, I have focused on original Japanese and its English translation texts. In this chapter, I examine Japanese as a target text produced in the opposite direction of translation. Through this process which facilitates a broader examination, I inquire whether the findings based on translations from Japanese as the source text are also found in Japanese as the translated text. Features examined express subjectivity-supported aspects, characters, and characteristics, all of which populate the otherwise empty self.

First, English and Japanese translation texts of a Russian novel are examined. Contrasting English and Japanese translation texts, i.e., *The Eye* (Nabokov 2010 [1965]) and *Me* (Ogasawara 1992), is expected to provide further evidence in support of my position. Second, a short story, *Auggie Wren's Christmas Story* (Auster 2000), is contrasted with two separate Japanese texts translated by a translator/scholar and a translator/novelist. I contrast English and Japanese texts paying attention to similarities and differences. Overall, the expressive gaps observed in contrastive pragmatics analyses conducted in Chapters 7 through 11 are evident in the reverse translations as well. Multiple aspects related to Japanese grammar and discourse, as well as characters realized through variations of character-speak are discovered in Japanese as translation text.

1   Aspects of Self and of Self's Onlooker in *The Eye*

The Eye is a novel written by Vladimir Nabokov in 1930. The work was translated into English by his son Dmitri Nabokov in collaboration with the author, and was published in 1965. The Japanese translation was prepared by Toyoki Ogasawara and originally published in 1968. The translation *Me*, literally eye(s), contains the statement "The book is published in Japan by arrangement through ORION PRESS, Tokyo, Japan." However, it is unclear whether Ogasawara, known to have studied Russian and translated many Russian novels, actually translated *Me* from Russian or from the then available English translation. Either way, the case of *The Eye* is useful for the present study, since it offers the opportunity to contrast two translation texts in two different languages.

The usefulness of *The Eye* is not limited to the above. Although the work received less attention than other Nabokov novels (Johnson 1985), it provides a narrative discourse where the theme concerning the self becomes the primary focus. *The Eye* is a story told by the narrator, a young Russian émigré in Berlin, who early in the story fatally shoots himself. The ensuing events take place in the imagination of the now ghostly narrator. Among the émigrés the narrator interacts with, one Smurov, a newcomer, comes to attention. It is revealed that Smurov, consisting of many different and contradictory images held by other dramatic persons, is the narrator himself. The narrator insists at the end of the novel that to be an onlooker, to be the "eye," is what makes him happy. For, I, the narrator, does not exist, but Smurov lives on. Zeman (2018) characterizes *The Eye* as a novel not representing a homogeneous perspective, but rather a fragmented polyphonic perspective of selves. She captures the essence of the self depicted in the novel by summarizing "(A)t the end, the disintegration of different selves leads the protagonist to the conclusion that he himself does not exist; what exists is only the distinct third-person reflections of his alter ego Smurov" (2018: 151).

In terms of narrative structure, Smurov is described from the third-person point of view as shown in (1) and (2). The modal verb *must* in (1) and the modal adverb *obviously* in (2) both echo the (deceased) narrator's voice. Here the self is clearly split into two, I (the narrator) and Smurov, whereby I (the observer) corresponds to the narrator's perspective, and me (the observed), to the dramatic person (i.e., Smurov). Counterparts to *must* and *obviously* in Japanese translation are *sooi nai* 'must' (*Me*, 201) and *akiraka ni* 'clearly' (*Me*, 212), both conveying the narrator's first-person point of view.

(1) *The Eye*, 45
    A brief silence followed. Smurov sat calmly stirring his tea. Yes, he **must** (*sooi nai*) be a former officer, a daredevil who liked to flirt with death, and it is only out of modesty that he says nothing about his adventures.

(2) *The Eye*, 46
    Smurov kept nodding approvingly as he listened. He was **obviously** (*akiraka ni*) a person who, behind his unpretentiousness and quietness, concealed a fiery spirit.

In the course of the novel, Smurov is identified as the narrator in the following way; "'Gospodin Smurov,' it said in a loud but hesitant tone. I turned at the sound of my name involuntarily stepping off the sidewalk with one foot" (*The Eye*, 110). Given this development, it is possible to identify referential expressions and roles including *I* (narrator, protagonist-live) and *I* (narrator, protagonist-deceased) who are further split into internal and external aspects. Additional roles include Smurov functioning as dramatic person, narrator, and protagonist-deceased, all viewed from the third-person perspective as *he*.

1.1   *First-Person Expressions*

In the examples to follow, (3) through (5) taken from *The Eye*, where English *I*, *my*, *me*, and *myself* appear, we find six different first-person references as given in parentheses in the Japanese version, *Me. Watashi* 'I' and other terms such as *ware* 'I (archaic and formal)', *waga mi* 'my self's circumstance (archaic and formal)' and *onore* 'self (archaic and formal)' index the objectified outer self reached from the outside. *Jibun* 'self' and *jishin* 'own self' both imply an inner self reached from the inside.

Notably, the choice here is not based on social or contextual information; rather, it is motivated by how and from where the narrating self views relevant aspects of the self. These expressions are socially motivated in that they originate in personal and interpersonal circumstances, but the choice in *The Eye* is primarily made for the purpose of narrative manipulation. In the Japanese version comparable to English texts (3) through (5), *watashi* and other self-referencing expressions appear. This seems to be influenced by the nature of the text, where the narrator is obsessed with the notion of the self, providing a context for the use of varied forms in the Japanese translation.

In (3), the phrase, *juxtaposition*, refers to the situation where a person needs to borrow some money but knows no one to ask. The Japanese translation (*Me*, 192) chooses the phrase *ware to waga mi* 'I and my self's circumstance'.

(3)   *The Eye*, 37
   However, now, as I indulged in this **juxtaposition** (*ware to waga mi*), I (*watashi*) did not feel a bit humiliated.

In the Japanese text (*Me*, 192) comparable to (4), we find *watashi* 'I' and *ima no watashi* 'current me', a case of *watashi* directly preceded by a modifier *ima no* 'current'. Here the self is viewed from the third-person point of view. In contrast with *In respect to myself* in the English counterpart in (4), the Japanese text uses *jishin ni tsuite yuu naraba* 'If I talk about my own self'. Here the term *jishin* 'own self', representing an objectified inner self, functions as the object of talking which is instigated by the self appearing as the zero-form. Varied first-person forms in Japanese communicate multiple aspects of the self not fully reflected in the English text.

(4)   *The Eye*, 37
      Ever since the shot—that shot which, in my opinion, had been fatal—I (*watashi*) had observed myself (*jibun to yuu mono*) with curiosity instead of sympathy, and my painful past—before the shot—was now foreign to me (*ima no watashi*). (...) **In respect to myself** (*jishin ni tsuite yuu naraba*) I (*watashi*) was now an onlooker.

Likewise, in the Japanese version (*Me*, 170) comparable to the English translation (5), we find *watashi*, *jibun jishin* 'self's own self', *jibun to yuu mono* 'person called the self', and *onore* 'self (archaic and formal)'. These variations convey the self viewed from outside and inside, illuminating the rich variability of the Japanese self.

(5)   *The Eye*, 17
      Yet **I** (*watashi*) was always exposed, always wide-eyed; even in sleep **I** (*watashi*) did not cease to watch over **myself** (*jibun jishin*), understanding nothing of **my existence** (*jibun to yuu mono*) growing crazy at the thought of not being able to stop being aware of **myself** (*onore*) (...)

Through varied forms associated with *watashi* and *jibun*, the Japanese translation reveals multiple aspects of the self introduced by a narrating self. These features are associated with multiple aspects of the self that play varying functional roles in the narrative discourse. Clearly refusing a holistic and homogeneous concept, the self in the Japanese text is realized in multiple ways, only to temporarily fill in the empty self. In the English version (5), we find *I*, *myself*, and *my existence*, which consistently bring forth the narrating self's descriptive perspective. Although in the English text varied forms are used, they do not fully portray aspects of the self communicated through Japanese self-referencing variations.

1.2   *Receptive and Perceptive Constructions*

The Japanese translation text shows a tendency toward a certain subjective personalization of discourse, especially by capturing events as receptive and perceptive experiences. Instead of maintaining a third-person perspective, the discourse bears features of shifting perspectives, often reflecting the rhetoric of *pathos*.

In (6), we find *he*, the objectified self viewed from the third-person perspective. In the English version, *he* refers to the narrator, but it is described as someone different from the narrating self. In the Japanese text (*Me*, 187), however, the zero-form is chosen, which implies that the self at the zero-point knew that person's shape. The clear shift in point of view in English is not realized in the Japanese version, where the event is ultimately perceived as an inner self's experience approached from the first-person perspective.

(6) *The Eye*, 33
I saw myself from the outside, treading water as it were, and was both touched and frightened like an inexperienced ghost watching the existence of a person whose inner lining, inner night, mouth, and taste-in-the-mouth, **he** (zero) knew as well as that person's shape.

Another method of expressing subjectivity in Japanese is the use of clausal constructions instead of nominal phrases, which is the case in the English text (7a). In the Japanese version (7b), the clausal choice successfully communicates the receptive self's experience with a personal emotive response, which contains the passive expression, *michibikarete* 'being lead'. Here the inanimate subject in the English translation, *my floating mechanical motion*, is avoided, and instead, a statement is made about *watashi*. The English text takes the third-person perspective while the Japanese version takes the emotionally involving receptive first-person perspective. A similar phenomenon is observed in the expression *Ever since the shot* in (4).

(7) a. *The Eye*, 33
My floating mechanical motion brought me to Weinstock's shop.
b. *Me*, 187
Tadayou yoona muishikiteki na ugoki ni **michibikarete**, **watashi** wa Wainsutokku no mise ni tadori tsuita.
[Being lead by some floating and almost unintended motion, I finally reached Wainsutokku's shop.]

(8a) illustrates a similar phenomenon where the nominal phrase *the sound of my name* appears. The Japanese version (8b) takes on the subordinate clause with a passive expression, *Jibun no namae o yobarete* 'I was called by my name'. Again, the choice of this sentence structure illustrates a preference for the Japanese way of subjectification, foregrounding the receptive self.

(8) a. *The Eye*, 110
"Gospodin Smurov," it said in a loud but hesitant tone. I turned at **the sound of my name** involuntarily stepping off the sidewalk with one foot. It was Kashmarin, Matilda's husband.

b. *Me*, 274

"Sumuurofu-san" to koedaka da ga, tamerai gachina chooshi de, dare ka ga yonda no dearu. **Jibun no namae o yobarete** watashi wa omowazu hodoo kara kataashi o fumi hazushi, furi muita. Sore wa ano Machiruda no otto, Kashimarin datta.

[(It was that) someone called "Mr. Sumuurofu" with a loud but hesitant tone. I was called by my name, and without thinking, I stepped off the sidewalk with one foot, and turned back. It was Machiruda's husband, Kashimarin.]

The preference in Japanese for perception verbs results in a sharp contrast with English. In (9b), *kikoeta* 'could be heard' is used, although we find, *I heard*, the agent-does structure in the English version (9a). In Japanese, a perceptive intransitive verb is chosen, which implies the existence of a hidden self.

(9) a. *The Eye*, 34

From somewhere down behind the counter **I heard** Weinstock's wheezing.

b. *Me*, 188

Kauntaa no mukoo no yuka no atari kara, Wainsutokku no zei zei yuu koe ga **kikoeta**.

[From somewhere from the floor behind the counter, Wainsutokku's wheezing sound could be heard.]

1.3 No da *Nominal Predicates*

Contrasting *The Eye* and *Me*, one is impressed by different predicate forms observed across the novel's two versions. In Japanese, although it is possible to end with simple verb forms, many sentences take nominal predicates, i.e., *no da* (and its variants) and *no dearu* expressions. As discussed in Chapter 9, *no da* offers multiple functions such as explanation, personalization, and cohesion. It should be added that being different from *da*, *dearu* conveys the self's confirming and declaring attitudes. A sentence with *dearu* gives the impression that the self is dramatically declaring or proclaiming a position (Maynard 1985).

In the Japanese text (*Me*, 278) comparable to (10), five cases of predicates with nominalization appear. It is possible here to use simple predicates instead, for example, *shiawase da* 'I am happy' instead of *shiawasena no da*, or *shiawasena no dearu*. This is what happens in English counterparts where expressions take simple predicate forms.

(10) *The Eye*, 113–114.

    And yet I am happy. Yes, happy (*no da*). I swear, I swear I am happy. I have realized that the only happiness in this world is to observe, to spy, to watch, to scrutinize oneself and others, to be nothing but a big slightly vitreous, somewhat bloodshot, unblinking eye (*no da*). I swear that this is happiness (*no dearu*). What does it matter that I am a bit cheap, a bit foul, and that no one appreciates all the remarkable things about me—my fantasy, my erudition, my literary gift ... I am happy (*no dearu*) that I can gaze at myself, for any man is absorbing—yes, really absorbing (*no daroo*)!

Predicates with nominalization evoke different aspects of the narrating self's presence, although this effect is not felt in the English version. Japanese subjective expressions remain complex and varied, and these strategies perpetually populate the empty self with multiple aspects.

1.4 Character-Speak and the Old-Man Character

In *The Eye*, different types of dramatic persons appear. The manner in which one character, Uncle Pasha, is presented is worthy of note. Here we witness a case of an old-man character-speak in the Japanese translation, although such speech style is not evident in the English version. Pasha, visiting Berlin from London, is uncle to Vanya whom Smurov is to marry. At his age of 80, he is mobile, noisy, and inquisitive. We concentrate on the conversation that takes place when Uncle Pasha meets Smurov in the English version (11a) and compare it with the Japanese version (11b).

    In the Japanese text, we find features stereotypically linked to the speech of an elderly male, such as Pasha's self-referencing form *washi* 'I' and its plural form *washira* 'we'. We also find expressions *no ka ne* '(is it that) it is the case, is it?' and *no kai* '(is it that) it is the case' associated with an old-man speech. *No ka ne* is formed with the nominalizer *no* followed by the question particle *ka* accompanied with an empathy-appealing *ne*. *No kai*, consisting of the nominalizer *no* and the question particle *kai*, gives an impression that the question comes from someone older who interacts in an inquisitive and polite manner. If a young person expresses a similar attitude of *no ka ne*, it would take something like *n daro* (or its formal version *n desho*) '(is it that) it is the case'. The use of the progressive tense expression *omottoru* 'thinking' and *ittoru* 'going well' instead of the usual *omotte iru* and *itte iru* also mark the speech as the kind stereotypically used by an elderly person, unless it is considered a dialect. Additionally, the emphatic particle *zo* is most typically used by male speakers.

(11) a. *The Eye*, 77
   "Oh, Smurov and I are old friends (...)" (...)
   "And you think we don't know ... We know all about it ..." (...)
   "I'll say one thing." (...)
   "Your job coming along well?"
   b. *Me*, 236–237
   "Aa, Sumuurofu-kun nara **washi** wa yoku shittoru **zo**." (...)
   "**Washira** ni wa wakara n to **omottoru no ka ne**." (...)
   "**Washi** no iitai koto wa hitotsu dake sa." (...)
   "Shigoto wa umaku **ittoru no kai**?"
   ["Ah, Mr. Sumuurofu, I know him well."] (...)
   ["So you think that we don't know?"] (...)
   ["What I want to say is just one thing."] (...)
   ["Is your work going well?"]

The features of character-speak observed in the Japanese version depict Uncle Pasha as an old man, and they clearly differ from speech styles of other males in the novel, including Smurov himself. In the English version (11a), it is difficult to trace the character-speak and as a result the old-man character is not depicted through speech as clearly as in the Japanese version. The contrast between *The Eye* and *Me* reveals different subjective expressions and character-speak features. Given that both works are linked to an identical Russian text, the contrast reveals essential and undeniable differences to be taken into consideration in our quest of exploring the self.

2   Expressivity in Two Translations of *Auggie Wren's Christmas Story*

This section examines two Japanese translation texts of an American short story, *Auggie Wren's Christmas Story* by Auster (2000). Both translations are titled *Oogii Ren no Kurisumasu Sutoorii*, and share common features, but differences are also found. I have chosen translation texts by Shibata and Murakami for the following reasons. Murakami is known for a style heavily influenced by the English language. In particular, his style seems to have been influenced by American novelists Raymond Carver, John Irving, J.D. Salinger, Truman Capote, and Scott Fitzgerald whose works Murakami has translated into Japanese. Murakami reflects that "(B)ecause I have created Japanese on my own, my style reflects the thought process influenced by foreign languages and foreign cultures" (Murakami and Shibata 2000: 218–219, my translation). He admits that when translating English novels into Japanese, foreign elements inevitably surface in the text. Murakami affirms, however, that his literary style is not exactly the same as his translation style, and that he has attempted a deconstruction of the translation style by changing the content while preserving the same structure.

Given this background, including Murakami's translation as data is expected to reveal a kind of variability otherwise difficult to unmask. I have come across a publication containing translations by Murakami and by Shibata, who is a scholar and translator of American literature. In what follows, first I compare the overall translation styles of Shibata and Murakami. Then I analyze first-person expressions, referential expressions of dramatic persons as well as *no da* and *no dearu* expressions across the two translations. I argue that even when the texts are produced by different and competent Japanese translators, the emergent self bears common features absent in the English source text.

2.1 Similarities and Differences across Two Translations

The source text, consisting of 191 sentences, is structured in such a way that the first-person narrator meets Auggie who tells him an interesting story. Auggie's story is based on what happens to him one Christmas day, and it occupies approximately half of the work. His story is presented in direct quotation, and in the data presentation to follow, all those sentences appear in quotation marks.

Similarities observed in translations by Shibata and Murakami include the tendency (1) to translate what is indirectly quoted into direct quotation, (2) to make use of verbs of giving in forms of *-te yaru* and *-te kureru*, and (3) to add the verb *naru* 'become'. Differences are observed in the choice of pronouns *boku* 'I' (primarily used by male speakers) and *watashi* 'I' in reference to the first-person narrator. In addition, compared with Murakami's, Shibata's translation of quotation tends to be colloquial with casual speech features, and overall his narrative style tends to be more conversational.

For example, in (12b), in *kozoo ni okuri kaeshite yaroo ka na* 'maybe I will send it back to that kid' and *kekkyoku zuru zuru* 'after all, dragging on', the use of *kozoo* 'kid' and *zuru zuru* 'dragging on' add to the conversational narrative tone. Murakami's translation (12c), avoiding colloquial phrases, incorporates a conversational style less frequently.

(12) a. *Auggie Wren's Christmas Story*, xii
"Every once in a while I'd get a little urge to send it back to him, but I kept delaying and never did anything about it."
b. Shibata's translation, 171
"Tokidoki, **kozoo ni okuri kaeshite yaroo ka na** tte yuu ki ni naru koto mo atta kedo, **kekkyoku zuru zuru** nani mo shi nakatta."

["Sometimes, there were occasions when I felt "Maybe I'll send it back to that kid (for the benefit of him)," but after all I kept dragging on and I did nothing about it."]
c. Murakami's translation, 155
"Ie ni okutte yara nakucha na to tokidoki omoi dasu n da kedo, tsui okuri sobirete, kekkyoku sono mama ni natte shimatta."
["Although now and then a thought occurred to me that I must send it back at his home address (for the benefit of him), I ended up delaying, and after all was left as it was."]

I should hasten to add, however, that in contrast with the English original, Japanese translations also reveal similarities in their use of conversational style. Comparing the source text (13) and comparable Japanese texts (Shibata, 171–172 and Murakami, 155–156), the following points are noted. In Shibata's translation, interpersonal particles *yo* and *na* in *mieru n da yo na* '(it is that) it can be seen', the use of nominalization and quotative qualification in *juugo wa aru n ja nai ka tte yuu* 'I think maybe there are fifteen', and the vocative *Robaato ya* 'my dear Robert' carry casual speech features. Likewise, in Murakami's translation, the interactional particle *yo* in *mawatte tari suru n da yo* 'do things like going over the same place' and the casual adverb *yattokosa* 'finally' add a conversational tone. Notably, Shibata's translation uses the verb of giving in *akete kureta* 'she opened (for the benefit of me)', but Murakami's translation, *akeru* 'open' shows a likeness closer to the original English. Both Shibata and Murakami use nominal predicates and particles while these strategies are unavailable in the source text.

The use of nonpast (*r*)*u*- and past *ta*-forms by Shibata and Murakami reveals an interesting contrast. In the English text (13), Auggie's talk which is directly quoted consistently uses the present tense. In Shibata's translation, the past tense appears five times (*oshita* 'pushed', *oshite mita* 'tried pushing', *kotaeta* 'answered', *itta* 'said', and *akete kureta* 'opened (for the self's benefit)'), maintaining the timeline and presenting information in chronological order. Murakami consistently uses the nonpast form which, partly because of being a root form and lacking modality, gives the impression that statements are made with less regard to the reader.

I should point out that Murakami uses *zoro zoro to ashi o hikizuri nagara* 'slowly dragging her feet' which is close in meaning to the original. In contrast, Shibata uses *noso noso to doa no mae ni yatte kuru* 'slowly comes toward the door' which does not fully reflect the image portrayed in the original word *shuffling*.

Now in terms of forms referring to the old blind woman, i.e., the mother of the young man in Auggie's story, Shibata uses *toshiyori no onna* 'old woman', followed by *baasan* 'grandmother-like old woman', expressing a moderate intimacy toward the dramatic person, while Murakami chooses neutral and distant expressions *toshi totta onna* 'elderly woman' and *onna* 'woman'. In English *an old woman* and *the old woman* appear.

(13) *Auggie Wren's Christmas Story*, xii
"Everything looks the same in the place, and you keep going over the same ground thinking you're somewhere else. Anyway, I finally get to the apartment I'm looking for and ring the bell. Nothing happens. I assume no one's there, but I try again just to make sure. I wait a little longer, and just when I'm about to give up, I hear someone **shuffling** to the door. **An old woman**'s (Shibata: *toshiyori no onna*, Murakami: *toshi totta onna*) voice asks who's there, and I say I'm looking for Robert Goodwin. 'Is that you, Robert?' **the old woman** (Shibata: *baasan*, Murakami: *onna*) says, and then she undoes about fifteen locks and opens the door."

In general, Shibata's translation is rich with linguistic subjectivity, and one senses that the narrating self tells the story as a performer, personally addressing the reader. Shibata's translation more closely reflects strategies and styles we have observed in Chapters 7 through 11. On the other hand, Murakami's clear, direct narration resembles the style Oda (1930) practiced when translating Hemingway's novel, and later adopted as the style featuring dry and crisp effects in Japanese literary genres (Inoue 2012). Regardless of differences, the two translators make a number of grammatical and stylistic adjustments in creating a narrative ambience most suitable to their personal preferences. Still, overall, Japanese texts use richer subjective expressions than the source text.

2.2 Person Expressions

Choosing the appropriate first-person reference form is a critical step in Japanese as discussed in Chapter 7. On the use of *watashi* 'I' and *boku* 'I (primarily used by male speakers)' in their translations, Murakami and Shibata (2000) offer the following reflection. Notably, both refer to themselves as *boku* in this talk.

> Murakami: One more thing. When I translated this work, I was very much concerned with personal pronouns. Regarding the choice between *boku* and *watashi*, I recall that for me the decision was difficult and quite bothersome. That, I remember. But in the end, I decided on *boku*. I felt that if I used *watashi*, it would seem too ordinary and expected. So I dared to use

> *boku*, I guess. Most people, probably 80% or 85% of them, would choose *watashi*, if they are translating this particular work.
>
> Shibata: I felt that perhaps *boku* is connected to the physical person, I mean, *boku* carries colorful personal features more than *watashi*. So, I wanted to use a phrase without those features, without the sense of a person. In truth, not using any phrase at all would be best, but I didn't think that would be quite acceptable, so, that's how I decided on *watashi*, I think.
>
> MURAKAMI and SHIBATA 2000: 183–184, my translation)

Clearly the choice of *boku* and *watashi*, since each adds different characteristics, establishes different aspects of the self. Murakami, while recognizing that *watashi* is more common, dares to choose *boku*. Shibata, not wishing to personalize the narrator, chooses *watashi*. Although Shibata hides the narrating self this way, overall, one senses the narrating self's voice reverberating more vividly in Shibata's translation style than in Murakami's.

Curiously, we find one case of *watashi* in Murakami's translation, *Watashi wa soko de rikai shita* 'I understood then' (Murakami, 151). Regarding this deviation in the translation of *Auggie Wren's Christmas Story*, Murakami admits that it was merely a result of carelessness.

> Murakami: About this, my feelings are that it didn't matter whatever decision I made. When I reread the work, *boku* was consistently used, except one time I spotted *watashi*. This happened because I translated the first half with *boku*, and then when I translated the second half, I used *watashi* by mistake. Realizing this, I made the necessary corrections. But I left one case of *watashi* uncorrected. That's what happened, so I think either *boku* or *watashi* is fine. It doesn't matter much, I think.
>
> MURAKAMI and SHIBATA 2000: 185, my translation

Regarding the narrating self's use of first-person pronouns in *Auggie Wren's Christmas Story*, Shibata's translation uses *watashi* in the narration, and *boku* in quotation. In Murakami's translation, *boku* is used both in narration and quotation. Contrasting the first-person reference in the narrative segment across Japanese and translation texts results in the following. The pronoun *I* appears 81 times in the English source text, *watashi* is used 47 times in Shibata's text, and *boku*, 38 times in Murakami's translation. The difference in frequency of first-person pronouns observed here results from the consistent appearance of *I* in English versus the frequent use of the zero-form and less frequent occurrences of *watashi* in Japanese. This supports the Japanese hidden self in contrast with

English consistently presented self. A commonality is observed in Shibata's and Murakami's translations, and yet some differences are noteworthy.

Let us observe here where *watashi* and *boku* across two translations create different narrative worlds. (14) is the initial sentence of *Auggie Wren's Christmas Story*. The first word is *I* in English, and in translation texts *watashi* (Shibata, 163) and *boku* (Murakami, 147) appear. When the story is told from the perspective of *watashi* versus *boku*, its narrative tone differs, the former being formal and distant, and the latter, more casual and personal. *Boku* also instantly activates the male character in the narrating self. The same effects are reinforced in the final sentence of the story as shown in (15). Here again, *watashi* (Shibata, 178) and *boku* (Murakami, 162) create different overall narrative impressions.

(14) *Auggie Wren's Christmas Story*, viii
  I (Shibata: *watashi*, Murakami: *boku*) heard this story from Auggie Wren.

(15) *Auggie Wren's Christmas Story*, xv
  I (Shibata: *watashi*, Murakami: *boku*) returned Auggie's smile with a smile of my own, and then I called out to the waiter and asked for the check.

Examining the source text (16) and the translation texts (Shibata, 177 and Murakami, 161), we find that Shibata chooses the zero-form and *watashi* in narration and *boku* when referring to himself in a question he was about to bring to Auggie. Murakami uses *boku* consistently. The two translations differ in how or whether the narration and conversation are separated. In Shibata's translation, the self in narration and the self in quotation reveal different characteristics associated with the zero-form, *watashi*, and *boku*, while Murakami's translation presents a consistent aspect of the self regardless of the self's role.

(16) *Auggie Wren's Christmas Story*, xv
  I (Shibata: zero, Murakami: *boku*) was about to ask him if he'd been putting me (Shibata: *boku*, Murakami *boku*) on, but then I realized he would never tell. I (Shibata: *watashi*, Murakami: *boku*) had been tricked into believing him, and that was the only thing that mattered.

As suggested by Murakami and Shibata (2000), the choice of *watashi* and *boku* brings different effects to the entire narrative. Although Murakami confesses that either one is fine, the reality is that the choice of self-reference forms is made for specific expressive purposes. Undeniably, the choice determines the manner in which the empty self is populated. In the English source text, this particular choice is absent, and a stable self is maintained.

Shifting our focus to dramatic persons, how is Auggie referred to? In English, *Auggie* appears 13 times, *he*, 47 times in narration, and *I* surfaces 103 times in Auggie's quotation. In Shibata's translation, *Oogii* appears 23 times, and *kare*, 19 times in narration; in quotation *ore* is used 35 times. In Murakami's translation, *Oogii* appears 17 times, and *kare*, 18 times in narration; in quotation *ore* is used 34 times. The sharpest contrast between the source and translation texts is observed in quotation where *Auggie* refers to himself as *I* in the original. In both Japanese translation texts, the frequency of *ore* is substantially less (Shibata 35 times and Murakami 34 times) just about one third of the time.

The old blind woman Auggie visits is translated in different ways. In addition to what is discussed regarding (13), Shibata uses *baasan* 'grandmother-like old woman' (Shibata, 176), and Murakami, *kanojo* 'she' (Murakami, 160). The repeated *baasan*, with familiarity and intimacy, augments the conversational and personalized nature of Shibata's translation style, while the use of *kanojo* 'she' in Murakami's translation communicates a sense of neutrality. In the original (17) and (18), *her* repeatedly appears, and Murakami's repetition of *kanojo* mostly corresponds to the English pronoun. This repetition of *kanojo* reminds the reader that Auggie is an American who, in his talk, is likely to use *her*. This may be intended by Murakami in that he presents translation as translation, or presents translation with a foreignization effect (Venuti 2004, 2008), revealing a case of shining through in a broad sense (Teich 2003). It may also reveal that his literary style has been substantially influenced by his experience in English-to-Japanese translation.

(17) *Auggie Wren's Christmas Story*, xiv
"I lied to **her** (Shibata: *baasan*, Murakami: *baasan*), and then I stole from her (Shibata: *baasan*, Murakami: *kanojo*). I don't see how you can call that a good deed."

(18) *Auggie Wren's Christmas Story*, xiv
"You made **her** (Shibata: *baasan*, Murakami: *kanojo*) happy."

Incidentally, it is of note that Murakami's writing anticipates translation into foreign languages. Hijiya-Kirschnereit (2012) introduces the concept of "pretranslation" as it applies to the works of Murakami. She points out that Murakami creates and edits anticipating that his novels will be translated into English and other languages. The pretranslation strategy may be one of the factors influencing Murakami's literary style.

2.3   No da *and* no dearu *Nominal Predicates*

We turn now to *no da* and *no dearu* nominal predicates in *Oogii Ren no Kurisumasu Sutoorii*. Comparing the two translation texts, sentence-final *no da* nominal predicates, including its colloquial *n da*, appear 28 times in both Shibata's and Murakami's translations. Given that the source text does not make use of nominal predicates, frequent use of *no da* in both translations reaffirms the subjective nature of the Japanese narrative style.

Although similarities are observed across two Japanese translations in contrast with English, a discrepancy is observed regarding the *no dearu* expression. The *no dearu* expression appears six times in Shibata's translation while Murakami does not use it at all. Let us contrast how the translations differ. In the source text, (19.2) offers justification for the position taken in (19.1). In the Japanese translation the sentence comparable to (19.2) is marked with the nominal predicate offering explanatory information. Shibata explains with *no dearu* (Shibata, 164) and Murakami, with *no da* (Murkami, 148). The *no dearu* construction nuances the self's dramatic declaration, but *no da* does not quite create this impression. Accordingly, one senses the self more vividly in Shibata's translation than in Murakami's.

(19) *Auggie Wren's Christmas Story*, viii
   1. I was no longer just another customer to Auggie. 2. I had become a distinguished person (Shibata: *no dearu*, Murakami: *no da*).

As a counterpart to English given in (20), Shibata (Shibata, 167) chooses *Watashi ni wa wakatta no da. Oogii wa jikan o totte iru no dearu* '(It was that) to me it was clear. (It was that) Oogii was taking pictures of time' with the use of *no da* and *no dearu*. Murakami (Murakami, 151) translates as *Oogii wa jikan o satsuei shite iru no da to boku wa satotta* 'I understood that (it was that) Oogii was photographing time', where *no da* appears within a subordinate clause. Although different in use, *no da* and *no dearu* are manipulations frequently chosen in Japanese, and statements with nominalized elements convey the self's subjective commentary perspective. Thus the narrating self who incorporates these strategies is more vividly portrayed although such a depiction is absent in the original English.

(20) *Auggie Wren's Christmas Story*, x
   Auggie was photographing time (Shibata: *no dearu*, Murakami: *no da*), I realized (Shibata: *no da*), both natural time and human time, and he was doing it by planting himself in one tiny corner of the world and willing it to be his own, by standing guard in the space he had chosen for himself.

For the translation of (21), again, the differences between the two translations become evident. Shibata uses (Shibata, 167) *no da* in the translation of *That was the subject of the story he told me*, and *no dearu*, for the translation of *I'm still struggling to make sense of it*. Here Shibata prefers to divide the original sentence into two, and to end both with nominalized predicates. For the first part of the English sentence, Murakami (Murakami, 151) structures the Japanese sentence closely to the source text, i.e., *Sore ga kare ga boku ni katatte kureta hanashi no shudai datta* 'That was the subject of the story he kindly told me', without a nominal predicate. And for the translation of the second part, Murakami chooses *no da*. Again, Shibata's preference for a commentary statement with *no dearu* is observed, where the narrating self's declaring and proclaiming aspect materializes.

(21) *Auggie Wren's Christmas Story*, x
That was the subject of the story he told me (Shibata: *no da*) and **I'm still struggling to make sense of it** (Shibata: *no dearu*, Murakami: *no da*).

Overall, Shibata's narrative style conveys more subjective expressivity, and generally incorporates Japanese features investigated in this work more than Murakami's. As a result, the narrating self with varied aspects materializes more vividly in Shibata's translation.

3 Reflections

This chapter has investigated Japanese as translation text by contrasting English and Japanese versions of a Russian novel as well as one English source text and two different Japanese translations. Features analyzed include (1) first-person reference forms, (2) perception verbs, (3) character-speak, (4) reference forms of dramatic persons, and (5) *no da* and *no dearu* nominal predicates. In these analyses, phenomena discussed in Chapters 7 through 11 are confirmed. These features absent in the source texts, repeatedly appear in Japanese as translation texts, despite differences observed between two different Japanese translation texts.

All the features of the Japanese language discussed in this chapter lead us to the concept of the empty self, being populated through varied devices and strategies. Japanese expressions make the character zone lively with emotive and attitudinal voices and varied features of the character-speak. The observed differences across English and Japanese translation texts guide us toward distinct ontological views in our exploration of the self across languages.

PART 4
Reflections

CHAPTER 13

Exploring the Self in Philosophical Pragmatics

1 **Empty and Populated Self: Summary**

Through philosophical contrastive pragmatics I have explored the concept of self as evidenced in the Japanese language in the contrastive context of translation texts. This process is based on linguistic and other related theories and frameworks developed in the West and Japan; ideas are mixed and integrated, resulting in a product of hybridity. At the same time, I have based my exploration of the empty and populated self on philosophical traditions and cultural phenomena primarily traced to Japan. In this sense, this work stands on the shoulders of many scholars associated with both Western and non-Western academic worlds.

The empty self proposed in this work is populated with its aspects, characters, and characteristics. The self is often place-sensitive, hidden, but perceptive of the situation and passive of the experience. The place is also empty, but becomes meaningful as it interacts with the self. The evidence supporting this conclusion is found in two related categories, linguistic subjectivity and character. Under these headings, extensive analyses of translation texts selected from literary genres are presented. I have taken the position that we are able to gain an understanding of the self by observing and interpreting translation gaps recognized across original and translation texts.

Aspects of the self revealed in this study are multiple and flexible. The self exists at a point of zero, experiencing what is happening in the place, foregrounding a stance both receptive and perceptive. The self is understood as being emotive, participatory, performatory, and interdependent. Also discussed in terms of perspectives are the inner, objectified, intersubjective, and transferred self, all portraying a fluid Japanese self. We have also come across poetic images of a flickering and transient self.

The Japanese self evidenced in the Japanese text in contrast with its translation is populated with characters and characteristics through the character-speak. The variations populating the self include age- and gender-associated varieties such as middle-aged male language, old-man language, youth language, the anti-social *yankii* language, as well as the effeminate *onee* language. Also discussed are regional and fictional dialects as well as stereotypical speech styles linked to characters such as a scholar and a feudal lord. With these features, the self emerges through moment-to-moment language use, while continuing with its populating process. The self, initially located in the empty place, is itself empty, but, through performance, transforms into a populated self consisting of a complex web of aspects, characters, and characteristics.

In the four chapters of Part 1, the general framework of this work is introduced. In Chapter 1, I have introduced the framework for philosophical contrastive pragmatics as a multidisciplinary area of contrastive study aiming to understand the ontological features of our language practice. I have placed this work in relation to the language-and-thought debate, and discussed the rationale for data selection. Chapter 2 reviews the Western thought from the traditional position to the postmodern and socially constructed views of the self. In Chapter 3, I have concentrated on subjectivity and character, the two key concepts for exploring the concept of self. Also reviewed are positions I have taken over the years, including my studies on Discourse Modality (Maynard 1993a), and the Place of Negotiation theory (Maynard 2000, 2002). Chapter 4 reviews the field of translation studies relevant to the data as well as the research in contrastive pragmatics.

In Part 2, Chapter 5 concentrates on the concepts of empty self and empty place in Japanese studies. Then, in Chapter 6, continuing with the Japanese context, I have discussed how Japanese language studies have explored linguistic and discourse phenomena related to the self.

In Chapter 7 through Chapter 11, I have analyzed grammatical phenomena including first-person references, intransitive verbs, and passives. Also explored are discourse aspects such as the topic-comment dynamism, varied types of quotation and inserted speech, and fictional and often stereotyped character-speak. My analyses have been guided by interpretive concepts developed in Japan and elsewhere and adapted from multiple fields. They include approaches to the self from philosophy, psychology, anthropology, and literary criticism. I have analyzed data qualitatively through context-based interpretation, making use of tools developed in multiple disciplines developed both in Western and non-Western scholarly traditions, including conversation analysis, pragmatics, discourse analysis, sociolinguistics, variation studies, literary studies, and translation studies. Different approaches are highlighted and applied to phenomena focused in specific chapters.

More specifically, Chapter 7 examines the empty self as presented through person-referencing terms such as the zero-form, self-referencing *watashi* 'I', *jibun* 'self', and *ore* 'I (blunt, primarily used by male speakers)' as well as different reference forms assigned to dramatic persons. Focused in Chapter 8 is Japanese grammar where the perceptive self as well as the receptive self are foregrounded as the self undergoes situated events and states. Chapter 9 explores the topic-comment dynamism, specifically by focusing on the use and

EXPLORING THE SELF IN PHILOSOPHICAL PRAGMATICS 243

non-use of the topic marker *wa* as well as nominal predicates. Varied manners of quotation and inserted speech are discussed in Chapter 10 where the self floats and is transferred across different perspectives. Chapter 11 explores how the self is populated with characters and characteristics through various devices functioning as character-speak. It is emphasized that all features analyzed in Chapters 7 through 11 are not fully reflected in the English translation.

Chapter 12 offers contrastive pragmatics of the Japanese language not as a source text but as a target text. These analyses reveal that the features discussed in earlier chapters repeatedly appear in Japanese as translation text. The Japanese texts created in an opposite translating direction provide further evidence that meanings and expressivity prioritized in Japanese significantly differ from English, suggesting different ontological foundations.

2 Translation and Expressive Gaps

2.1 *Complexities of Translation Gaps*

The gaps in translation span from propositional information to modality-based expressivity. Gaps in information are perhaps easier to overcome, while gaps in modal, subjective, and expressive meanings are more difficult. We have repeatedly observed that the English translation text fails to fully and consistently capture the force of emotion, attitude, perspective, relationship as well as feeling nuanced in the Japanese source text. Moreover, these aspects are deeply embedded not only in the aesthetics of the Japanese language and culture but also in the philosophical thinking of traditional and contemporary Japan. The gaps are linked to the self's creativity as well, which is difficult to transfer into another language.

Critically, readers of the English translated works will not know what they are missing. These ontological, subjective, and emotive meanings are not likely to be noted, since they are not present in the first place. For instance, once the English translation appears without those features Japanese character-speak conveys, the enhanced characters and characteristics of the self are absent or underrepresented; yet its expressivity is not actually "missed." This irreconcilable contradiction is a part of the reality of translation. Only careful contrastive pragmatics analyses can bring into the open these often ignored missing elements.

Most scholars of translation studies have lamented the difficulty and impossibility of translation. Obviously, translation involves much more than the transfer of corresponding words. Difficulties or the near impossibility of translation are serious because differences are rooted in different views toward the self. We are also aware that translation itself is influenced by current trends and the needs of society. In addition, factors not only in the nature of language, but also in the role language plays add to complexities. Still, all semantic and expressive discrepancies are transported and executed in the process of translation. Gaps involve more than what surfaces in the text, and ironically, what is absent in the text sometimes communicates more than its presence. Each of these points emphasizes the reality that translation is not a simple process, and unavoidable gaps are difficult to overcome.

Perhaps it is useful to recall Ricoeur (2006) who reminds us that we experience both gain and loss in the translation experience. Accuracy in translation is difficult to judge; what emerges as a translation is built only upon approximation. But Ricoeur also reminds us that this translation-like interpretation can occur within a single language as well. Language's capacity of what Ricoeur calls "linguistic hospitality" (the ability to explain the meaning by using the very language) is a process we generally utilize when interpreting. The difficulty in meaning is an intrinsic part of language itself, but our capacity for linguistic hospitality invites us to comprehend what may be difficult to understand. It is true that translations investigated in this study, no matter how "accurate" they may be, contain gaps that cannot be bridged. However, it is also the case that gaps in translation call attention to the essential difficulties of language itself and do so in an explicit manner than otherwise.

Difficulties in translation remind us of unresolved issues regarding machine translation and translation software. Google Translate, free translation software available to everyone who has access to digital devices, has undergone renovation in 2016 after 10 years of its service. Although, instead of the phrase-based translation, context- and collocation-based translation supported by AI technologies is in operation, Google Translate suffers from its shallowness of translation (Hofstadter 2018). Obvious, sometimes comical but other times serious, mistranslations occur across languages; machine translation is still far from a real understanding of human text.

Simple tests of Google Translate reveal that the gaps are of the kind discussed in this work, primarily involving subjective and intersubjective aspects as well as character-associated features (e.g., emotive expressions, person references, devices communicating perspective shifts, interactional particles, and variations). Testing of sample text from Japanese to English, and then to Japanese, result in the following. *Jibun wa watashi ga kiraida* (example 7 of Chapter 7) is translated into *I hate me*. Here the difference between *jibun* and *watashi* is not recognized, shortchanging the perspective differences of the Japanese first-person expressions. *Sore na noni konna ni shinken ni, sono negai o kanae yoo to shite kurete iru. Sono kuse kuwashii setsumei wa shite kure nai* (example 17a of

Chapter 8) is translated into *Nevertheless, he is trying to fulfill his wish so seriously. It doesn't give me a detailed explanation*. Here the error derives from a failure to interpret the zero-form and the *-te kureru* expression. Notably, the use of *it* fails to correctly identify the self in a cohesive manner and the interpersonal relationship realized by the verb of giving is not communicated. Variations in Japanese, character-speak including dialects, gender- and occupation-related varieties as well as style shifts pose another difficulty in Google Translate. *Kono kisha wa jissai doko made demo ikimasu ze* (example 4a of Chapter 11) is translated as *This train is going all the way*, which is then translated into Japanese as *Kono ressha wa zutto susunde imasu* 'This train is moving forward all the way'. The Google Translate version fails to reflect the effect of character-speak evident in the source text.

Translation gaps in computer-run programs may be associated not so much with the "deep learning" of a large set of data, but with cross-linguistic differences of philosophical foundations themselves. The day machine translation replaces human translation will not come until machines are capable of understanding, perceiving, receiving, experiencing, as well as performing the ever-changing creative and playful self across languages.

2.2   On Translation Texts as Data

Although I trust I have chosen reasonably reliable data, a few related issues must be raised. This work's starting point has been the sense that English translation is lacking in some way. However, the possibility of a research design from the opposite direction must be considered as well. If a reverse direction is taken, features evident in English but unrecognized in Japanese are likely to surface. Comparing the results of two studies approached from opposite directions is likely to bring new insight, although it is beyond the range of this work.

The translator's background is another factor. All works analyzed in this study are produced in the translator's native language. If the translator were a native speaker of the source language, would different translation texts result? If a Japanese native speaker translates works into English, will the translation text differ from the kind we have analyzed? This process may reveal different aspects of both languages, and they may provide different tools for exploring the self. In addition, we cannot dismiss the concern regarding the quality of the translation. As noted in this work, different qualities are observed, and this also applies to multiple translated texts of an identical original work. Translation texts always emerge under an ideological influence (Lefevere 2004 [1984]), and the rewriting process is likely to distort the nature of the text. These unresolved issues remain in the philosophical contrastive pragmatics involving translation texts.

I must insist, however, that undeniable benefits are found in using translation texts. By analyzing multiple works, despite any weakness found in an individual work, we are able to make meaningful generalizations. Choosing translation texts as data provides another benefit. Translated works are often popular among the general public of both source and target societies. In fact, it is often the popularity of the work itself that promotes the selection. They are likely to contain the speech variety widely used in everyday life of ordinary people. Instead of concentrating on classic literary works of high culture, which has been the case in past studies, popular works allow us access to our everyday language culture. I contend that it is particularly important to avoid an elitist view, and to focus on the language commonly used by the mass of contrasted language communities.

It is also true that different types of translation provide useful resources for contrastive pragmatics involving translation. Translations endorsed by the Skopos theory, and translations influenced by accommodation or foreignization approaches as well as overt and covert translations, for example, provide opportunities for comparing different kinds of translation texts. Or, glossing, paraphrasing, content-based translation, as well as back-translation offer ways for examining linguistic phenomena across different translation texts. Although it is beyond the scope of this work, analyzing different types of translation texts is expected to bring new insight not only to contrastive pragmatics but also to linguistics and literary studies.

Additionally, it should be reminded that the argument I develop in this work is based only on the select Japanese literary works as source and target texts. I do not present my view as applicable to all aspects of all Japanese or English texts for that matter. Broader contrastive studies focusing on parallel texts (not involving translation) across multiple genres are needed before fully answering the theme of exploring the self.

3   Overcoming the Ideologies of Metalanguage

Given that this work is heavily influenced by the Japanese language, the issue of linguistic ideologies should be addressed. Before going further, I should remind the reader, as I have alluded to earlier in this work, and as I argued in my earlier studies (Maynard 2002, 2016, 2017, 2019), of the fact that the universality of knowledge is customarily assumed when and if linguistic theories are built on and in Western languages. This sharply contrasts with studies conducted about or in non-Western languages which tend to be considered particular cases, with or without universal implications. Although academic knowledge about language is relative and bound by the metalanguage, linguistic theories presented in English are often exempt from the scrutiny of its inherent cultural embeddedness.

The issue regarding the relationship between the nature of linguistic theory and metalanguage falls under the notion of "linguistic ideologies" (Silverstein 1979; Kroskrity 2000, 2010). Linguistic ideologies as conceived by Silverstein refer to "any sets of beliefs about language articulated by the users as a rationalization or justification of perceived language structure and use" (1979: 193). Although I am writing this work in English, obviously my thought process is deeply influenced by Japanese, my native language. And examples are taken from Japanese literary works and translations. If a theoretically grounded paradigm is inevitably influenced by the metalanguage and the object language, what significance does my research bear? And, would differing or even opposing strands of theory building result if scholars analyzed varied languages based on different beliefs on language and pragmatics?

Recognizing limitations that the force of metalanguage imposes upon us both as speakers and researchers, I contend it is possible to pursue, with an open mind, the kind of philosophical contrastive pragmatics leading to an understanding of the self. Theoretical openness also encourages a reexamination of, if not a serious challenge to, available theories. We must not forget that in any research design, there is a level of collusion between the particular phenomenon selected for analysis and the specific academic tradition within which the very analysis is performed. In fact, what we think is new might have been there all along, but may only be newly discovered as a result of shifting popularities of available theories. We must remind ourselves that linguistic theories have often conveniently distorted reality, and this work is not entirely exempt from this blind spot.

I should mention that I have personally taken counter measures against this recognized linguistic ideology. Facing the risk of imposing certain research perspectives embedded in a particular language, I have incorporated both Japanese and Western research perspectives, and reached the conclusion of this work based on cross-linguistic data. Over the years I have also published my research results in both Japanese and English, and these studies are incorporated in this work. Although no text is culture-free, an attempt has been made to place the methodology and results of this work in a broader context of hybridity. And I agree with Suzuki (2014) who emphasizes the importance of presenting scholarly views in humanities and social sciences based on non-Western languages and academic traditions.

4 Beyond the *Nihonjinron* Debate

In Japanese studies approached from humanities and social sciences, the Japanese self has often been characterized as being in a state of interdependence (Doi 1971; Mori 1979; Markus and Kitayama 1991) in contrast with the self's state of independence in the West. It has been pointed out that the Japanese self attends to and strives to fit in with others, and a sense of harmonious interdependence is prized. Even in the so-called individual experience, self is mobilized in relation to others. As represented by Lebra's (1992, 2004) position that Japanese are most fully human in the context of others, the sense of interdependence has been generally emphasized.

In Maynard (1997b) I have explored the idea that the self can be captured in terms of the degree to which one is nurtured with "relationality," a sense of interpersonal relationships endorsed by society. Depending on when the relationality becomes critical in one's lifetime, varying linguistic and social behavioral preferences are experienced. For Japanese, early training tends to emphasize relationality through which a sense of group belongingness is encouraged, although as the self matures, an inner sense of freedom from relationality comes to play a part.

Terms used to label Japanese self and society include sociocentric, holistic, collective, contextual, and connected. A representative of this view can be found in Markus and Kitayama (1991) in which they contrast Japanese interdependent versus Western independent orientations. Markus and Kitayama make the following statement.

> The notion of an interdependent self is linked with a monistic philosophical tradition in which the person is thought to be of the same substance as the rest of nature. (...) As a consequence, the relationship between the self and other, or between subject and object, is assumed to be much closer. Thus, many non-Western cultures insist on the inseparability of basic elements (...), including self and other, and person and situation. (...) Thus, persons are only parts that when separated from the larger social whole cannot be fully understood. (...) Such a holistic view is in opposition to the Cartesian dualistic tradition that characterizes Western thinking and in which the self is separated from the object and from the natural world.
>
> MARKUS and KITAYAMA 1991: 227

Markus and Kitayama (1991) point out that the traditional Western independent self is most clearly exemplified by some sizable segment of American culture, as well as many Western European societies. They contend that the independent construal of the self is egocentric, self-contained, bounded, and remains apart from any social context. Others are important primarily for the purpose of social comparison. On the other hand, the interdependent self construal is interconnected with the social context, structured as a flexible entity, and is defined in relation to others in specific contexts (Markus and Kitayama 1991).

The concept of the Japanese self discussed above may unintentionally provoke a controversy over the "uniqueness" of Japan, associated with *Nihonjinron* (discussion of the Japanese people), specifically in reference to the assumption of a group-oriented collective society. *Nihonjinron* adheres, through an array of publications, to the idea that Japan is uniquely distinct from other cultures, featured primarily by its collectivism. Studies on Japanese language and culture presented with a hint of *Nihonjinron* have stirred criticism in Japan and especially in the West. For example, Dale (1986) characterizes Doi's (1971) theory of *amae* 'dependence' as "an explanation of the image of emotional, group-dependent relations among the Japanese" criticizing that it is "dependent on a Japanese kind of psychoanalysis" which is "inaccurate and incomprehensible in Western terms" (1986: 125). Based on a close reading of Doi (1971), I have argued that Doi does not necessarily fall into the *Nihonjinron* trap as characterized by the *Nihonjinron* critics (Maynard 1997b).

Through the years, concepts of group-orientation, collectivism, and interdependence have been criticized by a number of scholars. Matsumoto (1999) finds faults with the position taken by Markus and Kitayama (1991), specifically the concepts of independence versus interdependence, by pointing out the methodological error and overly accentuated differences. Takano and Osaka (1999), reviewing 15 studies which compare Japanese and Americans on the individualism versus collectivism scale, find counter-evidence or invalid interpretation in all of the studies. Reader (2003) criticizes Befu (2001) and Oguma (2002) pointing out that *Nihonjinron* studies lack rigorous research methods and cannot be considered academic work. He also criticizes that, although Befu (2001) and Oguma (2002) were published after 2000, they do not take into account the Japan in the 1990s and on.

In the context of criticism against *Nihonjinron* (Befu 1980), a critique of the criticism of *Nihonjinron* has also been presented. For example, Lebra (2004), in her book's epilogue titled *In Defense of Japan Studies* (Lebra translates *Nihonjinron* as Japan studies), laments the fact that many Japan specialists preface their texts with a short critical commentary on *Nihonjinron* as a means of dissociation. Lebra takes the position not so much to defend *Nihonjinron* as to "liberate Japan studies from the oppression that this label has created" (2004: 255).

Another critical point surrounds the concept of Japanese people as a unified group without giving consideration to internal variability (Okamoto and Shibamoto-Smith 2016). This is particularly true in contemporary Japanese society where ethnic, cultural, social, and linguistic variability is the norm. The controversy of *Nihonjinron* has been revisited by other writers as well (Takano 2008; Funabiki 2010). Funabiki (2010), clarifying *Nihonjinron*'s historical motivation, maintains that *Nihonjinron* was a necessary posture for Japan in the 1980s. Japanese scholars and travelers who went abroad were forced to define themselves to the world and *Nihonjinron* served such a purpose. As Funabiki suggests, Japanese no longer obsess about a singular cultural identity as they once did, and instead, now seem to welcome multiple identities.

More specifically regarding the concept of self in the context of *Nihonjinron*, I should touch upon Hasegawa and Hirose (2005). Hasegawa and Hirose criticize the Japanese collective view of self as being incompatible with essential features of the Japanese language. Based on their concepts of public and private self, they assert that contrary to the group model, Japanese are individualistic beings with a strong inner self-consciousness. In their view, what they call the "absolute" self is applicable to all languages, but the Japanese language has two aspects, private and public, with the former being expressed by *jibun* 'self' and the latter, by a number of expressions. They find fault with the group model for paying attention only to the public expressions involving social and interpersonal relations. On the absolute self, Hasegawa and Hirose (2005) state the following.

> We have seen that it is indisputable that all competent speakers of Japanese possess a clear and rigid concept of self, without which idiomatic Japanese is impossible. This absolute self is individualistic, neither part of a group nor interpersonal. Linguistically speaking, the absolute self is the one whose mental states the speaker can directly access and thus the one which the speaker is privileged to express without evidential sources—that is, it is essentially identical with the Cartesian notion of self. (...) It is significant that, if we define the term *self* in terms of locutionary subjectivity, it can hardly be language-specific; it should apply to all languages.
> HASEGAWA and HIROSE 2005: 235, original emphasis

Identifying the private self (i.e., absolute self) with the Cartesian notion of self as stated above is unconvincing. Their approach turns out to offer a supplement to the so-called Western self, which they accept as an *a priori* notion. Hasegawa and Hirose, without a further exploration into the essence of the Japanese self, prematurely claim that an absolute self is applicable to all languages. Unfortunately, the private and public self, being reminiscent of Cartesian dualism, remain separated, and their relationships, if any, are left unexplored. Their position does not convincingly resolve the issue of the Japanese self in the context of the *Nihonjinron* debate.

Liddicoat (2007) offers an interesting twist to the *Nihonjinron* debate. He finds that the internationalization education in Japan (such as teaching English in public elementary schools) is motivated not so much by the development of intercultural perspectives among Japanese, but more so to develop intercultural perspectives of others about Japan. With the term "other-transforming interculturality," Liddicoat concludes that "Japanese interculturality focuses on the inculcation, maintenance and entrenchment of a particular conception of Japanese identity" (2007: 41), and this can be associated with the discourse of *Nihonjinron* as well as its insemination to others.

As observed above, the debate over *Nihonjinron* continues. The disagreement on the features linked to Japanese people, society, and culture in contrast with other societies seems to originate from how a researcher qualifies his or her work. Writers of Japanese studies need to qualify their conclusions more carefully so that the scope of the work's applicability is clearly specified. At the same time, those commenting on Japanese studies need to pay attention to the broader academic context so that the work can be evaluated from open and multiple perspectives. The *Nihonjinron* debate may also benefit from broader cultural contrasts (e.g., Hofstede, 2001, Nisbett 2003) as a starting point for reevaluating the position itself. Both interpretive and empirical studies are called for before we come to understand the role the *Nihonjinron* debate plays in appreciating how different cultures approach conceptualizations of the self.

5   Toward an Embracing View of Self across Languages

In this work, I insist that concepts of empty self and populated self are critical for understanding the Japanese self. I also take the position that the construal of the self and others, as well as the relationship between them, are likely to differ across languages and cultures more substantially than previous scholarship has suggested. Different views of the self can systematically influence the self's cognition. emotion, and performance in varying degrees; the depth and the width of differences are not frivolous, to say the least.

Given my position stated above, two points should be noted regarding the question of whether my proposal is applicable to other languages and cultures. My answer here is mixed due to the following conflicting perspectives. First, recall the neo-Whorfian position discussed in Chapter 1, which endorses the undeniable connection between language and thought. The ontological views reached through a particular language or languages are expected to both resemble and differ from the views reached through other languages. This perspective opens the field; the Japanese self has the potential to be applicable, not universally, but relatively to some languages. Second, given the context of the *Nihonjinron* debate, a careful presentation of my position is necessary. My position is based on specific data and analyses, and does not claim its applicability across genres and disciplines. This implies that what I propose is unlikely to be applicable unless it is taken with these qualifications and conditions. Naturally, further studies are required before answering the question of the potential applicability of empty and populated self to other societies and regions.

I must emphasize, however, on the usefulness of the work such as this one in our effort of exploring the concept of self. For many cultures of the world including the Western cultures, the traditional notion of the self as a universal entity made of individualistic attributes is unlikely to provide an adequate or convincing understanding. The proposed self construal, although it is specific to the Japanese discourse in contrast with English, should not be carelessly discarded simply as a case of *Nihonjinron*.

This work has been an attempt to reach for one of the most fundamental issues in language and communication. Insisting on multiple aspects, characters, and characteristics that populate the self, I have provided my answer regarding the concept of self from a pragmatics perspective. After all, pragmatics has always been concerned with the language user. It is my view that ultimately, the purpose of pragmatics is to gain an understanding of the nature of and the meaning of the language-involving self. This is a formidable task, but philosophical contrastive pragmatics is uniquely positioned for such an enterprise (e.g., Ameka and Terkouraft 2019). In the kind of studies I envision, rich scholarship available in both Western and non-Western academic circles come to be fully appreciated in the spirit of hybridity and evaluated in the cycle of refutation and creation. By analyzing data associated with original and translated texts, it is possible to pinpoint difficulties of meaning within a single language as well as across multiple languages. By avoiding the pitfall of being overly influenced by prefabricated notions and concepts, and by closely examining literary works as source and target texts, I believe it possible to practice the kind of pragmatics that embraces a meaningful openness.

Given the ongoing political and religious conflicts that disrupt the postmodern world, a deeper understanding of the philosophy underlying different languages and cultures seems indispensable. A superficial grasp of communication is not sufficient for understanding the conflicts between and within the West and the non-Western regions. Understanding multiple religious traditions and belief systems in the globalized postmodern world would require appreciating translation gaps deeply hidden under the surface. Although I do not claim that philosophical contrastive pragmatics can offer some concrete answers to global issues, research under this framework is not without merit. Clearly, cautioning against self-righteousness, I must adhere to the principle of self-criticism through which I relativize my own theory as well as others; I myself must avoid falling victim to the naiveté of past studies. Still, what I have explored in this volume adds to our knowledge, if only as one possible path toward a deeper understanding of the way we experience the self in and across languages. I conclude this volume with optimism toward the further advancement of an open and embracing view toward the concept of self. By being more empathetic toward postmodernist and social constructionist views and going beyond the traditional ideologies through our exploration of the empty yet populated self, we may be able to transcend some of the theoretical limitations in linguistics and pragmatics.

As a final note, let me indulge in some personal thoughts. The proposed view of the self may offer insight toward seemingly unresolvable political, religious, as well as ideological conflicts we face today. As touched upon in Chapter 5, possible applications of the Japanese understanding of the self have been suggested by Machida (2003), Fukuoka (2009, 2011), and Maeno (2015). Although my position is more modest, it serves to remind ourselves that the priority of place over self encourages recognition of the particularity of place within and across diverse nations and regions. From a postmodern Japanese perspective, the self is far from being presupposed, universal, and unchanging. Like a flowing river, the self is a fluid state of being repeatedly reforming and transforming. The changing self is capable of embracing differences and particularities, not as subordination to or embeddedness within a traditional authoritative paradigm. The critical step may be taken, as suggested in this work, by appreciating the complex nature of language as well as the process of translation traceable to the core of the self. The humanistic approach taken in this work might open embracing pathways toward a meaningful exploration of the self, subjectivity, and character in our diverse multi-cultural worlds.

APPENDIX

Synopses of the Works Selected for Data

The works selected for analyses are well-known, and extensive information is available on the Internet. I am presenting synopses simply to provide context for the examples extracted from these works. Please be warned that synopses may contain spoilers. The works are presented in the order introduced in Chapter 1.

Kawakami, Hiromi: *Sensei no Kaban.*
Powel, Allison Markin: *The Briefcase.*

Tsukiko, an office worker, 38 years old and single, happens to run into her former high school teacher at a local drinking spot. Tsukiko only remembers him as *sensei* (i.e., teacher), a man 30 years her senior, retired, and a widower. At the same time Tsukiko refuses friendly advances from Kojima, a former classmate and divorcee. Tsukiko enjoys being with *sensei*, hunting for mushrooms, and viewing cherry blossoms. The relationship, in five years, develops from an enjoyable companionship to a sentimental love affair. Tsukiko and *sensei* enjoy seasonal changes and outdoor events together. At the end of their five-year romance, *sensei* passes away, leaving Tsukiko a briefcase, his treasured possession.

Oe, Kenzaburo: *Torikaeko Chenjiringu.*
Boehm, Deborah Boliver: *The Changeling.*

Kogito, a writer in his sixties and the protagonist, receives audio tapes from his childhood friend, filmmaker Goroo, who is his brother-in-law. One night Kogito, while listening to the tape on the player hears a loud thud. It turns out that Goroo has leaped to his death from the roof of a building. Kogito begins a far-reaching search to understand what drove Goroo to suicide. Kogito travels to Berlin (as a part of a lecture tour) looking for clues, only to discover Goroo's troublesome past. Kogito recollects youthful days spent with Goroo in the countryside of Ehime, as well as some politically-motivated violent incidents. At the end of the novel, through his wife's acceptance of her brother's death, Kogito is convinced that, instead of mourning the loss of his brother-in-law, he should treasure all lives that are yet to be born.

Yoshimoto, Banana: *Kitchin*.
Backus, Megan: *Kitchen*.

Mikage, the first-person narrator, is a young woman whose grandmother has recently passed away. She loves and finds comfort in the kitchen, particularly next to the humming refrigerator. Yuuichi, a young man who knew the grandmother, visits Mikage and asks her to come visit his apartment. At his apartment, Yuuichi introduces his "mother" (his biological father working as a host in a gay bar) who suggests that Mikage stay with them for a while. Mikage, after living with them for a while, decides to leave, now determined to be on her own and to find her favorite kitchen.

Yoshimoto, Banana: *Tsugumi*.
Emmerich, Michael: *Goodbye Tsugumi*.

Tsugumi is a sickly but feisty girl living in a small seaside town at the family inn. Tsugumi and her cousin Maria (the first-person narrator) who is visiting the inn, spend the summer together. They get involved in local incidents as they enjoy various adventures, and their friendship deepens. Tsugumi gets to know a young boy, Kyooichi, son of the owner of the new hotel to be built in the town. Kyooichi's dog is murdered by a local gang, and this incident unites Maria, Tsugumi, and Kyooichi. At the end of the summer, Maria and Kyooichi return to Tokyo, but soon Maria receives a desperate letter from Tsugumi, and returns to the seaside town.

Nomura, Mizuki: *"Bungaku Shoojo" to Shini Tagari no Dooke*.
McGillicuddy, Karen: *Book Girl and the Suicidal Mime*.

A bookish girl, Tooko Amano, a high school senior, is a literature-demon, a supernatural being who munches on torn-out pages from all kinds of literary works. The first-person narrator, Konoha Inoue, who was forced to join Tooko's literary club, ends up writing essays and stories to be consumed by Tooko as her daily snack. Konoha, with his painful past which involves being a published writer at an early age, begins a healing process as he observes and interacts with Tooko, and with other members of the club, Chiai Takeda, Kazushi Akutagawa, and Nanase Kotobuki. The high school life of these students is described through extensive references to *Ningen Shikkaku* by Dazai (1952) which gives guidance to vulnerable students, especially Chiai.

Nomura, Mizuki: *"Bungaku Shoojo" to Dookoku no Junreisha*.
McGillicuddy, Karen: *Book Girl and the Wayfarer's Lamentation*.

In this volume, Konoha's past is uncovered, in a plot development interwoven with *Ginga Tetsudoo no Yoru* by Kenji Miyazawa. With Tooko's high school graduation approaching, Konoha receives a letter from Nanase who is suddenly hospitalized. When Konoha visits the hospital, he is reunited with Miu, Konoha's childhood friend. When they were in the same junior high school, Miu jumped from the roof of the school building, and Konoha never found out what happened to her. Konoha had his first story published under the pen name of Miu Inoue, despite the fact that Miu on her own desperately wanted to be a writer. Konoha has suffered from a sense of guilt over the years, and now he and Miu are reunited. Konoha begins to feel relief thanks to Tooko's kindness and leadership. At the end of the story, they go to a planetarium to observe the Milky Way, and Tooko encourages everyone to be always hopeful despite painful memories.

Tanigawa, Nagaru: *Suzumiya Haruhi no Yuuutsu*.
Pai, Chris: *The Melancholy of Haruhi Suzumiya*.

As Kyon, the first-person narrator, enters high school, he meets an eccentric girl, Haruhi Suzumiya. Haruhi introduces herself by saying she is interested in getting to know aliens, espers, and time travelers. Haruhi, bored with ordinary high school life, forms a group, the SOS Brigade, and pressures Kyon to join. It turns out that Haruhi, although she herself is unaware, possesses the power to alter reality. To prevent Haruhi from getting involved in disturbing mischiefs, three other members join the SOS Brigade, shy and polite Mikuru Asahina, quiet and stoic Yuki Nagato, and a transfer student, Itsuki Koizumi. Despite Kyon's reluctance to go along, the five of them get involved in dangerous and supernatural incidents.

Higashino, Keigo: *Manatsu no Hooteishiki*.
Smith, Alexander O.: *A Midsummer's Equation*.

Manabu Yukawa, a physicist known as Detective Galileo, travels to Hari Cove, a small summer resort town. Kyoohei, an elementary school boy, also travels to Hari Cove to spend a few days at Ryokugansoo, a small hotel his uncle and aunt manage. Having met Kyoohei on the train to Hari, Yukawa decides to stay at Ryokugansoo. That night, one of the guests is found dead on the seashore. It turns out that the victim is Tsukahara, a former detective investigating a murder case (a woman was killed many years ago).

Detective Kusanagi in Tokyo requests Yukawa's assistance in investigating Tsukahara's death. As the story develops, it becomes clear that Tsukahara was murdered because he was about to discover that the daughter of the couple (Kyoohei's cousin) had stabbed a woman to death. Unfortunately, the action that Kyoohei and his uncle took that night was part of the murder plot. Although Yukawa learns who was involved in these two related murder cases, he decides not to reveal the truth. That would not make anybody happy, he thought. Yukawa warmly soothes Kyoohei's feelings of guilt, as Kyoohei leaves Hari Cove, heading back home with his father.

Miyabe, Miyuki: *R.P.G.*
Carpenter, Juliet Winters: *Shadow Family*.

A man's body is found in a new housing development in a residential neighborhood. The man murdered is Ryoosuke Tokoroda, a businessman, who lived with wife, son (Minoru), and daughter (Kazumi). But he had created an alternate fictitious family on the Internet. His shadow family (wife, Minoru, and Kazumi) were involved in a role-playing game, and they actually got together in real life as well. Detectives Takegami and Ishizu conclude that the murderer is someone close to the victim. Kazumi felt jealous toward the shadow family, and was deeply hurt to learn that his father did not care about his real family any more. Tokoroda's real family members and Kazumi's lover are questioned at police headquarter, but gradually Kazumi becomes the prime suspect.

Miyazawa, Kenji: *Ginga Tetsudoo no Yoru*.
Bester, John: *Night Train to the Stars*.
Neville, Julianne: *Night on the Galactic Railroad & Other Stories from Ihatov*.
Pulvers, Roger: *Eigo de Yomu Ginga Tetsudoo no Yoru*.
Sigrist, Joseph and D.M. Stroud: *Milky Way Railroad*.

Jobanni has a kindly friend, Kamupanerura, whom he admires. Jobanni's mother is sick and his father works away from home. One of the classmates, Zaneri, ridicules Jobanni's unfortunate family situation, and Jobanni feels a bit isolated. One evening, Jobanni notices a group of boys including Kamupanerura and Zaneri going to a festival, and feels bad that he cannot join them because of his responsibilities at home. Tired after hard work including his job at a printing office, Jobanni lies down on top of a hill and falls asleep. Suddenly he hears a strange announcement saying "This is the Milky Way Station." The next minute, Jobanni finds himself onboard a train, where he also finds Kamupanerura. Riding the train together, Jobanni and Kamupanerura meet interesting people such as a scholar, a bird-catcher, and a little girl. But then for no reason, Kamupanerura disappears. Jobanni now awoke on top of the hill, hears the news that a boy is missing who saved another boy from drowning in the river. Jobanni runs to the river, and learns that Kamupanerura, saving Zaneri, cannot be found. Kamupanerura's father confesses that his son has been missing so long that there is little hope of finding him alive.

Nabokov, Dmitri: *The Eye*.
Ogasawara, Toyoki: *Me*.

The first-person narrator, a young Russian émigré in Berlin, suffers from a beating from his mistress's husband, and in despair, he fatally shoots himself. The story develops based on a ghostly narrator who, while visiting émigré families and friends, encounters a newcomer, Smurov. Smurov interests the narrator, and the narrator sets out to discover the real Smurov, by collecting Smurov's diverse and contradictory images as portrayed by other dramatic persons. Most critical is the one created by Vanja whom both Smurov and the narrator are interested in. One day, the narrator encounters the mistress's husband who calls out the name Smurov, to which the narrator responds as he recognizes the name to be his own. It turns out that Smurov is the narrator; the narrator has been observing him (himself) all along; the narrator's "eye" has been alive. The narrator ends his account with an emphatic statement that he is happy, because, although the narrator does not exist, Smurov lives on. The story ends with the narrator's affirmation of the superiority of imagination as a source of happiness, particularly as being one's onlooker.

Auster, Paul: *Auggie Wren's Christmas Story*
Murakami, Haruki. *Oogii Ren no Kurisumasu Sutoorii*.
Shibata, Motoyuki: *Oogii Ren no Kurisumasu Sutoorii*.

The first-person narrator, a writer living in New York City, is looking for a Christmas story he was asked to submit for publication in a newspaper. He talks to Auggie Wren who works at a cigar shop, and Auggie invites him to come visit his place. There Auggie shows the writer 12 volumes of albums containing thousands of identical photos he has taken. At an eating place Auggie tells how he came to take those photos.

One day, a young man comes to Auggie's store and steals a paperback. Auggie chases him, and this man drops his wallet. On Christmas day, Auggie decides to return the wallet to this man (Robert) and visits his apartment, but an old blind woman comes to the door. The old woman mistakes Auggie for her son Robert, and they end up having Christmas dinner together. Then Auggie finds an expensive-looking camera in the bathroom, and steals it. Later, feeling guilty, Auggie revisits the old woman, only to find that she no longer lives there (perhaps because she has passed away). Since then, for 12 years, every morning, Auggie takes the same photo of a street crossing exactly at seven o'clock. The writer convinces Auggie that he did something good for the old woman, because he was there with her to celebrate her last Christmas dinner. He decides to write this story up as the Christmas story and to submit it to the newspaper.

References

Abe, Hideko Nonesu. 2014. Gei onee nyuu haafu no kotoba: Danseigo to joseigo no aida. *Nihongogaku*, 33, 1, 44–59.
Abe, Kobo. 1968. *Tanin no Kao*. Tokyo: Shinchosha.
Agha, Asif. 2005. Voice, footing, enregisterment. *Linguistic Anthropology*, 15, 1, 38–59.
Aihara, Hiroyuki. 2007. *Kyaraka Suru Nippon*. Tokyo: Kodansha.
Amagasaki, Akira. 1988. *Nihon no Retorikku*. Tokyo: Chikuma Shobo.
Amagasaki, Akira. 2002. Frame and link: A philosophy of Japanese composition. In *Japanese Hermeneutics: Current Debate on Aesthetics and Interpretation*, ed. by M.F. Marra. 36–43. Honolulu, HI: University of Hawai'i Press.
Ameka, Felix and Marina Terkouraft. 2019. What if …? Imagining non-Western perspectives on pragmatic theory and practice. *Journal of Pragmatics*, 145, 72–82.
Anzai, Tetsuo. 1983. *Eigo no Hassoo*. Tokyo: Kodansha.
Asano, Tomohiko. 2001. *Jiko e no Monogatariteki Sekkin: Kazoku Ryoohoo kara Shakaigaku e*. Tokyo: Keiso Shobo.
Asano, Tomohiko. 2005. Monogatari no aidentiti o koete? In *Datsu Aidentiti*, ed. by C. Ueno. 77–101. Tokyo: Keiso Shobo.
Auer, Peter and Aldo di Luzio, eds. 1992. *The Contextualization of Language*. Amsterdam: John Benjamins.
Baerveldt, Cor. 2014. On movements of language—within self, of self, about self, and between selves: Commentary on language and self. *Theory & Psychology*, 24, 4, 542–560.
Baker, Mona. 1992. *In Other Words: A Coursebook on Translation*. London and New York: Routledge.
Baker, Mona. 1993. Corpus linguistics and translation studies: Implications and applications. In *Text and Technology: In Honor of John Sinclair*, ed. by M. Baker, G. Frances and E. Tongnini-Borelli. 233–250. Amsterdam: John Benjamins.
Baker, Mona and Gabriela Saldanha, eds. 2009. *Routledge Encyclopedia of Translation Studies*. London and New York: Routledge.
Bakhtin, M.M. 1981. *The Dialogic Imagination*, ed. by M. Holquist, trans. by C. Emerson and M. Holquist. Austin, TX: University of Texas Press.
Bakhtin, M.M. 1986. *Speech Genres and Other Late Essays*, ed. by C. Emerson and M. Holquist, trans. by V.W. McGee. Austin, TX: University of Texas Press.
Bakhtin, M.M. 1993. *Toward a Philosophy of the Act*, ed. by M. Holquist and V. Liapunov, trans. and noted by V. Liapunov. Austin, TX: University of Texas Press.
Baumgarten, Nicole, Inke Du Bois and Juliane House, eds. 2012. *Subjectivity in Language and in Discourse*. Leiden: Brill.
Baumgarten, Nicole, Juliane House and Inke Du Bois. 2012. Introduction. In *Subjectivity*

in Language and in Discourse, ed. by N. Baumgarten, I. Du Bois and J. House. 1–13. Leiden: Brill.

Beaugrande, Robert de and Wolfgang Dressler. 1981. *Introduction to Text Linguistics*. London: Longman.

Befu, Harumi. 1980. The group model of Japanese society and an alternative. *Rice University Studies*, 66, 169–187.

Befu, Harumi. 2001. *Hegemony of Homogeneity: An Anthropological Analysis of Nihonjinron*. Melbourne: Trans Pacific Press.

Bell, Allan. 1999. Styling the other to define the self: A study in New Zealand identity making. *Journal of Sociolinguistics*, 99, 523–541.

Bellow, Saul. 1988. *Dangling Man*. New York: Penguin Books.

Benveniste, Émile 1971. *Problems of General Linguistics*. Coral Gables, FL: University of Miami Press.

Bertau, Marie-Cécile. 2014a. Introduction: The self within the space-time of language performance. *Theory & Psychology*, 24, 4, 433–441.

Bertau, Marie-Cécile. 2014b. On displacement. *Theory & Psychology*, 24, 4, 442–458.

Blommaert, Jan, ed. 1999. *Language Ideological Debates*. Berlin: De Gruyter Mouton.

Blommaert, Jan. 2007. Sociolinguistics and discourse analysis: Orders of indexicality and polycentricity. *Journal of Multicultural Discourses*, 2, 115–130.

Brown, Gillian and George Yule. 1983. *Discourse Analysis*. Cambridge: Cambridge University Press.

Buber, Martin. 1970. *I and Thou*. New York: Charles Scribner's Sons.

Bucholtz, Mary. 1999. You da man: Narrating the racial other in the production of white masculinity. *Journal of Sociolinguistics*, 99, 443–460.

Bucholtz, Mary and Kira Hall. 2009. Locating identity in language. In *Language and Identities*, ed. by C. Llamas and D. Watt. 18–28. Edinburgh: Edinburgh University Press.

Burdelski, Matthew. 2010. Socializing politeness routines: Action, other-orientation and embodiment in a Japanese preschool. *Journal of Pragmatics*, 42, 1606–1621.

Burke, Peter J. and Jan E. Stets. 2009. *Identity Theory*. Oxford: Oxford University Press.

Butler, Judith. 1990. *Gender Trouble: Feminism and the Subversion of Identity*. London and New York: Routledge.

Carter, Robert Edgar. 1996. *Watsuji Tetsurō's Rinrigaku*. Albany, NY: State University of New York Press.

Chafe, Wallace. 1976. Givenness, contrastiveness, definiteness, subjects, topics and point of view. In *Subject and Topic*, ed. by C.N. Li. 27–55. New York: Academic Press.

Chesterman, Andrew. 2004. Beyond the particular. In *Translation Universals: Do They Exist?*, ed. by A. Mauranen and P. Kujamäki. 33–49. Amsterdam: John Benjamins.

Chinami, Kyoko. 2003. Danwa sutoratejii to shite no jendaa hyooji keishiki. *Nihongo to Jendaa*, 3, 17–36.

REFERENCES

Christofaki, Rodanthi. 2018. Expressing the self in Japanese: Indexical expressions in the service of indexical thoughts. In *Expressing the Self: Cultural Diversity and Cognitive Universals*, ed. by M. Huang and K.M. Jaszczolt. 72–87. Oxford: Oxford University Press.

Clark, Herbert H. and Susan F. Haviland. 1977. Comprehension and the given-new contract. In *Discourse Production and Comprehension*, ed. by R.O. Freedle. 1–40. Norwood, NJ: Ablex.

Coulmas, Florian. 1986. Direct and indirect speech in Japanese. *Direct and Indirect Speech*, ed. by F. Coulmas. 161–178. Berlin: De Gruyter Mouton.

Cutler, Cecilia A. 1999. Yorkville crossing: White teens, hip hop and African American English. *Journal of Sociolinguistics*, 99, 428–443.

Dale, Peter N. 1986. *The Myth of Japanese Uniqueness*. New York: St. Martin's Press.

Daneš, František. 1974. Functional Sentence Perspective and the organization of the text. In *Papers in Functional Sentence Perspective*, ed. by F. Daneš. 106–128. Prague: Academic Publishing House of the Czechoslovak Academy of Sciences.

Dazai, Osamu. 1952. *Ningen Shikkaku*. Tokyo: Shinchosha.

Derrida, Jacques. 1974. *Of Grammatology*. Baltimore: Johns Hopkins University Press.

Derrida, Jacques. 1978. *Writing and Difference*. Chicago: University of Chicago Press.

Derrida, Jacques. 1981. *Dissemination*. Chicago: University of Chicago Press.

Descartes, René. 2001 [1901]. *Meditations on First Philosophy*, trans. by J. Veitch. *The Classical Library*. http://www.classicallibrary.org/indexhtm, accessed February 10, 2016.

Dilworth, David A. 1974. Watsuji Tetsuro (1889–1960): Cultural phenomenology and ethician. *Philosophy East and West*, 24, 1, 3–22.

Dilworth, David A., trans. 1987. *Last Writings: Nothingness and the Religious World View*. Honolulu: University of Hawai'i Press.

Doi, Takeo. 1971. *Amae no Koozoo*. Tokyo: Kobundo.

Dorr-Bremme, Donald W. 1990. Contextualization cues in the classroom: Discourse regulation and social control functions. *Language in Society*, 19, 3, 379–401.

Ducharme, Daphne and Roger Bernard. 2001. Communication breakdowns: An exploration of contextualization in native and non-native speakers of English. *Journal of Pragmatics*, 33, 825–847.

Eckert, Penelope. 2000. *Linguistic Variation as Social Practice: The Linguistic Construction of Identity at Belten High*. Oxford: Blackwell.

Eckert, Penelope. 2008. Variation and the indexical field. *Journal of Sociolinguistics*, 12, 4, 453–476.

Eckert, Penelope and Sally McConnell-Ginet. 1992. Think practically and look locally: Language and gender as community-based practice. *Annual Review of Anthropology*, 21, 461–488.

Eerland, Anita and Rolf A. Zwaan. 2018. The influence of direct and indirect speech in source meaning. *Collabra: Psychology*, 4, 1, article 5. https://online.ucpress.edu/

collabra/article/4/1/5/112959/The-Influence-of-Direct-and-Indirect-Speech-on?sea rchresult=1, accessed March 1, 2021.

Emmott, Catherine. 1997. *Narrative Comprehension: A Discourse Perspective*. Oxford: Clarendon Press.

Emmott, Catherine. 2002. Split selves in fiction and in medical life stories: Cognitive linguistic theory and narrative practice. *Cognitive Stylistics: Language and Cognition in Text Analysis*, ed. by E. Semino and J. Culpeper. 153–181. Amsterdam: John Benjamins.

Etelämäki, Marja. 2016. Introduction: Discourse, grammar and intersubjectivity. *Nordic Journal of Linguistics*, 39, 2, 101–112.

Evan-Zohar, Itamar. 2004 [1978, 1990]. The position of translated literature within the literary polysystem. In *The Translation Studies Reader*, second edition, ed. by L. Venuti. 199–204. London and New York: Routledge.

Everett, Caleb. 2013. *Linguistic Relativity: Evidence Across Languages and Cognitive Domains*. Berlin: De Gruyter Mouton.

Facchinetti, Roberta, ed. 2007. *Corpus Linguistics 25 Years On*. Amsterdam and New York: Rodopi.

Fauconnier, Gilles and Eve Sweetser, eds. 1996. *Spaces, Worlds, and Grammar*, second edition. Chicago: University of Chicago Press.

Fillmore, Charles J. 1976. Frame semantics and the nature of language. *Annals of the New York Academy of Sciences: Conference on the Origin and Development of Language and Speech*, 280, 20–32.

Finegan, Edward. 1995. Subjectivity and subjectivisation: An introduction. In *Subjectivity and Subjectivisation: Linguistic Perspectives*, ed. by D. Stein and S. Wright. 1–15. Cambridge: Cambridge University Press.

Firbas, Jan. 1964. In defining the theme in functional sentence analysis. *Travaux Linguistiques de Prague*, 1, 267–280.

Fløttum, Kjersti. 2006. *Academic Voices across Language and Disciplines*. Amsterdam: John Benjamins.

Fludernik, Monika. 2003. Chronology, time, tense and experientiality in narrative. *Language and Literature*, 12, 2, 117–136.

Fujii, Yoko. 2012. Differences of situated self in the place/*ba* of interaction between the Japanese and American English speakers. *Journal of Pragmatics*, 44, 5, 636–662.

Fujita, Yasuyuki. 2000. *Kokugo In'yoo Koobun no Kenkyuu*. Tokyo: Izumi Shoin.

Fujitani, Nariakira. 1934 [1767]. *Kazashishoo*, ed. by J. Matsuo. Tokyo: Okayama Shoten.

Fujitani, Nariakira. 1960 [1778]. *Ayuishoo Shinchuu*, ed. by I. Nakada and M. Takeoka. Tokyo: Kazama Shobo.

Fukuoka, Shin'ichi. 2009. *Dooteki Heikoo*. Tokyo: Kirakusha.

Fukuoka, Shin'ichi. 2011. *Dooteki Heikoo*, 2. Tokyo: Kirakusha.

Funabiki, Takeo. 2010. *"Nihonjinron" Saikoo*. Tokyo: Kodansha.

REFERENCES

Furuno, Yuri. 2002. Nihon no hon'yaku: Henka no arawareta 1970 nendai. *Tsuuyaku Hon'yaku Kenkyuu*, 2, 114–122.

Gambier, Yves and Luc van Doorslaer, eds. 2010. *Handbook of Translation Studies*, Vol. 1. Amsterdam: John Benjamins.

Gee, James Paul. 2012. *Social Linguistics and Literacies: Ideology in Discourse*, fourth edition. London and New York: Routledge.

Geertz, Clifford. 1984. From the native's point of view: On the nature of anthropological understanding. In *Culture Theory: Essays on Mind, Self, and Emotion*, ed. by R.A. Shweder and R.A. Levine. 123–136. Cambridge: Cambridge University Press.

Genette, Gérard. 1980. *Narrative Discourse: An Essay in Method*, trans. by J.E. Lewin. Ithaca, NY: Cornell University Press.

Gergen, Kenneth. 1996. Technology and the self: From the essential to the sublime. In *Constructing the Self in a Mediated World*, ed. by D. Grodin and T.R. Lindlof. 127–140. Thousand Oaks, CA: Sage.

Gergen, Kenneth. 2000 [1991]. *The Saturated Self: Dilemmas of Identity in Contemporary Life*. New York: Basic Books.

Giles, James. 1993. The no-self theory: Hume, Buddhism and personal identity. *Philosophy East and West*, 43, 2, 175–200.

Glaser, Barney G. and Anselm L. Strauss. 1967. *The Discovery of Grounded Theory: Strategy for Qualitative Research*. Chicago: Aldine.

Goffman, Irving. 1959. *The Presentation of Self in Everyday Life*. New York: Doubleday.

Gumperz, John J. 1982. *Discourse Strategies*. Cambridge: Cambridge University Press.

Gumperz, John J. and Stephen C. Levinson. 1996. *Rethinking Linguistic Relativity*. Cambridge: Cambridge University Press.

Gumperz, John J. and Debora Tannen. 1979. Individual and social differences in language use. In *Individual Differences in Language Ability and Language Behavior*, ed. by C. Fillmore, D. Kempler and W. Wang. 305–325. New York: Academic Press.

Haga, Yasushi. 1962. *Kokugo Hyoogen Kyooshitsu*. Tokyo: Tokyodo.

Haiman, John. 1995. Grammatical signs of the divided self: A study of language and culture. In *Discourse Grammar and Typology: Papers in Honor of John W.H. Verhaar*, ed. by W. Abraham, T. Givon and S.A. Thompson. 215–234. Amsterdam: John Benjamins.

Haiman, John. 1998. *Talk is Cheap: Sarcasm, Alienation, and the Evolution of Language*. Oxford: Oxford University Press.

Hall, Joan Kelly, Gergana Vitanova and Ludmila A. Marchenkova, eds. 2005. *Dialogue with Bakhtin on Second and Foreign Language Learning: New Perspectives*. Mahwah, NJ: Lawrence Erlbaum.

Hall, Stuart. 1996. Introduction: Who needs identity? In *Questions of Cultural Identity*, ed. by S. Hall and P. de Gay. 1–17. Thousand Oaks, CA: Sage.

Halliday, M.A.K. 1967. Notes on transitivity and theme in English, 2. *Journal of Linguistics*, 3, 199–244.

Halliday, M.A.K. 1985. *An Introduction to Functional Grammar*. London: Edward Arnold.
Halliday, M.A.K. and Ruqaiya Hasan. 1976. *Cohesion in English*. London: Longman.
Hanks, William, et al. 2019. Communicative interaction in terms of *ba* theory: Towards an innovative approach to language practice. *Journal of Pragmatics*, 145. 63–71.
Hansen, Sandra and Silvia Hansen-Schirra. 2012. Grammatical shifts in English-German noun phrases. In *Cross-linguistic Corpora for the Study of Translations: Insights from the Language Pair English-German*, ed. by S. Hansen-Schirra, S. Neumann and E. Steiner. 133–145. Berlin: De Gruyter Mouton.
Hansen-Schirra, Silvia, Stella Neumann and Erich Steiner, eds. 2012. *Cross-linguistic Corpora for the Study of Translations: Insights from the Language Pair English-German*. Berlin: De Gruyter Mouton.
Harada, Yohei. 2010. *Chikagoro no Wakamono wa Naze Dame na no ka: Keitai Sedai to "Shin Mura Shakai."* Tokyo: Kobunsha.
Hasegawa, Yoko and Yukio Hirose. 2005. What the Japanese language tells us about the alleged Japanese relational self. *Australian Journal of Linguistics*, 25, 219–251.
Hayakawa, Atsuko. 2013. *Hon'yakuron to wa Nani ka: Hon'yaku ga Hiraku Aratana Seiki*. Tokyo: Sairyusha.
Hayashi, Makoto. 1997. An exploration of sentence-final uses of the quotative particle in Japanese spoken discourse. *Japanese/Korean Linguistics*, 6, 565–583.
Hayashi, Shiro. 1992. Bunshoo to wa nani ka: Watashi no "bunshooron." *Nihongogaku*, 11, 4, 16–19.
Heidegger, Martin. 1962. *Being and Time*, trans. by J. Macquarie and E. Robinson. New York: Harper & Row.
Heidegger, Martin. 1971 [1959]. *On the Way to Language*, trans. by P.D. Hertz. New York: Harper & Row.
Held, Klaus. 1997. World, emptiness, nothingness: A phenomenological approach to the religious tradition of Japan. *Human Studies*, 20, 2, 153–167.
Herlin, Ilona and Laura Visapää. 2016. Dimensions of empathy in relation to language. *Nordic Journal of Linguistics*, 39, 2, 135–157.
Hijiya-Kirschnereit, Irmela. 2012. Pretranslation in modern Japanese literature and what it tells us about "world literature." In *Translation Studies in the Japanese Context*, ed. by N. Sato-Rossberg and J. Wakabayashi. 167–182. London and New York: Continuum.
Hinds, John. 1983. Contrastive rhetoric: Japanese and English. TEXT, 3, 183–195.
Hinds, John. 1984. Topic maintenance in Japanese narrative and Japanese conversational interaction. *Discourse Processes*, 7, 465–482.
Hinds, John. 1986. *Situation versus Person Focus*. Tokyo: Kuroshio Shuppan.
Hinds, John. 1987. Reader versus writer responsibility: A new typology. In *Writing across Languages: Analysis of L2 Text*, ed. by U. Connor and R. Kaplan. 141–152. Reading, MA: Addison-Wesley Publishing Co.

Hinds, John. 1990. Inductive, deductive, quasi-inductive: Expository writing in Japanese, Korean, Chinese, and Thai. In *Coherence in Writing: Research and Pedagogical Perspectives*, ed. by U. Connor and A.M. Johns. 89–109. Alexandria, VA: Teachers of English to Speakers of Other Languages, Inc.

Hinds, John, Shoichi Iwasaki and Senko K. Maynard, eds. 1987. *Perspectives on Topicalization: The Case of Japanese Wa*. Amsterdam: John Benjamins.

Hirako, Yoshio. 1999. *Hon'yaku no Genri: Ibunka o Doo Yatte Yakusu ka*. Tokyo: Taishukan.

Hirano, Keiichiro. 2009. *Doon*. Tokyo: Kodansha.

Hirano, Keiichiro. 2012. *Watashi to wa Nani ka: "Kojin" kara "Bunjin" e*. Tokyo: Kodansha.

Hiromatsu, Wataru. 1982. *Sonzai to Imi: Jiteki Sekaikan no Teiso*, Vol. 1. Tokyo: Iwanami Shoten.

Hirose, Yukio. 1995. Direct and indirect speech as quotations of public and private expression. *Lingua*, 95, 4, 223–238.

Hirose, Yukio. 1996. Nichieigo saiki daimeishi no saikiteki yoohoo ni tsuite. *Gengo*, 25, 7, 81–92.

Hirose, Yukio. 2000. Public and private self as two aspects of the speaker: A contrastive study of Japanese and English. *Journal of Pragmatics*, 32, 1623–1656.

Hirose, Yukio. 2014. The conceptual basis of reflexive constructions in Japanese. *Journal of Pragmatics*, 68, 99–116.

Hofstadter, Douglas. 2018. The shallowness of Google Translation. *The Atlantic*. https://www.theatlantic.com/technology/archive/2018/01/the-shallowness-of-google-translation, accessed January 2, 2020.

Hofstede, Geert. 2001. *Culture's Consequences: Comparing Values, Behaviors, Institutions, and Organizations across Nations*, second edition. Thousand Oaks, CA: Sage.

Holquist, Michael. 2002. *Dialogism*, second edition. London and New York: Routledge.

Holstein, James A. and Jaber F. Gubrium. 2000. *The Self We Live By: Narrative Identity in a Postmodern World*. Oxford: Oxford University Press.

Hopper, Paul. 1987. Emergent Grammar. *Proceedings of the Thirteenth Annual Meeting of the Berkeley Linguistic Society*, 139–157.

Horie, Kaoru and Heiko Narrog. 2014. What typology reveals about modality in Japanese. In *Usage-based Approaches in Japanese Grammar: Towards the Understanding of Human Language*, ed. by K. Kubota and T. Ono. 109–133. Amsterdam: John Benjamins.

Horii, Reiichi. 2015. Koshoo, ninshoo to shakai. In *Hitsuji Imiron Kooza Imi no Shakaisei*, ed. by H. Sawada. 57–70. Tokyo: Hitsuji Shobo.

House, Juliane. 2006. Text and context in translation. *Journal of Pragmatics*, 38, 3, 338–358.

House, Juliane. 2009. *Translation*. Oxford: Oxford University Press.

House, Juliane. 2010. Overt and covert translation. In *Handbook of Translation Studies*, Vol. 1, ed. by Y. Gambier and L. van Doorslaer. 245–246. Amsterdam: John Benjamins.

House, Juliane, ed. 2014. *Translation: A Multidisciplinary Approach*. Houndmills: Palgrave Macmillan.

Hume, David. 1963. A treatise of human nature. In *The Philosophy of David Hume*, ed. by V.C. Chappell. 11–311. New York: Random House.

Ide, Sachiko. 1979. *Onna no Kotoba Otoko no Kotoba*. Tokyo: Nihon Keizai Shinbunsha.

Ikeda, Yoshiharu. 2018. *Nishida Kitaro no Jitsuzairon: AI Andoroido wa Naze Ningen o Koerare Nai no ka*. Tokyo: Akashi Shoten.

Ikeda, Yoshiharu and Shin'ichi Fukuoka. 2014. *Fukuoka Shin'ichi, Nishida Tetsugaku o Yomu: Seimei o Meguru Shisaku no Tabi, Dooteki Heikoo to Zettai Mujunteki Jiko Dooitsu*. Tokyo: Akashi Shoten.

Ikegami, Yoshihiko. 1981. *"Suru" to "Naru" no Gengogaku*. Tokyo: Taishukan.

Ikegami, Yoshihiko. 1993. A grammar of the person as "affected sentient." *Sophia Linguistica Working Papers in Linguistics*, 33, 1–19.

Ikegami, Yoshihiko. 2004. Gengo ni okeru "shukansei" to "shutaisei" no gengoteki shihyoo, 2. *Ninchi Gengogaku Ronkoo*, 4, 1–60.

Ikegami, Yoshihiko. 2006. Shutaiteki haaku to wa nani ka, Nihongo washa ni okeru konomareru iimawashi. *Gengo*, 35, 3, 20–27.

Ikegami, Yoshihiko. 2011. Nihongo to shukansei shutaisei. In *Shukansei to Shutaisei*, ed. by H. Sawada. 49–67. Tokyo: Hitsuji Shobo.

Imai, Mutsumi and Reiko Mazuka. 2007. Language-relative construal of individuation constrained by universal ontology: Revisiting language universals and linguistic relativity. *Cognitive Science*, 31, 385–417.

Inoue, Fumio, Tsunao Ogino and Kotaro Akizuki. 2007. *Dejitaru Shakai no Nihongo Sahoo*. Tokyo: Iwanami Shoten.

Inoue, Ken. 2005. "Daisan no bungaku" to shite no hon'yaku bungaku: Kindai Nihon bungaku to hon'yaku. In *Hon'yaku o Manabu Hito no Tame ni*, ed. by T. Anzai, K. Inoue and A. Kobayashi. 173–202. Tokyo: Sekai Shisosha.

Inoue, Ken. 2012. On the creative function of translation in modern and postwar Japan: Hemingway, Proust, and Modern Japanese novels. In *Translation and Translation Studies in the Japanese Context*, ed. by N. Sato-Rossberg and J. Wakabayashi. 116–133. London and New York: Continuum.

Ishida, Hiroji. 2006. Learner's perception and interpretation of contextualization cues in spontaneous Japanese conversation: Back-channel cue *uun*. *Journal of Pragmatics*, 38, 1943–1981.

Ishiguro, Kei. 2007. *Yoku Wakaru Bunshoo Hyoogen no Gijutsu: Buntaihen*. Tokyo: Meiji Shoin.

Itabashi, Yūjin. 2018. Grounded on nothing: The spirit of radical criticism in Nishida's philosophy. *Philosophy East and West*, 68, 1, 97–111.

Itani, Reiko. 1997. A relevance-based analysis of hearsay particles: With special reference to Japanese sentence-final particle *tte*. In *Relevance Theory: Applications and Implications*, ed. by R. Carston and S. Uchida. 47–68. Amsterdam: John Benjamins.

Iwasaki, Shoichi. 1993. *Subjectivity in Grammar and Discourse: Theoretical Considerations and a Case Study of Japanese Spoken Discourse*. Amsterdam: John Benjamins.

Jakobson, Roman. 1960. Linguistics and poetics. In *Style in Language*, ed. by T.A. Sebeok. 350–377. Cambridge, MA: MIT Press.

Jakobson, Roman. 2004 [1959]. On linguistic aspects of translation. In *The Translation Studies Reader*, second edition, ed. by L. Venuti. 138–143. London and New York: Routledge.

James, William. 1904. A world of pure experience, 1 and 2. *Journal of Philosophy, Psychology, and Scientific Methods*, 530–543 and 561–570.

James, William. 1929. *The Varieties of Religious Experience: A Study in Human Nature*. London, New York and Toronto: Longmans, Green and Co.

James, William. 1984 [1890]. *The Works of William James: Psychology The Brief Course*. Cambridge, MA: Harvard University Press.

Jaszczolt, Kasia M. 2016. *Meaning in Linguistic Interaction: Semantics, Metasemantics, Philosophy of Language*. Oxford: Oxford University Press.

Jinnouchi, Masataka and Kenji Tomosada, eds. 2006. *Kansai Hoogen no Hirogari to Komyunikeeshon no Yukue*. Tokyo: Izumi Shoin.

Johnson, D. Barton. 1985. The books reflected in Nabokov's Eye. *The Slavic and East European Journal*, 29, 4, 393–404.

Johnson, Mark. 2018. The embodiment of language. In *The Oxford Handbook of 4E Cognition*, ed. by A. Newen, L. De Bruin and S. Gallagher. 623–640. Oxford: Oxford University Press.

Kamada, Osamu. 1988. Nihongo no dentatsu hyoogen. *Nihongogaku*, 7, 9, 59–72.

Kamada, Osamu. 2000. *Nihongo no In'yoo*. Tokyo: Hitsuji Shobo.

Kaplan, David. 1979. On the logic of demonstratives. *Journal of Philosophical Logic*, 8, 81–98.

Kataoka, Yoshio. 2012. *Nihongo to Eigo: Sono Chigai o Tanoshimu*. Tokyo: NHK Shuppan.

Kataoka, Yoshio and Yukiko Konosu. 2014. *Hon'yaku Mondoo: Eigo to Nihongo Ittari Kitari*. Tokyo: Sayusha.

Kato, Yoko. 2010. *Hanashi Kotoba ni Okeru In'yoo Hyoogen: In'yoo Hyooshiki ni Chuumoku Shite*. Tokyo: Kuroshio Shuppan.

Kawahara, Kiyoshi. 2011. Gaisetsusho ni miru hon'yakugaku no kihonteki ronten to zentaiteki taikei. *Hon'yaku Kenkyuu e no Shootai*, 5, 53–80.

Kawai, Hayao. 1982. *Chuukuu Koozoo Nihon no Shinsoo*. Tokyo: Chuo Koronsha.

Kecskes, Istvan. 2012. Is there anyone out there who really is interested in the speaker? *Language and Dialogue*, 2, 2, 285–299.

Kinsui, Satoshi. 2003. *Vaacharu Nihongo Yakuwarigo no Nazo*. Tokyo: Iwanami Shoten.

Kinsui, Satoshi, ed. 2007. *Yakuwarigo Kenkyuu no Chihei*. Tokyo: Kuroshio Shuppan.

Kinsui, Satoshi, ed. 2011. *Yakuwarigo Kenkyuu no Tenkai*. Tokyo: Kuroshio Shuppan.

Kinsui, Satoshi. 2013. Fikushon no hanashi kotoba ni tsuite: Yakuwarigo o chuushin ni. In *Hanashi Kotoba to Kaki Kotoba no Setten*, ed. by K. Ishiguro and Y. Hashimoto. 3–11. Tokyo: Hitsuji Shobo.

Kinsui, Satoshi. 2021 Popyuraakaruchaa no kotoba. *Nihongogaku*, 40, 1, 4–13.

Kleinke, Sonja and Birte Bös. 2018. Intermediate *us* and *them*: The complexities of referentiality, identity and group construction in a public online discussion. In *The Discursive Construction of Identities On- and Offline*, ed. by B. Bös, et al. 153–176. Amsterdam: John Benjamins.

Kokuritsu Kokugo Kenkyujo. 2000. *Shin "Kotoba" Shiriizu*, Vol. 12, *Gengo ni Kansuru Mondooshuu: Kotoba no Tsukaiwake*.

Koller, Werner. 2011. The concept of equivalence and the object of translation studies. *Target Online*. John Benjamins. https://benjamins.com/online/target/articles/target.7.2.02kol, accessed March 30, 2021.

Komaki, Osamu. 1986. *Watsuji Tetsuro*. Tokyo: Shimizu Shoin.

Kondo, Atsuko. 2002. Kaiwa ni arawareru "no da": "Danwa renketsugo" no shiten kara. In *Nihongogaku to Gengo Kyooiku*, ed. by H. Ueda. 225–248. Tokyo: Tokyo Daigaku Shuppankai.

Kondo, Ineko, trans. 1999. *Darowei Fujin*. Tokyo: Misuzu Shobo.

Konosu, Yukiko. 2018. *Hon'yaku tte Nan Daroo?: Ano Meisaku o Yakushite Miru*. Tokyo: Chikuma Shobo.

Kosulis, Thomas P. 2002. *Intimacy or Integrity: Philosophy and Cultural Difference*. Honolulu: University of Hawai'i Press.

Kozyra, Agnieszka. 2018. Nishida Kitaro's philosophy of absolute nothingness (*zettaimu no tetsugaku*) and modern theological physics. *Philosophy East and West*, 68, 2, 423–446.

Kranich, Svenja. 2014. Translation as a locus of language contact. In *Translation: A Multidisciplinary Approach*, ed. by J. House. 96–115. Houndmills: Palgrave Macmillan.

Kranich, Svenja. 2016. *Contrastive Pragmatics and Translation: Evaluation, Epistemic Modality and Communicative Styles in English and German*. Amsterdam: John Benjamins.

Krein-Kühle, Monika. 2014. Translation and equivalence. In *Translation: A Multidisciplinary Approach*, ed. by J. House. 15–35. Houndmills: Palgrave Macmillan.

Kristeva, Julia. 1980. *Desire in Language: A Semiotic Approach to Literature and Art*, ed. by L.S. Roudiez, trans. by T. Gora and A. Jardine. Oxford: Basil Blackwell.

Kroskrity, Paul V. 2000, ed. *Regimes of Language: Ideologies, Politics, and Identities*. Santa Fe, NM: School of American Research Press.

Kroskrity, Paul V. 2010. Linguistic ideologies: Evolving perspectives. In *Society and Language Use*, ed. by J. Jaspers, J.-O. Östman and J. Verschueren. 192–211. Amsterdam: John Benjamins.

Krueger, Joel. 2013. Watsuji's phenomenology of embodiment and social space. *Philosophy East and West*, 63, 2, 127–152.

Krummel, John W.M. and Shigenori Nagatomo, trans. 2012. *Place and Dialectic: Two Essays by Nishida Kitarō*. Oxford: Oxford University Press.

Kubota, Ryuko. 1997. A reevaluation of the uniqueness of Japanese written discourse: Implications for contrastive rhetoric. *Written Communication*, 14, 4, 460–480.

Kunihiro, Tetsuya. 1984. "Noda" no igi oboegaki. *Tokyo Daigaku Gengogaku Ronshuu*, 5–9.

Kuno, Susumu. 1972. Functional Sentence Perspective: A case study from Japanese and English. *Linguistic Inquiry*, 3, 269–320.

Kuno, Susumu. 1987. *Functional Syntax*. Chicago: University of Chicago Press.

Kuno, Susumu and Etsuko Kaburaki. 1975. Empathy and syntax. *Harvard Studies in Syntax and Semantics*, 1, 1–73.

Kuroda, S.-Y. 1973. Where epistemology, style, and grammar meet: A case study from Japanese. In *Festschrift for Morris Halle*, ed. by S. Anderson and P. Kiparsky. 377–391. New York: Holt.

Kurteš, Svetlana. 2008. An investigation into the pragmatics of grammar: Cultural scripts in contrast. In *Developing Contrastive Pragmatics: Interlanguage and Cross-cultural Perspectives*, ed. by M. Pütz and J.N. Aertselaer. 67–86. Berlin: De Gruyter Mouton.

Labov, William. 1963. The social motivation of a sound change. *Word*, 19, 3, 273–309.

Lafleur, William. 1978. Buddhist emptiness in the ethics and aesthetics of Watsuji Tetsurō. *Religious Studies*, 14, 237–250.

Lakoff, George. 1996. Sorry, I'm not myself today: The metaphor system for conceptualizing the self. In *Spaces, Worlds, and Grammar*, ed. by G. Fauconnier and E. Sweetser. 91–123. Chicago: University of Chicago Press.

Lakoff, George and Mark Johnson. 1980. *Metaphors We Live By*. Chicago: University of Chicago Press.

Lakoff, Robin. 1973. Language and woman's place. *Language in Society*, 2, 45–80.

Langacker, Robert W. 1990. Subjectification. *Cognitive Linguistics*, 1, 5–38.

Leavitt, John. 2011. *Linguistic Relativities: Language Diversity and Modern Thought*. Cambridge: Cambridge University Press.

Lebra, Takie S. 1992. Self in Japanese culture. In *Japanese Sense of Self*, ed. by N.R. Rosenberger. 105–120. Cambridge: Cambridge University Press.

Lebra, Takie S. 2004. *The Japanese Self in Cultural Logic*. Honolulu: University of Hawai'i Press.

Lee, Duck-Young and Yoko Yonezawa. 2008. The role of the overt expression of first and second person subject in Japanese. *Journal of Pragmatics*, 40, 733–767.

Lefevere, André. 1992. On the construction of different Anne Franks. In *Translation, Rewriting and the Manipulation of Literary Fame*, ed. by A. Lefevere. 59–72. London and New York: Routledge.

Lefevere, André. 2004 [1984]. Mother Courage's cucumbers: Text, system and refraction in a theory of literature. In *The Translation Studies Reader*, second edition, ed. by L. Venuti. 239–255. London and New York: Routledge.

Li, Charles N. and Sandra A. Thompson. 1976. Subject and topic: A new typology of language. In *Subject and Topic*, ed. by C.N. Li. 457–489. New York: Academic Press.

Liddicoat, Anthony J. 2007. Internationalizing Japan: *Nihonjinron* and the intercultural in Japanese language-in-education policy. *Journal of Multicultural Discourse*, 2, 1, 32–44.

Lucy, John A. 2016. Recent advances in the study of linguistic relativity in historical context: A critical assessment. *Wiley Online Library*. https://onlinelibrary.wiley.com/doi/10.1111/lang.12195, accessed November 11, 2020.

Lucy, John A. and James V. Wertsch. 1987. Vygotsky and Whorf: A comparative analysis. In *Social and Functional Approaches to Language and Thought*, ed. by M. Hickman. 67–86. Cambridge: Cambridge University Press.

Lukács, György. 1971. *The Theory of the Novel*, trans. by A. Bostock. Cambridge, MA: MIT Press.

Lunsing, Wim and Claire Maree. 2004. Shifting speakers: Negotiating reference in relation to sexuality and gender. In *Japanese Language, Gender, and Ideology: Cultural Models and Real People*, ed. by S. Okamoto and J. Shibamoto. 72–109. Oxford: Oxford University Press.

Lyons, John. 1982. Deixis and subjectivity: *Loquor, ergo sum?* In *Speech, Place and Action: Studies in Deixis and Related Topics*, ed. by R.J. Jarvella and W. Klein. 101–124. New York: John Wiley and Sons.

Lyons, John. 1994. Subjecthood and subjectivity. In *Subjecthood and Subjectivity: The Status of the Subject in Linguistic Theory. Proceedings of the Colloquium "The Status of the Subject in Linguistics,"* 9–17. Paris: Ophrys.

Macaulay, Ronald K.S. 1987. Polyphonic monologues: Quoted direct speech in oral narratives. *IPrA Papers in Pragmatics*, 1, 2, 1–34.

Machida, Soho. 2003. Jutsugoteki ronri to nijuuisseiki. In *"Aimai" no Chi*, ed. by H. Kawai and S. Nakazawa. 121–145. Tokyo: Iwanami Shoten.

Maeda, Shoichi. 2004. *Monogatari no Naratorojii: Gengo to Buntai no Bunseki*. Tokyo: Sairyusha.

Maeno, Takashi. 2015. *Shiawase no Nihonron: Nihonjin to Yuu Nazo o Toku*. Tokyo: Kadokawa Shoten.

Makino, Seiichi and Michio Tsutsui. 1989. *A Dictionary of Basic Japanese Grammar*. Tokyo: The Japan Times.

Makino, Seiichi and Michio Tsutsui. 1995. *A Dictionary of Intermediate Japanese Grammar*. Tokyo: The Japan Times.

Maree, Claire. 2003. *Ore wa ore dakara* (because I'm me): A case study of gender

REFERENCES

and language in the documentary *Shinjuku Boys*. http://www.gender.jp/journal/no4/ AIclaire.html, accessed May 1, 2014.

Maree, Claire. 2008. Grrrl-queens: *Onēkotoba* and the negotiation of heterosexist gender language norms and lesbo(homo)phobic stereotypes in Japanese. In *AsiaPacifiQueer: Rethinking Genders and Sexuality*, ed. by F. Martin, et al. 67–84. Champaign, IL: University of Illinois Press.

Maree, Claire. 2013. *Onee Kotobaron*. Tokyo: Seidosha.

Markus, Hazel Rose and Shinobu Kitayama. 1991. Culture and the self: Implications for cognition, emotion, and motivation. *Psychological Review*, 98, 224–253.

Marmaridou, Sophia. 2000. *Pragmatic Meaning and Cognition*. Amsterdam: John Benjamins.

Martin, J.R. and P.R.R. White. 2005. *The Language of Evaluation: Appraisal in English*. New York: Palgrave Macmillan.

Maruyama, Masao and Shuichi Kato. 1998. *Hon'yaku to Nihon no Kindai*. Tokyo: Iwanami Shoten.

Masuda, Kyoko. 2016. Style-shifting in student-professor conversations. *Journal of Pragmatics*, 101, 101–117.

Masuoka, Takashi. 1991. *Modariti no Bunpoo*. Tokyo: Kuroshio Shuppan.

Masuoka, Takashi and Yukinori Takubo. 1992. *Kiso Nihongo Bunpoo*. Revised. Tokyo: Kuroshio Shuppan.

Mathesius, Vilém. 1983 [1929]. Functional linguistics. In *Praguiana*, ed. by J. Vachek and L. Došková. 121–142. Amsterdam: John Benjamins.

Matsumoto, David. 1999. Culture and self: An empirical assessment of Markus and Kitayama's theory of independent and interdependent self-construals. *Journal of Social Psychology*, 2, 289–310.

Matsuoka, Kazuko. 2016. Hon'yaku to Nihongo. *Nihongogaku*, 35, 1, 2–5.

Mauranen, Anna and Pekka Kujamäki, eds. 2004. *Translation Universals: Do they Exist?* Amsterdam: John Benjamins.

Mayes, Patricia. 1990. Quotation in spoken English. *Studies in Language*, 14, 325–363.

Maynard, Senko K. 1980. Discourse Functions of the Japanese Theme Marker *Wa*. Ph.D. Dissertation. Evanston, IL: Northwestern University.

Maynard, Senko K. 1981. The given/new distinction and the analysis of the Japanese particle *wa* and *ga*. *Papers in Linguistics*, 14, 1, 109–130.

Maynard, Senko K. 1982. Theme in Japanese and topic in English: A Functional comparison. *Forum Linguisticum*, 5, 235–261.

Maynard, Senko K. 1983. Flow of discourse and linguistic manipulation: Functions and constraints of the Japanese and English relative clauses in discourse. *Proceedings of the XIIIth International Congress of Linguists*, ed. by S. Hattori and K. Inoue. 1028–1031. Hague: CIPL.

Maynard, Senko K. 1984. Functions of *to* and *koto-o* in speech and thought representation in Japanese. *Lingua*, 64, 1–24.

Maynard, Senko K. 1985. Choice of predicate and narrative manipulation: Functions of *dearu* and *da* in modern Japanese fiction. *Poetics*, 14, 369–385.

Maynard, Senko K. 1986a. On Back-channel behavior in Japanese and English casual conversation. *Linguistics*, 24, 1079–1108.

Maynard, Senko K. 1986b. The particle *-o* and content-oriented indirect speech in Japanese written discourse. In *Direct and Indirect Speech*, ed. by F. Coulmas. 179–200. Berlin: De Gruyter Mouton.

Maynard, Senko K. 1987a. Nichibei kaiwa ni okeru aizuchi no hyoogen. *Gengo*, 16, 11, 88–92.

Maynard, Senko K. 1987b. Thematization as a staging device in Japanese narrative. In *Perspectives on Topicalization: The Case of Japanese Wa*, ed. by J. Hinds, S. Iwasaki, and S.K. Maynard. 57–82. Amsterdam: John Benjamins.

Maynard, Senko K. 1989. *Japanese Conversation: Self-contextualization through Structure and Interactional Management*. Norwood, NJ: Ablex.

Maynard, Senko K. 1990a. *An Introduction to Japanese Grammar and Communication Strategies*. Tokyo: The Japan Times.

Maynard, Senko K. 1990b. Conversation management in contrast: Listener response in Japanese and American English. *Journal of Pragmatics*, 14, 397–412.

Maynard, Senko K. 1991a. Buntai no Imi: Datai to desu/masutai no kon'yoo ni tsuite. *Gengo*, 20, 2, 75–80.

Maynard, Senko K. 1991b. Pragmatics of Discourse Modality: A case of *da* and *desu/masu* forms in Japanese. *Journal of Pragmatics*, 15, 551–582.

Maynard, Senko K.1992a. Cognitive and pragmatic messages of a syntactic choice: A case of the Japanese commentary predicate *n(o) da*. *TEXT*, 12, 563–613.

Maynard, Senko K. 1992b. Where textual voices proliferate: A case of *to yuu* clause-noun combination in Japanese. *Poetics*, 21, 169–189.

Maynard, Senko K. 1993a. *Discourse Modality: Subjectivity, Emotion and Voice in the Japanese Language*. Amsterdam: John Benjamins.

Maynard, Senko K. 1993b. *Kaiwa Bunseki*. Tokyo: Kuroshio Shuppan.

Maynard, Senko K. 1994a. The centrality of thematic relations in Japanese text. *Functions of Language*, 1, 229–260.

Maynard, Senko K. 1994b. "To yuu" hyoogen no kinoo: Washa no hassoo, hatsuwa taido no kinoo to shite. *Gengo*, 23, 11, 80–85.

Maynard, Senko K. 1995. "Assumed quotation" in Japanese. In *Gengo Hen'yoo ni Kansuru Taikeiteki Kenkyuu Oyobi Sono Nihongo Kyooiku e no Ooyoo*, ed. by M. Tokunaga. 163–175.

Maynard, Senko K. 1996a. Contrastive rhetoric: A Case of nominalization in Japanese and English discourse. *Language Sciences*, 18, 933–946.

Maynard, Senko K. 1996b. Multivoicedness in speech and thought representation: The case of self-quotation in Japanese. *Journal of Pragmatics*, 25, 207–226.

REFERENCES

Maynard, Senko K. 1997a. *Danwa Bunseki no Kanoosei: Riron, Hoohoo, Nihongo no Hyoogensei.* Tokyo: Kuroshio Shuppan.

Maynard, Senko K. 1997b. *Japanese Communication: Language and Thought in Contrast.* Honolulu: University of Hawai'i Press.

Maynard, Senko K. 1997c. Manipulating speech styles in Japanese: Context, genre, and ideology. In *Proceedings of the Fifth Princeton Japanese Pedagogy Workshop,* ed. by S. Makino. 1–24.

Maynard, Senko K. 1997d. Meta-quotation: Thematic and interactional significance of *tte* in Japanese girls' comics. *Functions of Language,* 4, 23–46.

Maynard, Senko K. 1997e. Rhetorical sequencing and the force of the topic-comment relationship in Japanese discourse: A case of *mini-jihyoo* newspaper articles. *Japanese Discourse: An International Journal for the Study of Japanese Text and Talk,* 2, 43–64.

Maynard, Senko K. 1997f. Shifting contexts: The sociolinguistic significance of nominalization in Japanese television news. *Language in Society,* 26, 381–399.

Maynard, Senko K. 1997g. Synergistic structures in grammar: A case of nominalization and commentary predicate in Japanese. *Word: Journal of the International Linguistic Association,* 48, 15–40.

Maynard, Senko K. 1997h. Textual ventriloquism: Quotation and the assumed community voice in Japanese newspaper columns. *Poetics,* 24, 379–392.

Maynard, Senko K. 1998a. Patosu to shite no gengo. *Gengo,* 27, 6, 34–41.

Maynard, Senko K. 1998b. *Principles of Japanese Discourse: A Handbook.* Cambridge: Cambridge University Press.

Maynard, Senko K. 1998c. Ventriloquism in text and talk: Functions of self- and other-quotation in Japanese discourse. *Japanese/Korean Linguistics,* 7, 17–37. Stanford, CA: Center for the Study of Language and Information.

Maynard, Senko K. 1999a. A poetics of grammar: Playing with narrative perspectives and voices in Japanese and translation texts. *Poetics,* 26, 115–141.

Maynard, Senko K. 1999b. On rhetorical ricochet: Expressivity of nominalization and *da* in Japanese discourse. *Discourse Studies,* 1, 57–81.

Maynard, Senko K. 2000. *Jooi no Gengogaku: "Bakooshooron" to Nihongo Hyoogen no Patosu.* Tokyo: Kuroshio Shuppan.

Maynard, Senko K. 2001a. Falling in love with style: Expressive functions of stylistic shifts in a Japanese television drama series. *Functions of Language,* 8, 1–39.

Maynard, Senko K. 2001b. *Koisuru Futari no "Kanjoo Kotoba": Dorama Hyoogen no Bunseki to Nihongoron.* Tokyo: Kuroshio Shuppan.

Maynard, Senko K. 2001c. Kokoro no henka to hanashi kotoba no sutairu shifuto. *Gengo,* 30, 6, 38–45.

Maynard, Senko K. 2001d. Mitigation in disguise: *Te-yuu-ka* as preface to self-revelation in Japanese dramatic discourse. *Poetics,* 29, 317–329.

Maynard, Senko K. 2001e. Nihongo bunpoo to kanjoo no setten: Terebi dorama ni kaiwa bunseki o ooyoo shite. *Nihongo Bunpoo*, 1, 1, 90–110.

Maynard, Senko K. 2002. *Linguistic Emotivity: Centrality of Place, Topic-Comment Dynamic, and an Ideology of Pathos in Japanese Discourse*. Amsterdam: John Benjamins.

Maynard, Senko K. 2003. Danwa bunseki no taishoo kenkyuu. In *Asakura Nihongo Kooza*, Vol. 7, *Bunshoo, Danwa*, ed. by M. Sakuma. 227–249. Tokyo: Asakura Shoten.

Maynard, Senko K. 2004a. *Danwa Gengogaku: Nihongo no Disukoosu o Soozoo Suru Koosei, Retorikku, Sutoratejii no Kenkyuu*. Tokyo: Kuroshio Shuppan.

Maynard, Senko K. 2004b. Poetics of style mixture: Emotivity, identity, and creativity in Japanese writings. *Poetics*, 32, 387–409.

Maynard, Senko K. 2005a. Another Conversation: Expressivity of *mitaina* and inserted speech in Japanese discourse. *Journal of Pragmatics*, 37, 837–869.

Maynard, Senko K. 2005b. Kaiwa doonyuubun: Hanasu koe ga kikoeru ruiji in'yoo no hyoogensei. In *Gengo Kyooiku no Shintenkai: Makino Seiichi Kyooju Koki Kinen Ronshuu*, ed. by O. Kamada, et al. 61–75. Tokyo: Hitsuji Shobo.

Maynard, Senko K. 2005c. *Nihongo Kyooiku no Genba de Tsukaeru Danwa Handobukku*. Tokyo: Kuroshio Shuppan.

Maynard, Senko K. 2006. Shiji hyoogen no jooi: Katari no shiten sutoratejii to shite. *Nihongo Kyooiku*, 19, 55–74.

Maynard, Senko K. 2007. *Linguistic Creativity in Japanese Discourse: Exploring the Multiplicity of Self, Perspective, and Voice*. Amsterdam: John Benjamins.

Maynard, Senko K. 2008a. *Maruchi Janru Danwaron: Kan Janrusei to Imi no Soozoo*. Tokyo: Kuroshio Shuppan.

Maynard, Senko K. 2008b. Playing with multiple voices: Emotivity and creativity in Japanese style mixture. In *Style Shifting in Japanese*, ed. by K. Jones and T. Ono 91–129. Amsterdam: John Benjamins.

Maynard, Senko K. 2009. *An Introduction to Japanese Grammar and Communication Strategies*. Revised. Tokyo: The Japan Times.

Maynard, Senko K. 2011. *Learning Japanese for Real: A Guide to Grammar, Use, and Genres of the Nihongo World*. Honolulu: University of Hawai'i Press.

Maynard, Senko K. 2012. *Raito Noberu Hyoogenron: Kaiwa, Soozoo, Asobi no Disukoosu no Koosatsu*. Tokyo: Meiji Shoin.

Maynard, Senko K. 2013. Aizuchi no hyoogensei. *Nihongogaku, Rinji Zookangoo*, 32, 4, 36–48.

Maynard, Senko K. 2014. *Keetai Shoosetsugo Koo: Watashi Gatari no Kaiwatai Bunshoo o Saguru*. Tokyo: Meiji Shoin.

Maynard, Senko K. 2016. *Fluid Orality in the Discourse of Japanese Popular Culture*. Amsterdam: John Benjamins.

Maynard, Senko K. 2017. *Washa no Gengo Tetsugaku: Nihongo Bunka o Irodoru Barieeshon to Kyarakutaa*. Tokyo: Kuroshio Shuppan.

REFERENCES

Maynard, Senko K. 2019. *Nihongo Honshitsuron: Hon'yaku Tekusuto Bunseki ga Utsushidasu Sugata*. Tokyo: Meiji Shoin.
Maynard, Senko K. 2021. Raito noberu no katari: Kyarakutaa supiiku to kan janrusei no kanten kara. *Nihongogaku*, 40, 1, 38–47.
Maynard, Senko K. 2022a (to appear). Danwa to gengo no barieeshon: Sono kisokusei to soozoosei. In *Shakai Gengogaku Nyuumon*, ed. by F. Inoue and K. Tanabe. Tokyo: Kuroshio Shuppan.
Maynard, Senko K. 2022b (to appear). Style, character, and creativity in the discourse of Japanese popular culture: Focusing on light novels and *keetai* novels. In *Handbook of Japanese Sociolinguistics*, ed. by F. Inoue, M. Usami, and Y. Asahi. Berlin: De Gruyter Mouton.
McAdams, Dan P. 1985. *Power, Intimacy, and the Life Story: Personological Enquiries into Identity*. Homewood, IL: Dorsey Press.
McAdams, Dan P. and Kate C. McLean. 2013. Narrative identity. Current Directions. *Psychological Science*, 22, 3, 233–258.
McCarthy, Erin. 2010. *Ethics Embodied: Rethinking Selfhood through Continental, Japanese, and Feminine Philosophies*. Lanham, MD: Lexington Books.
McGloin, Naomi H. 1984. Danwa, bunshoo ni okeru "no desu" no kinoo. *Gengo*, 13, 1, 254–260.
Mead, George. 1967 [1934]. *Mind, Self, and Society: From the Standpoint of a Social Behaviorist*. Chicago: University of Chicago Press.
Menda, Masaru. 2012. Miyazawa Kenji no sekai no shinrigakuteki koosatsu. *Bukkyoo Daigaku Kyooikugakubu Ronshuu*, 23, 147–163.
Merleau-Ponty, M. 1962. *Phenomenology of Perception*, trans. by C. Smith. London: Routledge.
Metzinger, Thomas. 2003. *Being No One: The Self-Model Theory of Subjectivity*. Cambridge, MA: MIT Press.
Mey, Jacob L. 1993. *Pragmatics: An Introduction*. Oxford: Blackwell.
Milicia, Silvia. 2019. First-person Pronouns in Japanese Language: From Narrative Explanations to Actual Usage. Master's thesis. Universitetet I Oslo. https://www.duo.uio.no/bitstream/handle/10852/74165/First-person-pronouns-in-Japanese-language-Silvia-Milicia.pdf?sequence=11&isAllowed=y, accessed February 10, 2021.
Mio, Isago. 1948. *Kokugohoo Bunshooron*. Tokyo: Sanseido.
Mitani, Kuniaki. 1996. "Rashoomon" no gensetsu bunseki. In *Gendai Shoosetsu no "Katari" to "Gensetsu,"* ed. by K. Mitani. 197–237. Tokyo: Yuseido.
Miura, Tsutomu. 1976. *Nihongo wa Doo Yuu Kotoba ka*. Tokyo: Kodansha.
Miyake, Naoko. 2005. Kansaiiki gai ni okeru kansai hoogen no juyoo ni tsuite: Kooaku hyooka komento yori. In *Kansai Hoogen no Hirogari to Komyunikeeshon no Yukue*, ed. by M. Jinnouchi and K. Tomosada. 267–278. Tokyo: Izumi Shoin.
Miyawaki, Takao. 2018. *Hon'yaku Jigoku e Yookoso*. Tokyo: Aruku.

Mondada, Lorenza. 2019. Contemporary issues in conversation analysis: Embodiment and materiality, multimodality and multisensoriality in social interaction. *Journal of Pragmatics*, 145, 47–62.

Mori, Arimasa. 1979. *Mori Arimasa Zenshuu*, Vol. 12. Tokyo: Chikuma Shobo.

Moriguchi, Yasuhiko and David Jenkins. 1996. *Hojoki: Visions of a Torn World*. Berkeley, CA: Stone Bridge Press.

Morita Yoshiyuki. 1995. *Nihongo no Shiten*. Tokyo: Sotakusha.

Morita, Yoshiyuki. 1998. *Nihonjin no Hassoo, Nihongo no Hyoogen*. Tokyo: Chuo Koronsha.

Mueller-Vollmer, Kurt and Markus Messling. 2017. Wilhelm von Humboldt. In *The Stanford Encyclopedia of Philosophy* (spring 2017 edition), ed. by E.N. Zalta. https://plato.stanford.edu/archives/spr2017/entrieswilhelm-humboldt/, accessed January 10, 2021.

Munday, Jeremy and Meifang Zhang, eds. 2017. *Discourse Analysis in Translation Studies*. Amsterdam: John Benjamins.

Murakami, Haruki and Motoyuki Shibata. 2000. *Hon'yaku Yawa*. Tokyo: Bungei Shunju.

Nagae, Akira. 2009. Yankiiteki naru mono: Sono kigen to mentariti. In *Yankii Bunkaron Josetsu*, ed. by T. Igarashi. 32–51. Tokyo: Kawade Shobo.

Nagami, Osamu. 1981. The ontological foundation in Tetsurō Watsuji's philosophy: Kū and human existence. *Philosophy East and West*, 31, 3, 279–296.

Nagano, Masaru. 1986. *Bunshooron Soosetsu: Bunpooronteki Koosatsu*. Tokyo: Asakura Shoten.

Naganuma, Mikako. 2013. Hon'yaku kenkyuu ni okeru "tooka" gensetsu. *Tsuuyaku Hon'yaku Kenkyuu*, 13, 25–41.

Nagata, Takashi. 1999. Nihongo no shinwabun. *Nihongogaku Ronsetsu Shiryoo* 36, 4, 37–46.

Nakajima, Fumio. 1987. *Nihongo no Koozoo: Eigo to no Taihi*. Tokyo: Iwanami Shoten.

Nakamura, Akira. 1991. *Bunshoo o Migaku*. Tokyo: NHK Bukkusu.

Nakamura, Momoko. 2013. *Hon'yaku ga Tsukuru Nihongo: Hiroin wa "Onna Kotoba" o Hanashi Tsuzukeru*. Tokyo: Hakutakusha.

Nakamura, Yujiro. 1993. *Nakamura Yujiro Chosakushuu*, Vol. 7, *Nishida Tetsugaku*. Tokyo: Iwanami Shoten.

Nakamura, Yujiro. 1996. Basho no ronri to engekiteki chi. *Shinchoo*, 4, 291–307.

Nanba, Koji. 2009. *Yankii Shinkaron: Furyoo Bunka wa Naze Tsuyoi*. Tokyo: Kobunsha.

Narrog, Heiko. 2012. *Modality, Subjectivity, and Semantic Change: A Cross-linguistic Perspective*. Oxford: Oxford University Press.

Narrog, Heiko. 2014. Modariti no teigi o megutte. In *Hitsuji Imiron Kooza Modariti*, Vol. 1, *Riron to Hoohoo*, ed. by H. Sawada. 1–23. Tokyo: Hitsuji Shobo.

Narrog, Heiko. 2018. Modality in Japanese from a crosslinguistic perspective. In *Hand-

book of Japanese Contrastive Linguistics, ed. by P. Pardeshi and T. Kageyama. 611–634. Berlin: De Gruyter Mouton.

Nashima, Yoshinao. 2002. "Setsumei no no da" saikoo: Inga kankei o chuushin ni. *Nihongo Bunpoo*, 2.1, 66–88.

Neisser, Ulric. 1988. Five kinds of self-knowledge. *Philosophical Psychology*, 1, 35–59.

Nida, Eugene. 2004 [1964]. Principles of correspondence. In *The Translation Studies Reader*, second edition, ed. by L. Venuti. 153–167. London and New York: Routledge.

Nisbett, Richard E. 2003. *The Geography of Thought: How Asians and Westerners Think Differently ... and Why*. Eastbourne: Gardners Books.

Nishida, Kitaro. 1949. *Nishida Kitaro Zenshu*, Vol. 4. Tokyo: Iwanami Shoten.

Nitta, Yoshio. 1989. Gendai nihongobun no modariti no tenkai to koozoo. In *Nihongo no Modariti*, ed. by Y. Nitta and T. Masuoka. 1–56. Tokyo: Kuroshio Shuppan.

Noda, Harumi. 1997. *"No (da)" no Kinoo*. Tokyo: Kuroshio Shuppan.

Noda, Harumi. 2012. "No da" no imi to modariti. In *Hitsuji Imiron Kooza Modariti*, 11, *Jirei Kenkyuu*, ed. by H. Sawada. 141–157. Tokyo: Hitsuji Shobo.

Nogami, Toyoichiro. 1921. Hon'yaku kanoo no hyoojun ni tsuite. *Eibungaku Kenkyuu*, 3, 131–153.

Ochs, Elinor and Bambi Schieffelin. 1989. Language has a heart. TEXT, 9, 7–25.

Oda, Ritsu, trans. 1930. *Buki yo Saraba*. Tokyo: Tenjinsha.

Oe, Saburo. 1979. "Kanjoo doonyuu" ni kakawaru Nihongo no tokuchoo: Eigo to no hikaku o fukumete. *Kokugogaku Ronsetsu Shiryoo*, 16, 1, 198–208.

Ogi, Shojun. 2017. *Yakuse nai Nihongo: Nihonjin no Kotoba to Kokoro*. Tokyo: Arufaporisu.

Oguma, Eiji. 2002. *A Genealogy of "Japanese" Self-images*. Melbourne: Trans Pacific Press.

Oka, Motoyuki. 2013. *Basho no Gengogaku*. Tokyo: Hitsuji Shobo.

Okamoto, Shigeko and Janet S. Shibamoto-Smith. 2016. *The Social Life of the Japanese Language: Cultural Discourses and Situated Practice*. Cambridge: Cambridge University Press.

Onodera, Noriko. 2017. Goyooronteki choosetsu, bunpooka, koobunka no okiru shuuhenbu: "Koto" no hattatsu o rei ni. In *Hatsuwa no Hajime to Owari: Goyooronteki Choosetsu no Nasareru Basho*, ed. by N. Onodera. 99–114. Tokyo: Hitsuji Shobo.

Onodera, Noriko and Ryoko Suzuki. 2007. Historical changes in Japanese: With special focus on subjectivity and intersubjectivity. *Journal of Historical Pragmatics*, 8, 2, 153–169.

Onoe, Keisuke. 1999. Bunpoo o kangaeru, 7. *Nihongogaku*, 18, 1, 86–93.

Ortega y Gasset, J. 1959. The difficulty of meaning. *Diogenes*, 28, 1–17.

Osawa, Yoshihiro. 2010. *Gengo no Aida o Yomu: Nichieikan no Hikaku Bungaku*. Tokyo: Shibunkaku Shuppan.

Östman, Jan-Ola and Jef Verschueren, eds. 2010. *Variation and Change: Pragmatic Perspectives*. Amsterdam: John Benjamins.

Östman, Jan-Ola and Jef Verschueren, eds. 2011. *Pragmatics in Practice*. Amsterdam: John Benjamins.

Ota, Minoru, trans. 1971. *Chuuburarin no Otoko*. Tokyo: Shinchosha.

Otsuka, Tsuneki, ed. 1996. *Sakka no Zuisoo*, Vol. 8, *Miyazawa Kenji*. Tokyo: Nihon Tosho Senta.

Paltridge, Brian. 2006. *Discourse Analysis: An Introduction*. London: Continuum.

Paparella, Emanuel L. 1993. *Hermeneutics in the Philosophy of Giambattista Vico*. San Francisco: EMText.

Parks, Graham, ed. 1987. *Heidegger and Asian Thought*. Honolulu: University of Hawai'i Press.

Parks, Tim. 2007. *Translating Style: A Literary Approach to Translation, A Translation Approach to Literature*, second edition. Kinderbrook, NY: St. Jerome Publishing.

Peirce, Charles Sanders. 1992 [1868] *Essential Peirce: Selected Philosophical Writings*, ed. by N. Houser and C. Kloesel. 28–55. Bloomington, IN: Indiana University Press.

Pinker, Steven. 1994. *The Language Instinct: How the Mind Creates Language*. New York: W. Morris and Co.

Postgate, J.P. 1922. *Translation and Translations: Theory and Practice*. London: G. Bell and Sons.

Pullum, Geoffrey. 1991. *The Great Eskimo Vocabulary Hoax and Other Irrelevant Essays in the Study of Language*. Chicago: University of Chicago Press.

Pütz, Martin and JoAnne Neff-van Aertselaer, eds. 2008. *Developing Contrastive Pragmatics: Interlanguage and Cross-cultural Perspectives*. Berlin: De Gruyter Mouton.

Pütz, Martin and Marjolijn H. Verspoor, eds. 2000. *Explorations in Linguistic Relativity*. Amsterdam: John Benjamins.

Pym, Anthony. 2010. *Exploring Translation Theories*. London: Routledge.

Rampton, Ben. 1999. Styling the other: Introduction. *Journal of Sociolinguistics*, 3, 421–427.

Reader, Ian. 2003. Identity, *Nihonjinron*, and academic (dis)honesty. *Monumenta Nipponica*, 58, 1, 103–116.

Reiß, Katharina and Hans J. Vermeer. 2014. *Towards a General Theory of Translation Action: Skopos Theory Explored*, trans. by C. Nord. London and New York: Routledge.

Reines, Maria Francisca and Jesse Prinz. 2009. Reviving Whorf: The Return of Linguistic Relativity. *Philosophy Compass*, 4, 6, 1022–1032.

Ricoeur, Paul. 2006. *On Translation*, trans. by E. Brennan with an introduction by R. Kearney. London and New York: Routledge.

Sacks, Harvey, Emanual Schegloff and Gail Jefferson. 1974. A simplest systematics for the organization of turn-taking for conversation. *Language*, 50, 696–735.

Sadanobu, Toshiyuki. 2009. Onsei to hyoogen. In *Nihongo Hyoogengaku o Manabu Hito no Tame ni*, ed. by M. Itoi and K. Hanzawa. 118–131. Tokyo: Sekai Shisosha.

REFERENCES

Sadanobu, Toshiyuki. 2011. *Nihongo Shakai no Nozoki Kyarakuri: Kaotsuki, Karadatsuki, Kotobatsuki*. Tokyo: Sanseido.

Sadanobu, Toshiyuki. 2015. "Characters" in Japanese communication and language: An overview. *Acta Linguistica Asiatica*, 5, 2, 9–28.

Sadanobu, Toshiyuki. 2021. Kyara to wa nani ka. *Nihongogaku*, 40, 1, 14–25.

Saeki, Keishi. 2014. *Nishida Kitaro: Mushi no Shisoo to Nihonjin*. Tokyo: Shinchosha.

Saft, Scott. 2014. Rethinking Western individualism from the perspective of social interaction and from the concept of *ba*. *Journal of Pragmatics*, 69, 108–120.

Saito, Tamaki. 2009. Yankii bunka to "kyarakutaa." In *Yankii Bunkaron Josetsu*, ed. by T. Igarashi, 247–261. Tokyo: Kawade Shobo.

Saito, Tamaki. 2011. *Kyarakutaa Seishin Bunseki: Manga, Bungaku, Nihonjin*. Tokyo: Chikuma Shobo.

Sakahara, Shigeru. 2003. Voisu genshoo gaikan. *Gengo*, 32, 4, 26–33.

Sakai, Kiyoshi. 2005. *Jiga no Tetsugakushi*. Tokyo: Kodansha.

Sakai, Noaki. 1991. Return to the west/return to the east: Watsuji Tetsuro's anthropology and discussions of authenticity. *Boundary 2*, 18, 3, 159–190.

Sakai, Naoki. 1997. *Translation and Subjectivity: On Japan and Cultural Nationalism*. Saint Paul, MN: University of Minnesota Press.

Sakuma, Kanae. 1940. *Gendai Nihongo no Kenkyuu*. Tokyo: Koseikaku.

Salonen, Elise. 2018. Constructing personal identities online: Self-disclosure in popular blogs. In *The Discursive Construction of Identities On- and Offline*, ed. by B. Bös, et al. 57–80. Amsterdam: John Benjamins.

Sampson, Edward. 1989. The deconstruction of the self. In *Texts of Identity*, ed. by J. Shotter and K.J. Gergen. 1–19. London: Sage.

Sano, Kaori. 1997. "Jibun" no hatsuwa ito. *Kanda Gaikokugo Daigaku Daigakuin Kiyoo*, 1, 59–69.

Sasaki, Ken'ichi. 2002. Poetics of intransitivity. In *Japanese Hermeneutics: Current Debates on Aesthetics and Interpretation*, ed. by M.F. Marra. 17–24. Honolulu, HI: University of Hawai'i Press.

Satake, Hideo. 1995. Wakamono kotoba to retorikku. *Nihongogaku*, 14, 11, 53–60.

Satake, Hideo. 1997. Wakamono kotoba to bunpoo. *Nihongogaku*, 16, 4, 55–64.

Sato, Hiroshi, ed. 2007. *Miyazawa Kenji: Selections*. Berkeley and Los Angeles: University of California Press.

Saunders, Dale, trans. 1966. *The Face of Another*. New York: Alfred Knopf.

Saussure, Ferdinand de. 1966. *Course in General Linguistics*, ed. by C. Bally and A. Schehaye, trans. by W. Basken. New York: McGraw Hill.

Schafer, Roy. 1992. *Retelling a Life: Narration and Dialogue in Psychoanalysis*. New York: Basic Books.

Schegloff, Emanuel. 1968. Sequencing in conversational openings. *American Anthropologist*, 70, 1075–1095.

Senuma, Fumiaki. 2007. *Kyararon*. Tokyo: Studio Cello.
Sevilla, Anton Luis. 2016. The Buddhist roots of Watsuji Tetsurō's ethics of emptiness. *Journal of Religious Ethics*, 44, 4, 606–635.
Shibata, Takeshi. 1958. *Nihon no Hoogen*. Tokyo: Iwanami Shoten.
Shields, J.M. 2009. The art of *aidagara*: Ethics, aesthetics, and the quest for an ontology of social existence in Watsuji Teturō's *rinrigaku*. *Asian Philosophy*, 19, 3, 265–283.
Shimizu, Makoto and Masako Murata. 2007. Transitive verb plus reflexive pronoun/personal pronoun pattern in English and Japanese: Using a Japanese-English parallel corpus. In *Corpus Linguistics 25 Years On*, ed. by R. Facchinette. 333–346. Amsterdam and New York: Rodopi.
Shinmura, Izuru, ed. 1998. *Kojien*. Tokyo: Iwanami Shoten.
Shotter, John. 2014. From within the thick of it: Human beings doing being human in language worlds. *Theory & Psychology*, 24, 4, 592–605.
Shotter, John. 2019. Why being dialogical must come before being logical: The need for a hermeneutical-dialogical approach to robotic activities. *AI & Society*, 34, 29–35.
Silverstein, Michael. 1979. Language structure and linguistic ideology. *The Elements: A Parasession on Linguistic Units and Levels*, ed. by P.R. Clyne, W.F. Hanks and C.L. Hofbauer. 193–237. Chicago: Chicago Linguistic Society.
Silverstein, Michael. 2003. Indexical order and the dialectics of sociolinguistic life. *Language and Communication*, 23, 193–229.
SturtzSreetharan, Cindi L. 2009. *Ore* and *omae*: Japanese men's uses of first- and second-person pronouns. *Pragmatics*, 19, 2, 253–278.
Sunakawa, Yuriko. 1988. In'yoobun ni okeru ba no nijuusei ni tsuite. *Nihongogaku*, 7, 9, 14–29.
Sunakawa, Yuriko. 1989. In'yoo to wahoo. In *Kooza Nihongo to Nihongo Kyooiku*, Vol. 4, ed. by Y. Kitahara. 355–387. Tokyo: Meiji Shoin.
Suzuki, Akira. 1979 [1824] *Gengyo Shishuron*, ed. and noted by T. Kojima and M. Tsuboi. Tokyo: Benseisha.
Suzuki, Satoko. 1998. *Tte* and *nante*: Markers of psychological distance in Japanese conversation. *Journal of Pragmatics*, 29, 429–462.
Suzuki, Takao. 1978. *Japan and the Japanese*, trans. by A. Miura. Tokyo: Kodansha International.
Suzuki, Takao. 2014. *Nihon no Kansei ga Sekai o Kaeru: Gengo Seitaigakuteki Bunmeiron*. Tokyo: Shinchosha.
Tajfel, Henri. 1978. Social categorization, social identity and social comparison. In *Differentiation Between Social Groups: Studies in the Social Psychology of Intergroup Relations*, ed. by H. Tajfel. 61–76. London: Academic Press.
Takano, Yohtaro and Eiko Osaka. 1999. An unsupported common view: Comparing Japan and the U.S. on individualism/collectivism. *Journal of Social Psychology*, 2, 311–341.

REFERENCES

Takano, Yotaro. 2008. *"Shuudan Shugi" to Yuu Sakkaku: Nihonjinron no Omoichigai to Sono Yurai*. Tokyo: Shin'yosha.

Tanaka, Yukari. 2011. *"Hoogen Kosupure" no Jidai*. Tokyo: Iwanami Shoten.

Tanaka, Yukari. 2014. Vaacharu hoogen no san yoohoo: "Uchi kotoba" o rei to shite. In *Hanashi Kotoba to Kaki Kotoba no Setten*, ed. by K. Ishiguro and Y. Hashimoto. 37–55. Tokyo: Hitsuji Shobo.

Tanizaki Jun'ichiro. 2010 [1934]. Bunshoo dokuhon: Seiyoo no bunshoo to Nihon no bunshoo. In *Nihon no Hon'yakuron: Ansorojii to Kaidai*, ed. by A. Yanabu, A. Mizuno, and M. Naganuma. 256–262. Tokyo: Hosei Daigaku Shuppankyoku.

Tannen, Deborah. 1984. *Conversational Style: Analyzing Talk among Friends*. Norwood, NJ: Ablex.

Tannen, Deborah. 1988a. Hearing voices in conversation, fiction, and mixed genres. In *Linguistics in Context: Connecting Observation and Understanding*, ed. by D. Tannen. 89–113. Norwood, NJ: Ablex.

Tannen, Deborah. 1988b. Introduction. In *Linguistics in Context: Connecting Observation and Understanding*, ed. by D. Tannen. 1–14. Norwood, NJ: Ablex.

Tannen, Deborah. 1989. *Talking Voices: Repetition, Dialogue, and Imagery in Conversational Discourse*. Cambridge: Cambridge University Press.

Tanomura, Tadaomi. 1990. *Gendai Nihongo no Bunpoo*, Vol. 1, *"No da" no Imi to Yoohoo*. Tokyo: Izumi Shoin.

Taylor, Charles. 1985. *Human Agency and Language Philosophical Paper*, Vol. 1. Cambridge: Cambridge University Press.

Taylor, Charles. 2016. *The Language Animal: The Full Shape of the Human Linguistic Capacity*. Cambridge, MA: Harvard University Press.

Teich, Elke. 2003. *Cross-linguistic Variation in System and Text: A Methodology for the Investigation of Translation and Comparable Texts*. Berlin: De Gruyter Mouton.

Teshigawara, Mihoko and Satoshi Kinsui. 2011. Modern Japanese "role language" (*yakuwarigo*): Fictionalised orality in Japanese literature and popular culture. *Sociolinguistic Studies*, 5, 37–58.

Tipton, Rebeca and Louisa Desilla, eds. 2019. *The Routledge Handbook of Translation and Pragmatics*. London and New York: Routledge.

Tirkkonen-Condit, Sonja. 2004. Unique items—over- or under-represented in translation language? In *Translation Universals: Do They Exist?*, ed. by A. Mauranen and P. Kujamäki. 177–184. Amsterdam: John Benjamins.

Tokieda, Motoki. 1941. *Kokugogaku Genron*. Tokyo: Iwanami Shoten.

Tokieda, Motoki. 1950. *Nihon Bunpoo Koogohen*. Tokyo: Iwanami Shoten.

Tomasi, Massimiliano. 2004. *Rhetoric in Modern Japan: Western Influences on the Development of Narrative and Oratorial Style*. Honolulu, HI: University of Hawai'i Press.

Toury, Gideon. 1985. *Descriptive Translation Studies and Beyond*. Amsterdam: John Benjamins.

Toury, Gideon. 2012. *Descriptive Translation Studies and Beyond*. Revised. Amsterdam: John Benjamins.

Traugott, Elizabeth C. 1989. On the rise of epistemic meanings in English: An example of subjectification in semantic change. *Language*, 65, 31–55.

Traugott, Elizabeth C. 2003. From subjectification to intersubjectification. In *Motives for Language Change*, ed. by R. Hickey. 124–139. Cambridge: Cambridge University Press.

Tsuboi, Eiichiro. 2002. Jueisei to ukemi. In *Ninchi Gengogaku*, Vol. 1, *Jishoo Koozoo*, ed. by Y. Nishimura. 63–86. Tokyo: Tokyo Daigaku Shuppankai.

Tsuji, Daisuke. 1999. Wakamonogo to taijin kankei: Daigakusei choosa no kekka kara. *Tokyo Daigaku Shakai Joohoo Kenkyuujo Kiyoo*, 57, 17–40.

Tsunoda, Mie. 2004. *Nihongo no Setsu, Bun no Rensetsu to Modariti*. Tokyo: Kuroshio Shuppan.

Uchida, Tazuru. 2009. *Nihon Henkyooron*. Tokyo: Shinchosha.

Ueno, Chizuko. 2005. Datsu aidentiti no riron. In *Datsu Aidentiti*, ed. by C. Ueno, 1–41. Tokyo: Keiso Shobo.

Unami, Akira. 1991. *In'yoo no Soozooryoku*. Tokyo: Tojusha.

Vandelanotte, Lieven and Kristin Davidse. 2009. The emergence and structure of *be like* and related quotatives: A constructional account. *Cognitive Linguistics*, 20, 4, 777–807.

Venuti, Lawrence. 1998. The scandal of translation: Relevance and disciplinary resistance. *Yale Journal of Criticism*, 16, 2, 237–262.

Venuti, Lawrence, ed. 2004. *The Translation Studies Reader*, second edition. London and New York: Routledge.

Venuti, Lawrence, ed, 2008. *The Translator's Invisibility: A History of Translation*, second edition. London and New York: Routledge.

Vermeer, Hans J. 2004 [1989]. Skopos and commission in translational action. In *The Translation Studies Reader*, second edition, ed. by L. Venuti. 227–230. London and New York: Routledge.

Verschueren, Jef, ed. 1999. *Language and Ideology: Selected Papers from the 6th International Pragmatics Conference*. Antwerp: International Pragmatics Association.

Vico, Giambattista. 1965 [1709]. *On the Study Method of Our Time*, trans. by E. Gianturco. Indianapolis, IN: The Bobbs-Merrill Co. Inc.

Vollmer, Fred. 2005. The narrative self. *Journal for the Study of Social Behaviour*, 35, 2, 189–205.

Vološinov, V.N. 1973 [1929]. *Marxism and the Philosophy of Language*, trans. by L. Matejka, and I.R. Titunik. New York: Seminar Press.

Vygotsky, L.S. 1962 [1934]. *Thought and Language*. Cambridge, MA: MIT Press.

Wargo, Robert. 2005. *The Logic of Nothingness: A Study of Nishida Kitaro*. Honolulu: University of Hawai'i Press.

REFERENCES

Watabe, Naoki. 2015. *Shoosetsu Gijutsuron*. Tokyo: Kawade Shobo Shinsha.

Watanabe, Yoshiki. ed. 2007. *Miyazawa Kenji Daijiten*. Tokyo: Bensei Shuppan.

Watsuji, Tetsuro. 1935. *Fuudo, Ningengakuteki Koosatsu*. Tokyo: Iwanami Shoten.

Watsuji Tetsuro. 1990a [1962]. *Watsuji Tetsuro Zenshuu*, Vol. 9, *Ningen no Gaku to Shite no Rinrigaku*. Tokyo: Iwanami Shoten.

Watsuji, Tetsuro. 1990b [1962]. *Watsuji Tetsuro Zenshuu*, Vol. 10, *Rinrigaku Joo*. Tokyo: Iwanami Shoten.

Weber, T. 1997. The emergence of linguistic structure: Paul Hopper's Emergent Grammar Hypothesis revisited. *Language Science*, 19, 2, 177–186.

Weil, Henry. 1887 [1884]. *The Order of Words*, trans. by C.W. Super. Boston: Ginn and Company Publishers.

Wentker, Michael. 2018. Code-switching and identity construction in WhatsApp: Evidence from a (digital) community of practice. In *The Discursive Construction of Identities On- and Offline*, ed. by B. Bös, et al. 109–132. Amsterdam: John Benjamins.

Werth, Paul. N. 1999. *Text Worlds: Representing Conceptual Space in Discourse*. London: Longman.

Wertsch, James V. 1979. *The Concept of Activity in Soviet Psychology*. Armonk, NY: Sharpe.

White, P.R.R. 2003. Beyond modality and hedging: A dialogic view of the language of intersubjective stance. *Text and Talk*, 23, 259–284.

Whorf, Benjamin Lee. 1956. *Language, Thought, and Reality*. Cambridge, MA: MIT Press.

Wierzbicka, Anna. 2005. Empirical universals of language as a basis for the study of other human universals as a tool for exploring cross-cultural differences. *Ethos*, 32, 2, 256–291.

Wierzbicka, Anna. 2008. Why there are no "colour universals" in language and thought. *The Journal of the Royal Anthropological Institute*, 14, 2, 407–425.

Wolff, Phillip and Kevin J. Holmes. 2011. Advanced review: Linguistic Relativity. *WIRES Cognitive Linguistics*, 2, 3, 253–266. Wiley Online Library. https://onlinelibrary.wiley.com/doi/abs/10.1002/wcs.104, accessed February 12, 2021.

Yagishita, Takao. 2015. Kindai Nihongo ni okeru oobun chokuyaku hyoogen. *Nihongogaku*, 35, 1, 32–40.

Yamada, Yoshio. 1908. *Nihon Bunpooron*. Tokyo: Hobunkan.

Yamaguchi, Yoshiya. 2016. *"No da" no Bun to Sono Nakama Zokuhen: Bunkoozoo ni Sokushite Kangaeru*. Tokyo: Sanseido.

Yamazaki, Yoshiyuki. 1965. *Nihongo no Bunpoo Kinoo ni Kansuru Kenkyuu*. Tokyo: Kazama Shobo.

Yanabu, Akira. 2004. *Kindai Nihongo no Shisoo: Hon'yaku Seiritsu Jijoo*. Tokyo: Hosei Daigaku Shuppankyoku.

Yanabu, Akira. 2010. Nihon ni okeru hon'yaku: Rekishiteki zentei. In *Nihon no Hon'yakuron: Ansorojii to Kaidai*, ed. by A. Yanabu, M. Naganuma and A. Mizuno. 1–34. Tokyo: Hosei Daigaku Shuppankyoku.

Yasui, Minoru. 2000. Nihongo hyooki taikei no naka no katakana. *Gengo*, 29, 8, 113–120.

Yonekawa, Akihiko. 2002. Gendai Nihongo no isoo. In *Gendai Nihongo Kooza*, Vol. 4, *Goi*, ed. by Y. Hida and T. Sato. 46–69. Tokyo: Meiji Shoin.

Yonetani, Masafumi. 2000. *Watsuji Tetsuro: Ningen Sonzai no Rinrigaku*. Tokyo: Toeisha.

Yuasa, Yasuo. 1987. The encounter of modern Japanese philosophy with Heidegger. In *Heidegger and Asian Thought*, ed. by G. Parks. 155–174. Honolulu: University of Hawai'i Press.

Yusa, Michiko. 2002. *Zen and Philosophy: An Intellectual Biography of Nishida Kitaro*. Honolulu: University of Hawai'i Press.

Zanghellini, Aleardo and Mai Sato. 2020. A critical recuperation of Watsuji's *Rinrigaku*. *Philosophia*. https://link.springer.com/article/10.1007/s11406-020-00296-1, accessed March 10, 2021.

Zeman, Sonja. 2018. Expressing the selves: Subject splits and viewpoint hierarchies in multiple-perspective constructions. In *Expressing the Self: Cultural Diversity and Cognitive Universals*, ed. by M. Huang and K.M. Jaszczolt. 143–157. Oxford: Oxford University Press.

Zlatev, Jordan and Johan Blomberg. 2016. Embodied intersubjectivity, sedimentation and non-actual motion expressions. *Nordic Journal of Linguistics*, 39, 2, 185–208.

Data References

Auster, Paul. 2000. *Auggie Wren's Christmas Story*. In *Hon'yaku Yawa*, ed. by H. Murakami and M. Shibata. viii–xv. Tokyo: Bungei Shunju.

Backus, Megan. 1993. (Translation) *Kitchen*. New York: Grove Press.

Bester, John. 1996. (Translation) *Night Train to the Stars*. Tokyo: Kodansha International.

Boehm, Deborah Boliver. 2010. (Translation) *The Changeling*. New York: Grove Press.

Carpenter, Juliet Winters. 2004. (Translation) *Shadow Family*. Tokyo: Kodansha International.

Emmerich, Michael. 2002. (Translation) *Goodbye Tsugumi*. New York: Grove Press.

Higashino, Keigo. 2011. *Manatsu no Hooteishiki*. Tokyo: Bungei Shunju.

Kawakami, Hiromi. 2004. *Sensei no Kaban*. Tokyo: Bungei Shunju.

McGillicuddy, Karen 2010. (Translaton) *Book Girl and the Suicidal Mime*. New York: Yen Press.

McGillicuddy, Karen. 2012. (Translation) *Book Girl and the Wayfarer's Lamentation*. New York: Yen Press.

Miyabe, Miyuki. 2001. *R.P.G.* Tokyo: Shueisha.

Miyazawa, Kenji. 1961. *Ginga Tetsudoo no Yoru*. Tokyo: Shinchosha.

Murakami, Haruki. 2000. (Translation). Oogii Ren no Kurisumasu Sutoorii. In *Hon'yaku Yawa*, ed. by H. Murakami and M. Shibata. 147–162. Tokyo: Bungei Shunju.

Nabokov, Dmitri. 2010 [1965]. (Translation) *The Eye*. London: Longman.
Neville, Julianne. 2014. (Translation) *Night on the Galactic Railroad & Other Stories from Ihatov*. Long Island City, NY: One Peace Books, Inc.
Nomura, Mizuki. 2006. *"Bungaku Shoojo" to Shini Tagari no Dooke*. Tokyo: Entaburein.
Nomura, Mizuki. 2007. *"Bungaku Shoojo" to Dookoku no Junreisha*. Tokyo: Entaburein.
Oe, Kenzaburo. 2000. *Torikaeko Chenjiringu*. Tokyo: Kodansha.
Ogasawara, Toyoki. 1992. (Translation) *Me*. Taken from *Shijuusoo, Me*. 165–279. Tokyo: Hakusuisha.
Pai, Chris. 2009. (Translation) *The Melancholy of Haruhi Suzumiya*. New York: Hanchette Book Group.
Powell, Allison Markin. 2012. (Translation) *The Briefcase*. Berkeley, CA: Counterpoint.
Pulvers, Roger. 1999. (Translation) *Eigo de Yomu Ginga Tetsudoo no Yoru*. Tokyo: Chikuma Shobo.
Shibata, Motoyuki. 2000. (Translation) Oogii Ren no Kurisumasu Sutoorii. In *Hon'yaku Yawa*, ed. by H. Murakami and M. Shibata. 163–178. Tokyo: Bungei Shunju.
Sigrist, Joseph and D.M. Stroud. 1996. (Translation) *Milky Way Railroad*. Berkeley, CA: Stone Bridge Press.
Smith, Alexander O. 2016. (Translation) *A Midsummer's Equation*. New York: St. Martin's Press, Minotauer Books.
Tanigawa, Nagaru. 2003. *Suzumiya Haruhi no Yuuutsu*. Tokyo: Kadokawa Shoten.
Yoshimoto, Banana. 1991. *Kitchin*. Tokyo: Fukutake Shoten.
Yoshimoto, Banana. 1992. *Tsugumi*. Tokyo: Chuo Koronsha.

Author Index

Abe, H.N. 212
Abe, K. 91
Aertselaer, J.N. 91
Agha, A. 73, 211
Aihara, H. 74
Akizuki, K. 209
Amagasaki, A. 61n, 139n, 155n
Ameka, F. 252
Anzai, T. 56
Asano, T. 126, 127
Auer, P. 7
Auster, P. 24, 223, 230

Backus, M. 23
Baerveldt, C. 67
Baker, M. 77, 80, 81, 87n, 93
Bakhtin, M.M. 20, 21, 52, 64, 65, 66, 68, 183, 184, 190
Baumgarten, N. 52, 54
Beaugrande, R. 77
Befu, H. 249
Bell, A. 45
Bellow, S. 91
Benveniste, É. 49, 50
Bernard, R. 7
Bertau, M.-C. 66, 67
Bester, J. 23
Blomberg, J. 11n, 59n
Blommaert, J. 33, 45n, 46
Boehm, D.B. 23
Bös, B. 75n
Brown, G. 168
Buber, M. 31
Bucholtz, M. 33, 45, 46, 47
Burdelski, M. 11
Burke, P.J. 43
Butler, J. 211

Carpenter, J.W. 23
Carter, R.E. 121, 123, 124, 125
Chafe, W. 168
Chesterman, A. 94
Chinami, K. 206
Christofaki, R. 135
Clark, H.H. 168
Coulmas, F. 182n
Cutler, C.A. 45

Dale, P.N. 249
Daneš, F. 168
Davidse, K. 181, 200
Dazai, O. 256
Derrida, J. 32, 39, 40, 41, 103, 119n
Descartes, R. 30
Desilla, L. 77
Dilworth, D. 107, 121
Doi, T. 248, 249
Door-Bremme, D.W. 8
Doorslaer, L. van 77
Dressler, W. 77
Du Bois, I. 52, 54
Ducharme, D. 7

Eckert, P. 44, 45, 73, 211
Eerland, A. 181, 182n
Emmerich, M. 23
Emmot, C. 136
Etelämäki, M. 53
Evan-Zohar, I. 78
Everett, C. 13, 14

Facchinetti, R. 95
Fauconnier, G. 136
Fillmore, C.J. 111n
Finegan, E. 50, 54
Firbas, J. 168
Fløttum, K. 136n
Fludernik, M. 187
Fujii, Y. 58n
Fujita, Y. 182
Fujitani, N. 117
Fukuoka, S. 105, 115, 253
Funabiki, T. 250
Furuno, Y. 85

Gambier, Y. 77
Gee, J.P. 10
Geertz, C. 29, 40
Genette, G. 190
Gergen, K. 32, 42, 43
Giles, J. 34
Glaser, B.G. 48
Goffman, I. 68, 69
Gubrium, J.F. 33, 43, 44, 127n
Gumperz, J.J. 7, 8, 13, 40n, 122n

AUTHOR INDEX

Haga, Y.   217, 218
Haiman, J.   50, 51
Hall, J.K.   67, 68
Hall, K.   33, 36, 47
Hall, S.   126
Halliday, M.A.K.   77, 91, 168
Hanks, W.   58n
Hansen, S.   95
Hansen-Schirra, S.   95
Harada, Y.   74
Hasan, R.   77
Hasegawa, Y.   128n, 250
Haviland, S.F.   168
Hayakawa, A.   92
Hayashi, M.   182
Hayashi, S.   164
Heidegger, M.   16, 17, 18, 29, 32, 37, 38, 39
Held, K.   103, 104
Herlin, I.   53, 119n
Higashino, K.   4, 23
Hijiya-Kirschnereit, I.   236
Hinds, J.   61n, 139, 167
Hirako, Y.   86
Hirano, K.   128, 129
Hiromatsu, W.   104, 105n
Hirose, Y.   128n, 143, 250
Hofstadter, D.   244
Hofstede, G.   60n
Holmes, K.J.   15, 16
Holquist, M.   65
Holstein, J.A.   32, 43, 44, 127n
Hopper, P.   119
Horie, K.   57, 79
Horii, R.   134
House, J.   8, 52, 54, 80, 91
Hume, D.   32, 33, 34, 102, 103, 165

Ide, S.   211
Ikeda, Y.   105, 109
Ikegami, Y.   55, 104n
Imai, M.   14
Inoue, F.   209
Inoue, K.   85, 86, 233
Ishida, H.   7
Ishiguro, K.   148n
Itabashi, Y.   108
Itani, R.   182
Iwasaki, S.   53n, 54, 167

Jakobson, R.   51, 82
James, W.   32, 34, 35, 36, 110, 115, 165
Jaszczolt, K.M.   135
Jefferson, G.   40n
Jenkins, D   101
Jinnouchi, M.   71
Johnson, D.B.   224
Johnson, M.   11, 59n, 118n, 136

Kaburaki, E.   54
Kamada, O.   182, 200
Kaplan, D.   135
Kataoka, Y.   86
Kato, S.   84
Kato, Y.   182
Kawahara, K.   21
Kawakami, H.   4, 22
Kawai, H.   105
Kecskes, I.   4
Kinsui, S.   72n, 75, 148
Kitayama, S.   248, 249
Kleinke, S.   75n
Kokuritsu Kokugo Kenkyujo   202
Koller, W.   81
Komaki, O.   120
Kondo, A.   175
Kondo, I.   98
Konosu, Y.   86, 135
Kosulis, T.P.   60n
Kozyra, A.   106
Kranich, S.   22n, 77, 94, 96n, 98, 199n, 210
Krein-Kühle, M.   81
Kristeva, J.   183
Kroskrity, P.V.   45n, 249
Krueger, J.   123
Krummel, J.W.M.   107, 108, 109, 111
Kubota, R.   61n
Kujamäki, P.   93, 95, 96n, 98, 199n, 210
Kunihiro, T.   175
Kuno, S.   53n, 54, 55, 167
Kuroda, S.-Y.   53n, 54, 55
Kurteš, S.   91

Labov, W.   44
Lafleur, W.   121
Lakoff, G.   135, 136
Lakoff, R.   44
Langacker, R.W.   51
Leavit, J.   13

Lebra, T.S.   248, 249
Lee, D.-Y.   135
Lefevere, A.   82, 83, 84, 245
Levinson, S.C.   13
Li, C.N.   176
Liddicoat, A.   251
Lucy, J.A.   13, 18, 19
Lukács, G.   20
Lunsing, W.   212
Luzio, A. di   7
Lyons, J.   13, 49, 50, 53

Macaulay, R.   181, 200
Machida, S.   104, 105n, 253
Maeda, S.   190
Maeno, T.   105, 253
Makino, S.   156n
Marchenkova, L.   67, 68
Maree, C.   212
Markus, H.R.   248, 249
Marmaridou, S.   11, 59n, 118n
Martin, J.R.   52
Maruyama, M.   84
Masuda, K.   7
Masuoka, T.   7, 57, 211
Mathesius, V.   167, 168
Matsumoto, D.   249
Matsuoka, K.   135
Mauranen, A.   93, 95, 96n, 98, 199n, 210
Mayes, P.   181, 200
Maynard, S.K.   9, 15, 18, 22, 23n, 31, 40n, 48,
    50, 53n, 54, 55, 56, 57, 58, 59, 62, 63, 72,
    73, 74, 75, 91, 92n, 97n, 104n, 106, 118,
    133, 134n, 138n, 139, 148n, 156n, 158, 166,
    167, 168, 170, 175, 181n, 182, 183, 194, 197,
    211, 212, 217, 218, 228, 242, 246, 248, 249
Mazuka, R.   14
McAdams, D.P.   127n
McCarthy, E.   121, 122n
McConnell-Ginet, S.   44, 45
McGillicuddy, K.   23
McGloin, N.H.   175
McLean, K.C.   127n
Mead, G.   41, 42, 68
Menda, M.   112, 113
Merleau-Ponty, M.   10, 11, 59n
Messling, M.   17n, 122n
Metzinger, T.   41
Mey, J.   6, 68

Milicia, S.   134n
Mio, I.   167, 171
Mitani, K.   190, 191
Miura, T.   167
Miyabe, M.   4, 23
Miyake, N.   209
Miyawaki, T.   213
Miyazawa, K.   23, 27, 101, 112, 113, 114, 115, 116
Mondada, L.   11, 59n, 118n
Mori, A.   248
Moriguchi, Y.   161
Morita, Y.   104n
Mueller-Vollmer, K.   17n, 122n
Munday, J.   91
Murakami, H.   24, 230, 231, 232, 233, 234,
    235, 236, 237, 238
Murata, M.   96

Nabokov, D.   24, 223
Nagae, A.   205
Nagami, O.   124, 125
Nagano, M.   167
Naganuma, M.   95
Nagata, T.   142
Nagatomo, S.   107, 108, 109, 111
Nakajima, F.   57, 104n
Nakamura, A.   140
Nakamura, M.   87
Nakamura, Y.   112
Nanba, K.   205
Narrog, H.   57
Nashima, Y.   175
Neisser, U.   139
Neumann, S.   95
Neville, J.   23
Nida, E.   79
Nisbett, R.E.   60n
Nishida, K.   27, 37, 101, 104, 106, 107, 108, 109,
    110, 111, 114, 119n, 120
Nitta, Y.   57
Noda, H.   175
Nogami, T.   85
Nomura, M.   23

Ochs, E.   51
Oda, R.   85, 233
Oe, K.   4, 23
Oe, S.   56
Ogasawara, T.   24, 223

AUTHOR INDEX

Ogi, S.   86
Ogino, T.   209
Oguma, E.   249
Oka, M.   58n
Okamoto, S.   211, 250
Onodera, N.   62
Onoe, K.   158
Ortega y Gasset, J.   70
Osaka, E.   249
Osawa, Y.   22
Östman, J.-O.   68
Ota, M.   92
Otsuka, T.   27

Pai, C.   23
Paltridge, B.   10
Paparella, E.L.   32
Parks, G.   37n
Parks, T.   96, 97, 98
Peirce, C.S.   73
Pinker, S.   13
Postgate, J.P.   85
Powell, A.M.   22
Prinz, J.   15
Pullum, G.   13
Pulvers, R.   23
Pütz, M.   13, 91
Pym, A.   80, 81

Rampton, B.   45
Reader, I.   249
Reiß, K.   77, 80
Reines, M.F.   15
Ricoeur, P.   82, 83, 244

Sacks, H.   40n
Sadanobu, T.   71, 72, 75
Saeki, K.   106
Saft, S.   58n
Saito, T.   74, 76
Sakahara, S.   158
Sakai, K.   113
Sakai, N.   86, 122n
Sakuma, K.   166
Saldanha, G.   77
Salonen, E.   75n
Sampson, E.   29
Sano, K.   143n
Sasaki, K.   6in

Satake, H.   207
Sato, M.   122n
Saunders, D.   91
Saussure, F. de   39, 73
Schafer, R.   127n
Schegloff, E.   40n
Senuma, F.   75
Sevilla, A.L.   122n
Shibamoto-Smith, J.S.   211, 250
Shibata, M.   209, 230, 231, 232, 233, 234, 235, 236, 237, 238
Shibata, T.   24
Shields, J.M.   122n, 125
Shimizu, M.   96
Shinmura, I.   134
Shotter, J.   67
Sigrist, J.   23
Silverstein, M.   46, 247
Smith, A.O.   23
Steiner, E.   95
Stets, J.E.   43
Strauss, A.L.   48
Stroud, D.M.   23
SturtzSreetharan, C.L.   135
Sunakawa, Y.   182, 200
Suzuki, A.   117, 118, 119
Suzuki, R.   62
Suzuki, S.   182
Suzuki, T.   133
Sweetser, E.   136

Tajfel, H.   44
Takano, Y.   249, 250
Takubo, Y.   211
Tanaka, Y.   209
Tanigawa, N.   23
Tanizaki, J.   84
Tannen, D.   7, 40n, 50, 122n, 181, 200
Tanomura, T   175
Taylor, C.   19
Teich, E.   22n, 80n, 152
Terkouraft, M.   252
Teshigawara, M.   72n
Thompson, S.A.   176
Tipton, R.   77
Tirkkonen-Condit, S.   94
Tokieda, M.   27, 57, 58n, 111n, 118, 119, 120
Tomasi, M.   6in, 84
Tomosada, K.   71

Toury, G.   78, 80, 93
Traugott, E.C.   62
Tsuboi, E.   158
Tsuji, D.   129, 207
Tsunoda, M.   175
Tsutsui, M.   156n

Uchida, T.   105
Ueno, C.   125, 129
Unami, A.   183

Vandelanotte, L.   181, 200
Venuti, L.   78, 84, 210
Vermeer, H.J.   77, 78, 80
Verschueren, J.   45n, 68
Verspoor, M.H.   13
Vico, G.   32, 68n
Visapää, L.   53, 119n
Vitanova, G.   67, 68
Vollmer, F.   127
Vološinov, V.N.   52, 183, 184
Vygotsky, L.S.   18, 19, 66, 68

Wargo, R.   106
Watabe, N.   199
Watanabe, Y.   114, 115
Watsuji, T.   27, 37, 120, 121, 122, 123, 124, 125, 129
Weber, T.   119n

Weil, H.   167
Wentker, M.   75n
Werth, P.N.   136
Wertsch, J.V.   18, 19
White, P.R.R.   52
Whorf, B.L.   12, 13, 14
Wierzbicka, A.   94
Wolff, P.   15, 16

Yagishita, T.   84
Yamada, Y.   57
Yamaguchi, Y.   175
Yamazaki, Y.   167
Yanabu, A.   85
Yasui, M.   148n
Yonekawa, A.   207
Yonetani, M.   122, 123
Yonezawa, Y.   135
Yoshimoto, B.   23
Yuasa, Y.   37
Yule, G.   168
Yusa, M.   107, 108, 112

Zanghellini, A.   122n
Zeman, S.   33, 45, 224
Zhang, M.   91
Zlatev, J.   11n, 59n
Zwaan, R.A.   181, 182n

Subject Index

a bundle of perceptions   33–34
A Midsummer's Equation   93, 155, 156, 157, 162, 188
a subject in transit   86
affect   52
anti-Cartesian views   31–41
Appropriation   17
aspects of self   136–139
Auggie Wren's Christmas Story   231, 233, 235, 236, 237, 238

back-translation   97
Being   17, 29, 37–39
betweenness   123–125
boku   134
Book Girl and the Suicidal Mime   148, 193, 194, 208
Book Girl and the Wayfarer's Lamentation   149, 164
borrowed style   72
Buddhist theory of no-self   102–104
"Bungaku Shoojo" to Dookoku no Junreisha   164
"Bungaku Shoojo" to Shini Tagari no Dooke   193, 194

Cartesian view   30–31
   Vico's opposition to   31–32
character   4, 70–76
   definition of   70
   in Japanese society   74–76
character-speak   70–73
   contrasting with role language   71–72
   definition of   70–71
   middle-aged-man language   28, 202–205
   old-man language   202–205
   onee language   28, 211–214
   yankii language   205–207
   youth language   28, 207–209
character zone   65–66, 184–185, 190, 222
characteristic   70
   definition of   70
complimentary schismogenesis   7
constructed dialogue   181

context   6–7
   external   6
   internal   6
contextualization   7–12
   definition of   7
   of self   9–10
contextualization cues   7–9
contrastive pragmatics   90–96
   involving translation   90–96
   of Japanese translation texts   91–93
corpus-based studies   95–96
covert translation   79–80, 91

data   4–5, 20–26
   limitations of   5
   literary works as   20–22
   presentation of   24–26
   selection of   22–24
   translation as   21–22, 245–246
deconstruction   36–41, 125–127
   of self by Derrida   39–41
   of self by Heidegger   37–39
Descriptive Translation Studies   93
dialect   28, 209–211
dialogical   64–68
dialogical self   67
dialogicality   52, 66–68
différance   39
difference   39
Discourse Modality   57
dividual   128–129
domestication   78
dynamic equilibrium   105
dynamic flow   105

Eigo de Yomu Ginga Tetsudoo no Yoru   88, 89, 152, 153, 154, 158, 161, 204, 205
embodiment   11
emptiness   104–112, 125
empty and populated self   26, 241–243
empty place   3, 27, 106–112
empty self   106–112
equivalence   79–82
   dynamic   79
   formal   79
   textual   81

explicitation 93–94, 96n
external evidence 8

fashions of speaking 14–15
first-person expression 133–145, 225–226
    contrasting *watashi* and *jibun* 136–137
    jibun and inner self 142–145
    variability of 133–136
    zero form 139–142
floating self 189–194
foreignization 78
futaku 139, 155

Ginga Tetsudoo no Yoru 88, 89, 152, 153, 154, 157, 160, 161, 177, 204
given information 167
Goodbye Tsugumi 172, 189, 206
Google Translate 244–245

heteroglossia 52, 68
hidden self 170–179
    and nominal predicates 174–178
    and staging effect 170–174
humanistic linguistics 32, 50

identity 125–127
    deconstruction of 125–127
    deconstruction of Japanese 126
inserted speech 183–189, 196–200
    as monologue 190–191
    in the novel 183–185
    transferred self in 196–200
    transferring self in 185–189
inter-genre expressivity 48, 71
internal conversation 194–195
    adjacency-pair 194
    quoted-speech-responding 194
    solitary 194
    thought-presenting 194
internal evidence 8
internal monologue 189–194
intersubjectification 62
intersubjectivity 52–54, 62–63
intertextuality 48, 71

jibun 27, 136–137, 142–145
    and inner self 142–145

Katakana 147–148
Kitchen 140, 141, 143, 214, 220, 221
Kitchin 144, 220, 221

Language-as-Process theory 118
Language and ontological views 18–19
language crossing 45
language has a heart 51
linguistic hospitality 83, 244
linguistic relativity 12–16
linguistic subjectivity 49–54
literary stylistics 96–98

Manatsu no Hooteishiki 93, 155, 156, 162, 188
Me 227, 228, 230
metalanguage 246–247
middle-aged man language 202–205
Milky Way Railroad 88, 89, 152, 153, 154, 155, 158, 161, 204, 205
missing translation 89–90
mistranslation 88–89
Miyazawa's view of self 112–116
    echoes of Western thought 115–116
    flickering self 112–114
monologue 28, 189–194
    across narration 191–194
    inserted speech as 190–191
mosaic philosophy 34
Murakami's *Oogii Ren no Kurisumasu Sutoorii* 232

narrating self 214–221
    and character-speak 214–216
    and style shifts 219–221
Neo-Whorfian scholars 13–14
new information 167
Nihonjinron 28, 248–251
    criticism of 248–250
    debate 250–251
Night on the Galactic Railroad & Other Stories from Ihatov 88, 89, 152, 153, 154, 158, 161, 204, 205
Night Train to the Stars 88, 89, 152, 153, 154, 158, 161, 177, 178, 179, 204, 205
Nishida's philosophy 106–112
    place of nothingness 107–108
    predicational universal 110–112
    pure experience 106–107

SUBJECT INDEX

no da 28, 174–179, 228–229, 237–238
   avoidance of 178–179
   use of 178–179
no dearu 237–238
nominal predicate 174–179
no-self theory 34, 102–114

old-man language 202–205, 229–230
onee language 211–214
ontological relativity 19
ontological view 16–20
   language and 18–20
ore 134
overt translation 79–80, 91

passive sentence 158–161
pathos
   rhetoric of 59–60
   in contrast with *logos* 61
perceptive verb 151–156, 226–228
performance 68–70
performatory 5, 68–70
person expressions 145–149, 233–236
philosophical contrastive pragmatics 3–6, 48
philosophical pragmatics 4
place
   Maynard's view of 58–59
   Nishida's concept of 107–108
   Tokieda's situated 118–120
Place of Negotiation theory 58–59
place of nothingness 3, 107–108
polysystem 78
populating self 202–222
   and dialect 209–211
   and variation 212–222
   with character-speak 202–222
postmodern approach to self 36–41
pragmatics 6
predicating universal 110–112
pure experience 34–36, 106–107

quotation 28, 181–189
   background 181–183
   transferring self in 185–189

R.P.G. 163, 186, 187, 191, 203
recontextualization 8–9
refraction 83

rheme 167–168
rhetoric of *logos* 61
rhetoric of *pathos* 59–60
role language 72
saturated self 42
self 9–12
   as flickering light 113–114
   as performer 10
   as betweenness 123–125
   aspects of 136–139
   embodied 11
   emotive 117–118, 158–162
   empty 106–112
   deconstruction of 39–41
   definition of 10
   floating 189–191
   hidden 170–179
   interdependent 120–125
   participatory 118–120
   perceptive 151–156, 226–228
   place-sensitive 147–149
   receptive 158–162, 226–228
   transferred 145–147
   transient 112–113
   unmentioned 156–158
Self-as-Multiple theory 125–129
self-contextualization 9–10
   contextual interpretation 9
   contextual transformation 9
self in self-narrative 126–127
sense-based expression 156–158
Sensei no Kaban 169
Shadow Family 138, 163, 186, 187, 192, 203, 208
Shibata's *Oogii Ren no Kurisumasu Sutoorii* 231, 232
shining through 79–80
simplification 94
situated place 118–120
Skopos theory 80, 77–78, 246
social construction of self 41–44
   social identity 44–45
   social identity and language 45–47
spoken and written language unification 84
staging effect 170–174
style 217–219
style shift 219–221
subjectification 51

subjectivity 4, 49–63
   in Japanese discourse 58–63
   in Japanese grammar 54–58
   linguistic 49–54
subjectivity expressions 54–58
Suzumiya Haruhi no Yuuutsu 159, 160, 193, 195, 203
systemic functional linguistics 79, 91

-te kureru expression 161–165
te-ni-o-ha particles 117
textual equivalence 81
The Briefcase 169, 170
The Changeling 146, 147, 173, 174, 197, 198, 200, 210, 211
The Eye 224, 225, 226, 227, 228, 229, 230
The Melancholy of Haruhi Suzumiya 159, 160, 193, 195, 196, 203, 208, 214, 215, 216, 219
theme 167–168
Tokieda's view of self 118–120
   in situated place 118–120
   participatory 118–120
topic marker 166–168
topic-comment dynamism 28, 168–170
   and the place 169–170
topicalization 166–168
Torikaeko Chenjiringu 197, 198, 199, 200
translation
   absence of 5
   as data 445–446
   covert 79–80, 91
   difficulties of 8, 82–84, 243–245
   gaps 5, 8, 26, 79n, 243–245
   missing 89–90
   mistranslation 88–89
   overt 79–80, 91
   types of 79–80
   universal 93–96
translation equivalence 79–82
   dynamic 79
   formal 79
   textual 81

translation gaps 79n, 243–245
   significance of 243–245
translation into Japanese 84–87
   influence on language 84–86
   stereotyped expressions 87
translation studies 77–82
   corpus-based 95–96
   equivalence in 79–82
   overview 77–78
translation universal 93–96
Tsugumi 188, 189

utterance character 72

variation
   age-associated 202–203, 207–209
   gender-related 211–214
   place-evoking 209–211
   stereotyped 87
verbs of giving 56, 161–165
voices from the heart 117

wa 142–145, 166–167
   and *jibun* 142–145
   and zero-form 144–145
watashi 136–139
Watsuji's view of self
   as betweenness 123–125
   in and with language 121–123
   interdependent 120–125
Whorfian hypothesis 13–16
   contrast with Vygotsky's view 19–20
   fashions of speaking 14–15
Whorfianism 15
   Habitual 15
   Ontological 15

yankii language 205–207
youth language 207–209

zero-form 25, 27, 139–142